The River Congo

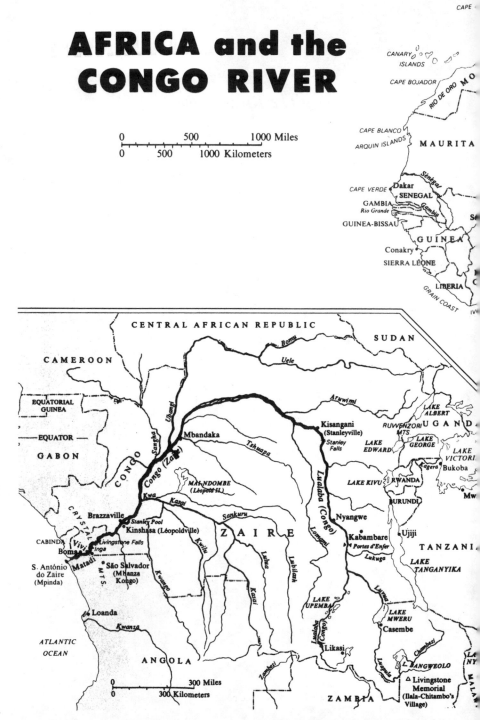

AFRICA and the CONGO RIVER

0   500   1000 Miles

0   500   1000 Kilometers

CAPE

CANARY ISLANDS

CAPE BOJADOR

RIO DE ORO   MO

CAPE BLANCO

ARQUIN ISLANDS   MAURITA

MAURITA

Senegal

CAPE VERDE   Dakar

SENEGAL

GAMBIA

Rio Grande   Gambia   Se

GUINEA-BISSAU

GUINEA

Conakry

SIERRA LEONE

LIBERIA

C

GRAIN COAST

IV

CENTRAL AFRICAN REPUBLIC   SUDAN

Bomu

CAMEROON   Uele

EQUATORIAL GUINEA

Aruwimi

LAKE ALBERT

Kisangani (Stanleyville)

RUWENZORI MTS.   UGANDA

EQUATOR

Sangha

Ubangi

Mbandaka

Stanley Falls

LAKE EDWARD

LAKE GEORGE

LAKE VICTORIA

GABON

Congo (Zaire)

Tshuapa

Kagera   Bukoba

CONGO

LAKE KIVU   RWANDA

MAINDOMBE (Léopold II)

BURUNDI

Kwa

Kasai

Lualaba (Congo)

Nyangwe

Mw

CRYSTAL

Brazzaville

Sankuru

Kabambare   Ujiji

Stanley Pool

Kinshasa (Léopoldville)

Z A I R E

Portes d'Enfer

TANZANI

CABINDA

Livingstone Falls

Vivi

Matadi

Boma

Inga

Kwilu

Lualaba

Lukuga

LAKE TANGANYIKA

S. António do Zaire (Mpinda)

São Salvador (M'banza Kongo)

MTS.

Kwango

Kasai

Lukenie

Lomami

Luvua

ATLANTIC OCEAN

Loanda

Kwanza

LAKE UPEMBA

LAKE MWERU

Casembe

ANGOLA

Lualaba (Congo)

Likasi

Chambezi

L. BANGWEOLO

LA NY

MALA

300 Miles

300 Kilometers

Zambezi

ZAMBIA

△ Livingstone Memorial (Ilala-Chitambo's Village)

Also by Peter Forbath

SEVEN SEASONS

THE
RIVER CONGO

The discovery, exploration and exploitation
of the world's most dramatic river

Peter Forbath

Houghton Mifflin Company

BOSTON

For Piry and John

Copyright © 1977 by Peter Forbath

All rights reserved

Published by arrangement with HarperCollins Publishers

Epilogue and portions of this book originally written
by Peter Forbath for Newsweek Books' *The Congo*, published in Newsweek Books' Great Rivers
of the World Series.
Copyright © 1977 by Newsweek, Inc.

The author has drawn in part and expanded upon material originally prepared for Newsweek
Books. The author thanks the editors of Newsweek Books for their courtesy.

CIP data is available.

ISBN 0-395-56725-4 (pbk.)

Printed in the United States of America

AGM 10 9 8 7 6 5 4 3 2 1

Houghton Mifflin Company paperback, 1991

CONTENTS

Part Four: THE EXPLOITATION

PROLOGUE

Congo: the two sudden syllables beat on the imagination like the beat of a jungle drum, calling up nightmare visions of primeval darkness, unfathomable mystery, dreadful savagery. No other word has quite that power; no other symbol stands more vividly for the myth and magic of Africa than the fabulous river those two barbaric syllables name. And for hundreds and hundreds of years, from the time *Congo* first entered the geography and literature of Western civilization in the fifteenth century, this has been so.

For one age, it was the primitive splendor of the Kingdom of Kongo, which a Portuguese caravel captain discovered at the river's mouth, that charged the word and place with its awesome connotations. For another, it was the horrible cruelties of the European slave trade, which ravaged the river basin's forests for more than three hundred years. For still another, there were the terrifying tales the explorers told of their epic journeys on the river, and, for yet another, the unspeakable atrocities committed by sadistic adventurers in the service of an infamous Belgian king. For our age, and certainly for me, the chilling images the name and the river still have the power to evoke come from those ghastly years of tribal and civil wars that followed the Belgian Congo's independence in 1960.

I first saw the Congo during one of the bloodiest moments in those violent years. The place was Stanleyville (now called Kisangani); the time, the Simba uprising of 1964. For 110 days in the fall of that year, the Simbas (Swahili for *lions*), a jungle army of cannibal warriors, doped up on *mira*, dressed out in monkey skins, armed with poisoned arrows, and in the thrall of a witchdoctor's *dawa*, had held Stanleyville in a reign of terror, which was finally broken by a lightning military strike of Belgian paratroopers and white mercenary soldiers. And by the time I got there, as a journalist covering the liberation, the city was a charnel house.

Thousands had been massacred. Mutilated corpses lay in the streets, some partially devoured. The stench of death and decay hung sickeningly in the oppressively hot and humid air. And fear was everywhere. The Simbas had fled but no one could be sure how far and for how long. They might still be lurking in the dark rain forests that surrounded the city, awaiting only their witch doctor's hissing signal to return. The population cowered in dread. The silence was uncanny.

I went down to the river then. The waterfront was deserted, the wrecked warehouses and sheds along the harbor abandoned. An old paddle-wheel steamer, some rusting barge hulks and derelict tugs creaked against the pier. Overhead, a fish eagle suddenly emitted its eerie cry, and from somewhere in the distance a woman, driven mad by terror, echoed the call. And the river flowed by unheedingly between its dark forested banks, silvery gray, glinting malevolently under the beating jungle sun, empty of all but its own implacable movement, moving agelessly down to the sea. In that atmosphere, the effect was hypnotic. In that moment, all the centuries of the West's trembling fascination with the Congo was there for me to understand, and it was then, I suppose, that I first began imagining this book.

The book I imagined, however, was not one I intended to write. It was one I wanted to read. When I had first come out to Africa I had read those two superb classics by Alan Moorehead, *The White Nile* and *The Blue Nile,* which had told me more about the myth and magic of *that* river than any I had read before or have read since, and it was for just that sort of book on the Congo that I began hunting after that astonishing day in Stanleyville. Now, there is, to be sure, a monumental literature on the Congo scattered in libraries and archives all over the world. There are books on the river's hydrography and the river basin's flora and fauna. There are monographs on the Kingdom of Kongo and the pygmies of the rain forest. There are chronicles of the earliest voyagers to the Congo, biographies of the later European explorers, accounts of their stupendous adventures, and volumes on various aspects of the river's recent politics. But oddly enough there is no book that tells the story of the Congo as Moorehead told the story of the Nile, the story of the river's discovery, exploration, and exploitation by Europe told as that seamless narrative of incredible adventure which more than anything else explains the

special place the Congo holds in the Western imagination. This then
is meant to be that book.

In writing it, I had, at the outset, to face a nagging problem of
nomenclature. For many, indeed most, of the place names involved
have been changed—and not least of all the name of the river itself.
Since 1971, as part of the *authenticité* campaign of a nationalistic
African government intent on erasing the last traces of European colonial rule, the river has been called the Zaire. It is, of course, not
difficult to understand and indeed sympathize with the sentiment behind the replacement of such obviously European names as Leopoldville, Stanleyville, and Elizabethville by such authentically African
ones as Kinshasa, Kisangani, and Lubumbashi. But the change from
Congo, a word so inarguably authentically African, to Zaire, which is
not only not an authentic African word but no kind of real word at
all—it is the clumsy Portuguese mispronunciation of the ancient Kikongo *nzadi* or *nzere,* meaning "the river that swallows all rivers"—is
bound to make one wonder. Until one is reminded again, as I was
reminded a few years ago, of the powerful connotations the word
Congo still carries.

The occasion was while I was traveling on a *vedette* up the river's
estuary from Banana Point to Matadi and had fallen into a conversation with a young Zairois official, a government veterinarian,
who frequently made the trip to inspect the livestock of the tribal
villages along the banks. At one point in our aimless, friendly chatter,
I happened to refer to the river as the Congo. His expression stiffened
and he corrected me pointedly, calling it the Zaire. I was surprised and
apologized but took the opportunity to question him on what I regarded as the foolishness of the name change. No, it was not foolish, he
replied firmly. "You will understand me, my friend, when I say that
Congo is a very heavy word. It is a word far too heavy for a people like
ourselves to bear in this modern age. When I was a student in Europe,
I never liked to say I was Congolese. I pretended I was Guinean. Because there in Europe and also in your America and, yes, even here
in Africa, *Congo* has come to stand for all the things we are now struggling so hard to leave behind, for all the savage and primitive things
of our past."

There is no way in the world that I can quarrel with that sentiment. Indeed, it is one that I have no trouble at all subscribing to. But

as it is precisely that past, which Zaire is struggling to leave behind, that this book is about; as it is the story of the Congo when it was truly the Congo that I am writing here, I feel it will be understood that no insult is intended to present-day sensibilities that I have chosen to go on calling that marvelous river by its evocative ancient name.

Part One

THE VOYAGES

1

THE RIVER THAT SWALLOWS
ALL RIVERS

The river rises in southeastern central Africa, more than 1000 miles south of the equator, more than 1000 miles from the continent's coasts, more than 5000 feet above the level of the sea. This is flat, open country, a highland savanna thinly covered in scrub and twisted thorn trees, solitary silver baobabs and yellow elephant grass, and spotted with those giant sandcastle-like structures that the driver ants build. The vast bowl of the sky, ablaze with the fierce white heat of the African sun during the day, a chilling star-washed velvet at night, falls in a dizzying arc here to immensely distant horizons, where rough brown hills, another 500 or 600 feet above the sea, seem to mark off the edge of the world.

This was once a land of great herds of wild game—zebra and giraffe, antelope and wildebeeste and elephant, and prides of lions hunting in the yellow grass—but it is no longer. For this plateau, which forms the southern rim of the 1.5-million-square-mile saucerlike depression in the heart of Africa that is the Congo River basin, lies in the continent's copper belt and contains astonishingly rich deposits of malachite ore. The Baluba and Balunda tribesmen of this region mined and smelted it, using the giant ant hills for their ovens, as long ago as the fourteenth century and founded a succession of rather wonderful savanna kingdoms on that industry. But in the twentieth century the European colonizers of the plateau, exploiting the ore on a mammoth scale, scarred the savanna into an ugly moonscape with their huge open-pit mines and killed or drove off the magnificent herds and the traveler now can count himself lucky to catch a glimpse of a lone gazelle, startled from the bush by a passing Land-Rover, or a gang of angrily shrieking baboons scattering through a bamboo grove, or a few ostriches loping away with their dignified ladylike gait across the harshly monochromatic landscape.

The tribal villages are also by and large gone. Those lovely groupings of thatched-roof huts with their kraals and palisades and broom-swept avenues and their feathered, spear-bearing warriors, which David Livingstone visited in the nineteenth century as the first European to reach the Congo headwaters, have been displaced by dreary modern mining towns. The tribesmen now wear plastic hard hats and khaki shorts and carry lunch buckets, and row upon row of identical cinderblock houses and empty, sun-dazzled streets sprawl across the grassland. Railways follow the old game trails; mountains of waste tailings tower over the giant ant hills; power lines slice down from the river's earthenwork dams to the black metal sheds of the electrolytic copper refineries perched on the edges of the mines. And fires can be seen burning everywhere, burning through the grass, blackening the earth, destroying the land. Plumes of dust, whipped off the charred and cracked earth by sudden gusts of hot wind, blow hard against you in the dry season, tearing at your eyes and choking in your mouth. And, in the rainy season, ferocious thunderstorms lash across this ruined highland plain, flooding its lakes and rivers and turning huge tracts of it into swamp.

This is not the landscape one ordinarily associates with the Congo. It is not yet that region of gloom-haunted rain forests which Conrad called the heart of darkness and which do, in fact, dominate the greater part of the river's basin. Nor is the river we find here the one its name traditionally evokes. For here it has the appearance of a lively stream, crystal clear and emerald green, hardly ever much more than a hundred feet wide, splashing brightly over pebble-strewn rapids, tumbling through narrow gorges in bursts of brilliant white spray, rushing swiftly between sharply twisting and turning banks, marking a fertile green path through the austere yellow grassland. Here it is still a river on a human scale, an approachable river, a river you'd be tempted to swim in or fly-cast for fish in, a young river still free of the silent, lurking dangers to be found in its broad, deep, ominously slow-moving waters later on. And here, appropriately enough, it goes by other names.

The Congo begins its tremendous journey to the Atlantic Ocean—a journey of nearly 3000 miles, the fifth longest in the world (after the

Nile, the Mississippi-Missouri, Amazon, and Yangtze) —as the Chambezi. It originates just south of Lake Tanganyika in Zambia and meanders southwestward for a few hundred miles to vanish into Lake Bangweolo. Draining the marshes of the lake's southern shore, it re-emerges as the Luapula, and then, turning northward, flows for over 300 miles along the frontier between Zambia and Zaire until it enters the southern end of Lake Mweru. As Mweru's outlet, now lying wholly in Zaire, it is called the Luvua and flows northwestward from the lake's northern end for another couple of hundred miles to join the Lualaba.

There is an argument over whether this circuitous riverine and lacustrine system is the Congo's true watershed and many geographers, bothered by its complexities, prefer to leave it aside altogether and assign the distinction straightaway to the Lualaba. To choose it, instead of the Chambezi, as the Congo's ultimate beginning is to shorten the river by about three hundred miles (and drop it in the world ranking to seventh or eighth place), but the choice does have the virtue of simplicity. For the Lualaba is a strong and straight stream. Its source lies about 250 miles south of the confluence with the Luvua, in those rough brown hills rimming the Shaba (formerly Katanga) Plateau near Zaire's southern border with Zambia, and once upon it the traveler has no trouble following its course. It flows almost directly due north, making none of those reversals in direction that the Chambezi and Luapula make, never vanishing into lakes as they do, and by the time it is joined by the Luvua it is a considerable river in its own right. Indeed, at this point, it is twice the river the Luvua is and anyone standing at their confluence would be hard pressed not to see the Lualaba as the mainstream and the Luvua as the tributary instead of the other way around.

But this is an academic argument and here the traveler can put it behind him, for at the confluence of the Lualaba and Luvua the headwaters of the Congo end and the river, under the name of the Lualaba, but in everything except name the Upper Congo, begins its long descent from the highland savanna toward the rain forests of its immense basin, a basin that encompasses more than one-tenth of the land surface of the African continent and includes all of the modern nations of Zaire and Congo-Brazzaville, most of the Central African Republic and parts of Zambia, Angola, Tanzania, Cameroon, and Gabon.

The Lualaba's course into this great basin continues as it began, almost directly due north, a course that it will now follow for nearly 1000 miles and follow so relentlessly that it appears to be journeying not to the Atlantic Ocean, which after all lies over 1000 miles to the west of it, but straight up the entire length of the continent to the Mediterranean Sea. Not until it crosses the equator will it at last turn away from this misleading course and, describing a remarkable counter-clockwise arc first to the west and then to the southwest, flow back across the equator and on down to the Atlantic.

In this the Congo is exceptional. No other major river in the world crosses the equator even once, let alone twice. Indeed, so astounding a geographical curiosity is this that for centuries no one could believe that even the Congo did. Until barely a hundred years ago, when Henry Morton Stanley proved otherwise, the idea that the relentlessly northbound Lualaba and the southwestward flowing stream that exits to the Atlantic over half a continent away had anything whatsoever to do with each other was inconceivable. They were perceived as two quite separate and distinct rivers, the former, for example, being taken for the mainstream of the Nile by no less an explorer than David Livingstone and the latter as the mouth of the Niger by Mungo Park, the discoverer of the Niger itself.

Something else needs to be mentioned about this astonishing course. The fact that the Congo flows in both the northern and southern hemispheres of the globe means that some part of it (and its network of tributaries) is always in a zone of rain, and thus it does not experience those great periodic rises and falls in its level which are characteristic of all other major rivers. It is, depending on how you choose to look at it, either always in flood or never in flood, because the flooding caused by the rainy season on one side of the equator is always compensated for by the drought caused by the dry season on the other. Thus, the Congo's flow is amazingly constant all the year round. And that flow is the second most powerful in the world (after the Amazon's), pouring almost 1.5 million cubic feet of water every second down to the sea.

The river's descent from the highland savanna to the rain forests occurs over a distance of some 500 miles. In places, it makes the descent in sudden, dramatic steps, plunging into a trough, rushing down a series of rapids, cutting through a gorge. But mostly it proceeds on its relentless northward course across open, gently sloping country, growing always stronger and wider as tributaries feed into it on both banks, and the descent is perceptible mainly by the steadily increasing richness of the vegetation. The grass becomes thicker; stands of acacia trees form into shady woods, in which weaverbirds nest in great chattering flocks; the baobabs put out broad shiny leaves; and one begins to see palms and lotus and the mangos of the old slave trails. The copper belt is now far behind us, and the alert traveler is now likely to spot game: impala that have come down to the river to drink, a family of hippo bathing in the mud of its banks, just possibly a leopard or cheetah bolting through the high grass, or the carrion eaters that follow the game—hyenas and jackals, or vultures circling overhead. Far off to the east is Lake Tanganyika, and beyond, the Ruwenzoris, the legendary Mountains of the Moon, whose highest peaks, snow-capped the year round, soar to over 16,000 feet and form the Congo River basin's eastern rim just as the copper-belt plateau forms its southern.

The Lualaba in its course through these lower savannas is not yet the great riverine commercial highway that it will soon become, but in long stretches it is by now wide enough to be used by the people living along its banks. Here we begin to see the dugout canoes which become such a permanent feature of the Congo's life and scenery. They are long, narrow craft, carved from single tree trunks and gracefully river-worthy. The tribesmen paddle them standing up, with long-handled oars whose blades are shaped like gorgeous palm leaves, and one sees them here gliding swiftly along the river carrying bunches of green bananas or sugar cane to a market day at some village, or trailing fishing nets in the glassy waters of some quiet cove.

But at Kongolo the river suddenly funnels into the Portes d'Enfer, the Gates of Hell, a startling gorge in the floor of the savanna a half mile deep and barely one hundred yards wide, where the waters boil up alarmingly and turn into impassable rapids for nearly seventy-five miles. And, where they emerge from the gate, the jungle begins.

Strictly speaking, it is not a jungle. Botanists tell us that there is no such thing as a jungle in Africa, only in Asia and South America, and what the river now enters is properly called an equatorial rain forest. But there is a far more dramatic ring to the word *jungle* and no one who has been in the Congo forest would hesitate to use it to describe this incredible realm.

It is seemingly endless. It stretches east to west across the Congo basin, some 4 degrees of latitude to the north and 4 degrees to the

south of the equator, covering very nearly 1,000,000 square miles of
the heart of Africa and enclosing very nearly 2000 miles of the river's
course. The Congo's counter-clockwise journey twice across the equator occurs entirely within this jungle and this is the reason, above all
others, why the river's remarkable course remained an insoluble mystery for so many centuries. For it is a killing place, a region so forbidding, a barrier so formidable that it blocked every attempt to unlock
the Congo's geographical secret until a mere hundred years ago.

Traveling into it upon the river, Conrad wrote in *Heart of
Darkness,*

was like travelling back to the earliest beginnings of the world, when vegetation rioted on the earth and the big trees were kings. An empty stream, a
great silence, an impenetrable forest. The air was warm, thick, heavy,
sluggish. There was no joy in the brilliance of sunshine. The long stretches
of the waterway ran on, deserted, into the gloom of the overshadowed distances. On silvery sandbanks hippos and alligators sunned themselves side
by side. The broadening waters flowed through a mob of wooded islands;
you lost your way on the river as you would in a desert . . . this stillness of
life did not in the least resemble a peace. It was the stillness of an implacable force brooding over an inscrutable intention. It looked at you with
a vengeful aspect.

Moving into the brooding silence, downstream from the exit of
the Gates of Hell, the river flows by Nyangwe. Today it is only a
scattering of fishermen's mud huts on the Lualaba's right bank, but it
was once a considerable town, the easternmost trading station of the
Arab slavers and ivory hunters whose caravans penetrated Africa from
Zanzibar and the Indian Ocean coast until a century ago, and the
farthest any outsider—Arab or European—had ever dared go into the
Congo forest until then.

We are here at an elevation of a little more than 2000 feet; the
bright horizons of the savanna vanish and the heavy humid heat of the
jungle closes down oppressively. It is true that the temperature rarely
reaches much above 90 degrees Fahrenheit, but it never goes down
much below it either. Between the height of the day and the depth of
the night, the thermometer will show a drop of barely 10 degrees, and
the mean temperature difference between the hottest and coldest
months of the year is less than 5 degrees. Moreover, there is no clear
distinction here between a rainy and a dry season; rain can fall in any

month, several times a day, nearly 100 inches of it a year. And in this climate oak, mahogany, ebony, red cedar, walnut, and rubber trees grow to heights of over 200 feet, forming dense canopies overhead that shut out the sky and plunge the forest into a perpetual twilight. A dozen varieties of fruit and palm trees proliferate, linked together in strangleholds of lianas and flowering vines. Giant orchids cling to the tree trunks, and lichens and mosses hang down from their branches like ghostly drapery. Rain and dew in the oppressive humidity of the suffocating air drip from everything.

There are pythons in those trees, and cobras and puff adders, and day and night you hear the hysterical screams of hordes of monkeys swinging through the upper branches, fleeing the deadly ambushes of the snakes. Elephants, of a breed smaller than those found on the savanna highlands, plod through the great stagnant pools made by the constant rainfall, and crocodiles slither in the marshes and ooze of the river's banks, their hooded eyes hypnotically watching the long-legged white water birds that step precariously around them—cranes and herons. There are bats and rats and civet cats. And dreadful diseases— malaria and sleeping sickness, bilharzia, river blindness, and black- water fever—breed invisibly in the silent, humid gloom.

Only the Pygmies live deep in the forest, but the traveler along the river is unlikely to see any of them. There are relatively few left (fewer than 300,000 scattered throughout the Congo basin) and they rarely come down to the river. They live in nomadic bands of ten or twenty families; their beehive-shaped huts, made of sticks and leaves and often set high in the trees, are built and abandoned from month to month as they keep on the move, hunting with bows and arrows, spears and nets, fearful of all other humanity. The people one does see along the river are of an entirely different race. They are Bantu speakers who migrated into the river basin from the surrounding grassland plateaus and, driving the Pygmies always deeper into the forest, settled along the banks of the Congo and its tributaries a thou- sand years ago. Very little has changed for them since.

When Stanley first came down the river these people were canni- bals, and they are known to indulge in the grisly practice occasionally still, for ritual reasons, out of hunger, simply for the taste of it. Theirs is an extremely primitive existence. The villages here are desperately poor places, four or five huts made of bamboo plastered with mud or covered with dried palm leaves, perched on the river's muddy shore.

Small patches of manioc and maize are cultivated in painfully hacked-out clearings, and here and there you'll see a few banana trees and pineapple plants. But because of the riot of vegetation and the lack of sunlight it is extremely difficult to raise anything more than a subsistence crop, and what little is raised is forever being destroyed by the elephants that trample through the forest. The tribesmen hunt the elephants; they dig pit traps, cover them with brush, and when an unlucky beast falls into one they pounce upon it with spears and tear it to pieces in a blood-spattering orgy. They also hunt the monkeys that chatter in the trees and the hairy forest pigs that root in the underbrush, amazingly accurate shots with their bows and arrows and slingshots, but their main source of life is the river, and they can be seen from dawn to dusk in their dugout canoes, fishing with immeasurable patience for the river's huge catfish and *capitaines*.

The river, fed by dozens of tributaries, has widened now to a half mile or more and, rolling ever northward, has taken on the glinting, greasy-gray color of the heavy, lowering sky. Islands, some quite large and heavily forested and with villages on them, begin appearing in the stream, but the channels around them are navigable, and, in fact, a steamer nowadays makes the 200-mile trip between Kindu and Ubundu from time to time. But at Ubundu (formerly called Ponthierville) the Stanley Falls begin, and the only sensible way downriver now is by the railroad the Belgians built around these falls early in the century.

Falls is a misnomer if the word calls to mind the magnificent plunge of the Zambezi over Victoria Falls or the Blue Nile's over the Tisisat Falls. What we have here rather is a series of seven cataracts and rapids, which in the course of some sixty miles drop the river to an elevation of about 1500 feet. They begin mildly enough. Just below Ubundu, reefs of slate and rose-colored granite jut out like fingers from the forested banks, breaking up the river's ponderous flow and creating eddies and whirlpools. But by the time we reach the last of them, the river is a roaring mass of white-water turbulence, rushing in several directions at once, throwing up waves five and ten feet high, boiling over boulders and reefs and crashing on the beaches of forested islands. It is called the Wagenia Cataract, after the tribe of fishermen who live along its banks, a tall, handsome, muscular people who have learned to negotiate the cataract in their long dugouts to set fish traps in its boiling waters. They paddle standing up in crews of ten, wearing bright-colored sarongs and keeping the beat of their powerful strokes with wonderfully savage chants, like warriors setting out for battle. And, in the midst of the most turbulent rapids, hanging on with amazing grace, they erect elaborate structures of bamboo poles, and from these suspend conical raffia baskets, the mouths of which they face upstream to catch the hapless fish that come tumbling over the falls.

Wagenia lies just north of the equator and marks the end of the Lualaba or Upper Congo. Here the river, called now the Middle Congo, is turned away from its northbound course by the Cameroon Highlands, which form the river basin's northern rim, and begins its great sweeping arc to the west. And here we find the city of Kisangani.

Kisangani (formerly called Stanleyville) is the first real city one meets traveling down the river and, by African standards, it is a large one, with a population of around 200,000. It nevertheless retains much of the brooding, threatening atmosphere of the dark forests around it. For, since Stanley's passage around the river's great bend, it has suffered a history of almost ceaseless violence. The Zanzibari Arabs, who followed Stanley down the Lualaba, built a slaving depot on the site. The Belgians, whom Stanley brought back up the river, used it as a military garrison in their campaign to drive the Arabs out of the region. After that it became the main river port for shipping out the rubber and ivory that the Belgians harvested in the surrounding forests under the brutal conditions so vividly described in *Heart of Darkness*. In recent years, it was the scene of some of the most horrible atrocities committed during the tribal and civil wars following the Congo's independence in 1960.

The specter of that violence still seems to haunt the city. In the oppressive jungle heat, the thick, sweet scent of exotic flowers reminds one alarmingly of the stench of decaying flesh. The district along the waterfront, which was once the European quarter, is ruined; the large, luxurious villas are either abandoned or occupied by squatters, and their gardens are wildly overgrown as if the jungle were pressing in to reclaim them. There are very few whites in the city; in colonialism's heyday some 6000 lived here, but now there are no more than 200 or 300, mainly missionaries, contract technicians, a polyglot of traders and adventurers, who seem always vaguely on the alert for the recurrence of violence, ready on an instant's notice to flee.

The river here is almost a mile wide. Dugout canoes, fitted with outboard motors, serve as ferries between the city's left- and right-bank settlements, and the riverfront harbor is a jumble of barge hulks, derelict paddle-wheel steamers, tugs tied up to creaking piers, rusting warehouses, and huge tripod cranes. A busy marketplace of kiosks operates just outside the harbor gate, and there large crowds, in bright-colored shirts and blouses, gather to wait for the boat that will take them downriver.

We are here at the beginning of the longest navigable stretch of the Congo, a 1000-mile journey around the river's great bend and back across the equator to Kinshasa (formerly Leopoldville), the capital of Zaire. This is the main stem of a great inland waterway system; the tributaries that feed the Middle Congo, some like the Ubangi as large as the Congo itself is here, form a network of some 8000 miles of navigable rivers, fanning out, like the veins of a leaf, throughout the Congo basin and the passenger boats, cargo barges, ferries, tugs, and canoes which ply these waterways often provide the only practical means of transport and communication in the equatorial rain forests. The steamer one takes from Kisangani is something called an "integrated tow boat." Its main unit is a four-deck pusher boat containing, besides the bridge, officers' and crew's quarters, and engine room, some first-class passenger cabins. To its squared-off prow, lower-class passenger and cargo barges, at least one but sometimes two or three, are lashed, and the assembled long-nosed, high-backed, rather cumbersome-looking vessel pushes out into the river, often with as many as 1000 people aboard.

The journey that took Stanley seven weeks now takes about seven days. Throughout it the river steadily widens. It is difficult to judge just how wide it is at any point because the Congo in this stretch is studded with thousands of sizable islands (4000 by some accounts), which sometimes appear to form the opposite bank and at others the confluence with tributaries, but at its widest it measures over nine miles across. The channels the boat follows form naturally under the force of the river's current (running here as much as six to eight knots), shifting with the shifting silt and mud of its bottom. Survey teams keep track of these changes and post channel markers—barrel buoys in the river, signals on the trees along its banks—to show the way. During the daylight hours, these are easy enough to see; at night the riverboat captain sweeps the water and shoreline with searchlight beams in order to find them and if, for some reason, he can't, he stops.

The villages along the river now belong mostly to the Lokele. They are a relatively small tribe but they are settled in a thin line along the banks of this portion of the Congo and dominate the river's trade. They are famous for their "talking" drums, which one hears day and night sending messages of boats' progress downriver, so that at every village we pass the Lokele are expecting us and come out in their canoes loaded with goods to trade with the boat's passengers. They are quite relentless in this trade; throughout the journey, the riverboat is never without at least a dozen and often as many as a hundred dugout canoes tied up alongside, and what the Lokele bring aboard for sale or barter reflects the changing nature of the lands we pass through. First there are manioc and sugar cane, then bananas and avocados; pineapples and coconuts are replaced by tangerines and peanuts. At one point palm oil is brought aboard, at another baskets of live grubs; freshly caught fish give way to smoked fish and live eels, then smoked eels and fresh-killed monkeys, then smoked monkeys, live forest pigs, crocodile eggs, and dressed-out antelope.

This trade is the chief occupation and entertainment of the journey. The lower decks and cargo barges turn into thriving marketplaces, floating bazaars. Stalls are set up to barter or sell manufactured goods, barbers go into business, laundries materialize, butchers prepare the animals and fish brought aboard, restaurants serve meals from open fires, beer parlors spring into existence complete with brassy music from transistor radios, and the buying and selling goes on around the clock. And in this way the produce of the Congo rain forest makes its way to the outside world, and the manufactured goods of the outside world—salt, cigarettes, matches, cloth, wire, nails, tools, soap, razor blades—find their way into the forest.

Where the river recrosses the equator stands Mbandaka (formerly Coquilhatville), the only other sizable city on the river before Kinshasa. A few miles below it the Ubangi joins the Congo on the right, and from here the river marks the frontier between the Congo Republic on the right bank and Zaire on the left.

Rain, or the threat of rain, is always with us during the journey. The mornings dawn shrouded in fog, which never entirely burns off, and with the advance of the day the overcast sky lowers suffocatingly

until, toward afternoon, the light fades and there is the eerie gloom of
a false night. A wind springs up, sweeping the decks with a fine drizzle,
and up ahead you can see a luminous gray sheet of rain slanting down
across the jungle. Then suddenly there will be a stunning flash of
lightning, a crash of thunder, and the torrential downpour is upon us.
The boat slows in the face of the furious onslaught. The captain
switches on the searchlights and sweeps the beams into the curtain of
rain, hunting for the channel markers. But it's no use; nothing can be
seen, and, reversing the engines, the captain backs away as if from the
pounding sheet of rain itself and eases the boat toward an island, there
to anchor and wait out the storm.

It will last for perhaps an hour or two and then, as abruptly as it
began, the rain lets up and the clouds clear away just in time for us to
see the sun set. It is a great blood-orange sphere, painting a stripe of
the same color across the rippling surface of the river; elsewhere the
river is a pale purple under the smoky blue sky, and the forests have
turned indigo. A glowing moon comes out and then the stars, and for
a few hours the air seems fresh and washed. But then the steaming
humidity emerges from the gleaming, dripping jungle, and the oppressive heat closes round again.

But one morning you wake up and go on deck and you discover
that the jungle has thinned away and there are high, rugged yellow
limestone hills rearing up on both banks. These are the Crystal Mountains, which form the western rim of the Congo basin. We are here at
the entrance to the Stanley Pool (now called the Malebo Pool) , a vast,
lakelike expanse in the river, 15 miles across at its widest, more than
20 miles long, which marks the end of the Middle Congo. As we sail
into it with the day's first light, the pool might be the river's mouth
with the Atlantic Ocean lying just beyond, shrouded from view for the
moment by the morning's lingering mists. But then in the distance
you see the skyline of Kinshasa on the left bank and that of Brazzaville, the capital of the Congo Republic, on the right and slowly begin
to make out the low distant roar of what Stanley named the Livingstone Falls. And you know you are still over 300 miles from the sea
and nearly 1000 feet above it.

Kinshasa is a booming modern metropolis. It has a polyglot population of detribalized Africans and denationalized Europeans of close
to 1.5 million. Downtown is a complex of towering skyscrapers; motor
traffic rockets wildly along its broad boulevards. There are outdoor

cafés, rows of airline offices, apartment blocks, international hotels, fashionable boutiques, supermarkets, neon signs, expensive suburbs, and the outlying *cités* have the look and feel of urban slums. Its waterfront is vibrantly alive, with tugs and ferries, barges and day liners, steamers and cargo boats, and miles of piers, cranes, petroleum tank farms, dry docks, shipyards, warehouses, chandleries. More than one million tons of cargo and ten times that many passengers pass through this port each year. It is the great Congo terminus. All the river's traffic ends or begins here. For the river has now reached the single most difficult obstacle, even including the rain forest, that its geography placed in the way of its discovery, exploration, and exploitation: the Livingstone Falls, by which the river cuts its way through the western rim of its basin, the Crystal Mountains, and rushes the last thousand feet down to the level of the sea.

Again, if what we are thinking of is some Victoria or Niagara, then Livingstone *Falls* is a misnomer. Like the Stanley Falls, what we have here is a series of rapids and cataracts, but with that all comparison must end. For the Livingstone Falls cover some 220 miles and include at least 32 cataracts, and their violence is a hundred times more terrible. They thunder through narrow gorges and ravines, boil up in vicious yellow waves 30 and 40 feet high, crash over giant boulders, rip giant trees and islands of sod from the river's banks, twist and turn and whirl around to create terrifying whirlpools and dreadful, fathomless holes. No tribesmen would dare, as the Wagenia do on the Stanley Falls, to venture into these cataracts in a dugout canoe. Indeed, no vessel of any design could hope to live in these waters. The force is so great that a hydroelectric power dam complex, currently being built on just one of the cataracts, Inga, will produce three times Italy's total annual electrical output, five times China's, twelve times Belgium's. All 32 cataracts have as much power potential as all the rivers and falls of the United States put together.

The only way down this stretch of the river is by the road or railway the Belgians built around it at the beginning of this century. Before that there was no way, in either direction. For 400 years after Europe discovered the Congo's mouth, every attempt to get up the river was defeated by these cataracts and by the mountains that enclose them. And when Stanley at last thought to come *down* the river, they very nearly killed him.

The last of the cataracts is called the Cauldron of Hell, and at this point the river, emerging from the Crystal Mountains, flows into a coastal plain. It is still about 100 miles from the ocean, but in this, its final course, known as the Lower Congo, it is again wholly navigable, the only major African river to reach the sea via an estuary (the Nile and the Niger, for example, exit via unnavigable deltas). Just below the Cauldron of Hell stands Matadi, Zaire's seaport, which the largest ocean-going vessels are able to reach by sailing up this estuary. And ferries, which regularly make the trip to Banana Point at the river's mouth, take the traveler down it.

From Matadi to Banana, the river marks the border between Zaire on the right bank and Angola on the left. It steadily widens, in some places to as much as five miles, and once again we find sizable islands standing in its stream. Its banks are heavily forested, now mainly with palm trees and mangroves and jungles of giant water ferns. The people on this stretch of the river are the Bakongo, descendants of the inhabitants of that once great African kingdom that gave its name to the river. Their villages are larger than those we have seen until now, their houses more substantial, and they cultivate maize and manioc on a more ambitious scale. There are flocks of goats and pigs and chickens, and herds of cattle stand in the shallow water of the marshland of the river's edge. Naked children rush down to the bank to watch the ferry go by, and the tribesmen, dressed in mission shorts and colorful shirts, are everywhere in their canoes, trawling for fish with nylon nets.

Two sandy peninsulas, some 15 miles apart and arcing out into the Atlantic like the opposing jaws of a giant crab's claw, form the Congo's mouth. The river, now moving with a current of some nine knots and swollen to a flow of nearly 1.5 million cubic feet a second, rushes to it and through it and then well beyond it. For geologists tell us that this immensely powerful river has cut a submarine canyon in the ocean's floor, in some places 4000 feet deep, for another 100 miles out to sea. And we can see the river's waters, in their unrelenting flow, staining the ocean's surface for scores of miles offshore with the mud and vegetation carried down on the long journey from the savanna highlands.

That stained ocean—the muddy red sea offshore, the muddy yellow surf breaking on the coastline's beaches, the islands of vegetation riding the river's current far out in the Atlantic—was the first view that

Europeans ever had of the Congo. It was a sighting first made by a Portuguese caravel captain toward the end of the fifteenth century, a decade before Columbus discovered America, and it began an epoch of nearly 400 years of exploration by Europe, during which the rest of the great African river was ultimately found.

The history of that discovery and exploration is inextricably bound up in the geography which we've been following here. Indeed, it is a history so profoundly shaped by the astonishing direction of the river's course, by the forbidding nature of the land it passes through, by the murderous cataracts on its stream that it is virtually impossible to follow without a fair grasp of that geography. But the history begins with yet another geographical fact: the Congo's location in the heart of Africa, utterly remote from Europe and in no way ever touching upon it.

This was not true, for example, of the Nile or even the Niger, those two other great African rivers with whose histories the Congo's can best be compared. Europe had always been in contact with the Nile. The river's delta and lower valley had been visited by classical Greeks and conquered by Imperial Rome; its ancient civilizations had taught Europe how to be civilized; its history had been intertwined with Europe's since well before the Christian era. The Nile's great geographical mystery was the location of its source and, to be sure, it took centuries to find it. But Europe always knew it was there, always considered it vital to find, and searched for it for nearly 2000 years. The Niger too was a river of abiding fascination. Although no European actually laid eyes on it until the early nineteenth century, it was part of Europe's mythology from the earliest Middle Ages. For the Niger was the river of Timbuktoo, the fabled golden city from whence the Saharan caravans brought the precious merchandise of Bilad al-Sudan, the land of the blacks, to the Barbary Shore and the courts of the European kings. And for this, if for nothing else, it was a river to be sought, a lure compelling enough to have tempted adventurers on daring voyages of discovery for hundreds of years.

The Congo played no comparable role, offered no such tempting prizes, held no such place in Europe's literature. For, because of its remote geography, its very existence was unknown. No one could dream of setting out to find it because no one could dream that it was even there. Its discovery was an accident, the fruit of Europe's other quests, its quests for the gold of the Niger and the secret of the Nile, for the silks of far Cathay and the spices of the Indies, for knowledge, for light in the darkness that lay beyond its circumscribed world, for allies against the dangerous mysteries of the unknown, but, in the first instance, for the legendary kingdom of Prester John.

2

THE QUEST FOR PRESTER JOHN

The first we hear of Prester John is in the twelfth century, a perilous time in medieval Christendom's history. The Pope, Eugenius II, had been driven from the Vatican by a popular revolt in Rome; the rift between the Roman and Byzantine branches of the Church had widened into open hostility and occasional warfare; and the conquests of the First Crusade, which had won for the Roman Church such strongholds in the Moslem world as Jerusalem, Tripoli, Antioch, and Edessa, were in the process of being reversed. Imad-al-Din Zengi, a Seljuk Turk general, had united the Moslem emirates of Syria and the Holy Land into a jihad against the Crusader states, and in 1144 his army of desert horsemen swept down on Edessa, captured it, and put all its defenders to the sword.

The news of this disastrous defeat was brought to the Pontifical Court, then in Viterbo, by Hugh, the Bishop of Jabala. Otto, the Bishop of Freising, was present, and it is in his *Historia de Duabus Civitatibus*, which includes an account of what transpired at the audience between Hugh and Eugenius, that we first read the name of the mysterious Christian priest-king of the Orient.

Hugh's main purpose at Viterbo was to persuade the Pope to call for a second crusade. There was already some enthusiasm for the idea—Conrad III of Germany and Louis VII of France had indicated that they were willing to take up the cross against the Saracens—and Hugh did all he could to inflame the passion. He described in grisly detail the atrocities committed by the Seljuk Turks at Edessa and warned that the capture of that city presaged the fall of all the other Latin states in the Holy Land, up to and including Jerusalem and the

Holy Sepulchre itself. Because of the enmity with Constantinople, the Latin knights could expect no help from the armies of Byzantium; only a great legion of Crusaders from Europe could stem the Moslem tide. Then, to further excite enthusiasm, Hugh, according to the account in the Bishop of Freising's *Historia,* told the following story:

Not many years ago a certain John, a king and priest who lives in the extreme Orient, beyond Persia and Armenia, and who like his people is a Christian . . . made war on the brothers known as the Samiardi, who are the kings of the Persians and the Medes, and stormed Ecbatana, the capital of their kingdoms. . . . When the aforesaid kings met him with Persian, Median and Assyrian troops, the ensuing battle lasted for three days. . . . At last Presbyter John, for so they customarily call him, put the Persians to flight. . . . He is said to be a direct descendant of the Magi, who are mentioned in the Gospel, and to rule over the same peoples they governed, enjoying such glory and prosperity that he uses no sceptre but one of emerald. Inspired by the example of his forefathers, who came to adore Christ in his cradle, he had planned to go to Jerusalem.

While this is the first *written* reference to Presbyter or Prester John that historians have managed to find, it is safe to presume that Bishop Hugh wasn't the inventor of this legendary figure. The belief that a Christian king and kingdom existed somewhere beyond Persia and Armenia, somewhere beyond the domains of the infidel Mohammedans, somewhere in the unknown realm of the extreme Orient, was in fairly wide circulation from at least the time of the First Crusade. Bishop Hugh, in raising the hope that this rich and powerful Christian monarch could prove a valuable ally in a second crusade, may have been quite deliberately seeking to exploit the belief for his own purposes, but he wasn't trying to gull the Pope with it. He himself surely believed the story he told at Viterbo, for there was, as is usually the case in matters like this, a basis in fact for it.

Because of the stupendous success of Mohammed and the incredible speed with which his faith spread out of Arabia, we think of Christianity as cut off from Africa and Asia from the eighth century onward, and therefore the idea that a Christian kingdom might have existed somewhere out in those remote parts in the Middle Ages seems utterly fanciful. What we tend to overlook is that in Christianity's first centuries, before the rise of Islam, Christian missionaries had wandered far and wide from the Holy Land. Indeed, at least apocryphally, Thomas the Apostle is believed to have gone to the land of the Magi, there to baptize the kings of the Indies, Balthazar, Melchior, and Gaspar, and, similarly, Matthew is said to have traveled to Abyssinia to convert that kingdom to Christianity. Whatever the historical worth of such tales, it is certainly true that by the fifth century Christian missionaries, albeit heretical ones, had reached those lands, and beyond.

For example, the Council of Ephesus, in 431, in deposing Nestorius, the Patriarch of Constantinople, for teaching that Christ had a dual nature, equally human and divine, drove him and his followers, the Nestorians, into exile in Persia. From there they moved ever eastward, on through India, making converts and building churches along the way, and by the eighth century had reached and settled in Far Cathay. The Council of Chalcedon, in 451, pronouncing on yet another heresy, that of Monophysitism, which maintained a single nature of Christ, partly divine and partly human, as taught by the monk Eutyches, set loose another group of wandering heretical preachers, one of whom, St. Frumentius, is credited with establishing the Coptic Church (as the Monophysite sect is called today) in Abyssinia.

With the rise of Islam, these sects were cut off from European Christendom, but reports of their existence and activities, although in highly fragmentary and distorted forms, did manage to filter through to the Mediterranean world. The knights of the First Crusade, for example, surely saw Monophysite pilgrims from Abyssinia in Jerusalem, and we know, from contemporary documents, that someone who represented himself as the Patriarch of the Indies, a Nestorian, appeared in Rome in 1122 and lectured Pope Calixtus II on the miracles performed by the uncorrupted body of St. Thomas, which he claimed rested in a shrine of his church. Whatever else was made of this in Europe, there was certainly a realization that Christianity, in one form or another, existed in that unknown world beyond Islam. It is not hard to see how out of this realization the idea of a mighty Christian king of the extreme Orient might have arisen, especially at a time when the wish for such an ally against the infidel was most pressing.

It was against this background of belief that Bishop Hugh could speak of Prester John at the Pontifical Court in Viterbo and be listened to with complete credulity. But it was because of a specific event at the time that he could go beyond merely reiterating the existence of

Prester John and claim that the priest-king, having defeated a Mohammedan army, was now on the move to aid Jerusalem—and be
listened to with equal credulity.

Just a few years before the fall of Edessa, in 1141 to be specific, a
great battle had been fought at Samarkand between Sanjar, the Seljuk
Turk ruler of Persia (of which Samarkand then was a vassal), and a
certain Yeh-lu Ta-Shih, the prince of a Manchurian tribe called Khitai
(which had once ruled China and from whose name Cathay derives),
with the latter emerging victorious. Now this Yeh-lu Ta-Shih was anything but a Christian (he was, most probably, a Mongol Buddhist),
but the fact that he had defeated the Persian army of the feared and
hated Seljuk Turks qualified him as an enemy of Islam, and by the
time the news of his victory had traveled out of the steppes of Central
Asia from Samarkand and reached the beleaguered Crusader states in
the Holy Land, this Manchurian enemy of Islam had been converted
into the Christian king of Bishop Hugh's tale.

So, when the Second Crusade was launched, it was with the expectation that an army of a mysterious Christian ally from the Orient was
then also on the march against the Saracens. But that army never
materialized, Prester John did not come to the aid of the Crusaders,
and the ill-conceived adventure ended in unmitigated disaster. The
knights of Conrad III and Louis VII were defeated at the siege of
Damascus and the advance of Islam continued unabated. Zengi was
followed by Noureddin, and he in turn was succeeded by Saladin,
whose fierce cavalry overran the Crusader states one by one, ultimately
capturing Jerusalem and the Holy Sepulchre.

And then, at this moment of darkest despair and defeat, Europe
once again heard of the fabulous priest-king of the Orient. This time,
though, word came in a far more remarkable manner: a letter from
Prester John himself arrived. This astonishing document was addressed to Manuel Comnenus, Emperor of Byzantium, but we know
from contemporary chronicles that copies of it also reached the Pope,
the Holy Roman Emperor Frederick Barbarossa, and other kings and
princes of Europe around 1165.

John the Presbyter [it began], by the grace of God and the strength of
our Lord Jesus Christ, king of kings, lord of lords, to his friend Manuel,
Governor of the Byzantines, greetings, wishing him health and the continued enjoyment of the divine blessing. Our Majesty has been informed
that you hold our Excellency in esteem, and that knowledge of our great-

ness has reached you. . . . If indeed you wish to know wherein consists our great power, then believe without doubting that I, Prester John, who reign supreme, exceed in riches, virtue and power all creatures who dwell under heaven. Seventy-two kings pay tribute to me. I am a devout Christian and everywhere protect the Christians of our empire, nourishing them with alms. We have made a vow to visit the sepulchre of our Lord with a great army, as befits the glory of our Majesty, to wage war against and chastise the enemies of the cross of Christ, and to exalt his sacred name.

Our magnificence dominates the Three Indias, and extends to Farther India, where the body of St. Thomas the Apostle rests. It reaches through the desert toward the place of the rising of the sun, and continues through the valley of deserted Babylon close by the Tower of Babel.

The letter then goes on to describe the wonders of this realm. We are told that "every kind of beast that is under heaven" can be found there, that milk and honey abound, that "no poison can do harm and no noisy frog croaks" in this kingdom. A river called the Physon, emerging from Paradise, winds through one province and is full of emeralds, sapphires, topazes, onyxes, beryls, and other precious stones.

Images of Africa: strange men (from an edition of Pliny's *Natural History*, Frankfurt, 1582)

There is a kind of worm there

which in our tongue are called salamanders. These worms can only live in
fire, and make a skin around them as the silkworm does. This skin is carefully spun by the ladies of our palace, and from it we have cloth for our
common use. When we wish to wash the garments made of this cloth, we
put them into fire, and they come forth fresh and clean.

The palace "in which our sublimity dwells" has a roof of ebony,
gables of gold, gates of sardonyx inlaid with the horn of a serpent,
windows of crystals, columns of ivory, a courtyard paved in onyx.

Our bed is of sapphire, because of its virtue of chastity. We possess the
most beautiful women, but they approach us only four times in the year
and then solely for the procreation of sons, and when they have been sancti-
fied by us, as Bathsheba was by David, each one returns to her place.

We feed daily at our table 30,000 men, besides casual guests. . . . .
This table is made of precious emerald, with four columns of amethyst
supporting it; the virtue of this stone is that no one sitting at the table can
fall into drunkedness. . . . During each month we are served at our table
by seven kings, each in his turn, by sixty-two dukes, and by three hundred
and sixty-five counts. . . . In our hall there dine daily, on our right hand,
twelve archbishops and on our left, twenty bishops and also the Patriarch
of St. Thomas, the Protopapas of Samarkand and the Archprotopapas of
Susa, in which city the throne of our glory and our imperial palace are
situated.

As for Prester John's military power, the letter informs us,

When we ride forth to war, our troops are preceded by thirteen huge and
lofty crosses made of gold and ornamented with precious stones, instead
of banners, and each of these is followed by ten thousand mounted soldiers
and one hundred thousand infantrymen, not counting those who have
charge of the baggage and provisions.

And finally, anticipating a question that must have been in the minds
of its readers, the letter says,

If you ask how it is that the Creator of all things, having made us the most
supreme and most glorious over all mortals, does not give us a higher title
than presbyter, priest, let not your wisdom be surprised on this account,
for here is the reason. At our court we have many ministers who are of
higher dignity than ourselves in the Church, and of greater standing in
divine office. For our household steward is a patriarch and a king, our
butler is an archbishop and a king, our chamberlain is a bishop and a king,

our marshal is a king and an archbishop, our chief cook is a king and an abbot. And therefor it does not seem proper to our Majesty to assume those names, or to be distinguished by those titles with which our palace overflows. Therefore to show our great humility, we choose to be called by a less name and to assume an inferior rank. If you can count the stars in the sky and the sands of the sea, you will be able to judge thereby the vastness of our realm and our power.

The letter was, of course, a forgery, albeit a wonderfully imaginative one. We don't know who the forger was or how the letter was delivered, but, no matter how preposterous it may seem to us 800 years later, it was taken for genuine, and the impact it had on medieval Europe was electrifying.

Almost surely the main purpose of the letter's author, as was Bishop Hugh's two decades before, was to bolster Europe's morale in a dark time and incite it to yet another crusade against the Saracens. (For this reason scholars tend to guess that the perpetrator of the forgery was Frederick Barbarossa, a keen champion of a Third Crusade.) In this it succeeded, providing much of the inspiration that sent the ill-fated Barbarossa, Richard the Lion-Hearted, and Philip Augustus of France to cross swords with Saladin at the gates of Jerusalem. But, inadvertently, at least for its author's original intent, the letter accomplished much more.

In one bold stroke, the existence of a Christian king and kingdom somewhere on the other side of the world seemed confirmed. Out of the cloudy swirl of rumor and fantasy and travelers' tales, which had circulated for almost a century, the legend of Prester John crystallized and took such hypnotic hold on the medieval imagination that it was to persist unshakably for nearly 500 years and set off a quest—as romantic and quixotic and rich in consequence as the search for the Golden Fleece or the Holy Grail or the Fountain of Youth—that was to be the great energizing force behind Europe's first great age of exploration and discovery. To find that shining and ever-elusive Kingdom of Prester John, with its fabulous wealth and magical powers, proved a sufficiently seductive goal to lure adventurous men of the Middle Ages out of the severely circumscribed limits of the known world into the dangerous enterprise of penetrating always farther into the unknown.

One is almost tempted to suggest that the legend arose expressly to serve this purpose, that some communal unconscious, mythic intelligence within medieval Europe gave birth to the idea of a fabulous priest-king because of its need and desire at the time for knowledge of the world, knowledge to dispel the terrors of the geographical darkness that pressed all around, knowledge to promote its expansion. And the most cunning part of the idea was that the goal sought wasn't there to be found, so that the quest for it would have to go on for a long time and range in every conceivable direction. In time, other reasons would develop to promote European exploration, most of them far more material and practical. But throughout the greater part of the Middle Ages it was the quest for the legendary kingdom of Prester John that served as the preeminent motivation for Europe's geographical discoveries, including the Congo.

As no other piece of writing in that illiterate age, Prester John's letter was remarkably widely circulated. Thousands of copies were made, and it was translated out of the original Latin into most of the vernacular languages of medieval Europe. As it passed through the hands of the copyists and translators it was elaborated and distorted to become an anthology of all the myths and marvels and fables of the Middle Ages and the single most popular piece of literature of the times. Ants as big as foxes with the skins of panthers, the wings of sea locusts, and the tusks of forest boars, which burrowed in the ground and heaped up piles of gold, were said to be found in Prester John's kingdom. So too were unicorns that killed lions, serpents with "two heads and horns like rams and eyes which shine brightly as lamps," amazons and centaurs and "horned men, who have but one eye in front and three or four in back." In that realm was the nation of Gog and Magog, whose people were cannibals and whom the priest-king employed as soldiers, granting them permission "to eat our enemies, so that of a thousand foes not one remains who is not devoured and consumed, but later we send them home because, if we let them stay longer with us, they would eat us all."

We learn that Prester John made annual pilgrimages into the desert to pay homage at the tomb of the prophet Daniel, "accompanied by ten thousand priests and the same number of knights, and two hundred towers built on elephants which also carry a turret to protect us against the seven-headed dragons." Standing outside the priest-king's palace, we discover, is a tower thirteen stories high and at its top an enchanted mirror in which is reflected the whole of the world. There too is the Fountain of Youth. "A person who bathes in this fountain," we're told, "whether he be of a hundred or a thousand years, will regain the age of thirty-two. Know that we were born and blessed in the womb of our mother 562 years ago and since then we have bathed in the fountain six times." Which helps to explain how it was that men would quest for Prester John for hundreds of years and continue to believe he was still there to be found.

But found where? In 1177, more or less in response to Prester John's letter, Pope Alexander III sent his personal physician, a Master Philip, on an embassy to the priest-king. He vanished without a trace; we don't know what happened to him or, for that matter, in which direction he traveled. The letter provided precious few clues where to look for the fabulous kingdom. Its mention of Babylon (a city of Mesopotamia near present-day Baghdad in Iraq), of Susa (several hundred miles farther east in present-day Iran), and of the Physon (cited in Genesis as one of the four rivers flowing out of Eden, which medieval geographers believed to be the Indus) only served to confirm the notion that Prester John's realm lay somewhere beyond Persia.

As for the reference to "the Three Indias," over which his magnificence dominated, that was of little more help. For twelfth-century Europe, real and practical knowledge of the world didn't extend much farther than the North African littoral, Asia Minor, and a portion of the Near East, and everything beyond was generally referred to as the Indies or the Orient. The geographers of the time often tried to make themselves seem more knowledgeable than they actually were, and on some maps of the twelfth century we find fanciful demarcations of the vast unknown into three parts. On one such map, we see an *India Ultima* comprising what might be today's Afghanistan and West Pakistan, and *India Inferior* marking out a region that would include today's India, and an *India Superior* ranging from the Ganges to the Caucasus across what today would be China. On another, Nearer India seems to cover the northern half of the Indian subcontinent, Farther India its southern half, and Middle India is roughly where Ethiopia and East Africa are today. On still another, *India Prima* is indicated as "the land of the pygmies," *India Secunda* "faces the land of the Medes," and *India Ultima* "occupies the ends of the earth with the ocean on one side and the realm of darkness on the other." Thus, anyone setting off to find Prester John had to be prepared to travel beyond Persia to the uttermost edge of the world.

Ironically, it was one of the deadliest perils that Christendom was ever to face that turned the quest for the priest-king initially in the direction of Far Cathay and so opened that unknown part of the world to Europe. In 1221, with the Fifth Crusade shattered in the defeat at Cairo, Jacques of Vitry, the Bishop of Acre, last of the Crusader states to survive, wrote to Pope Honorius III that "A new and mighty protector of Christianity has arisen. He is King David of India, who has taken the field of battle against the unbelievers at the head of an army of unparalleled size." This King David, who according to Bishop Jacques was commonly called Prester John, was believed to be the son or grandson of the Prester John who had been awaited at the time of the Second Crusade (giving rise to the sensible idea that "Prester John" was the title of a dynasty of Christian priest-kings in the Indies rather than a marvelously long-lived individual). But, whatever his lineage, ancestry, or relationships, one thing was certain: this Prester John was a mortal foe of Islam. For once again, out of the mysterious lands of the Indies where Nestorian Christians were known to reside, a great king was leading an invincible army of ferocious horsemen and scoring victory after victory over the Saracens. This king, it was to turn out, was Genghis Khan, lord of the Mongols, scourge of Asia.

It wasn't until the Golden Horde, under Genghis's successors, having routed the Moslems of Asia and Asia Minor, thundered down on the Christian kingdoms of Eastern Europe and massacred their populations that Europe suspected that it might be mistaken about this protector of Christianity. By then, though, the belief that Prester John's kingdom was to be found in Cathay had taken firm root and, under the Pax Mongolica of Kublai Khan, monks and friars and traders began venturing along the caravan routes deep into that exotic realm in search of it. It was quickly apparent to these travelers that the Great Khan himself, in his pleasure dome at Karakorum, wasn't Prester John. But they also realized that Kublai Khan wasn't the only king in the Indies; there were hundreds of lesser khans throughout the immense Mongol empire, and the Europeans, wandering about it endlessly, were very willing to believe that any one of these might be the Christian priest-king. What strengthened them in this hope was their discovery that Nestorian Christians served in the highest ranks of the Mongol courts, as generals and counselors, and often as wives of the Tatar chieftains. So it seemed likely that one day they would come upon a chieftain who was a Christian himself.

The most famous of the European travelers in Cathay was Marco Polo, a Venetian merchant who was employed by Kublai Khan. He roamed widely over the Mongol empire for 17 years and his wonderful account of his adventures, *Il Milione,* was Europe's most comprehensive and accurate report on the Orient for 250 years. In *Il Milione,* Marco Polo writes of Prester John as "that king most famous in the world" and identifies him as the monarch of a kingdom of the Indies which opposed the Mongols and which was defeated in battle against the Golden Horde. And then he reports that in this battle the long-sought Christian priest-king was killed. Other travelers in Cathay at roughly the same time, notably the Franciscans Giovanni de Piano Carpini and William of Rubruck and the Dominican Ascelin of Lombardy, reported very much the same shocking news. This was late in the thirteenth century, more than 100 years after Prester John's letter had arrived, and it would seem reasonable to conclude that this would be the end of the story. But it wasn't.

It is a measure of the hypnotic hold that his legend had on medieval Europe that, despite repeated "eyewitness'" accounts to the contrary, it would simply not let Prester John be killed. The will to believe in the Christian priest-king's fabulous realm and the need to quest after it were too compelling. Europe steadfastly refused to believe that Prester John was dead. The most that it would concede was that his kingdom, after all, might not be in Far Cathay. When the Pax Mongolica shattered with the rise of the Ming dynasty and, as a result, Europeans were expelled from Cathay, the caravan routes to that land were closed, and the eastern half of Asia was cut off from Europe for the next 200 years—when, in short, it was no longer feasible to search for Prester John in that part of the world—the quest turned to another mysterious realm: Africa.

This shift in geography seems to have occurred gradually. We see on what was called Fra Paolino's map, dated around 1320, Prester John's realm still situated in what we would consider Asia. But on the map of Angelino Dulcert of 1339 the mythical kingdom is placed in what we would regard as East Africa, in the vicinity of Ethiopia (or Abyssinia, as it was then called). In the 1330s, a Dominican friar, Jordanus of Severac, who had traveled in China and India and described his adventures in *Mirabilia Descripta,* identified the Emperor of Ethiopia as Prester John. And this idea is repeated and promoted in such accounts as *The Book of Knowledge of all the Kingdoms, Lands and Lordships that are in the World* by an anonymous Spanish Franciscan published in the 1350s, which placed Prester John's realm in a region beyond the Mountains of the Moon, and in the *Travels* of the Florentine aristocrat Giovanni de' Marignolli, published in 1355.

That Prester John might be the Emperor of Ethiopia didn't violate the fundamental beliefs that he was a Christian and that he was a monarch of the Indies. For, as we have seen, in medieval geography, in which there was only the vaguest realization that an ocean separated the Indian subcontinent from the east coast of Africa, Ethiopia was considered part of the Indies. And, as we also have seen, Europe had known, since the time of the First Crusade, when Christian knights had seen Monophysite pilgrims in Jerusalem, that the Coptic Church was the religion of Ethiopia and her Emperor. So the only problem now was to discover where Ethiopia was and how to get there.

For fourteenth-century Europe, Africa was totally unknown. Indeed, no European had so much as set foot on it since the days of the Roman Empire. The North African littoral was occupied by the infidel Moors, the desert beyond was firmly in the control of warrior Mohammedan Berber tribes, and what lay beyond that even the Moslems themselves had only the vaguest notion. In the geography of the times—mainly the work of Arab geographers of the preceding three centuries—a mighty river, flowing east to west, thought to be the western branch of the Nile but in reality the Niger, was said to mark the end of the Sahara. The lands south of it, wherein the kingdom of Prester John was assumed to lie, were referred to variously as Ethiopia or Guinea or the Sudan. These were extremely imprecise, always shifting and often interchangeable terms, having nothing to do with the nations that bear those names today but rather demarking a vast unknown into roughly eastern, central, and western parts, and all meaning, in the corruption of one vernacular or another, the land of the men with burnt faces, the land of the blacks. To be sure, Arab traders and travelers had made some contact with sub-Saharan Africa by this time, sailing out of the Red Sea down the East African coast, pushing up the Nile into the Sudan and trading with the black tribes on the southern edge of the desert. But whatever useful geographical information they had gathered was hidden away in the libraries of Moslem sultans and merchants, and what little filtered out to Europe only served to feed its fantasies about Prester John's realm.

This was the land that Pliny, writing in the first century, had

called "the middle of the earth, where the Sunne hath his way and
keepeth his course, scorched and burnt with flames." And there, he
said, lived the mantichora, "which has a triple row of teeth, meeting
like the teeth of a comb, the face and ears of a human being, grey eyes,
a blood-red colour, a lion's body, inflicting stings with its tail in the
manner of a scorpion, with a voice like the sound of a pan-pipe
blended with a trumpet, of a great speed, with a special appetite for
human flesh." Solinus, in the third century, had entitled a chapter of
his geography "Of Aethyop, of the filthy fashion of the people of that
Countrey, of their monstrous shape, of the Dragons and other wylde
beastes of wonderful nature there," and then proceeded with great
gusto to spin out fabulous stories altogether in keeping with this eye-
popping rubric.

The tales of Arab travelers in the succeeding centuries further
embroidered the fantastic nature of the realm in Europe's imagination. For example, al-Idrisi, writing in the twelfth century, told of a
kingdom in the land of the blacks whose king was "the most just of all
men" and in whose palace there was "an entire lump of Gold, not cast,
nor wrought by any instrument, but perfectly formed by the Divine
Providence only, of thirty Pounds Weight, which has been bored
through and fitted for a Seat to the Royal Throne." Moreover, this
king had an "abundance of rich ornaments, and Horses, with most
sumptuous trappings, which on Solemn Days were led before him. He
had many Troops who march each with their Colours, under his
Royal Banner; Elephants, Camels and various kinds of animals, which
are found in the Negroes Countries, precede him." Ibn-Batuta two
centuries later described a city he had visited as made entirely out of
gold; it was called Timbuktoo. And in the Catalan Atlas, prepared for
Charles the Wise in 1375 by the Majorcan Jew Abraham Cresques and
derived from Arab sources, we read of a certain Mansa Musa, who was
"the richest and most noble lord because of the abundance of gold
found in his country."

So the lure of Prester John remained and, as his kingdom was now
said to lie in Africa, Europe was drawn to the continent in its enduring quest.

3

---◆•◦•◆---

A HERO IN BARBARY

"I shall not find a better opening for this chapter than the recital of the remarkable conquest of the great city of Ceuta, a celebrated victory which glorified the heavens and favoured the earth."

In this way a fifteenth-century Portuguese chronicler, Gomes Eannes de Azurara, begins his account of the capture of the Moroccan citadel on the Barbary Shore by his countrymen in 1415. And it can serve equally well for the opening of this chapter because that celebrated Portuguese victory over the infidel forces of the Moorish Kingdom of Fez marked Europe's first step into Africa since Roman times and the start of its discovery of the mysterious "Ethiopia" beyond the Sahara where Prester John was thought to reside.

That it was Portugal, one of the smallest nations of medieval Europe (its population was much less than one million at the time), which showed Europe the way into Africa is not one of history's larger puzzles. We only have to remember that for nearly 700 years before that Portugal had been fighting the Moors in the great *Reconquista* by which it, along with Castile, Aragon, Navarre, and the other Christian Kingdoms of the Spains, drove the North African Mohammedans step by step out of the Iberian peninsula, which they had overrun in the eighth century. In addition, during much of the same period, Portugal had also been fighting Castile in order to retain the independence it was winning back from Islam. In 1385, with the Moors safely reduced to a single caliphate on the peninsula—Granada, Portugal under João of Aviz scored a stunning victory over Castile at the battle of Aljubarrota. During a pause in the hostilities, while the astonished Castile tried to decide whether to accept the defeat as the end of its ambitions against Portugal, João married Philippa, daughter of John of Gaunt, and the alliance with England, which the marriage signified, settled the matter for Castile. In 1411, a peace treaty was signed between the two kingdoms, the new and vigorous Aviz dynasty was established on the Portuguese throne, and a confident, triumphant Portuguese army stood in the field spoiling for new worlds to conquer.

Azurara, in his chronicle, explains how it then came to passs that Portugal launched that army across the Straits of Gibraltar into Africa. It wasn't João's idea. We read in Azurara that, to commemorate the peace with Castile and occupy his restless soldiers, the new king planned a magnificent tournament in which all the *fidalgos* of the kingdom would participate and at which his three eldest sons—the Infantes Dom Duarte, Dom Pedro, and Dom Henrique—were to win their knighthoods. But, Azurara tells us, this scheme didn't appeal to the youngest of these princes, Dom Henrique. He felt that a fanciful joust in an arena for a fair maiden's favor was no way for a noble prince to gain his knighthood. For him, the only proper way was in a true test of arms, on the field of battle, at war against a worthy enemy. As he was only seventeen at the time, the hot-blooded prince had missed out on the fighting with Castile and, as Portugal had also made peace with Granada, the last Moorish stronghold in Iberia, the times seemed to offer no opportunity for such valorous display.

But Henrique had a solution. According to Azurara, it was the young prince who suggested the idea that, in place of a tournament, his father should attack Ceuta. King João, we read, was taken aback; the audacious idea had never occurred to him and, at the outset at least, he resisted it adamantly. Henrique, however, proved persuasive. Again and again he returned to his father with new arguments for the enterprise: As Ceuta was the port from which the Moors had originally invaded Iberia, its conquest would cripple Islam's ambitions against the Spains. As Ceuta was also the port from which the corsairs of the Barbary pirates sailed, its conquest would end their raids on European shipping and put Portugal in command of the western Mediterranean. And as Ceuta was known to be one of the wealthiest Moorish cities, its conquest would enrich the royal treasury, whereas the tournament would only deplete it. And, finally, Henrique argued, there could be no more glorious enterprise by which to celebrate the ascendancy of the Aviz dynasty and to employ its conquering army than by carrying Christendom's war against the Moor, so long fought on the soil of the Spains, into the infidel's own land.

At last, Azurara tells us, King João relented. In great secrecy, an armada of 33 galleys, 27 triremes, 32 biremes and 120 pinnaces, carrying 50,000 men-at-arms and 30,000 mariners was assembled on the Tagus before Lisbon and, sailing under a Papal Bull, which bestowed all the privileges and indulgences of a Crusade, assaulted the walled fortress of Ceuta in August of 1415.

You may imagine the ardour of the combatants on either side [Azurara writes]. The din of battle was so great that there were many persons who said afterwards that it was heard at Gibraltar . . . the rage of the Moors was such that at times, even without arms, they threw themselves upon the Christians; and their despair and their fury were so great that they did not surrender themselves, even if they found themselves alone before a multitude of enemies; and many of them, already lying on the ground, and with their souls half severed from their bodies, still made movements with their arms as though they would deal mortal blows to those who had vanquished them. . . . In this conquest the Infante Dom Henrique was the captain of a very great and powerful fleet, and, as a valiant knight, he fought all that day on which the city was taken from the Moors . . . the first royal captain who touched land near the walls of Ceuta was he of whom I write, and his square banner was the first to pass the gates of the city, the Infante himself being not far from its shadows. And the blows he dealt the enemy that day were noteworthy among all others, since for five hours he fought without respite, and neither the heat, which was great, nor the fatigue of such an effort could persuade him to depart and take some rest.

As initiator and hero of this victory over Islam, which gave Europe its first permanent possession in Africa in more than 700 years (and which Portugal kept for another 560 years), Dom Henrique was duly rewarded. Not only did he gain his knighthood in the bloody manner he coveted but he was also appointed Duke of Viseu (Portugal's premier duchy), Master of the Order of Christ (the Portuguese branch of the rich and famous Knights Templar), and Governor of Ceuta. In view of the profound impact it was to have on the young prince, the last must be judged the most valuable prize that he won.

In his role as governor, Dom Henrique returned again and again to the Moroccan citadel. In the first years after the conquest, his main interest was in employing the port as a base from which armed Portuguese *barinels* could patrol the western Mediterranean and clear it of the corsairs of the Barbary pirates. Later, he became involved in defending the city against attacks by the Berber tribesmen of the Moroccan Atlas. And, still later, he entertained schemes for using this Portuguese stronghold in North Africa for further, more ambitious campaigns against the Kingdom of Fez. But, Azurara tells us, during all these visits, the prince also spent much of his time questioning the city's inhabitants, wandering in its streets and marketplaces, perusing the libraries and archives of its sultans and merchants, and developing an ever keener curiosity about the vast unknown continent that stretched away from the citadel's walls, across the forbidding wasteland of the desert, toward the mysterious realm of Prester John.

Ceuta at this time was at the height of its splendor, a gorgeous city built upon seven rolling hills (from which, Septa, its name derives), and sprawling in indolent luxury down to the glittering white beaches of the blue Mediterranean. It contained the flower of Moorish architecture; handsome watch towers, massive arches and gates, delicate minarets and gold-leafed domes of its mosques and palaces adorned the winding walled streets. Its bazaars overflowed with jewels and gold, silver and jade, ivory and amber, silks and spices, carpets and porcelain, incense and pearls, and its port bustled with the feluccas of Arabia and the galleys of Venice and Genoa. It was Islam's richest trading emporium on the western Mediterranean, terminus of the great Arab caravans.

Europe had long known, and always envied, the caravan routes from the Orient that the Moslems controlled—those that wound out of Cathay across the Central Asian steppes to the Black Sea, those that came from India to the Persian Gulf and on from there either through the Tigris and Euphrates valleys to Baghdad and Damascus or up the Red Sea to Cairo and Alexandria—all bringing their fabulous riches to the Moslem ports of Asia Minor and North Africa, such as Ceuta. But what Europe had not known, or at best had only heard vague rumors of, was that there was yet another set of caravan routes under Islam's control—those that crossed the burning wastes of the Sahara from the Negro lands of Ethiopia and Guinea and the Sudan, beyond the so-called Western Nile, which brought riches to the Moorish ports every bit as fabulous as those from the Orient. And Dom Henrique also discovered this in Ceuta.

Wandering in the caravanseries of the city, pushing through the exciting crush of camel trains and bearded Arab merchants on donkeys and white-robed tawny Moors called Azenegues from the

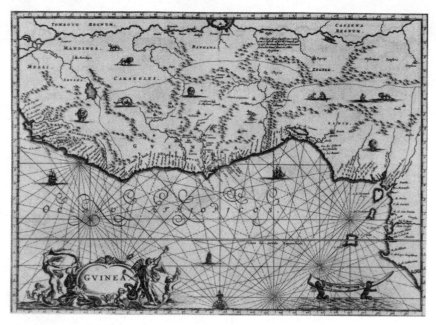

Ancient map of Guinea

farthest Sahara, his eyes darting from one wonder to another amid the
tumble of stalls in the bazaars, the Portuguese prince could see for
himself the precious goods that the trans-Saharan caravans brought.
Bags of gold dust spilled open so as to glitter seductively under the
desert sun; pyramids of elephant tusks and rhinoceros horns were
stacked as tall as a man; there were ostrich feathers arranged in flowery
bouquets, oryx skins stretched over warriors' shields; malaguetta
peppers and civet furs; and huddles of mournful blacks waiting to be
sold into slavery.

And, in his ceaseless questioning of Arab merchants and camel
drivers and captive blacks and Berber traders, he heard of the kingdoms of Mali and Ghana and Songhai; the royal cities of Timbuktoo
and Gao and Cantor, from whence those precious goods had come; the
line of oases across the waterless desert by which trade to those distant
places was made possible; and the way that trade was conducted once
the caravans got there. He heard, for example, of the Silent Trade,
which Herodotus was the first to mention, claiming that the Cartha-
ginians had participated in it, and which Alvise da Cadamosto, a
young Venetian merchant adventurer who was later to enlist in
Dom Henrique's service, gives an account of in his fifteenth-century
chronicle.

Deep in the Sahara, the prince was told, many weeks from Ceuta, there are rock-salt mines at an oasis called Taghaza. The Berber Moors of that region mine the salt, load it on camels, and take it for forty days southward, from oasis to oasis, across the desert to Timbuktoo, on the shores of the Western Nile, where they sell it to the Negro king for gold. But it is known that this king of Timbuktoo does not himself possess the gold which he exchanges for the salt. For he, in his turn, takes the salt and has it packed into blocks to be carried on men's heads, and they march with it still farther to the south, to the land of the Wangara. The Wangara, who are people said to have the heads and tails of dogs, are never seen. For the salt is laid down in their land, and the men who have brought it go far out of sight and light a fire. When the Wangara see the smoke of the fire, and when they are sure that the men from Timbuktoo are sufficiently distant, they come up to the salt and place by each block as much gold as they judge to be its equivalent. Then they go away out of sight too. Now the men from Timbuktoo return and look at the gold, and if they think it represents a fair price for their salt, they take the gold and go away for good. But if, on the other hand, the gold seems too little, they leave both the gold and the salt and go away to wait. Now the Wangara, coming up again, take away the salt where the gold for it has been accepted; but where it hasn't they add more gold. This process continues until both sides finally are satisfied that the amount of gold given is equal to the amount of salt taken away. "There is perfect honesty on both sides," Herodotus wrote of this Silent Trade. "The gold is never touched until it equals in value the salt that has been offered for it and the salt is never touched until the gold has been taken away."

Not everything Dom Henrique learned in Ceuta was accurate or even credible. Much of it, he realized, was wildly embroidered, but all of it so obviously contained a hard core of truth that, Azurara tells us, it fixed him in his determination to reach those lands beyond the Sahara, to take up the quest for the Kingdom of Prester John.

Throughout his life he never entirely gave up the idea of getting there by direct onslaught against Islam. That crusading zeal, that warrior temperament, that hatred of the infidel, which had led him to instigate the conquest of Ceuta, never completely left him, and from time to time he involved himself in Portuguese campaigns against the Kingdom of Fez in the hope of thus taking control of the Moor's trans-Saharan caravan routes and so opening the way to the Christian priest-

Prince Henry the Navigator

king in black Africa. But he must have realized early on that this would prove a futile course. The capture of Ceuta hadn't shaken the Moor's hold on North Africa, and the later attacks on Tangier and Arzila ended in total disaster. So it is likely that soon after the conquest of Ceuta, when he was still a regular visitor to the Moroccan citadel, Dom Henrique dreamed up his plan to turn Islam's flank by sailing down the Atlantic coast of Africa, bypassing the Moslem-controlled Sahara, and then striking inland from there to the Kingdom of Prester John—the audacious enterprise to which he would devote his life and for which historians of a later age would give him the title Prince Henry the Navigator.

This noble prince was of middle stature [Azurara tells us], a man thickset with limbs large and powerful, and bushy hair; the skin was white but the travail and the battles of life altered its hue as time went on. His aspect, to those who beheld him for the first time, was severe; when anger carried him away his countenance became terrifying. He had force of mind and acute intelligence in a high degree. His desire to accomplish great deeds was beyond all comparison.

There is some controversy over exactly what great deeds Henry desired to accomplish. Very much after the fact, historians have credited him with setting out not only to reach the Ethiopia of Prester John by sailing down the West African coast but also to go on and circumnavigate the African continent and so open a sea route to the Indies, break into the rich trade with the Orient, and found an overseas empire for Portugal. To be sure, these ultimately were to be direct consequences of the enterprise he launched. But Azurara, despite his desire to extol the virtues and accomplishments of his prince, doesn't mention any of them. He lists only these: (1) to find "the Christian king or seigneur, outside this kingdom, who, for the love of our Lord Jesus Christ, was willing to aid him" in the wars against the Moors; (2) to "increase the holy faith in Our Lord Jesus Christ, and to lead to His faith all souls desirous of being saved"; (3) to discover "the power of the Moors of this land of Africa . . . because every wise man is moved by the desire to know the strength of his enemy"; (4) to learn "if in these territories there should be . . . any harbours where men could enter without peril so that they could bring back to the realm many merchandises . . . and in like manner carry to these regions merchandise of the realm"; and (5) "to know what lands there were beyond the Canary Isles and a cape which was called Bojador."

For medieval Europe, these were stupendously daring goals. Indeed, the very idea of sailing into the Atlantic beyond Cape Bojador seemed utterly mad. For, if the heart of Africa was then a fantastic, unexplored mystery, it at least was believed to contain, for the brave adventurer, wonders as well as terrors. But the Atlantic Ocean, which was every bit as unknown as Africa at the time, contained in the medieval imagination nothing but terrors.

It is altogether likely that this wasn't always so. In the histories of Herodotus, for example, we find recounted the story of an expedition of Phoenician sailors, dispatched by Pharaoh Necho II of Egypt, which was said to have circumnavigated Africa around 600 B.C., sailing southward down the Red Sea and returning through the Pillars of Hercules three years later, having apparently passed through the Atlantic without incident. Herodotus also tells us of a certain Persian nobleman, Sataspes, who in order to escape execution for a crime against Xerxes, agreed to sail once around the continent, and though he didn't make it, the fact that he was willing to try suggests that the

Atlantic was not considered an impassable sea at the time. Similarly, Pliny records the exploits of Hanno, an admiral of Carthage, who in 450 B.C. sailed down the Atlantic coast of Africa to what appears to have been the Senegal, where "savages, bodies all over hairie" attacked his ships with stones. And in Strabo we can read of Eudoxus of Cyzicus, a Greek navigator who around 130 B.C. discovered the prow of a fishing boat from Cádiz on the East African coast and from this concluded that a vessel could sail from Spain clear around the continent without encountering any particular danger in the Atlantic.

But, by Prince Henry's time, the lore of the ancients was either lost or disbelieved. Even the notion that Africa was surrounded by oceans and thus could be circumnavigated at all, on which so much of this ancient lore was based, was wildly in doubt. Claudius Ptolemy's geography had been an overpowering and paralyzing influence on geographers since the second century, and in his elegantly symmetrical picture of the world, which was promoted by the Church because it placed Jerusalem at the center of the earth, Africa was not a continental island but a great land mass that extended southward to the ends of the earth, merging with what today we know as Antarctica.

Since the days of Necho's Phoenicians or of Hanno, Sataspes, or Eudoxus, if indeed even then, there had been no ocean-going expeditions ambitious enough to prove Ptolemy wrong. It is true that the Arabs had been sailing from the Red Sea around Cape Guardafui into the Indian Ocean and part way down the East African coast since at least the seventh century. But Europe didn't know about those voyages. And, besides, the Arabs themselves never ventured into the monsoon seas south of Madagascar, so even they didn't have any first-hand evidence that the Indian and Atlantic oceans flowed together at the southern tip of the continent.

On the other coast of Africa, geographical knowledge was even dimmer. The great European sailors of the time were those of the Italian city-states—Genoa, Venice, Pisa, Amalfi—who had gained their seamanship in the "carrying trade," that is, shipping the riches of the Orient from the Moslem ports of the Black Sea and the Barbary Shore across the Mediterranean to Europe. Their constant exposure to this wealth tempted many of them to try to short-circuit the Arab's overland caravan routes and get to the Orient via the Atlantic. We know, for example, of a certain Lancelot Malocello who is credited with sailing as far as the Canary Islands in 1270 (and, in a sense, rediscovering them, for they are believed to be the Fortunate Isles of Greek mythology), but he lost his nerve in the face of the Atlantic and turned back. In 1281 (or possibly 1291), the Genoese galleys of Tedisio Doria and the brothers Vivaldi are said to have set off "to go by sea to the ports of India to trade there" and, apparently following Malocello's route, were never heard of again. Others may have tried in subsequent years—a Portuguese galley is supposed to have visited the Canaries in 1341, a Catalan ship from Majorca is said to have been lost in 1346 after passing Cape Bojador, a French vessel is said to have reached the cape in 1402—but there is no record of anyone getting any further. As Azurara tells us, "up to that time no one knew, whether by writing or the memory of man, what there might be beyond this cape."

What was commonly believed to be beyond this cape was the Mar Tenebroso, the Ocean of Darkness. In the medieval imagination, this was a region of uttermost dread. We see it pictured on the maps of the time as a place of monsters and monstrous occurrences, where the heavens fling down liquid sheets of flame and the waters boil, where ferocious tempests and mountainous waves and terrible whirlpools rage, where serpent rocks and ogre islands lie in wait for the mariner, where the giant hand of Satan reaches up from the fathomless depths to seize him, where he will turn black in face and body as a mark of God's vengeance for the insolence of his prying into this forbidden mystery. And even if he should be able to survive all these ghastly perils and sail on through, he would then arrive in the Sea of Obscurity and be lost forever in the vapors and slime at the edge of the world.

That, despite the terror with which the Atlantic was viewed, Prince Henry nevertheless proposed to sail beyond Cape Bojador is certainly a measure of the audaciousness of his enterprise. But that he should propose to do this in light of the primitive state of the art of seamanship at the time gives a far better sense of the magnificent daring of his conception.

For example, one only has to remember what sorts of vessels were available. There were the galleys, three-masted merchantmen propelled by banks of oars, used by the Venetians and other Italians in the carrying trade, which were far too frail to venture very far into the Mar Tenebroso and which besides, because they required such a large crew of oarsmen, couldn't carry enough provisions for a prolonged ocean voyage. Then there were the *naos* and *barchas* of the Portuguese fleet—the former, broad-beamed cargo vessels used in the trade with England; the latter, fishing boats that worked the Atlantic shoals off the Iberian coast. Both were single masted with square-rigged sails and sturdy enough to ride out the rough weather and seas of the Atlantic. Their trouble was their awkwardness except in a following wind; they couldn't be tacked and were ill equipped to beat off a lee shore and had to run for shelter in a storm or contrary wind. The Portuguese had also developed the *barinel*, which combined the single square-rigged sail of the *barcha* and the oarsmen of the galley, and as far as long ocean voyages were concerned compounded the drawbacks of both. Also available, though mainly in the eastern Mediterranean, was the Arab felucca. It had a triangular, lateen-rigged sail and a raked mast, copied from the Indian Ocean dhows, and could sail much closer to the wind than any square-rigged vessel; but it too was far too lightly built to take on the rigors of the Atlantic.

Moreover, and by whichever vessel, sailing in those days meant coasting. Captains rarely, if ever—and then only for the shortest periods possible and in the most familiar waters—sailed out of sight of land. Navigational knowledge and equipment just weren't up to it. For example, there was no way of determining longitude. And, while the astrolabe was available, which calculates latitude from the height of the Polar Star above the horizon, the trouble here was that the length of a degree of latitude was not known with any accuracy. The compass was in use, having reached Europe from China via the Arabs, but its value was limited to sea charts that indicated compass bearings between visible landmarks and was of no value on the high seas, where pilots had to rely on dead reckoning.

For vessels and navigational equipment of this sort, the Atlantic coast of Africa posed formidable problems of seamanship. To be sure, the currents, flowing southward from Portugal, and the prevailing winds, northeast trades, favored the outbound leg of the voyage well enough. The trouble was the nature of the shoreline along which the craft were obliged to coast. This was, of course, the Sahara coast, a burning waste which, as far as anyone knew at the time, might stretch on forever, offering very few good anchorages and no food or water, and made treacherous by shoals and unpredictable tides and winds that no one had ever charted.

But these problems were minor compared with those that faced the mariner who hoped to return from the journey. For now he would have to sail *into* the current and *against* the winds. The *naos* and *barchas,* which were sturdy enough in construction to venture out on the voyage in the first place, simply could not manage to beat against the winds and currents with their square-rigged sails and return home along the route they came. There was, in fact, only one way they could hope to get back to Portugal once they were beyond Cape Bojador and that was by sailing away from the African coast and describing a bold arc out into the mid-Atlantic, where they could pick up the westerlies and the eastward-running current. To do this would take incredible nerve. For it meant sailing out of sight of land for days, even weeks, at a time. And it meant sailing on an unknown sea without any reliable navigational aids.

So, even had the seamen not feared the legendary terrors of the Mar Tenebroso, they had reason enough to fear the real terrors the ocean posed. And yet, when Prince Henry called on them to go, they sailed out onto the Ocean of Darkness after all.

4

ON THE OCEAN OF DARKNESS

Sagres, "where endeth the land and beginneth the sea," as the medieval Portuguese epic poet Camões wrote, is a tiny peninsula, barely 500 yards wide and 1000 yards long, that juts southward into the Atlantic from Cape St. Vincent in Portugal's Algarve and points like a finger from Europe's extreme southwest corner down the west coast of Africa. A barren outcropping of jagged rock, spotted with stunted junipers, it is lashed by the Atlantic's thundering surf and, when the simoon sweeps the Sahara, by the sands of Africa as well. It was originally called the Sacred Promontory because legend has it that the guardians of the relics of St. Vincent, fleeing the Moslem conquest of the saint's place of martyrdom in Zaragoza, landed on this peninsula and buried the holy remains there. For centuries afterward the deep coves in the cliffs of its shoreline provided safe anchorage for ships coasting from the Mediterranean to the English channel ports.

The desolation and holiness of the place suited Prince Henry's temperament, and its geography was perfect for his Atlantic enterprise. In the early 1420s he set about establishing there his famous School of Navigation, which in the course of the next four decades was to become the Cape Canaveral of West African exploration. In time, the best of the world's mathematicians and astronomers, cartographers and cosmographers, pilots and ships' captains, makers of nautical instruments and shipwrights would be gathered at Sagres, and the finest available maps, atlases, sea charts, scientific treatises and travel literature would be collected in its libraries. Princes would come there eager to invest in the enterprise, and it would eventually win the official patronage of the crown and the Pope's blessing. A city would grow up on the once-deserted promontory; a fortress, observatory, churches, and dockyards would be built. New maps would be drawn, unknown coastlines charted, currents and winds plotted, navigational instruments invented, and new ships designed that would overcome the problems posed by the Atlantic and step by step strip away its mysteries.

But, before any of this would happen, the first expeditions had to be launched into the terror of the Ocean of Darkness. As he enjoyed only token royal support for his enterprise at the outset, Prince Henry was required to finance the first voyages out of his own personal treasury. Moreover, he had to use the open, clumsy *naos, barchas,* and *barinels* as the vessels for those voyages, and as captains had to rely on the young, adventurous *fidalgos* of his own household, the knights and squires who had fought with him in North Africa and on whose courage he could count but who had little seafaring experience.

In the course of the next decade or so, Henry dispatched these *fidalgos* on expedition after expedition down the West African coast, each with instructions to sail beyond Cape Bojador. But none of them ever did. Most, on reaching the North African shore, spent their time attacking the pirate corsairs and raiding Barbary for booty. And, on their return to Sagres, Azurara, who lived there at the time, tells us, they explained their failure in this way:

How shall we pass beyond the limits established by our elders? What profit can the Infante win from the loss of our souls and our bodies? For plainly we should be like men taking their own lives. . . . This is clear; beyond this cape there is no one, there is no population; the land is no less sandy than the deserts of Libya, where is no water at all, neither trees nor green herbs; and the sea is so shallow that at a league from the shore its depth is hardly a fathom. The tides are so strong that the ships which pass the cape will never be able to return.

Azurara reports that the Prince dealt with these captains with great patience,

never showing them any resentment, listening graciously to the tale of their adventures, and rewarding them as those who were serving him well. And immediately he sent them back again to make the same voyage, them or others of his household, upon his armed ships, insisting more and more strongly upon the mission to be accomplished, and promising each time greater rewards.

In 1433, when his own squire Gil Eanes, "overcome by dread," also returned to Sagres without doubling the cape, Henry addressed him in this manner:

My son, you know that I have brought you up since you were a small boy and that I am confident you will serve me well. For this reason I have chosen you to be captain of this ship to go to Cape Bojador and discover what lies beyond. You can not meet there a peril so great that the hope of reward shall not be even greater.

This speech obviously made the necessary impression on the young squire. Azurara tells us that "having heard these words Gil Eanes promised himself resolutely that he would never again appear before his lord without having accomplished the mission with which he had been charged." And in 1434, "disdaining all peril," he became the first European to pass beyond the dreaded Cape Bojador. As we know that he made it back again, we can assume that he was also the first of Henry's captains daring enough to sail that bold arc out into the Atlantic, well out of sight of land, and, on a reach to the Azores, find the favoring currents and westerlies that sent his *barcha* home again.

With the jinx of the cape broken, with the terror of the unknown ocean somewhat diminished, and with the trick of getting home again learned, Henry and his young captains' hopes momentarily soared. Gil Eanes went out again and this time pressed 100 miles beyond Cape Bojador. Henry's cupbearer, Affonso Gonçalves Baldaya, took a *barinel* 50 miles further, and in the next couple of years four or five other voyages explored the West African coast still another some 50 miles southward. But progress was painfully slow, and, what was worse, the shore continued to be an unyielding, unpopulated, waterless desert. It seemed that there would never be any end to it, that the Sahara of Islam could never be bypassed. What's more, all that could be found of even the slightest value was herds of sea lions nesting on the arid, rocky outcroppings in the sea. These, from time to time, the captains hunted for their skins and oil, so that there might be some reward from the undertaking. But how paltry a reward this appeared when compared with the shining goal of reaching the fabulous kingdom of Prester John.

Henry grew impatient; the cost of the expeditions put an intolerable strain on his personal finances, which the occasional hauls of seal skin and seal oil did little to relieve. So, at this point, we find him turning away from his West African enterprise and taking up that old scheme of penetrating to the legendary Ethiopia beyond the Sahara by direct onslaught against the Moors.

By this time, King João had died and Henry's eldest brother, Duarte, was on the throne, a rather weak figure, who was easily persuaded to renew the war against the Kingdom of Fez. Henry was given command of the Portuguese army and in 1438, with his youngest brother, Affonso (who forever after was to be known as the Unfortunate), as his second-in-command, he led an assault on Tangier. It was an unmitigated disaster. The Portuguese army was routed and Affonso was taken prisoner, to end his days in Moorish captivity. Blame for both catastrophes fell heavily on Henry's shoulders and he fled back to Sagres.

The Tangier debacle and the fate of his youngest brother had an even more devastating impact on Duarte; he died of a broken heart within a year of the Moroccan defeat. As his son, the heir apparent, was only six at the time, the second brother of the Aviz dynasty, Pedro, was named regent. The appointment was fortunate for Henry. Pedro had been a great traveler in his youth and had always taken a great interest in his brother's enterprise. And now as regent he did everything to promote royal support for it.

In 1441, this at last began to seem worthwhile. For in that year one of Henry's young *fidalgos*, Antao Gonçalves, commanding a *barcha*, sailed 120 leagues beyond Cape Bojador and, at Río de Oro in present-day Spanish Sahara, made contact with the first people ever encountered on the desert West African shore. They were Sanhaja Tuaregs, Arabic-speaking Moslem Berbers of the extreme Sahara, whom the Portuguese had seen in Ceuta and whom they called Azenegues.

At the sight of the Portuguese, the Azenegues fled, but the young *fidalgo* was ecstatic. "Oh how fair a thing it would be if we . . . would meet with the good fortune to bring the first captives before the face of our Prince for it would give great satisfaction to our Lord for from them he would learn much of the people who live in these parts." With this end in mind, Gonçalves landed a war party on the coast. Pressing inland, the Portuguese came upon two encampments of some twenty Azenegues, and "when our men had come nigh to them, they attacked very lustily, shouting at the tops of their voices St. James for Portugal, the fright of which so abashed the enemy that it threw them all into disorder," and in the ensuing battle ten prisoners were taken.

At this point the *caravel* enters the picture. Dissatisfied all along with the *naos, barchas,* and *barinels* that he was forced to use and blaming their inadequacies for the slow progress of the coastal exploration, Henry had put his Sagres shipwrights to work experimenting with new hull constructions and sail riggings. In the early 1440s they came up with a ship design which for the next two centuries, in one variation or another, would carry Portuguese explorers to the ends of the earth and back again. In fact, the caravel was probably the single most important contribution made at Sagres to the discovery of the world.

By modern standards, it was a cockleshell. In its first version, the vessel had a draft of from 50 to 100 tons (and never much more than 200 tons even 100 years later), measuring some 20 to 25 feet in the beam and from 60 to 100 feet stem to stern. It was a round-bottomed ship with a hybrid hull adapted from fishing boats, strengthened to withstand ocean storms and rough seas, stout-decked, with a high poop and a castle in the stern, and fitted out with first two, then three, and finally four masts (when they were called *caravelas de armada*). But the key innovation in its design was its lateen-rigged triangular sails borrowed from the Arab feluccas of the eastern Mediterranean and the Indian Ocean dhows. With these, the ship could sail close to the wind and was capable of advancing in a side wind as well as tacking, and thus wasn't compelled to await a fair breeze to make headway. By the standards of the time, the caravel was extremely fast, developing speeds up to ten knots with the wind on the quarter or aft. Moreover, they were easy to handle—they carried crews of fewer than thirty and there's an account where only three sailors and two cabin boys sailed one 1000 miles home in an emergency—and were very well adapted for nosing in and out of the inlets and among the countless shoals of the West African coast.

The first caravel we hear of was commanded by Nuno Tristão. Sometime around 1443, unfurling the caravel's lateen sails like the wings of a great bird, he took his fast and maneuverable ship past the Río de Oro, across the Tropic of Cancer, around Cape Blanco and then 25 leagues beyond to discover the islands of the Arguin archipelago (off what is today Mauritania). The Arguin islands were then inhabited by Azenegues, and when Tristão first saw them they were

A port with caravels in harbor

paddling dugout canoes with their feet so that "our men, looking at them from a distance and quite unused to the sight, thought they were birds skimming over the water." The Portuguese, still full of the mythology of this unexplored region, apparently were perfectly prepared to come upon such marvelous creatures, and it wasn't until Tristão sailed the caravel closer that they realized what they were looking at was a reasonably natural scene. What the Azenegues thought of the caravel, in their turn, we have some idea from a report by Cadamosto a few years later:

This much is certain, that when they first saw the ships of Dom Henrique sailing past, they thought them to be birds coming from afar and cleaving the air with white wings. When the crews furled sail and drew into shore, the natives changed their minds and thought they were fishes. When they made out the men on board of them, it was much debated whether these men could be mortal; all stood, stupidly gazing at the new wonder.

In the case of Tristão's ship, that stupefaction cost them dearly. Using the same reasoning that had motivated Gonçalves at Río de Oro, Tristão ordered an attack on the astonished Azenegues and with comparative ease captured 29 to take back to Sagres for Henry's edification.

Tristão's return with his captives so soon after Gonçalves' similar success, coupled with the availability of the excellently seaworthy caravel, sparked a surge of interest in Henry's enterprise. Until then, the prince's voyages had been looked on with indifference,

and the worst of it was [Azurara informs us] that besides what the vulgar said among themselves, people of more importance talked about it in a mocking manner, declaring that no profit would result from all this toil and expense. But when they saw the first Moorish captives brought home and the second cargo that followed these [both by Gonçalves from the Río de Oro], they became already somewhat doubtful about the opinion they had at first expressed; and altogether renounced it when they saw the third consignment that Nuno Tristão brought home, captured in so short a time, and with so little trouble.

In renouncing their adverse opinion, these people of importance, merchants and nobles, became quite eager to get in on Henry's enterprise.

The first of these was Lancarote de Freitas, an officer of the Royal Customs at the port in Lagos, just up the Algarve coast from Sagres. He organized a private trading company with several Lagos merchants, and in 1444, with Henry's permission, he hired Gil Eanes and sent six caravels to the Arguin islands. While the ships stood off, five boats with some thirty soldiers were lowered into the waters at sunset. They rowed all that night until they reached an island village. At dawn, they attacked and

saw the Moors with their women and children coming out of their huts as fast as they could, when they caught sight of their enemy; and our men, crying out St. James, St. George and Portugal, fell upon them, killing and taking all they could. There you might have seen mothers catch up with their children, husbands, their wives, each one trying to flee as best he could. Some plunged into the sea, others thought to hide themselves in the corners of their hovels, others hid their children underneath the shrubs that grew about there, where our men found them. And at last our Lord God, who gives to all a due reward, to our men gave that day a victory over their enemies, in recompence for all their toil in His service, for they took, what of men, women and children, one hundred sixty-five, not counting the slain.

The Portuguese attacked several other villages and, when they returned to Lagos, they had 235 captives with them.

The Europeans trading with the Africans

On the next day, August 8, 1441, very early in the morning, the captives were disembarked from the caravels and marched to a meadow on the outskirts of town. And there was held Europe's first slave market. Azurara was present.

What heart [he tells us], even the hardest, would not be moved by the sentiment of pity on seeing such a flock; for some held their heads bowed down, and their faces were bathed with tears; others were groaning grievously, lifting their eyes to heaven, fixing them upon the heights, and raising an outcry as though imploring the Father of Nature to succour them; others beat upon their faces with their hands and cast themselves at length upon the ground; others raised their lamentations in the manner of a chant, according to the custom of their country; and although the words uttered in their language could not be understood by us, it was plain that they were consonant with the degree of their grief.

Then, as though the more to increase their suffering, came those who were commanded to make the division; and they began to part them one from another in order to form companies, in such manner that each should be of equal value; and for this it was necessary to separate children from their parents, and women from their husbands, and brothers from brothers. There was no law in respect of kinship or affectation; each had perforce to go whither fate drove him . . . consider how they cling one to another, in such wise that they can hardly be parted! Who, without much travail, could have made such a division? So soon as they had been led to their place the sons, seeing themselves removed from their parents, ran hastily towards them; the mothers clasped their children in their arms, and holding them, cast themselves upon the ground, covering them with their bodies, without heeding the blows which they were given!

The market was an enormous success. And, as Azurara tells us, Henry without delay "made Lancarote knight, loading him with benefits according to his merits and valour. And he likewise granted benefits to all the other captains, so that over and above the gain they had of their captures they had others which rewarded them right well for all their fatigues." Predictably, this further promoted interest in the enterprise, and in the next year alone, four privately sponsored expeditions, forming an armada of 27 ships, headed back to the Arguin hunting grounds and attacked villages all along the Mauritanian coast, killing and capturing Africans for the Lagos slave market.

In that same year, 1445, a *fidalgo* named Dinis Dias, in a lone caravel, sailed past Cape Blanco and the Arguin islands down the coast to the mouth of the Sénégal River and then beyond to reach and double Cape Verde, the westernmost point of Africa (where Dakar stands today). In accomplishing this feat, he attained the goal that Prince Henry had set for his enterprise more than a quarter of a century before. Here at last was sub-Sahara Africa. The desert and Islam had been bypassed, the Moslem flank turned at last. The people Dias encountered were no longer Moorish Azenegues but Waloffs, pagan Negroes. Here, some 450 leagues (1350 miles) south of the once-dreaded Cape Bojador, began the grasslands and forests of the Guinea coast. And from here, Henry could believe, if one traveled far enough into the continent's interior, perhaps along the Sénégal River, which was taken to be the "Western Nile" of the Arab geographers, one would at last come to the Kingdom of Prester John.

But slaving fever had seized the coasting captains; the profit and adventure of it had become a more powerful lure than the search for geographical knowledge, than even the quest for the fabled Christian priest-king's realm. And by 1448 more than 50 ships had gone to Guinea and returned with nearly 1000 slaves.

Slaving, however, became increasingly dangerous. Word of what the Portuguese came for traveled swiftly, and soon enough the blacks all along the coast were up in arms. Gonçalo de Sintra, sent by Henry to explore beyond Cape Verde but unable to resist making a bit of profit on the way (as very few of his fellow captains could), stopped off to slave at the Sénégal mouth, was ambushed by a party of blacks, and so earned the distinction of being the first European to be killed in sub-Saharan Africa. Nuno Tristão, who in a way started it all with his slave raid in the Arguin islands, did sail beyond Cape Verde, past the mouth of the Gambia and on to discover the Río Grande. And, though it is unclear whether he had any slaving in mind, when he sailed into the mouth of that river, in what can be seen as a case of poetic justice, he and his party were also ambushed and killed.

The blacks realized, of course, that the white men in their strange boats came to kidnap them but, as none ever returned to tell the tale, they didn't know why. So they invented their own explanation, an explanation that Cadamosto, the Venetian merchant adventurer who joined in on the enterprise when it became so profitable, discovered. He and a Genoese merchantman had sailed their caravels to the mouth of the Gambia River. Before proceeding upstream, they decided to send a scout ahead to get the lay of the land, but "the poor wretch," Cadamosta tells us, "had no sooner swum ashore than he was seized and cut to pieces by armed savages." Then suddenly a war party in native canoes attacked the caravels. The blacks shot their arrows; the caravels, Cadamosta tells us, replied with their cannon. As the natives fled, Cadamosta had one of his interpreters shout after them: "Why have you greeted us in this unfriendly way? For we are men of peace and seek only to trade with you." And they replied: "We have heard of your visits to the Senegal and we know that you Christians eat human flesh and buy black men only to make a meal of them. We do not want peace on any terms. We hope only to make an end of you and give all you possess to our chief."

While it is true that the Portuguese started the West African slave trade, it has to be said that they didn't practice it, at least at this stage, with the despicable and degrading brutality that was employed in later centuries. They treated their captives with a measure of decency and humanity, converting them to Christianity, teaching them trades, occasionally granting some their freedom, and not infrequently marrying them off to their white servants. Moreover, and perhaps more importantly, they did not conduct the traffic on the horrendous scale it was to attain a hundred years later. During Prince Henry's lifetime, the total number of slaves landed in Portugal could still be counted in the thousands. This was, of course, before the discovery of the New World, before the colonization of the Americas and the West Indies with their slave-run plantations, so the demand for slaves was not great. And, after the first flush of slaving fever subsided, the merchant sailors began seeking for other profit.

To be sure, slaving never ceased. But gradually slaves became only one, and not always the most valuable of several commodities that the Portuguese acquired along the West African coast. And gradually they began acquiring those products in a manner quite different from the initial slave raids. For they learned that the Azenegues of Cape Blanco and the Arguin islands and the Waloffs and other tribesmen of the Guinea coast were prepared to enter into peaceful trading relations given half a chance. So soon enough an orderly, profitable commerce developed, the caravels bringing out cloth, beads, brass wire, manufactured items, tin, coral, and bloodstone, and taking back slaves, ivory, and gold.

As commerce flourished, coastal exploration waned. A few intrepid caravel captains pushed south to what today would be Conakry, but the consuming interest in discovery now was less what lay further down the coast and what lay further inland from it. The Portuguese were aware that the people they traded with on the coast traded in their turn with peoples of the interior and that it was from there that the gold and ivory and slaves came. The temptation was great to try to circumvent the coastal middlemen and make direct contact with the black kingdoms of the interior. And the prospect that one of these might turn out to be the Kingdom of Prester John was always a lure to draw the Portuguese on. Several attempts were made. None, however, succeeded. Inland from Cape Blanco, for example, was the desert, and the Moslems controlled the caravan routes and oases there. Inland from the Guinea coast, fever-ridden swamps and jungles and deadly, unknown tropical diseases turned the Portuguese back.

Prince Henry doesn't seem to have been terribly disappointed. At the time of his death in 1460, he appears to have been quite satisfied with what he had wrought. And he had good reasons: Cape Bojador had been doubled, the desert of Islam had been bypassed by sea, some 2000 miles of previously unknown coastline had been charted, Portugal had broken into the Moslem trade with black Africa, and the Christian faith had been extended if only to the poor slaves brought back to Portugal. In fact, of the five goals Azurara cites for Henry's enterprise, the Prince had failed to reach only one: the Kingdom of Prester John.

5

THE PERFECT PRINCE

Affonso V, son of King Duarte and nephew of Prince Henry, took the sobriquet *O Africano*. It was ill deserved and, certainly from the point of view of the daring Portuguese voyages of exploration under way during his reign, grossly misleading. The Africa to which it referred was North Africa, where Affonso conducted campaigns against the Moors of little consequence and less long-lasting significance. As for the Africa which his uncle's captains discovered and which was to be the cornerstone of an incredible Portuguese empire, Affonso expressed hardly any interest at all.

As a king and a human being, Affonso was rather a failure. There was something peculiarly unstable in his temperament, an impetuous witlessness, a callow dilettantism; he exhibited the delusionary boldness of the weakling, easily influenced and even more easily disloyal. When he reached his majority—at the tender age of fourteen—and formally ascended the throne in 1446, he turned against his regent, Dom Pedro, who had governed wisely in his stead since the death of Duarte in 1438, and put himself under the malevolent tutelage of the Duke of Braganza. The duke was the bastard son of João of Aviz, the offspring of a youthful romantic fling, who was never treated as the equal of his younger but legitimate half-brothers, Duarte, Pedro, and Henry, and who harbored bitter resentments against them throughout his life. One visualizes him as a dark, brooding man, hardening in his bitterness as he grew older, suffering what he fancied as insults, forever intriguing against the crown (and, indeed, passing his bitterness down through the generations until it ripened into the successful vengeance that put the House of Braganza on the Portuguese throne in the seventeenth century). From the moment of Duarte's death, the duke plotted to secure power over the new boy-king, first clashing with Pedro in an attempt to win the regency for himself and then, when Affonso was crowned in his own right, provoking a bloody quarrel between the monarch and his regent. What character flaw Braganza recognized in the young Affonso, what weakness, what ambition, what vice he played to, it is hard to say, but the sour fruit of his work was a civil war and the murder of Dom Pedro by Affonso's soldiers at the castle of Affarrobeira in 1449. From this inauspicious beginning Affonso went on to torment his reign with other infamous adventures.

For example, a Crusade. It seemed just the thing to the foolish, vainglorious king. The Ottoman Turks were on the rampage in the East. In 1453, the army of Mohammed II conquered Constantinople, opening the way across the Dardenelles for the latest infidel scourge to strike into Europe. And once again the cry for a Crusade was heard in Christendom. But this time no one answered the call. Except Affonso. Eager to make a name for himself, thrilled by the prospect of grandeur, and ignorant of the uselessness of the venture, the young king assembled an armada and assaulted Alcazar on the Moroccan shore in 1458. Though the Portuguese were victorious, the conquest did nothing to stem the Turk's advance up the Danube half a world away. Nevertheless, the victory went to Allonso's head and, thirsting for more glory, he launched additional campaigns against the Kingdom of Fez, culminating with a victory at Tangier in 1471 for which he dubbed himself The African.

It was a title he retained for the rest of his life and with which he went into the history books, but even he eventually recognized its meaninglessness. As had been the case at Ceuta, these North African conquests did nothing to loosen the Moor's hold on the Barbary Shore, and the cost of defending the cities against ceaseless Moorish counterattacks came close to bankrupting the Royal Treasury. By 1475, Affonso the African had given up, if not his sobriquet, his ambitions in Africa and looked for new fields of glory and adventure. He found it in that other traditional enemy of Portugal: Castile.

Affonso had married Juana la Beltraneja, daughter of King Henry IV of Castile. In some circles she was considered the heiress to the Castilian throne, but it was more widely believed that she was an illegitimate child, and when the Castilian king died the crown went to her aunt Isabella. As usual, however, Affonso was not to be discouraged by rhyme or reason. He claimed the Castilian throne for himself and plunged Portugal into a war with Castile (and with Aragon as well, since Isabella was by then married to Ferdinand of that kingdom) which was to rage for five bloody years and end in 1479 with Affonso's total defeat and humiliation.

Not surprisingly then, with O Africano so thoroughly preoccupied with everything but West Africa, exploration along the continent's Atlantic coast came to a virtual standstill in the years after Prince Henry's death. Sagres itself, without the Navigator to serve as its magnetizing force, deteriorated. No more than two or three voyages of discovery sailed from its harbor after Henry died; the last in 1462. That caravel was captained by Pero de Sintra, son of the same Gonçalo de Sintra who had been killed on a slave raid at the Sénégal River some seventeen years before. Perhaps with the idea of avenging his father's memory, the young fidalgo sailed beyond Cape Verde, beyond the Gambia, and discovered the coast of Sierra Leone (so named because he was said to have heard the roar of lions atop the mountains there). It was the final contribution to West African exploration by the famed School of Navigation of Sagres. In the following years, the astronomers and mathematicians, pilots and cartographers, whom Henry had gathered together, drifted away. The city Henry had built was abandoned, the dockyards fell into disrepair, the fortress and observatory crumbled. This isn't to say, of course, that ships no longer sailed to West Africa. They did, and in increasing numbers. But they were the ships of the private trading companies, little interested in running the risks of further explorations southward when they could traffic so profitably in slaves, ivory, and gold along the coast already discovered. And they sailed now from Lagos and Lisbon, leaving Sagres to the dusts of history.

Since 1454, when Pope Nicholas V recognized Portugal's claim to all new lands on or near the West African coast and forbade all Christians to traffic there without Portugal's permission, the West African trade had been a crown monopoly. And while Henry was alive, he guarded that monopoly, as Cadamosta tells us, "with no small care." Any merchant who wanted to partake in the trade had to get a royal commission and strike a deal with the prince.

After Henry's death, however, with King Affonso so little interested in the enterprise, the guarding of the crown's West African trade monopoly became increasingly lax. Most Portuguese merchants still went through the formality of applying for a royal commission but now, as there was no authority to check on the merchandise they brought back, they quite brazenly cheated the crown out of its share. Worse, foreign merchants, mainly from the Italian city-republics and the Spains, didn't bother even to go through the formality of applying for a royal commission. They sailed from their own Mediterranean ports, traded along the African coast, and returned without paying Portugal anything whatsoever for the privilege.

After nearly a decade of this abuse, someone finally called Affonso's attention to the vast sums in potential revenue that were being lost to the royal treasury. Affonso's response was characteristic: rather than take the responsibility of enforcing the crown's authority, he decided to turn the monopoly over to a private entrepreneur in return for a fixed annual payment. In this way, Affonso reckoned, he would be guaranteed at least some revenue from the trade without having to bother involving himself in it and distracting himself from his other adventures.

Fernão Gomes, a Lisbon merchant, was that lucky entrepreneur. In 1469, he contracted a five-year lease with Affonso for exclusive trading rights (pieces of which he could sell off, if he wished, to other merchants) along the Guinea coast and at Arguin for a rent of 300,000 reis per year. There was one condition, however. And it is to Affonso's everlasting credit—or to that of some unknown advisor—that he included this stipulation in the contract: Gomes had to explore 100 leagues (about 300 miles) of new coastline in every year of his lease. And it is to Gomes's credit that he fulfilled this condition most faithfully. In the five years the Lisbon merchant held the West African franchise, his captains discovered and charted nearly 2000 miles of the continent's Atlantic shore—as much as Prince Henry's captains had in the twenty years after Gil Eanes doubled Cape Bojador. They sailed from Sierra Leone into the Bight of Benin, through the full length of the Gulf of Guinea to the Bight of Biafra, and raised the richest part of West Africa in the process: the Ivory, Gold, and Malagueta coasts. And they raised another tantalizing prospect as well.

Whether or not Prince Henry had ever consciously aimed at finding a sea route to the Indies when he started sending his ships down the West African coast, the idea that Africa might after all be a circumnavigable island, no matter what Ptolemy said, had gained adherents in the years of exploration since. Now, thanks to Gomes's captains, the idea became more than wishful fancy. For, in their very first push into unknown waters from Sierra Leone, they found that the West African coast, which had been followed steadily southward since Gil Eanes's day, turned to the east. Inevitably, this sparked the belief that the continent in fact had already been rounded, that the Ivory and Gold coasts were the bottom of Africa, and that by sailing far enough eastward now ships would enter the Indian Ocean and the seaway to the Indies. It was a belief that persisted for four years, and it wasn't until a caravel captain named Fernão Po in 1473 reached 9 degrees of longitude east, near the island in the Bight of Biafra which bears his name, that the coastline once again turned southward and the belief had to be abandoned. But this experience, the finding and rounding of Africa's great western bulge, fatally undermined the Ptolemaic picture of the continent and freed the Portuguese to seek the Indies by way of the Atlantic. So it was with a new eagerness that Gomes's captains pushed southward now, and by the time the Lisbon merchant's lease expired in 1474 one of them, Rui de Sequiera, had crossed the equator and sailed 2 degrees of latitude south of it to Cape St. Catherine on today's Gabon coast.

Gomes was well rewarded for his good work. He acquired great wealth exploiting the established and developing the new coastal trade and, into the bargain, was knighted for his discoveries of new lands. One would imagine that his franchise would have been renewed quite automatically. But it wasn't. Gomes himself didn't really want it. For, in point of fact, it had ceased being an exclusive franchise. Privateers, foreign merchantmen from the Spains and Flanders, Venice, and Genoa had, despite the Papal Bull expressly forbidding it, taken to openly poaching on the West African trade in ever-increasing numbers as soon as it was no longer even nominally under the direct supervision of the Portuguese crown. And there was nothing the Lisbon merchant could do about it. So when the time came to renegotiate the lease he refused to agree to the annual rental the king demanded, and Affonso passed the West African enterprise to his son and heir, the 19-year-old Prince John.

Utterly unlike his father in every trait of character and temperament, John seemed a throwback to the generation of his granduncle, Prince Henry. He was earnest and sensible, an astute politician and clever diplomat, intellectual, religious, visionary, physically strong, and ruthlessly determined; he came to be called the "Perfect Prince." Though still a child when Henry died, he grew up with a keen interest in the Navigator's work (as king, he would add "Lord of Guinea" to his royal titles) , and when Gomes failed to renew his franchise John eagerly importuned his father for it. As the chronicler of his reign, Rui de Pina, wrote, "He was a good Catholic anxious for the propagation of the faith, and a man of inquiring spirit desirous of investigating the secrets of nature."

But at the moment he was put in charge of the West African enterprise there was little he could do with it. For it was just at this time that his father embarked on his ill-fated intrigues for the Castilian crown, and it fell to the Perfect Prince to save Affonso and the kingdom from this fiasco. Indeed, by the time of Affonso's humiliating defeat by Castile in 1479, and still two years before his death, *de facto* if not *de jure* rule of the realm had passed into John's far more capable hands.

When he formally ascended the throne in 1481 as King John II, the kingdom, thanks to Affonso's hare-brained adventures, was in a sorry mess. The royal treasury was virtually bankrupt and, what was worse, the feudal nobles, and most especially the Duke of Braganza, having won so much power under Affonso, were in a free-wheeling mood to defy the new king. A plot was already afoot, hatched by Braganza with Castile's connivance. Fearing John's strength of character and his ability to rule Portugal as Affonso never had, Braganza schemed to have the new king assassinated and his cousin Diogo, the Duke of Viseu, another pliant weakling like Affonso, put on the throne in his place. When John got wind of the plot, he moved with the decisive dispatch that was to characterize his reign. Unintimidated by the Duke's power, he had Braganza arrested, tried for treason, and executed, all in a matter of days. As for the co-conspirator, Diogo, this was slightly more complicated but no less directly taken care of. Since Diogo was of the blood royal, John could not have him arrested, so he invited his young cousin to his private apartment at the palace at Sintra. Present at the royal interview were three of John's most trusted *fidalgos*—and no one else. We do not know what John said to Diogo, whether he accused him or behaved as if nothing were amiss. Nor do we know how Diogo acted, whether he pleaded or was defiant, whether his eyes darted anxiously to the three *fidalgos* standing silently aside in the otherwise suspiciously empty royal chamber. But what we do know is that, not long after the interview began, John suddenly unsheathed a short dagger from his girdle and stabbed Diogo

King John II of Portugal

to death. Such then was the man who was now in charge of Portugal's West African enterprise.

As a king, John was able to bring far greater resources to the enterprise than Prince Henry ever could. More important, he also brought to it a far more ambitious vision, seeing a potential that his granduncle had, at best, only sensed. John, of course, had the benefit of the Navigator's pioneering work. Thanks to more than a half century of voyages, the Atlantic was no longer the Mar Tenebroso of legendary terror, the profit that could be gained by sailing upon it had been amply demonstrated, the seamanship it required was well advanced, the map of Africa was taking accurate shape, and the discovery of a sea route to the Indies seemed a realistic prospect. But because of his boldness and intelligence, John, as few men of his time could, was able to seize on these accomplishments and form them into a plan for Portugal's greatness. Virtually turning his back on Europe, he made the West African enterprise the top priority of his reign and set it the specific tasks of exploiting the Guinea trade to its fullest, circumnavigating the African continent and breaking into the Indies trade, establishing an overseas Portuguese empire, and finding Prester John.

Prester John? It was now over 300 years since Europe had received that marvelous letter from the legendary Christian monarch, and it would seem that, considering how much had been learned of the world since, Europeans, and especially one so estimable as King John II, would have given up the quest as rather old-fashioned and foolish. But the legend continued to exert its hypnotic hold and, as a matter of fact, on no one quite so obsessively as the Portuguese king.

It is true that by this time the vision of the priest-king was considerably less wonderful and the geography of his realm far more modest. Prester John now was quite specifically assumed to be the Emperor of Ethiopia, and his kingdom was fairly well understood to lie hidden somewhere in the mountains off the East African coast. But as yet no European had ever been there or, at least, no European who had ever returned to tell the tale. (In fact, as was later to be discovered, a handful of questers had managed to reach Ethiopia in the middle and late fifteenth century but, though they were treated with much honor, they were never allowed to leave again.) So Europe still hoped that Prester John, if no longer invested with quite the magical powers and magnificence he was once believed to possess, would nevertheless prove a potent Christian ally in the wars against the latest infidel scourge, the Ottoman Turks. As a good Christian, John II shared fervently in this hope. But he had another, more self-serving reason for seeking Prester John. As he believed Prester John's kingdom extended to the East African coast, he hoped that the Ethiopian monarch, as a brother in Christ, would assist him in his ambition to circumnavigate Africa, by providing information on how and where the Indian and Atlantic oceans merged and by allowing Portuguese ports of call to be established in his realm for the long voyage from there to the Indies.

Perhaps the most famous of the Portuguese quests for Prester John was that of Pedro da Covilhã and Afonso de Paiva, two courtiers whom King John II dispatched by an overland route in the early years of his reign. They traveled together to Alexandria, where, disguised as Moorish traders, they joined a caravan of Muslim merchants. In this way they were able to pass through the domain of the Ottoman Turks to Cairo and from there on to the Red Sea, where they secured passage on an Arab dhow sailing to Aden. In Aden, they parted company. Covilhã was to attempt to reach India while Paiva was to go on to Ethiopia. They agreed that on their return each would wait for the other in Cairo.

Covilhã met with remarkable success. Traveling with Arab merchants who plied the Indies trade, he sailed from Aden across the Indian Ocean to the Malabar Coast of India, where Hindu traders brought the spices and other merchandise they collected throughout the Orient. These the Arab merchants bought and, with the dhows laden, Covilhã now sailed with them to the Persian Gulf and Arabia. Then, following the age-old caravan routes, he crossed the Arabian desert to the Red Sea, sailed back to Aden and returned to Cairo. By that time, Paiva had also returned to Cairo. But he was dead, of the plague. And, as Covilhã soon realized, he had died before he had had a chance to give anyone an account of his travels.

One must admire Covilhã's fidelity to his king at this point. He had a wife and children in Portugal, he had been traveling for more than two years under the most dangerous circumstances and must have been aching to get home. Yet he didn't. He realized that the most important part of the king's mission had been Paiva's, the discovery of Prester John's realm, and not his, the reaching of India. And, as there was no way of knowing whether Paiva had accomplished it, the faithful Covilhã took the task on himself. He had the presence of mind first to send a detailed description of what he had discovered on his travels (and which doubtless proved of great value to the king's ambitions to break into the Indies trade), and then he set off for Ethiopia. We know that Covilhã, in fact, did succeed in reaching Axum. But the king never heard of it. For the same fate befell Covilhã that had befallen all Europeans who managed to reach Ethiopia in those days. He was treated with great esteem, given an honored place in the emperor's court, provided with a harem, a house, and servants, but never allowed to leave again. Thirty years later, when the Portuguese did at last establish relations with the Emperor of Ethiopia, Covilhã was found there, an old man but alive and well and living in the lap of luxury, no longer especially eager to return to Portugal.

Covilhã's disappearance didn't diminish the Portuguese king's zeal to find Prester John, and he set about trying to reach the African Christian kingdom by striking inland across the continent from the West African coast. For, if the continent's outline was becoming better known, its breadth was still very much underestimated, and it seemed likely that a few months' march into the interior would bring a traveler to Ethiopia. So John instituted a policy of having Christianized black slaves landed at various promising places along the coast, dressed in the best silks and bearing gifts of gold and silver, with instructions to go inland and proclaim the greatness of the Portuguese king and his desire to communicate with Prester John.

A flurry of excitement was generated when word was brought back from the Benin coast that a powerful monarch called Ogane lived 20 moons' march inland (reckoned to be about 900 miles, which, in the geography of the times, could put him in Ethiopia) and held sovereignty over all the other kings and chiefs of the region. In fact, before any of these other kings and chiefs could be crowned, it was said, they first had to send ambassadors to Ogane and gain his acceptance. João de Barros tells us in his chronicle *Decadas de Asia:*

As a sign of his approval Prince Ogane used to send to the kings of Benin, not a scepter and a crown, but a helmet of shining brass such as the Spaniards wear and a staff of the same metal. And he sent them also a cross of brass to wear on their hearts. And all the time the ambassadors were at the Court of Ogane they never caught sight of the Prince; they saw only silk curtains behind which he placed himself. And when the time came to say goodbye, he showed one foot beneath the curtain to satisfy them that he was there and to this foot they made reverence as to a holy thing. And when he presented the insignia of office, the leader of the embassy received a small cross of the same kind sent to the king.

It was, of course, the cross that excited King John's hopes. But, alas, this Ogane (he probably was the Oni of Ife), as with all Prester Johns to date, was not found, and the Portuguese king at last concluded that if he ever was to be found it would be accomplished only by rounding Africa and approaching his realm from the continent's east coast. And so the voyages of exploration were resumed.

At that time, as we have seen, the most distant landfall in West Africa was Cape St. Catherine at 2 degrees of latitude south. From now on, ships would be sailing always further south of the equator, which raised some new seafaring problems. For example, the North Star vanishes in the southern skies, so the established practice of shooting it with a quadrant or astrolabe in order to determine latitude was no longer possible. What's more, south of the equator the coastal current sets to the north and the winds are southerlies, just the reverse of what they are north of the line, requiring entirely new sailing procedures. How John set about dealing with these new problems would have made Prince Henry proud. For the king gathered around him the best navigators, astronomers, mathematicians, and map makers of his time, assembling a sort of mini-Sagres at his palace in Sintra. And there men like Joseph Vizinho and Abraham Zacuto developed the new navigational and sailing techniques—such as the method for calculating the height of the sun above the horizon at noon and for preparing tables of declination so that latitude could be worked out without a North Star in the heavens—which made voyaging south of the equator a less risky adventure.

Then John clamped a vise of the closest secrecy on the enterprise. Not for him was Prince Henry's practice of swapping information and skills for a share of the profits with foreign merchantmen. Believing he was on his way to rounding the continent and breaking into the rich Indies trade, John didn't want other European vessels following in the wake of his caravels. They were not to know where to go or how to get there, and to throw them even further off course John not only wouldn't make accurate information available, he wasn't above putting about false information. In one case, the king deliberately caused a rumor to be circulated that "round ships," that is, those whose length measured only three or four times their breadth, could never return from south of the equator, a breath-taking lie, since the caravel was itself a round ship. But John was prepared to go to any length to make the enterprise exclusively Portugal's. And to assure his claim to the discoveries, he outfitted his expeditions with stone pillars. Until now, the caravel captains had signified the discovery of new lands—if they signified them at all—by casually carving a marking on a tree or erecting a wooden cross. This was a far too informal and impermanent method for John. His captains were to erect a *padrão*, a shaft of limestone or marble some five feet high, topped with a stone cross and inscribed with the royal coat of arms, the king's name, and that of the commander of the expedition.

Part Two

THE DISCOVERY

6

THE STONE PILLARS

The first expedition commander to carry King John's stone pillars was Diogo Cão, a naval captain who had made a name for himself fighting privateers on the West African coast. Unlike Prince Henry, John did not count on amateur *fidalgos* for the captains of his expeditions. He could get the best and most experienced seamen of the time, and Cão was just that. He was later knighted for his discoveries, and genealogists then invented a noble pedigree for him, but there's every reason to believe that he was very much a commoner to begin with, descended from a bailiff at the Villa Real in Trás-os-Montes, Portugal's most primitive province, the son and grandson of ordinary soldiers. He probably enlisted in the Royal Fleet as a boy, made his way up through the ranks, and came to the king's attention with daring exploits against privateers. In any case, it was to him that John gave his first stone pillars, and commanded him to go further south down the Atlantic coast of Africa than anyone had ever gone before.

Cão set sail from the Tagus, in front of Lisbon, in May or June of 1482. We know little of his ship or, for that matter, ships—it would not have been unusual for John to fit out this expedition with more than one, considering the distances he hoped it would travel. One must have been a three-masted caravel, and if there was another it might have been a pinnace, serving as a store ship. We can assume that Cão followed what was by then a well-traveled route to West Africa, sailing with the winds and currents to the Canaries, then on to Arguin (where he may have called to revictual), then around Cape Verde to Beziquiche, where he certainly stopped to take on fresh water, before making the long haul past Sierra Leone into the Gulf of Guinea, there to catch the eastward-running current that carried him to Elmina on the Gold Coast. This leg of the journey probably took about two months, and Cão may have spent a few more weeks at Elmina reprovisioning. Then came the run through the Bights of Benin and Biafra and across the equator to Cape St. Catherine, where he probably arrived in early August.

Now Cão's seamanship was tested. The current, setting to the north, and the prevailing winds were hard against him and the sailing was made all the more difficult by sudden squalls and thundershowers. Moreover, he couldn't run for the shore in case of trouble or even sail very close along it, for it was bound for the most part by high red clay cliffs, affording few safe anchorages, and the surf on its narrow beaches was rough and heavy while the beaches themselves sloped off so gradually that the offshore waters were very shallow for some distance out. Making judicious use of land and sea breezes, Cão had to inch his way along, standing off from the coast by as much as 15 miles at times and keeping his glass glued on the shoreline. For everything he saw now had never before been seen by a white man.

And then he spotted what appeared to be a bay or inlet. Squinting through the shimmering, humid haze of an August day, he made out the points of two spits of land, arcing out into the Atlantic like the opposing jaws of a giant crab's claw and forming what seemed a natural, safe deep-water harbor perhaps 12 to 15 miles across. The landfall was flat and featureless; the parapet of red clay cliffs had abruptly ended here and mangrove and palm trees stretched away from the shoreline's narrow beach of gleaming sand in a dark, unyielding forest to the horizon, where the vague blue outline of mountains could be seen.

But Cão's practiced seaman's eye would have immediately picked out the other, more startling features of this landfall. For the waves breaking on the beach here were an astonishing yellowish brown in color, and the ocean all around the ship was of a thick muddy-red hue as far as the eye could see. What's more, as he sailed toward this inlet, he found he was running against an amazingly powerful seaward current, four, six, or as much as nine knots the closer he got to shore. And dozens of floating islands, some of considerable size, came rushing past his ship, riding the strong muddy current far out to sea. We know that Cão had a sample of the ocean taken and tasted because on a map drawn by Cristoforo Soligo directly after Cão's voyage we see that the ocean is indicated as being sweet, not salt, for scores of miles off the coast.

Cão must have instantly recognized the significance of these odd conditions. What lay ahead was not a bay or an inlet but the mouth of a great river,

so violent and so powerful from the quantity of its water, and the rapidity of its current [as a Portuguese chronicler recorded not long after], that it enters the sea on the western side of Africa, forcing a broad and free passage, in spite of the ocean, with so much violence, that for the space of 20 leagues it preserves its fresh water unbroken by the briny billows which encompass it on every side; as if this noble river had determined to try its strength in pitched battle with the ocean itself, and alone deny it the tribute which all other rivers in the world pay without resistance.

Diogo Cão had discovered the Congo.

We can be certain of the date of this discovery and confidently credit it to Cão because he erected one of John's stone pillars on the southern bank of the river's mouth; that *padrão* was found centuries later and its inscription deciphered:

In the year 6681 of the World and in that of 1482 since the birth of our Lord Jesus Christ, the most serene, the most excellent and potent prince, King John II of Portugal did order this land to be discovered and this pillar of stone to be erected by Diogo Cão, an esquire in his household.

That Cão chose to erect the very first of John's pillars here, though he had so far journeyed barely 6 degrees of latitude south of the equator and hardly 280 miles from Cape St. Catherine, when his instructions were to sail as far south as he possibly could, is a measure of the importance Cão attached to the discovery. For here was, far and away, the most powerful river any white man had ever set eyes upon until that time. And, what's more, it had an estuary that appeared to offer a way, the first practical way that had been found in over 60 years of exploration, into the interior of the continent.

Cão sailed slowly into the river's mouth, making use of the afternoon sea breeze, his leadsmen anxiously sounding the fathoms, finding the channels around the islands that spotted the estuary, staying close to the bank, aware of the flocks of parrots chattering in the palm trees, the fishing eagles and terns and herons, the crocodiles along the shore, aware too of the people emerging from the forests, silently watching the progress of the birdlike caravel. When the sea breeze dropped toward dusk, Cão anchored in a mangrove-shaded cove a few miles upstream. Then he had the stone pillar offloaded from the ship and erected on the river's left bank while the local blacks gathered in great crowds around him. There may have been a few anxious moments. Cão had with him a few Christianized black slaves from the Guinea coast to serve as his interpreters, but though the people here looked much like the Guineans it turned out that they spoke a completely different language. Quickly enough, however, by means of signs and gestures and wide happy grins, the locals managed to make their friendly intentions known and their desire to become acquainted with the unusual newcomers. In the simple, direct and open way that strangers made friends in those far parts of the world in those distant times, the blacks and whites were soon trading with each other, lengths of wool and cotton cloth for elephant tusks, with Cão inviting aboard his ship those among the blacks whom he judged to be chiefs or headmen.

It makes a pretty picture to imagine the grizzled caravel captain attempting to parlay with the natives, squatting with them on the ship's deck while his sailors crowded around, no one quite understanding the other, everyone trying out various words in various languages, making signs and gestures, pointing at things, bringing out other things to show, grinning, touching. There must have been a lot of touching. These were the first white men the Bakongo had ever seen, and we know from the experiences of other voyagers that the blacks were always utterly baffled at the first sight of them. "The negroes came stupidly crowding around me," Cadamosta wrote, "wondering at our Christian symbols, our white color, our dress, our Damascenes, garments of black silk and robes of blue cloth or dyed wool all amazed them; some insisted that the white color of the strangers was not natural but put on." He goes on to tell us that the natives spat on his arm and tried to rub off the white paint, and then they wondered all the more when they found the skin itself was white.

Probably the first thing Cão wanted to find out was the name of the river he had discovered. The Bakongo called it *nzere* or *nzadi*, which in their language, Kikongo, meant "the river that swallows all rivers," a grandiose enough appellation to confirm Cão in his belief that he had made a major discovery. But he couldn't pronounce the Kikongo word and, with his tongue stumbling over it, it came out Zaire. And that was the name by which the river was to be known for the next two centuries. It wasn't until the eighteenth century that it would be commonly called the Congo, from the name of the tribe that dominated its estuary.

But surely a far more exciting piece of information Cão gathered, amid all the gesturing, pointing, and grinning, was that these people were inhabitants of a great kingdom, the Kingdom of Kongo. Some unspecified distance into the interior, Cão learned, southeast from the river, through the rain forest, upon a high mountain, was a royal city called Mbanza Kongo, and there resided a most powerful king, known as the ManiKongo, Lord of the Kongo, to whom all other kings and chieftains paid homage and under whose rule all the people lived. We cannot doubt that Cão's first thought was of Prester John. And he immediately set about making arrangements to contact this monarch. He would not go himself or send any of his white crew, not at first; to march into the unknown of the steaming rain forest would be far too dangerous. He wanted first to have a better idea of who this Mani-Kongo was and what might be expected of him, so he selected four of his Christianized slaves to serve as his ambassadors. He had them dressed in Portuguese clothing, loaded them down with whatever impressive gifts he could find on board, and dispatched them to Mbanza in the company of local guides. The understanding—or at least the understanding Cão hoped he had managed to convey to the Bakongo —was that the ManiKongo would respond to Cão's ambassadors by returning them to the river in the company of his own emissaries, and in this way indicate his desire to enter into friendly relations with the Portuguese.

We don't know how long Cão remained in the river's estuary. His contacts with the natives probably developed over a number of weeks, beginning with a first tentative exchange of gifts, turning into a rather lively trade and culminating in the revelation of the ManiKongo's existence and the dispatch of emissaries to Mbanza. Cão realized that it might take them weeks, perhaps months, to reach the ManiKongo and return, and he was not willing to wait around that long. His own king had commanded him to sail as far south as he possibly could, and so, after perhaps a month at the Congo's mouth, he continued his journey of exploration. We know he sailed nearly 500 miles further along the West African coast to 13 degrees of latitude south and erected the second of King John's *padrões* at Cape St. Mary on what is today the Angola shore. It is probable that he went no further because he was

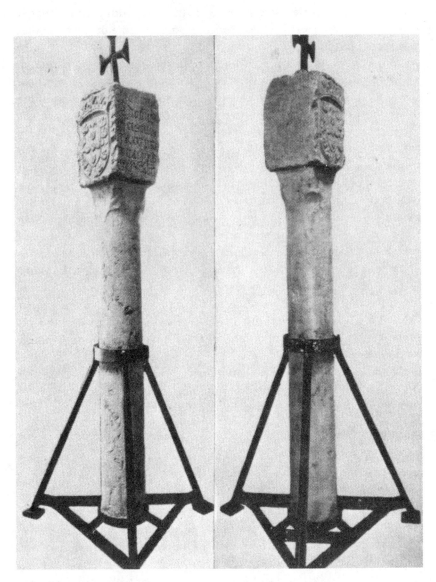

The Pillars of Diogo Cão

running low on provisions and was concerned about the long journey home that still faced him. But it also is possible that he was eager to discover what his emissaries had learned about the ManiKongo, and so we find him now speedily returning to the Congo's mouth.

But his emissaries were not there. Nor was there any word from them or the ManiKongo. Cão was enraged. He couldn't make head or tail of what the natives had to say about what had happened. They seemed to have forgotten about the whole thing and were only anxious to resume trading for the white men's wonderful merchandise, swarming out to the caravel in their dugout canoes, waving and smiling and holding up elephant tusks. Cão suddenly saw in all the happy, friendly faces a terrible duplicity. He was mistaken; as was to be learned later, his emissaries had been greeted with much delight and treated excellently by the ManiKongo and hadn't been returned with the monarch's own ambassadors only because of a misunderstanding due to a lack of a common language. But at that moment Cão feared the worst. He imagined that his emissaries had been imprisoned and, reverting to the old habits of a fighting naval captain, he had four of the Bakongo seized as hostages and had a message sent to the Mani-Kongo warning him that these people would be freed only in exchange for his own men. Then, promising to return, he sailed for Lisbon on the next favoring tide.

Cão arrived in Portugal in March or April of 1484. In making him a *cavalheiro,* awarding him a coat of arms charged with the two *padrões* he had erected and granting him a lifetime annuity of 10,000 *reis,* John expressed his extreme pleasure over Cão's accomplishments. He was ecstatic about the news of the Kingdom of Kongo. He seems to have been firmly convinced that the ManiKongo, if not himself the fabled Prester John, would know of him and prove a valuable ally in the endless quest for him. And, in a show of that innovative statesmanship that characterized his reign, John prepared for that alliance by treating the four hostages Cão had brought home as if they were, albeit unwitting and unwilling, ambassadors from the Kingdom of Kongo to the Portuguese court. It was an astonishing approach. For the first time, blacks seized on the West African coast were not automatically enslaved. Rather, they were provided with apartments at the palace, fitted out with the wardrobe of courtiers, set to studying Portuguese and Christianity, and given tours of the realm. John's intention was to return the quartet to Mbanza so bedazzled by Portugal that the ManiKongo would be eager to enter an alliance and assist John in his aims.

John was equally enthusiastic about the geographical discoveries of Cão's voyage. He had every reason to believe that, in the Congo River, his captain had found a great highway into the African interior, a natural artery to lands never reached by Europeans before, promising access to untold riches. And in having traveled nearly 800 miles further southward down the West African coast, Cão, by John's calculations, had come close to rounding the continent and finding the sea route to the Indies.

Yet, despite all the excitement, we find John delaying the dispatch of Cão on a second expedition. Why, one can't help wondering. And then we realize that it was just at this time that a young Genoese seaman turned up at the palace at Sintra. He was called in Portugal Christovao Colom, and João de Barros describes him as "a man expert, eloquent and a good Latinist" who came to John with the request to "give him some vessels to go and discover the Isle Cypango by the Western Ocean."

Christopher Columbus had been living in Lisbon for about eight years at this time, in the Genoese community which had flocked there to partake in the West African trade. He had married a Portuguese noblewoman and had himself made a fair share of voyages in Portuguese and Genoese merchantmen to the Guinea coast. When exactly he first conceived the idea of reaching Isle Cypango (as Marco Polo had named Japan) and the Indies by sailing straight westward across the Atlantic, instead of southward around Africa, as the captains with whom he had sailed dreamed, we cannot say, but it was fully formed when he presented it to King John in 1484.

John was the first person to whom Columbus brought his *Emprêsa de las Índias*. As the only monarch of the time with the resources for and commitment to this sort of daring ocean exploration, John was the only one from whom the Genoese seaman could hope to get an intelligent hearing. And an intelligent hearing he got. John turned Columbus's amazing proposition over to his assembly of experts (which now included Diogo Cão) for their consideration and advice. But, as Barros tells us, "They all considered the words of Christovao Colom as vain, simply founded on imagination or things like Marco Polo's Isle Cypango." For his part, "the king," Barros reports, "as he observed this Christovao Colom to be a big talker and boastful in setting forth his accomplishments, and more puffed up with fancy and imagination about his Isle Cypango than certain of the things he told about, gave him small credit."

It is, of course, pure nonsense that, as popular histories would have it, Columbus was turned down because the Portuguese believed the earth was flat. After all their experience sailing the Atlantic, seeing ships hull-down over the horizon, no intelligent man among them, and certainly not King John or his experts, doubted for a moment that the world was a globe. The problem with Columbus's proposition lay elsewhere. He grossly underestimated the distance across the Atlantic and grossly overestimated the size of the Asian continent. Thus he made the trip from the Canaries to Japan one of only 2500 miles when in fact it is over 10,000 and that to the China coast only 3500 miles when it is in reality nearly 12,000. And somehow the Portuguese sensed the error. They simply would not believe that the voyage Columbus proposed could possibly be as short as Columbus said. Besides, as we've seen, John was satisfied that Diogo Cão had reached within a few days' voyaging of the Indian Ocean, so it made little sense for him to gamble the heavy investment of a westward expedition by the Genoese seaman when he felt he had a sure thing in hand by the southerly route. So Columbus was dismissed (to go on, of course, to John's father's old *bêtes noires*, Isabella and Ferdinand of Spain) and John set about outfitting Diogo Cão with a fleet for his second expedition.

Because of a lack of records, there is some confusion about Cão's second voyage. We know that he sailed from the Tagus sometime late in 1485 with at least three vessels. And, since he was again carrying John's stone pillars, we know how far he journeyed: one of the *padrões* was erected at what is today Cape Negro on the Angola coast, nearly 16 degrees latitude south of the equator, and a second was planted at nearly 22 degrees latitude south, just short of the Tropic of Capricorn, at what is today Cape Cross on the Namib Desert coast of South-West Africa. Thus, though he failed to make that "few days' journey" round the continent, he uncovered 700 miles more of African coastline, for a total of 1500 miles in just two voyages (as compared with the 2000 miles in the 5 years of Gomes's lease and in the 20 years of Prince Henry's enterprise).

What we also can be certain of is that Cão on this journey again called in at the Congo mouth. Aboard were the four hostages from the first voyage, now speaking Portuguese, probably Christianized, and dressed like *fidalgos*. Cão landed them, according to Rui de Pina, to the great surprise and joy of the natives who had gathered to watch the return of the caravels. They were carried off to Mbanza, bearing sumptuous gifts from King John to the ManiKongo, with the request that the African monarch return Cão's four men along with envoys and ambassadors of his own. While waiting for this exchange of envoys to take place Cão decided to make a more thorough exploration of the river, to find how deep into the African interior it would take him. We know that he sailed up the full length of the estuary to a point just above today's Matadi, because we can find his name inscribed on a rock of an overhanging ledge there.

It was a trip of about 100 miles, across the coastal plain to the foothills of the Crystal Mountains. Though the river steadily narrowed and was studded with sizable islands, it remained completely navigable, and Cão had little difficulty finding his way. But at Matadi, where the river was barely one half mile wide, the Crystal Mountains abruptly and dramatically reared up on both banks, and the river, making a sudden sharp bend, was cut off from view. One can imagine Cão taking his little cockleshell of a vessel around that sharp bend into the narrow, spectacular mountain gorge—and encountering the Cauldron of Hell, the last of those 220 miles of thundering cataracts and rapids of the Livingstone Falls, over which the Congo roars through the Crystal Mountains before emerging into the coastal plain and flowing down to the sea. And this was the end of Cão's exploration of the Congo. For there was no possibility that his little caravel could sail through that ferocious white water. The disappointment for Cão must have been crushing, and it was surely with a heavy heart that he turned his caravel back toward the sea.

The confusion we have about this voyage concerns the sequence of the events. According to Rui de Pina, Cão called in at the Congo on the outbound leg of his journey, and it was then that he landed his hostages and discovered the Cauldron of Hell. After this, rather than wait until the hostages reached Mbanza and returned with his men and the ManiKongo's ambassadors, he went on to sail south and erected the *padrões* at Cape Negro and Cape Cross. In this account of the voyage, we have Cão calling in again at the Congo on the homeward leg, as he had on his first expedition; but this time he finds his men happily waiting for him on the riverbank along with a group of envoys from the ManiKongo's court, and he gathers everyone up and sails home to Portugal with them.

The only trouble with this seemingly plausible sequence is that Diogo Cão, made so much of until now, abruptly vanishes from the chronicles, never to be heard of again. One explanation for his sudden disappearance is that, upon Cão's return to Lisbon, King John was so enraged at learning that his captain had failed to round the African continent, which he believed was merely a matter of a few days' voyaging, that he had Cão imprisoned and possibly executed. Given John's ruthless character and the bloody nature of the age, there is some merit in this explanation. But there's another which may be just a bit more plausible, and that is that Cão, after calling in at the Congo, landing his hostages, and discovering the Cauldron of Hell, went on to reach Cape Cross—and died there, shipwrecked on the barren, waterless wastes of the Namib Desert coast. How then, we must ask, did Cão's men and the ManiKongo's envoys reach Lisbon? For we know, as a matter of fact, that they did reach Lisbon, sometime in 1488. And the best answer is that Bartholomeu Dias de Novais took them there.

With Cão vanished without a trace, for whatever reason, Dias was the best sea captain around. So it was to him that John turned to accomplish what Cão had failed to do: round the continent and find the seaway to the Indies. Dias was put in command of two caravels and a store ship to carry sufficient water and provisions for the long voyage along the desert coast beyond Cape Cross, which may have been what defeated Cão. John put his experts to work on another problem Cão had encountered: that, beyond the Congo's mouth, the contrary winds and currents grew progressively stronger the further one sailed southward. Using the logic that had been applied successfully to the problem of beating against winds and currents north of the equator—but in reverse—the experts suggested that by sailing southwest in a wide enough arc away from the coast into the Atlantic, Dias might be able to pick up westerlies to carry him around the continent.

So, in the fall of 1487, Dias led his ships out of the Tagus roadstead. Following Cão's wake, he sailed beyond Cape Cross and put into a sheltered bay at 29 degrees latitude south, now called Alexander Bay near the mouth of the Orange River in present-day South Africa. By now the winds were blowing so strongly out of the south and southwest that his clumsy store ship could make no headway. Dias decided to leave it in the bay and for the next five days beat against the winds along the coast. But this eventually proved impossible even for the handier caravels.

Then Dias made his daring move. Rather than give up in face of the adverse winds and current and return to Portugal a failure, he took the risk of sailing away from the coast and stood out on a tack into mid-ocean in hopes of finding the westerlies. For thirteen perilous days his ships scudded before a gale with shortened sails and then, at about 40 degrees latitude south, those winglike lateen sheets picked up the winds out of the west, driving the ships back toward Africa. Day after day, Dias watched for the continent's west coast to reappear, running north and south along the horizon. But it didn't. So Dias turned his vessels north and after several anxious days, he at last sighted a landfall. But, as the line of mountains rose along the horizon now, Dias had what must have been a heart-stopping revelation: the coastline was running not north and south but east and west. This was the bottom of Africa; he had turned the continent.

Dias's first landfall was what is today Mossel Bay, 200 miles beyond the Cape of Good Hope. To make dead certain that he had rounded the continent, he sailed along the shore some distance beyond today's Port Elizabeth, where the coast made a distinct turn to the north, revealing itself unquestionably as the east coast of Africa. We know that Dias wanted to press on still further, perhaps into the Indian Ocean and all the way to India, but his crew prevented him. The caravels were leaky, the rigging was in shreds, provisions were low; and there was a dreadfully long way to go before they would be home again. The seamen threatened to mutiny, so Dias turned back. Homeward bound, he stopped at Alexander Bay to recover his store ship. Then, by many accounts, he called in at the Congo mouth, where Cão's men and the ManiKongo's envoys were waiting and took them aboard for the journey to Lisbon. Sixteen months after departing, he crossed the Tagus roadstead with the emissaries from the Kingdom of Kongo in his ships.

Understandably, the great excitement in Lisbon on Dias's return focused mainly on the sea route he had found around the African continent (and which, in 1497, Vasco da Gama would follow to open Portugal's trade with the Indies). But the king had lost none of his enthusiasm for the quest for Prester John, and he took a great personal interest in the men who had been brought back from Mbanza Kongo. The envoys whom the ManiKongo had sent were the sons of nobles of the Kongo court, led by a prince named Nsaku who had brought gifts of ivory and palm cloth to the Portuguese king and expressed his desire to learn the arts of the European kingdom. John was quick to seize the opportunity. As he had the four hostages Cão had brought to the palace, he treated this retinue of Kongo nobles with extraordinary extravagance. And, as Rui de Pina tells us, when it came time for their conversion to Christianity, John personally stood sponsor at Nsaku's baptism, where, amid great pomp and solemnity, he was christened Dom João da Silva (John of the Woods), and an unprecedented and honorable, though tragically brief, alliance between the European and African kingdoms was inaugurated.

7

KINGDOM OF KONGO

Sometime around the birth of Christ, give or take a few hundred years, a mysterious migration of peoples began in central Africa. It was comparable in extent and historical consequence to the "Indian" exodus from northern Asia that provided the American continents with their first populations, one of those not-quite-explicable but truly stupendous shifts of humanity that have periodically revolutionized the earth's demography. Here it was the Bantu-speaking blacks of the savanna highlands of the central Benue River valley, in what is today the frontier region between Cameroon and Nigeria, who embarked on the enigmatic journey away from their homeland and who, traveling south and southeast in the course of the first millennium A.D., fanned out and established themselves as the dominant people of the southern third of the African continent.

What exactly set them off is a matter of academic speculation, but a safe if rather simplistic guess is that it had to do with a drastic shortage of land. We know that in the preceding centuries these early Iron Age peoples had acquired the rudiments of agriculture, probably from the civilizations of the Upper Nile Valley, based on Sudanic millet or sorghum grain and employing the slash-and-burn technique of farming, at which they proved extremely proficient—in fact just a bit too proficient for their own good. For we know that not long afterward the Bantus experienced one of the most spectacular population explosions in human history. Coupling the profligate use made of land in slash-and-burn farming with the rapid rise in the numbers of people, it is not hard to see how the Bantus might have come under a terrific land pressure within a few generations.

Sub-tribes would have formed and hived off from the main tribal groupings and ventured always further afield in search of new lands, until eventually the homeland savanna had been overrun and the rain forests of the Congo River basin bordering the highlands on the south had been reached. Then, with land and population pressures still mounting relentlessly behind them, the Bantus would have had little choice but to press on into this alien landscape as well. No doubt some settled or attempted to settle in the forest, but, for all its riot of vegetation, they would have found it a very inhospitable place. Their Sudanic millets and sorghum grains, so fecund in the high, open grasslands, would not grow in that close, wet climate, and the forest's indigenous crops were inadequate to support the sizable populations. So the mainstream of the migration pushed on, instinctively following the streams and tributaries of the Congo drainage system, until at last one day they emerged from the forests and reached the Katanga (or Shaba) Plateau, there to discover a highland savanna remarkably like the one they had left behind.

We can assume there was then a hiatus in the migration while the Bantus settled this familiar grassland and reestablished their traditional slash-and-burn agricultural society. But the hiatus would have been relatively short-lived. Almost certainly within a century, and surely in less than two, the whole cycle of population boom and land shortage would have begun again, and again the Bantus would have been on the move, expanding now across the Shaba Plateau and down through what is today Zambia, Rhodesia, and Mozambique, all the way to the Indian Ocean coast.

And there something of a miracle occurred. In the vicinity of the mouth of the Zambezi River, the Bantus found food plants of southeast Asia, notably the banana, Asian yam, and taro (or coco yam). One theory explaining how these plants came to be there holds that they were brought by Indonesian mariners who had blown across the Indian Ocean on the monsoons and established settlements on the East African coast in the third or fourth century A.D. Whether the Bantus actually contacted these settlements or whether they simply found the plants proliferating in the wild we really don't know. What we do know is that the introduction of the Asian plants into African agriculture revolutionized the Bantu migration. The bananas and yams would thrive in the hot, moist climates where the Sudanic sorghum and millet were useless, and thus they allowed the Bantus to expand into regions until then hostile to them, up the East African coast, into the areas of the great lakes of present-day Tanzania, Kenya, and Uganda, and then, in the tenth century A.D., back to the Congo River basin, through which they had passed a millennium before. By the twelfth and certainly no later than the thirteenth century, Bantus occupied virtually every part of the Congo forests and, having absorbed the indigenous aboriginal Pygmies or driven them into the most remote regions, settled into the tribal societies from one of which the Kingdom of Kongo arose.

There are no written records of this Bantu kingdom before the arrival of the Portuguese, and all we can know of its origins comes from its oral tradition, historical memory and myths. One of these, which the Portuguese heard on their arrival and which was later recorded by missionaries, concerns a certain Nimi a Lukeni, the son of a chief of a small Bantu tribe called the Vungu or Bungo, that had settled on the bank of the Congo near today's Stanley Pool. He was young, strong, ambitious, a fearless warrior, impatient for command but with little prospect of succeeding to the rule of his tribe, so, with a band of armed followers, he withdrew from his village and set himself up at a ford on the river, to collect tolls from all who wished to cross. One day, the legend relates, a sister of the chief, Nimi a Lukeni's aunt, came to the ford and sought to cross over. Nimi a Lukeni demanded the payment of a toll. She refused, invoking her privileges as the chief's sister, and when she set out to cross the river anyway, Nimi a Lukeni leapt upon her and disemboweled her.

It was an awesome, atrocious act and, in the legend's countless retellings, it echoes with all the symbolic horror that we find in so much of Greek mythology. For by this act, this killing of kin, we are told, Nimi a Lukeni violated all that was sacred, defied every tradition and broke irretrievably with the normal order of life. By his murder of the chief's sister he declared himself outside the restraints of tribal law, an exceptional being, godlike in his apartness, fearsome in his violence, incomparably courageous in his defiance, a figure of awe and power. He was, legend tells us, the founder-king of the Kingdom of Kongo, the first ManiKongo.

There is no way of knowing when or, for that matter, if this terrible event occurred. But there is evidence that sometime in the first decades of the fourteenth century a young outcast Bantu chieftain of towering, mythic authority—be he Nimi a Lukeni or someone else—

gathered a band of followers and, in the tradition of a millennium of Bantu migration, led them southwestward away from the vicinity of Stanley Pool in search of new lands. This was now no longer the simple matter of finding and moving into unoccupied regions. By this time the Bantus had pretty much taken over all the forest, so Nimi a Lukeni had to acquire his new lands by conquest. In a series of wars, he is said to have subdued the region of a people called the Mbundu and Mbwela lying south of the Congo estuary (in present-day Angola) and there, on a high hill about 100 miles from the river, built his *mbaji* or *mbanza*, court of justice and palaver place. Legend, as transcribed by a seventeenth-century Italian Capuchin missionary, Giovanni Antonio Cavazzi, says that "Such great respect the inhabitants of the country had for this place in the forest . . . that those who passed nearby dared not turn their eyes in that direction. They were convinced that should they do so, they would die on the spot."

Nevertheless, we learn from the legends, the military conquest, and the fear and respect inspired by that conquest, were not enough. For Nimi a Lukeni was a stranger to this new land; it did not contain the spirits of his ancestors, and so he could not truly control it. He had no power over its fertility, or over the rains and the crops; he could not regulate the sowing and the reaping or govern the hunt. This control, this power, we are told, belonged still to the land's original occupants, whose ancestors were buried there, and to ignore them, to refuse to solicit their cooperation and their ritual mediation, was to run the risk of catastrophe. Yet Nimi a Lukeni did ignore them. And one day, legend says, he was struck down by *laukidi,* the convulsions of a madman.

So his followers went to the priest of the conquered people. They knelt down before him and said, "Lord, we know that you are the elder, he who first occupied this region, who was first at the nostrils of the universe. Our chief has fallen into convulsions; bring him peace again." At first the priest looked angry and protested against what he called an intrusion. At last, however, he consented to accompany them to their chief. Nimi a Lukeni said to him, "You are the eldest among us. Strike me with the *nsea,* the buffalo tail, that my convulsions may cease." By this request he accepted the religious authority of the land's original occupants, and he sealed the peace by taking for his first wife the priest's daughter. And so the Kingdom of Kongo was born.

In the roughly 150 years between then and the arrival of the Portuguese, at least five but perhaps as many as eight ManiKongos, all presumably descendants of the mythic Nimi a Lukeni, ruled in Mbanza. By a similar process of military conquest and religious alliance, they extended the boundaries of the realm to encompass more than 200,000 square miles and upward of 4 or 5 million people. At its height, it may have reached as far north as the Ogowe River in modern Gabon, eastward from the Atlantic beyond Stanley Pool to the Bateke Plateau and the Kwango River in today's Zaire, and south across the Kwanza River in today's Angola. By the time the Portuguese got there, however, the kingdom had somewhat diminished. The peoples on the northern and southern peripheries had broken away and formed rival kingdoms, and while some of these may have still paid tribute as vassals to the ManiKongo, he exercised true sovereignty only over a realm bounded by the Congo River on the north, the Kwango in the east, the Dande in the south, and the Atlantic Ocean on the west.

We speak of this realm as a kingdom, rather than, say, a paramount chieftainship, which might seem more appropriate to Africa. But, as long as we understand that what we are referring to here is a state of feudal principalities owing allegiance to a central hereditary authority, *kingdom* is a perfectly accurate description. For the ManiKongo ruled as supremely as any European king in those Middle Ages. He was regarded as a semi-divine, sacred personage surrounded by a court of nobles, retainers, slaves, and wives and a royal protocol every bit as elaborate as any in Europe at the time. Those who wanted to approach him had to prostrate themselves and crawl forward on all fours. He could not be observed eating or drinking, under pain of death, and when he chose to do either a slave would strike two iron staffs together and all present would fling themselves face down on the ground. Whenever he traveled, no matter for how short a distance, he was carried on a litter and escorted by a bodyguard, and whenever he stopped, the ground was swept clean and mats strewn all about, for it was regarded as a sacrilege for his feet to touch bare earth. He had a palace and a throne and all the fabulous insignia of sovereignty. He maintained a monopoly on the currency of the realm—cowrie shells, called *nzimbu,* "mined" from the sea floor of the Atlantic coastline—and extracted tribute from all his subjects. And it was from his loins, and only his, that the successor ManiKongo could spring.

Nevertheless, for all his power and exalted standing, the Mani-

Kongo, as in any feudally organized state, had to take into account and contend with strong rival centers of power. The kingdom consisted of separate provinces or principalities—there were six at the time of the Portuguese arrival: Soyo, Mpemba (where the capital of Mbanza was located), Mbamba, Mpangu, Mbata, and Nsundi—each of which corresponded to a once independent state conquered by the ManiKongos and each of which was further divided into districts, and the districts, in turn, into villages and towns. Each of these political units had its own chief, enjoyed a large degree of autonomy, and retained a very real sense of separate tribal identity. The ManiKongo formally appointed the chiefs or lords (manis) of the provinces (who in turn appointed the district chiefs and so on down the political ladder) and they served at his pleasure, but undoubtedly he felt that prudence obliged him to honor regional traditions. Thus, the kingdom was a confederation of fiefdoms and the province chiefs feudal lords. They swore their fealty to the king, acknowledged his suzerainty, gathered tribute for his royal treasury, raised armies to fight his wars, and served as the nobles of his court and the ministers of his cabinet. At the same time, they had their own very real bases of power and it was not unknown for them to challenge or even rebel against a king.

One needs to be careful neither to overvalue nor to undervalue this kingdom. Certainly its political structure was remarkably sophisticated. Moreover, some arts and crafts were developed there to an impressive degree. For example, iron ore, which was found in the form of ferruginous rock, was mined, smelted, and, with well-designed hammer, anvil, and bellows, worked into a wide array of handsome and effective weapons, tools, ornaments, musical instruments, and other devices. The Bakongo also forged copper and apparently knew the lost-wax process, casting this metal into statuettes, fetishes, and jewelry.

In addition, they were brilliant weavers. They used vegetable fibers, stripped primarily from the leaves of the raffia palm tree, which they wove into fabrics with such fine skill and variety that on seeing them for the first time the Portuguese took them to be velvet and damask, brocade, satin, and taffeta. They also made a very usable cloth by beating the bark of trees; fashioned beautiful baskets, nets, and furniture from split vines and wicker; carved wood and ivory; made pottery; and cured hides with which to dress themselves and furnish their lives. Thus, in no sense can we imagine the Bakongo as a naked savage. He was handsomely dressed in his marvelous cloths, beauti-

A contemporary river scene

fully adorned with his skillfully crafted jewelry, outfitted with excellent tools and implements, and surrounded by the finest of artifacts.

But, for all this, he remained a member of an essentially primitive society, a society based on subsistence farming. The Bakongo cultivated the yams and bananas his ancestors had brought into the forest, gathered indigenous legumes and fruits, made excellent use of the native palm trees, from which he derived oil, wine, vinegar, and a kind of bread. He kept domesticated goats, pigs, and cattle and, using nets and baskets, harpoons and poisons, fished the Congo and its tributaries. But everything he caught or raised he ate. The concept of commodity farming, of a cash crop, of producing more than the immediate need for barter or sale, had not been developed. Indeed, the whole idea of trade outside the immediate neighborhood, which would involve a system of storage and transportation, had not yet caught hold on any extensive scale when the Portuguese arrived. And, without extensive trade, without the need for accounting records, storehouse inventories, and the like, there was no writing.

There also was no calendar, no means of telling time. And there was no wheel. A network of trails crisscrossed the forest, with bridges of sturdy vines slung over the rivers and ravines, but there were no carts or carriages. What is perhaps more curious, the Bakongo never thought to use his domesticated animals to carry things or people, or even to pull the hoes with which he worked his fields. The only vehicles of transport available, if they can be called that, were the wooden horse and the litter, the first being a log fitted with a hide saddle for the traveler to straddle while being carried by slaves, the latter a skin slung between poles also carried by slaves, in which the nobles of the kingdom rode. Everyone else walked and carried their goods on their heads.

Yet, despite its limitations, the Kingdom of Kongo probably was the most highly advanced civilization on the west coast of Africa at the time. It certainly was the most highly advanced civilization that Europeans had come in contact with in sub-Sahara Africa up to that time, and the excitement generated by its discovery was immense, provoking a fabulous degree of exaggeration. The Portuguese imagined the kingdom as being far greater and more magnificent than it really was, and in the earliest chronicles we see its boundaries described as extending as far north as Benin (in modern Nigeria), as far south as the Cape of Good Hope, and reaching to the east all the way to Ethiopia, the realm of Prester John. And, if the ManiKongo was himself not the fabled Christian priest-king, the Portuguese were certain that he could show them the way to that long-sought kingdom. King John II quite specifically believed that the great river whose mouth Diogo Cão had discovered flowed from a huge lake in the highlands of Ethiopia and by following it upstream to its source one could cross Africa all the way to the Indian Ocean. So, even before dispatching Vasco da Gama to follow the sea route around the Cape of Good Hope that Bartholomeu Dias had found and so opened the seaway to the Indies, he first dispatched an expedition to the Congo.

Gonçalo de Sousa was given command of a fleet of three caravels. A dozen priests, a contingent of soldiers, masons, carpenters, printers, farmers, and various other artisans, even including a few women skilled in the domestic arts such as bread baking and sewing, along with the tools of their trades, sacerdotal objects, ornaments, gifts, and building materials were loaded aboard the vessels. And then, with Nsaku and the other Bakongo nobles who had been residing in Portugal for the past two years, the expedition set sail in December 1490 on the extraordinary mission of establishing diplomatic relations with the Kingdom of Kongo and entering into an alliance of mutual aid with it.

It proved a grim voyage. The plague, which was raging in Lisbon at the time of the expedition's departure, had been carried aboard, and before the journey was half done, it had taken a deathly toll, killing among others Nsaku and Gonçalo de Sousa. Rui de Sousa, a nephew of the expedition's leader, assumed command and reached the mouth of the Congo at the end of March 1491. The ships anchored in the lee of the south bank of the river's estuary, not far from where Diogo Cão had erected his *padrão*, near the village of Mpinda. In subsequent years, Mpinda became the first port of the Congo (it is today Angola's Santo António do Zaire) and was at the time of the arrival of de Sousa's expedition the capital city of the kingdom's province of Soyo and the residence of the chief of the province of Soyo, the ManiSoyo.

"The ManiSoyo, with demonstrations of great joy, met the Portuguese with all his followers," a contemporary chronicler, Duarte Lopes, tells us. Three thousand warriors, armed with bows and arrows, naked to the waist, painted in various colors, and wearing headdresses of parrot feathers, assembled to the sound of drums, ivory trumpets, and stringed instruments. After three days of grand revelry, feasting, and dancing, they took the Portuguese to Mbanza Kongo to meet their king. It was a journey of a hundred miles along a footpath snaking through dense forests, across streams and ravines, along precarious ridges, through marshes and swamps, and always ascending to a plateau some 1700 feet above the sea in the Crystal Mountains. It took very nearly three weeks, and throughout the journey, Duarte Lopes tells us,

So great was the multitude who ran to see the Portuguese Christians, that it seemed as if the whole country were covered with people, who loaded them with kindness, singing and making sounds with cymbals and trumpets, and other instruments . . . after three days on the road they met the king's escort, who presented them with all manner of refreshments, and paid them great honor, as did other nobles sent by the king to meet the Christians.

When they came within three miles of Mbanza, at a place called Mpangala, which was something of a suburb of the royal capital,

all the Court came to meet the Portuguese with great pomp, and with music and singing . . . and so great was the crowd that not a tree or raised place but was covered with people running together to see these strangers.

Unfortunately, there are no contemporary descriptions of the kingdom's royal capital at the time of the Portuguese arrival. Duarte Lopes, unaccountably, fails us in this regard and all later descriptions of the city unavoidably include alterations made by the Portuguese. However, Monsignor Jean Cuvelier, the preeminent student of the ancient kingdom, has attempted to reconstruct what it must have looked like when Rui de Sousa became the first European to enter it. Because of its elevation, it was well up out of the worst of the jungle's humid heat and had a relatively mild and healthy climate for a population that must have numbered in the tens of thousands.

The streets were not laid out in straight lines [Cuvelier reckons]. Narrow paths ran in all directions through the tall grass. . . . The houses were of unadorned straw, except for their interiors, where there were mats with designs. . . . The dwellings of the notables were distinguished from those of ordinary people by a little more room and a greater number of painted mats. They were surrounded by walls of perennial trees. . . . To the north the mountain was crowned by a dark forest, a kind of sacred wood in which the sound of the axe was never heard. . . . It was in this wood that the former kings were buried. The founder of the kingdom, Nimi a Lukeni, was buried there. To the south lay a large square which was known as *mbasi a nkanu,* court of justice, because under the great wild fig tree . . . which shaded one corner of this square, the kings were accustomed to dispense justice. It provided a large open space where people assembled to receive the benediction of the king, or to attend dances and triumphal reviews of the troops. Not far from the public square was the residence or enclosure of the king. . . . This was made of stakes tied together with vines. . . . At the different gates of entry, the king's guard and a few trumpeters were stationed. Inside the enclosure there was a large yard; then there was another palisade which enclosed the dwelling of the king, which was approached through a maze.

At the end of this maze, Duarte Lopes tells us, the ManiKongo awaited the approach of the Portuguese embassy. His name was Nzinga a Nkuwu; he was perhaps sixty years old and was seated on a throne made of wood inlaid with ivory, which had been placed on a raised platform. He was draped in beautifully tanned, glossy hides and leopard and civet furs, and around his waist, affixed as a sort of apron over his skirt of palm cloth, he wore a piece of European damask which Diogo Cão had sent him nearly ten years before. His arms were laden with bracelets of copper, the tail of a zebra hung from his shoulder, an ironwood baton and a bow and arrows lay across his lap, and on his head he wore a cap of palm cloth resembling velvet and embroidered with the figure of a snake. Assembled around him were his queen and lesser wives, the nobles of his court, the chiefs of the provinces—including his sons, Mbemba a Nzinga, chief of Nsundi and the heir apparent, and Mpanzu a Nzinga, chief of Mpemba province.

Rui de Sousa approached and, in the European custom, knelt before the monarch and kissed his hand. The ManiKongo responded by taking up a handful of dust, pressing it first against his heart and afterward against the Portuguese. Then Rui de Sousa called forward his porters and presented the gifts he had brought from the king of Portugal—lengths of satin, silk, and linen, brocade and velvet fabrics, silver and gold jewelry, trinkets and plate, and a flock of red pigeons. Duarte Lopes tells us,

After this the king rose from his seat, and showed by words and countenance the great joy he felt at the arrival of the Christians, and sat down again in presence of his people. These last, immediately after the speech of the king, with songs and music, and other signs of delight, also manifested their satisfaction with the embassy, and as an act of submission, prostrated themselves three times on the ground, and lifted their feet, according to the custom of those countries, praising and approving their king.

Then, using as his interpreter one of the Bakongo nobles who had returned from Lisbon, Rui de Sousa proceeded to explain his mission—the desire of King John II that the ManiKongo and his people accept the Christian faith and enter into an alliance with the kingdom of Portugal. We are told that this explanation occupied the rest of that day and most of the night. De Sousa described the virtues of Christianity and the wonders of Portuguese civilization, illustrating his lecture with the tools and equipment and sacerdotal objects he had brought—and by having his soldiers fire off a salute with their rifles. The ManiKongo, Duarte Lopes reports

listened with great attention. . . . Then the king retired and gave lodgings to the ambassadors in a palace set apart for them, and the rest were lodged in various houses of the nobles, with every provision for their comfort.

The ManiKongo couldn't have been anything but overwhelmingly impressed by Rui de Sousa's presentation. He obviously realized that he had come in contact with a superior civilization from which, as an ally, he and his kingdom could gain immense benefit and from which, as an enemy, they might suffer considerable harm. His, therefore, couldn't have been a difficult decision to make, and whether he made it with quite the alacrity the early Portuguese chroniclers would have us believe, there can be no doubt that he must have made it very soon after Rui de Sousa's arrival.

The next day, Duarte Lopes reports, the ManiKongo

sent privately for all the Portuguese, when they devised the manner in which the baptism of the king was to take place, and how to effect the conversion of these people to the Christian faith. After much discourse, it was decided first to build a church, in which to celebrate with great solemnity the rite of baptism and other services, and meanwhile to instruct the king and the people of the court in the truths of the Christian religion.

One thousand Bakongo, we are told, the ManiKongo himself included, joined the Portuguese masons and carpenters and artisans in the construction of the church, gathering rocks, lime and wood from as far as ten miles away, and by the first week of May the cornerstone was laid.

The church was built in the amazingly short time of two months but, as it turned out, before its completion an insurrection erupted within the realm. The ManiKongo's son and heir, the chief of Nsundi, Mbemba a Nzinga, was sent to deal with the rebels but soon returned to Mbanza in need of reinforcements. One might cynically suggest that part of the ManiKongo's eagerness to become a Christian and an ally of the Portuguese was connected with the impression their firearms had made on him. In any case, he insisted that the baptismal rites be performed before the church's completion.

A wooden hut was hastily raised and, according to some chroniclers, 100,000 people gathered in Mbanza to witness the historic event. The ManiKongo, in honor of the king of Portugal, took the Christian name John, his wife took that of the Portuguese Queen Eleanor, and his son and heir, Mbemba a Nzinga, that of the Portuguese heir to the throne, Affonso. Other lords of provinces and nobles were also baptized at the same ceremony, but it is important to note that a number were not. There were members of the ManiKongo's court who disapproved of the king's hasty embrace of the newcomers and their religion, who feared the impact of the strangers on their traditional society, and who would have preferred to drive them out of the kingdom straight away while their numbers were still small. Among these was the ManiKongo's other son, the chief of Mpemba, Mpanzu a Nzinga. The Portuguese, however, were not disturbed by this. Everything was being done in haste anyway. The ManiKongo was eager to get on with the baptism so he could enlist the Portuguese in subduing the rebellion. Convincing and converting Mpanzu and other hostile nobles would have to wait. Now was a time for war. Here would be the practical proof of the power of Christianity. Rui de Sousa presented the ManiKongo with a banner with a cross embroidered on it, said to have been blessed by Pope Innocent VIII, and commanded his soldiers to fight in the black monarch's army as if on a crusade against infidels.

There is some confusion about who the rebels were and where the ManiKongo's battle against them took place. Duarte Lopes calls them Anzichi, living on islands in the Congo where "this great river, being restrained by falls, is greatly swollen and expands into a large and deep channel," and other chroniclers say the rebels lived on the banks of the Congo's "Great Lake." In both cases the reference seems to be to the Stanley Pool, the lakelike expanse above the Livingstone Falls, which would mean that the Anzichi rebels were probably the Bateke, then vassals of the ManiKongo. If it is true that the battle did occur at the Stanley Pool, it means that the Portuguese soldiers who fought in the battle accomplished, although surely unwittingly, the feat at which Diogo Cão ten years previously had failed, and that is to reach the Congo River further upstream than the Cauldron of Hell, a feat that would not formally be recognized as having been accomplished until Stanley did it nearly four hundred years later.

Born of conquest, the Kingdom of Kongo was a fiercely militaristic state at the time. Duarte Lopes tells us that the king's bodyguard consisted of some 20,000 warriors. Besides this, every able-bodied man in the realm considered himself a soldier of the king and, Lopes estimates, the ManiKongo could call up an army of more than 100,000 warriors virtually at a moment's notice. To assemble such a formidable army, the king needed but to order the war drums to be sounded. Hearing the signal, the men would take up their arms and run to the royal enclosure, where the king would appear and, flourishing his weapons, leap about in a war dance of sham combat. His officers and nobles would join in, and then, as the mood would catch hold, the people would take up the ferocious war chants, working themselves into a blood lust, soon to be joined by the fetishers, banging wooden bells and rattles that were meant to obtain the assistance of the ancestors. After three days of this, the army was in a fit state to set off for battle—camouflaged in palm leaves; armed with bows and iron-tipped arrows, ironwood clubs, knives, lances, and assegais; wearing feathered headdresses, with iron-link chains hanging from their necks; and carrying shields of buffalo hide or bark.

Duarte Lopes tells us:

They fight only on foot; they divide their armies into several units, adapting themselves to the terrain and brandishing their emblems. . . . The movements of the combat are regulated . . . by different ways of beating the drum and sounding the trumpet. . . . In front of the fighters march valiant sturdy men who leap about, beating their bells with wooden sticks, firing the courage of the soldiers, and warning them of the weapons being launched against them and the dangers they face. When the fighting begins, the ordinary soldiers run into the fray in scattered formation, shooting their arrows from afar, turning and dodging this way and that, darting in all directions to avoid being hit. . . . When they have fought a certain length of time and the captain decides they are tired, the signal for retreat is given by the ringing of bells; when they hear this, they retrace their steps and other soldiers take their place in combat, until their armies are engaged with all their forces in the general melee.

A single battle usually was the war, for the army went into combat without provisions. They would fight for a couple of hours or so, and whichever side weakened first would then flee and the stronger side would give chase, killing the oldest men, taking the younger ones prisoners, pillaging the villages of the defeated, and shouting all the while, "We have won the war." In this way, the ManiKongo, fighting under the cross and with the help of Portuguese firearms, won his war against the rebels at Stanley Pool and marched triumphantly back to Mbanza with his prisoners and plunder.

Rui de Sousa departed for Lisbon with every reason to feel well-satisfied. A stone church stood in Mbanza Kongo, the ManiKongo and leading members of his entourage had accepted the Gospel, and the power of Portugal's arms had been demonstrated. What's more, he took back with him a number of young Bakongo nobles as ambassadors to the Portuguese court and left behind a number of Portuguese to promote the new alliance: four priests, several lay brothers and artisans, a contingent of soldiers. "There also remained," Rui de Pina, the official chronicler of King John II's reign, tells us, "other persons of distinction ordered to go and discover other distant countries, with India and Prester John as their objectives." Presumably this was to be done by following the Congo River into the heart of Africa.

It is not unlikely that a party of soldiers and *fidalgos,* following the route of the ManiKongo's army, did find their way once again over-land through the forests and mountains around the Livingstone Falls back to Stanley Pool. But almost certainly they didn't get much farther than that. The jungle, the oppressive climate, fevers and un-known diseases, hostile tribes living outside the frontiers of the King-dom of Kongo would have stopped them and they must have perished. For they were never heard from again.

Meanwhile the Portuguese back in Mbanza were running into troubles of their own. With the conversion of the ManiKongo and the first military victory under the banner of the cross, the European settlers had unquestionably made an auspicious beginning. The king set aside a special quarter of the royal capital for the Portuguese, directly across from his own enclosure, where they built themselves comfortable houses, often of stone, and set about what they regarded as their main civilizing mission in this primitive kingdom: the conver-sion of the people to Christianity. The priests and lay brothers pur-sued the task with zeal and, taking the lead from their king, the Bakongo flocked to the missionaries. The mysterious rituals, the mar-velous sacerdotal objects, the images and paintings of the Virgin and the saints, the splendid processions, the solemn ceremonies in the church excited and delighted the people, and they came to view the religion, a chronicler wrote, "as a gay and pompous pageant, in which it would be an amusement to join." But soon enough the zeal-ous priests tried to get beyond the pretty formalities and teach the faith's doctrines, precepts, duties, and obligations. And in that they came into conflict with traditional Bakongo beliefs.

The Bakongo, as a matter of fact, did believe in a high god, a supreme being called *Nzambi ampungu,* whom they perceived as the creator of all things. But they also believed that, by virtue of this god's very highness, he was exceedingly remote, quite beyond the influence of men, and therefore, useless to worship. It was the lesser gods, gods closer to men and earth, more intimately involved with the matters of daily life, who could be placated and bribed and who deserved the worshiper's attention. So it was nature spirits, ghosts of ancestors, and shades of every sort, along with the attendant witchcraft and sorcery, medicine men and diviners, fetishes, idols, and magical rituals, that constituted the Bakongo religion and which they, even after their ostensible conversion to Christianity, refused to give up.

The Portuguese felt obliged to try to force them to give it up, resorting to flogging individuals they couldn't otherwise convince, setting fire to fetishes, destroying idols and holy places. In one history we read of a priest who

having met one of the king's wives, and finding her inaccessible to all his instructions, determined to use sharper remedies and, seizing the whip, began to apply it to her majesty's person. The effect he describes as most auspicious; every successive blow opened her eyes more and more to the truth, and she at length declared herself wholly unable to resist such forcible argument in favour of the Catholic doctrine. She hastened to the king, however, with loud complaints respecting the mode of spiritual illumination, and the missionary henceforth lost all favour both with the king and the ladies of the court.

The Portuguese found other ways to fall from favor. As with missionaries in Africa ever since their time, these priests were appalled by the sexual behavior of the Bakongo. In fact, however, the Bakongo were hardly a licentious people. Rape, incest, and adultery were severely punished, sometimes by wrapping the culprits in dried banana leaves and setting them afire, sometimes by selling them into slavery. The defloration of a virgin required reparation payments to her family; the proper vocabulary for sexual matters was indirect and allusive; the courting procedure was complex and dignified; and the ultimate marriage ceremony was an elaborate and serious business.

Nevertheless, the Bakongo exhibited a refreshing candor about the realities and the pleasures of sex, and this is what seems to have incited the Portuguese priests. They would fly into rages at the sight of the Bakongo dances, which were often explicit pantomimes of sexual intercourse, at the fact that masturbation was considered quite normal, that young couples were allowed to live and sleep together in preparation for their marriages. But the practice the priests attacked most vehemently was polygamy. "Appalled by the host of wives that surrounded every prince or chief, and whom, as they fulfilled for him all public as well as domestic services, it had been his constant study to multiply," a historian wrote, the Portuguese "called upon their converts to select one, and to make a sweeping dismissal of the rest." It proved the most unwise move of all. For polygamy was central to the political and social structure of the Kongo, and the attack on it "was considered an unwarrantable inroad on one of the most venerable institutions of the realm." To the ManiKongo and his nobles, a multiplicity of wives was a measure of their prestige, power, and wealth. It was also a vital political instrument; alliances were made through marriages, transforming rival feudal lords into in-laws. Moreover, it wasn't only the men who supported the practice. As the wives were the primary workers in households, performing a wide variety of domestic chores, they quite liked the idea of being part of a harem; indeed, the larger the harem the better, because this meant the work was shared out among more people.

So, as the Portuguese pressed uncompromisingly for observance of Church doctrine, disaffection with the new religion steadily grew, and so did the anti-Christian, anti-Portuguese faction led by Mpanzu a Nzinga, the ManiKongo's second son. Gathering always more closely around the ManiKongo, warning of the disorders and calamities that would befall the kingdom because of the abandonment of traditional customs, the betrayal of ancestors, the violation of powerful fetishes, this faction ultimately gained the upper hand in the kingdom. Mbemba a Nzinga, the heir apparent, baptized Affonso, remained faithful to the Church and led the Christian faction at the court, and, in the best tradition of court intrigue, Mpanzu set out to destroy his half-brother's influence with their father. Duarte Lopes tells us that Mpanzu "gave the king to understand that Affonso favoured the Christian religion in order to usurp his place." He claimed that Affonso came every night and slept with one of the king's wives, that he used the magic taught by the Portuguese priests to dry up the rivers and injure the fruits of the earth so that the king's territories might not yield their usual revenues.

At last the ManiKongo had had enough. Sometime around 1495 the king renounced the Christian faith and banished Affonso, along with all the Portuguese remaining in Mbanza, to Affonso's province of Nsundi on the banks of the Congo River. It seemed that the Portuguese experiment of alliance with an African kingdom had ended, and quickly, in failure.

We don't know exactly how many new Portuguese expeditions were dispatched to the Congo during this period of anti-Catholic reaction. The chronicles seem to suggest two or three, but in any case there were relatively few. The ManiKongo's apostasy was only partly responsible. For during this period, too, King John II, the great Congo enthusiast, died (in 1495) and his cousin, Manuel the Fortunate, on ascending the throne, sent Vasco da Gama on his successful voyage opening the sea route to India. Then, in 1500, Pedro Álvares Cabral, following da Gama, inadvertently discovered Brazil, and the Congo no longer seemed quite so important. Portuguese ships, money, men, ingenuity, and energy were now diverted to exploiting the rich Indies spice trade, establishing trading posts on the East African and Malabar coasts, and exploring the possibilities of the South American continent.

Affonso, however, even in his exile, remained unshakable in his attachment to Christianity and Portugal. He is said to have destroyed fetishes and driven the fetishers out of his province, observed the mass daily, and taken instruction from the handful of Portuguese priests, soldiers, and artisans who were left with him. Despite his isolation, he appears to have been convinced that his day would come. And it did.

In 1506 or thereabouts, the ManiKongo died. Though Affonso was the rightful heir to the throne, his exile had thrown the succession open to other pretenders, and there was no doubt that Affonso's half-brother, Mpanzu, as leader of the dominant anti-Christian faction, would attempt to seize the crown. A war of succession, between the Christian, modernist faction of Affonso and the pagan, traditionalist faction of Mpanzu, was inevitable as soon as the news of the old Mani-Kongo's death was out. And Affonso was at the disadvantage in this fight: he was far from the capital and he had fewer forces at his command.

But, when the day of reckoning arrived, Affonso found he had a powerful ally in Mbanza. Queen Eleanor, the ManiKongo's principal wife and Affonso's mother, is said to have remained a faithful, if secret, Catholic during the years of the pagan reaction. Be this as it may, it is obvious that she would have wanted her son, rather than the son of one of the ManiKongo's other wives, to inherit the crown. So she conspired to keep the death of the king secret for three days, long enough for Affonso to get to the capital. Duarte Lopes tells the story this way:

In a secret manner she informed her son by runners, who, placed at convenient distances, like posts, are always ready to carry the commands of the king throughout the kingdom, of the death of his father, and that she would keep it secret till he arrived, begging him to come without delay, and with as great haste as possible to the court. Therefore, by means of these same posts, and being carried by slaves, according to the custom of the country, day and night, he accomplished with marvelous speed the journey of two hundred miles, and suddenly appeared in the city.

Once there, he revealed the news of the ManiKongo's death and announced his own succession to the throne. And, with amazing aplomb, he then arranged that his father, the old pagan monarch who had exiled him for his Christianity, be given a Christian burial.

Mpanzu, of course, did not accept this passively. Duarte Lopes tells us that he "collected a great force, and came armed against his brother, bringing with him the greater part of his subjects, to the number of nearly 200,000 men." This army was positioned around the royal city, cutting off all the roads leading to and from it. Then Mpanzu sent word to Affonso and all who were with him that, if they did not immediately surrender, recognize him as king, and abandon Christianity, they would all be slain. Although Affonso, along with the handful of Portuguese soldiers who still remained with him, had been able to raise an army of barely 10,000 men to stand against Mpanzu's hordes, the ultimatum was refused. And so the battle was joined.

On the following dawn, we read in Duarte Lopes's account, Mpanzu

led the assault with furious impetus on the side of the city that faces to the north. . . . Here Dom Affonso, and his handful of men, were ranged against the pagans and his brother; but before the latter had come face to face with the king, he was suddenly and entirely routed, and put to flight. Seeing himself conquered, Mpanzu was greatly amazed, not understanding the cause of his defeat. Notwithstanding, he returned next day to the assault in the same place, and again was discomfited in like manner. . . . Therefore, the people in the city mocked the pagans, and taking heart from such a victory, no longer feared, but became eager to attack their adversaries, who told them that they had not won the day themselves, but owed their victory to the presence of a lady in white, whose dazzling splendour blinded the enemy, whilst a knight riding on a white palfrey, and carrying a red cross on his breast, fought against them and put them to flight. On hearing this, Dom Affonso sent to tell his brother that these were the Virgin Mary, the mother of God, whose faith he had received, and St. James, who were sent from God to his aid.

Nonetheless, Duarte Lopes tells us, Mpanzu continued to fight, attempting to assault the city from two different positions. But the results were the same; the miracle of Christianity was unassailable, and finally,

being overcome by fright, Mpanzu rushed headlong into the ambush covered with stakes, which he had himself prepared for the Christians, and there, almost maddened with pain, the points of the stakes being covered with poison, and penetrating his flesh, ended his life.

This is, of course, a Portuguese Christian account of the event, written at a time of militant Catholicism, and obviously needs to be taken with a grain of salt. The miracle that allowed Affonso's inferior forces to prevail against the pagan hordes of his half-brother was more likely the presence of Portuguese firearms in his ranks than the visions of the Virgin and saint in the clouds. But no matter; Affonso's astonishing victory over his half-brother was perceived as a victory for Portuguese and Christian power, a power that the new ManiKongo, King Affonso, had allied to himself. And so, with his ascendancy to the throne, Europe got an unparalleled opportunity on the African continent.

8

THE FOREST OTHELLO

"A native of the Congo knows the name of only three kings; that of the present one, that of his predecessor and that of Affonso."

So wrote a Catholic missionary, Father Antonio Barroso, more than 300 years after the coronation of this ManiKongo. That long-lasting fame was well deserved, for Affonso was an extraordinary figure, not only in terms of his own kingdom or even of Africa, but, in a special way, on the world stage as well. He was as imposing and memorable as an Othello in his pride and ambition, and in his innocence and tragic betrayal as well, a man not merely years but literally centuries ahead of his time.

There is no way we can write a biography of this remarkable African monarch; the materials simply are not available from so remote a time and place. What we can safely assume, though, is that he was in his late twenties or early thirties when he ascended the Kongo throne. We can imagine him as tall and muscular, clean shaven, with his hair close cropped, noble in feature as befits the descendant of at least a half a dozen Bakongo kings. We can assume that he was physically strong, tempered as he was in jungle wars, and we know that he was intellectually brave, considering how fiercely he held to Christianity, suffering for his beliefs and persisting in them until he finally triumphed. We also know that, in a way no African would be until the European colonists of the twentieth century started sending their charges to Oxford and the Sorbonne, he was an educated and literate man in the strictest European sense.

Some fifteen years had passed between his baptism and his coronation, and throughout those years, especially during his exile, he studied with the Portuguese priests and artisans whom he had kept close around him, learning everything he could of the civilization of Christian Europe. A Portuguese priest, Rui d'Aguiar, in the early years of Affonso's reign, described him in a letter to King Manuel of Portugal in this way:

May Your Highness be informed that his Christian life is such that he appears to me not as a man but as an angel sent by the Lord to this kingdom to convert it, especially when he speaks and when he preaches. For I assure Your Highness that it is he who instructs us; better than we he knows the prophets and the Gospel of Our Lord Jesus Christ and all the lives of the saints and all things regarding our Mother the Holy Church, so much so that if Your Highness could observe him yourself, you would be filled with admiration. He expresses things so well and with such accuracy that it seems to me that the Holy Spirit speaks always through his mouth. I must say, Lord, that he does nothing but study and that many times he falls asleep over his books; he forgets when it is time to dine, when he is speaking of the things of God.

It is impossible to gauge the true depth of Affonso's belief in the Catholic faith. Unquestionably he professed and practiced it with zeal, and equally unquestionably he understood it not only in its ceremonial and miraculous aspects but in its finest metaphysical nuances as well. But whether this means that he was convinced of its eternal truth we really don't know and, in fact, have some reason to doubt. But what cannot be doubted is that he recognized in a way that his predecessor had not—and as no African leader would until the twentieth century—that European knowledge, which was embodied then in the Catholic Church, was of immense potential value to himself and to his people. In his time and place, Affonso was a modernist, an apostle of new ideas, a bold innovator and reformer, and one can only wonder where he got that from. He believed in education, admired technology, wanted trade, and throughout his reign he remained steadfastly dedicated to bringing these benefits of European civilization to the Kongo. And he was convinced that the way to do it was by the evangelization of his kingdom.

His reign began auspiciously. To be sure, after the fratricidal war by which he won his throne, there was a brief bloody period during which Affonso's pagan enemies were put to death or driven into exile. But Affonso was anxious not to split his kingdom into warring factions, and he moved quickly to heal the wounds of the religious war. For example, he singled out the *ne vunda,* the chief earth priest and witch doctor in the kingdom, who, in his natural opposition to Christianity, had been Mpanzu's major ally, and not only granted him a pardon but restored him to religious power in the capital by putting him in charge of the construction and maintenance of the churches and the furnishing of the holy water for the baptismal rites.

Moreover, in another effort to win over the pagan faction, he agreed to a particularly grisly ceremony, which traditionally confirmed the ascendance of a new ManiKongo. Harking back to the sacredly violent act of a Nimi a Lukeni, by which the legendary founder of the kingdom established his divine isolation, the rite required the new sovereign to bury alive one of his relatives and so demonstrate his position above the common law. That Affonso performed this ritual and participated in other pagan practices—he was, for example, almost surely polygamous throughout his life—may justify questioning just how deeply his Christian convictions ran. But it may be fairer to recognize even in this his remarkable modernism. For, as the Church itself was to do elsewhere in similar circumstances, he was sensible enough to bend the rules of Christianity to make it compatible with older sacred forms and thus give it a better chance of flourishing.

Central to Affonso's plans was restoration of relations with Portugal. The band of Portuguese who had been left behind by Rui de Sousa had dwindled to a mere handful; if Affonso was to realize his ambition of bringing European Christian civilization to the Kongo he needed to have more priests and artisans and teachers. And, as fate would have it, not long after his coronation—it appears to have been in 1507—one of those caravels which Portugal occasionally dispatched to the Congo, commanded by a certain Gonçalo Rodrigues Ribeiro, called at the river's mouth. Affonso seized the opportunity. He loaded Ribeiro's ship with gifts—copper jewelry, elephant tusks, parrots, civet cats, raffia cloth, and slaves—for King Manuel and sent to Lisbon aboard it the last remaining Portuguese priests in his kingdom along with his own son, baptized Henrique, and some other young Kongo nobles. The priests he charged with asking the Portuguese king for more missionaries and technicians; as for the youths, he asked the Portuguese king to provide them with a full education in Christianity and Portuguese civilization.

Portuguese enthusiasm for the alliance with the Kingdom of Kongo never revived to the level that had existed under King John II.

Manuel was far too busy with the burgeoning Indies trade and the development of Brazil, and the experience with the apostasy of the previous ManiKongo had been a souring one. Nonetheless, the arrival of Ribeiro's caravel with its rich cargo of gifts and the message from the long-lost Portuguese priests about Affonso's devout Christianity and zealous desire for Portuguese aid sparked a renewed interest to which Manuel couldn't help but respond. Affonso's son Henrique and the other Kongo nobles were enrolled in the college of the Santo Eloi cloister in Lisbon, and 15 priests from there, along with a company of artisans, craftsmen, soldiers, and teachers, were sent to Mbanza.

The Christianization of the Kongo was underway. Determined to create a literate class, Affonso concentrated on education. As early as 1509, we are told, mission schools for 400 students, including, remarkably enough, women, had been built in Mbanza, and by 1516, the priest Rui d'Aguiar reported the presence of more than 1000 students in the capital, "sons of noblemen" who were not only learning to read and write but were studying grammar, the humanities, and technology "as well as the things of faith." Moreover, in those first few years of Affonso's reign, every Portuguese ship that called at the Congo returned to Lisbon carrying Bakongo youths to be educated at Santo Eloi. At the same time, the conversion of the people grew apace. Duarte Lopes tells us that the priests "with much charity and zeal, disseminated the Catholic faith, which was received alike by everyone in the kingdom. The priests themselves were treated with as great reverence as if they were saints, being worshipped by the people on their knees, who kissed their hands and asked benediction every time they met them."

Using the technology of the Portuguese artisans, Affonso undertook something of an urban development program in the royal capital. The city was enclosed by a wall and both the Portuguese quarter and the king's enclosure were also walled off. Churches were built, the streets were straightened and lined with trees, houses were constructed of ironstone and came to cover an area of over 20 square miles, and the population there grew to more than 100,000. In addition, Affonso had the Portuguese introduce new food plants to improve his people's diet, including such fruit-bearing trees as the guava, lemon, and orange as well as maize, manioc, sugar cane, which Portuguese expeditions had brought back from Brazil and Asia. And they imported their tools and weapons, sabers and swords, muskets and mortars, and taught the Bakongo how to manufacture and use them.

As for Affonso personally, he seems to have become more and more "Portuguese," at least in formal appearance and behavior, with every passing year. For example, he and his court adopted the Portuguese style of dress, wearing, as Duarte Lopes reports, "cloaks, capes, scarlet tabards, and silk robes. . . . They also wear hoods and capes, velvet and leather slippers, buskins, and rapiers at their sides. . . . The women also have adopted the Portuguese fashions, wearing veils over their heads, and above them black velvet caps, ornamented with jewels, and chains of gold around their necks." Portuguese titles were taken up: the king's sons became princes, the chiefs of the principal provinces dukes, while lesser nobles became marquises, counts, and barons. And Portuguese rules of etiquette and protocol were introduced. For example, Affonso abandoned the traditional rule that the ManiKongo could not be seen eating or drinking. Instead, imitating the Portuguese custom, he ate in public and, as Duarte Lopes notes,

Preparations for the coronation of the ManiKongo

"he always eats alone, no one ever sitting at the table with him, and the princes stand around with heads covered." He even adopted a royal coat of arms, prepared for him by the Portuguese, "for us to use as ensigns on our shields," we read in a letter Affonso wrote to the lords of his provinces around 1512, "as the Christian kings or princes of those lands generally carry so to show to whom they belong and whence they come."

One needs perhaps to step back for a moment and remind oneself what a really astonishing thing all this was. For here was the start of a genuine partnership, an alliance struck in peace and friendship, based on mutual respect between two nations an ocean apart, in which the two monarchs treated with each other as equals despite the difference in the color of their skins and in the character of their civilizations. One cannot help wondering what might have been, how Europe and America's relations with Africa would have been influenced in the centuries that followed, if this promising start, forged almost single-handedly by Affonso, had become what this remarkable African king's soaring vision dreamed it could be. But it didn't. It was doomed to fail almost at the outset. And what doomed it was the slave trade.

One must be very quick to say that neither Portugal nor any other European nation introduced slavery to Africa. African tribes and kingdoms, and not least among them the Kingdom of Kongo, slaved for as long ago as there is any record or memory. But one must be just as quick to point out that there was a vast difference between the slavery of Iron Age Africa and the slavery brought to Africa by Europe in the sixteenth century.

The African's slave was of course not a free man and his status certainly was inferior to that of a free man. But he was not a chattel slave as that term came to be understood in the subsequent centuries; he was not stripped of his property or human dignity or all his rights. He was rather what might more appropriately be called a serf or vassal or perhaps an indentured servant, a condition common enough to Christians during the Middle Ages. And it was a status to which he fell in much the same way Christians did in feudal Europe: in punishment for a crime—thieves, murderers, and adulterers were usually enslaved—by being taken prisoner in a war, or by being offered as tribute from a subjugated tribe to a dominant one. Once his status as a free man had been lost in some manner such as these, the slave or serf was required to perform work for his master (as a vassal peasant, for in-

stance, or artisan, soldier, or house servant) . But the amount of work
he performed and, more importantly, the duration of his enslavement
depended on the way he had become a slave in the first place. Africa
did not have the concept of perpetual enslavement. Slavery there was
almost always for a specified period of time, much like a prison sentence, commensurate with the nature of the crime, the circumstances
of capture, or the conditions agreed on between tribes. What's more,
every slave enjoyed the possibility of earning time off for good behavior or purchasing freedom outright with goods acquired during
that free time in which he was not required to work for his master.
Moreover, during his servitude the slave could not be abused; he was
regarded with respect and often became a confidant or trusted advisor of his master. And he was always free to marry, raise children,
and run his own household.

It is true that Islam introduced a much harsher form of slavery to
Africa. The Moslem traders, feeling no restraint in dealing with infidels, did take blacks into perpetual slavery, castrating the men and
totally denying them rights to property or anything else. But these
slavers had not yet succeeded in penetrating the forests of the Congo
River basin, and the Kingdom of Kongo was unaware of such cruel
practices. It was left to the Portuguese to teach it to them.

As we've seen, the Portuguese began slaving in Africa in a comparatively benign manner. After a brief, initial period of violent,
chaotic slave raids, the caravel captains settled down to a rather organized and peaceable trade, buying from African middlemen who
brought slaves—enslaved under the accepted rules and traditions of
Africa—down from the interior to the Portuguese posts on the coast.
The numbers remained limited; the greater trading interest still lay
in the gold dust, ivory, pepper, and other more seemly natural products of the continent. What's more, the slaves that were taken back to
Portugal were treated with a measure of human dignity. That they
were regarded as human beings and not as some highly developed
species of animal, as they would be later, is testified to by the fact that
the Portuguese always insisted on converting them to Christianity.

This was all to change from the beginning of the sixteenth
century onward, and what brought about the change was, of course,
the European discovery of new worlds. The opening of the rich Indies
trade sharply diminished Portuguese interest in Africa's comparable
natural products, making slaves the single most valuable commodity

the continent had to offer. And the settlement of the West Indies and the Americas, with their slave-worked mines and plantations, drastically escalated the demand for this valued commodity. No longer would the modest numbers of slaves taken from the coast be sufficient; therefore, no longer would the methods used to acquire these numbers be sufficient. Slaving was to become big business, the main business for Europe in Africa for the next four hundred years. Slaving fever, hyped by the huge profits to be made in the bloody business, was to seize white men everywhere near or on the continent, and the changed nature of slaving would doom Affonso's dream and destroy his kingdom.

It began on São Tomé, an island in the Gulf of Guinea some 600 miles northwest of the Congo's mouth off the coast of present-day Gabon. The Portuguese discovered it in the 1470s and, because it was uninhabited and had a relatively healthy climate, attempted to settle it beginning in the 1490s. It was first used as a penal colony. Later, criminals were granted freedom if they accepted exile there, and they were soon followed voluntarily by adventurers and disreputable characters of every stripe who needed, for whatever reason, to flee Portugal. With the opening of the sea route to the Indies, São Tomé became a major port-of-call for the Indiamen and its economy boomed. The settlement grew to about 10,000. Sugar and coffee plantations were established, and to work them the São Tomistas began buying slaves along the Benin coast. Then, when the colonization of the Americas escalated the demand for slaves, the island's traders got into the business in a big way, moving always further southward down the coast, until by the early 1500s they were plying the trade in the Kingdom of Kongo.

In order to encourage the island's development at the outset, the Portuguese crown had leased it to a chartered trading company organized by a certain knight of the court named Fernão de Mello. As donatário (proprietor-general) of the company, de Mello was in effect governor of São Tomé. Formally, he was a subject of King Manuel, but Portugal was just too far away to exercise any real control over him. De Mello was the law on the island—indeed, very much a law unto himself. He ignored the crown with impunity and ruled his settlement of rogues and vagabonds with an iron hand, very much as he pleased.

By all accounts, he was a viciously avaricious and venal man. He was determined to monopolize all the trade with the adjacent African coast and exploit the slave trade particularly to its fullest potential. Not for him was the traditional modest business of sending ships to the established slaving posts on the coast, such as the one that had developed at Mpinda at the Congo's mouth, there to buy the limited number of slaves that African middlemen had brought down from the interior for sale. De Mello's traders opened their own slaving depots and, bypassing the coastal middlemen, struck inland to do their business at the traditional slave markets of the interior. And they introduced new ways of doing that business. Since prisoners of war could be enslaved, they fomented wars. Since criminals could be enslaved, they promoted crime. They corrupted chiefs and headmen with gifts of firearms, cloth, and alcohol, developing in them a lust, almost an addiction, for these goods, and then used them as they chose. They led Africans on slave raids, induced rebellions against the vested authorities, and in short enough order began wreaking havoc in the Congo forests.

As early as 1511, we find Affonso appalled at what the São Tomé slavers were doing in his realm. In the first of what was to be a virtually endless stream of letters to reigning Portuguese monarchs, of which twenty-two have survived, the ManiKongo requested King Manuel to send a Portuguese ambassador to the Kongo with the power to control the atrocious behavior of the white men in his kingdom. Manuel responded to this request but he responded for reasons of his own, reasons which Affonso, in his noble innocence, never entirely grasped. For, with the boom in the demand for slaves, Manuel had taken a new interest in the Kongo. Slaving the kingdom, he realized, could prove an immensely profitable commercial proposition, which he did not enjoy seeing fall into the hands of the greedy, defiant *donatário* of São Tomé. He wanted it for himself. De Mello's activities were to be limited to the Guinea coast; the Kongo was to become a trade monopoly of the Portuguese crown. And the best way to accomplish that, Manuel decided, was by shoring up his alliance with the ManiKongo, an alliance which he still considered as one between equals.

"Most powerful and excellent king of Manycongo," Manuel wrote in reply to Affonso's request, "We send to you Simão da Silva, nobleman of our house, a person whom we most trust. . . . We beg you to listen to him and trust him with faith and belief in everything he says from our part." Da Silva was sent out in command of an expedition of five ships, the largest ever dispatched to the Kongo, which carried to Affonso more missionaries, technicians, soldiers, books, tools, church furniture, and above all, a *regimento,* a fascinating document that Manuel had designed to formalize relations between the European and African kingdoms. It was cast in the form of instructions to da Silva, who was to serve as the Portuguese ambassador to the Kongo court. The first group of instructions outlined the kind of assistance Portugal was prepared to extend to the Kongo in such matters as education, missionary work, political, technical, and military affairs. The next group addressed itself directly to the abuses of which Affonso had complained. Saying "our plans can be carried out only with the best people," Manuel empowered da Silva to arrest and expel those Portuguese in the Kongo who did not lead exemplary lives.

But a group of instructions also dealt with the Kongo's obligations to Portugal in return for this assistance. "This expedition," Manuel wrote, "has cost us much; it would be unreasonable to send it home with empty hands. Although our principal wish is to serve God and the pleasure of the Manikongo, nonetheless you [da Silva] will make him [Affonso] understand—as though speaking in our own name— what he should do to fill the ships, whether with slaves or copper or ivory." In addition, da Silva was instructed to get Affonso to make regular annual payments of such commodities to Portugal in return for the aid. And finally da Silva was ordered to determine the present and potential value of the Kongo trade and set about organizing it as a royal monopoly between the Portuguese and Kongo kings, cutting de Mello and his São Tomistas out of it entirely.

The da Silva expedition reached the Congo's mouth in 1512. On the outbound journey, however, it called at São Tomé, as did all ships sailing these seas at that time, so de Mello, through his spies and informers, had learned the contents of Manuel's *regimento,* and by the time da Silva's first ship reached Mpinda the São Tomista slavers there were ready to stir up trouble. Exactly what kind of trouble it is hard to make out from the chronicles, but it was evidently so threatening that da Silva refused to leave his ship and instead sent the ship's physician to Mbanza to secure some protection from Affonso. But, by the time that protection could reach him, da Silva was dead of fever, and so it fell to the captain of the expedition's second ship, Álvaro Lopes, to deliver the *regimento* to Affonso, take up the office of ambassador at the ManiKongo's court and set about trying to enforce its provisions. It proved an impossible task. De Mello and the São Tomistas had defied the Portuguese king before and they were prepared to defy him now. Certain that Manuel was too far away to protect the crown's trading monopoly, their slaving gangs arrogantly ravaged the Kongo's forests, sowing violence, creating terror, inducing tribal chiefs and province lords, in their turn, to defy their king. What's more, taking advantage of São Tomé's geography astride the seaway to and from Portugal, they set about interposing themselves between Affonso and Manuel. De Mello had every ship bound from the Kongo to Lisbon searched, and he wasn't above delaying, turning back, or even imprisoning, enslaving, or killing messengers and ambassadors from the ManiKongo to the Portuguese king, ultimately cutting off the royal brothers of the alliance from each other.

The Portuguese in Mbanza were swiftly infected by São Tomé's defiance and slaving fever, and they split into bitterly contending factions on the issue of the crown's trading monopoly. There were some who remained loyal to Manuel and Affonso but the far larger number joined the São Tomistas, unable to resist the huge profits to be made in the freebooting slave trade. The masons, carpenters, teachers, and other artisans in the royal capital bought or took payment in slaves and assembled the coffles in caravans to be driven down to Mpinda for sale to the slaving caravels from the island that called there. Even the priests, men initially so revered by the Bakongo as to be treated as saints, soon followed the lead of their secular colleagues. They abandoned their cloister, set up housekeeping with black concubines and joined in the bloody business with zeal, not only neglecting but in fact enslaving their catechists.

The story is told that de Mello bribed one of these corrupt priests, who then, using the threat of excommunication, set about the evil work of sowing discord among the nobles of Affonso's court and luring them into the São Tomista camp. His activities so infuriated Álvaro Lopes, the Portuguese ambassador there, that, in a fit of rage, he killed the priest. The murder played right into the São Tomistas' hands. Expressing self-righteous indignation, they demanded the crime be punished, and Lopes was exiled to the penal colony on São Tomé, never to be heard from again. Then the São Tomistas contrived to have one of their own number installed as the Portuguese ambassador, and the ugly situation in the capital deteriorated even further.

One can visualize Mbanza turning into a sort of wide-open frontier boom town: The priests living with mistresses, their missionary work an utter sham, and every white man in the place neglecting his duties to make his fortune out of human flesh. Corrals were built in the main square, hard by the churches, in which slaves were assembled before being driven down to the coast. As the methods as well as the intensity of the trade got further beyond the pale, slave revolts became commonplace. We read of one slave caravan, organized by a priest and some masons, that rebelled and ran amok through the royal capital, setting fire to and pillaging the Portuguese quarter.

Although, at any one time, there probably were never more than 200 Portuguese in Mbanza, their impact was all out of proportion to their numbers, and the corruption they brought spread quickly to the Bakongo. The nobles of the court and the educated elite, aping the Portuguese in dress and manners, conspired with the contending white factions for or against Affonso, sold their servants and members of their households, and organized slave raids with Portuguese gunmen. The hundreds, and then thousands, of mulatto offspring of the loose-living whites who swarmed the capital became agents of the slave traders, bully-boy enforcers, petty officials, and lesser members of the corrupted clergy. From their female ranks, prostitutes were recruited for the Mbanza brothels, and with the introduction of that profession, until then unknown in the Kongo, was introduced what the Bakongo called *chitangas*, venereal diseases, which ravaged the black population as the tropical diseases ravaged the white, heightening the terrible mood of moral decay. "The climate is so unhealthy for the foreigner," a Portuguese trader in Mbanza wrote in 1515 (and by climate we can take him to mean the word in its broadest definition),

that of all those who go there few fail to sicken and of those who sicken few fail to die, and those who survive are obliged to withstand the intense heat of the torrid zone, suffering hunger, thirst, and many other miseries, for which there is no relief save patience, of which much is needed, not only to tolerate the discomforts of such a wretched place but what is more to fight the barbarity, ignorance, idolatry, and vices which seem scarcely human but rather those of irrational animals.

It was at this point that Portugal can be said to have betrayed Affonso. For, having issued his *regimento*, blueprinting the alliance of equals between the two kingdoms and the obligations each owed the other, Manuel failed to live up to his part of it. Neither he nor his successor—King John III ascended the Portuguese throne in 1521—made any move to control the rapacious São Tomé slavers or discipline the defiant Portuguese in Mbanza. Rather, they stood aside and watched with cold, calculating eyes the havoc wreaked.

Once again one must note the increasing demands made on the Portuguese crown by its other overseas enterprises, its heavy expenditures in ships, men, and material for the development of the Indies, Brazil, and East Africa. But that serves as only a partial explanation for Portugal's betrayal of the bargain it struck with Affonso. Bluntly put, no sooner had the *regimento* been formulated than the Portuguese crown decided that to honor it was not really in its own best interest. The hard commercial truth of the matter, which quickly enough dawned on the Portuguese king, was that the chief value of the Kongo was as a source of slaves. The hope that the Congo River would prove a pathway to the kingdom of Prester John and the Indian Ocean was no longer operable; the Indian Ocean had been reached years before, and Ethiopia, the realm of the Christian African monarch, had by this time been entered from the East African coast. No, what the Kongo had of special and increasing worth was its population, and, to exploit it, the *regimento* was hardly necessary. Quite the contrary; the modernization of the Kongo, the evangelization and education of its peoples, could only make the slaving more difficult, both in practice and in conscience. The Portuguese king's only regret was that it was de Mello and the São Tomistas who were harvesting those slaves and not he. But that too could be changed—and in time it was. In 1522, the Portuguese king disenfranchised de Mello, and took over São Tomé as a crown colony. The ruthless slave trade continued unabated—by the 1530s at least 5000 slaves a year were being shipped from Mpinda alone—and, except for sporadic, empty gestures, Portugal abandoned Affonso.

It was at this point that Affonso revealed the tragic extent of his innocence. For he seemed unable or at least unwilling to grasp Portugal's motives and intentions; he refused to believe that the Portuguese kings could betray the Christian principles they professed. Again and again we find him, heartbreakingly and naïvely, appealing to his royal brother to heed those principles, to honor their alliance.

As early as 1515, Affonso asked the Portuguese king to simply hand over to him in fief the island of São Tomé so that he could control its abuses. When this request was ignored, he then asked for a ship of his own. This was to be a recurring theme in his correspondence with the Portuguese crown. "Most powerful and most high prince and king my brother," a letter of 1517 begins, "I have already written to you how much I need a ship, and telling you how grateful I would be if you would let me buy one." He obviously believed that with his own ship he would be able to circumvent São Tomé and enter into direct communication with Portugal without the hated island's interference. "Most high and most powerful prince and king my brother, it is due to the need of several things for the church that I am importuning you. And this I would not probably do if I had a ship, since having it I would send for them at my own cost." But no matter how he couched his request for a vessel, or for the means of building one of his own, it was always refused or ignored.

Affonso sought to break out of his geographical confinement by trying to contact the only other European power he had any specific knowledge of—the Vatican His son Henrique had been in Rome since 1513 and, with Manuel's agreement, the ManiKongo arranged to have the youth consecrated a bishop by Pope Leo X in 1518. It was a truly historic event; no black man would attain such an exalted rank in the Church for another four centuries. But Affonso's hope that this would open a new avenue for him to Christian Europe was quickly dashed. The Portuguese would allow Henrique to be named only an auxiliary to the Bishop of Madeira, who had his seat on São Tomé, so the Bishop of the Kongo, on returning to Mbanza in 1521, found himself taking his instructions from the hated island. Affonso's subsequent attempts to reach the Pope were also blocked. "We beg you to lend us five thousand *cruzados*," he wrote to John III at one point, "to provide for the expenses for our brother and ambassador . . . who on our behalf goes to see the Holy Father, accepting in exchange one hundred and fifty *cofos* of coins of our Kingdom with which slaves can be bought [in repayment for the loan]." It was refused.

But perhaps the clearest illustration of Portugal's betrayal of Affonso came with its steadily diminishing willingness to provide technical aid and material for the modernization and evangelization of the African realm. Affonso year after year wrote in vain requesting priests and missionaries, teachers and technicians, church artifacts and tools.

It happens that we have many and different diseases which put us very often in such a weakness that we reach almost the last extreme; and the same happens to our children, relatives and others owing to the lack in this country of physicians and surgeons. . . . We have neither dispensaries nor drugs which might help us in our forlornness. . . . We beg you to be kind and agreeable enough to send two physicians and two apothecaries and one surgeon.

They were not sent. The grand experiment of Europeanizing the African kingdom ground to a halt and, because of the ravages of the slavers, the Kongo fell into a state far more chaotic and primitive than it had ever been before the Portuguese arrived.

By 1526 the situation was catastrophic. The Portuguese were totally out of hand but, worse yet, the Kongo nobles and chieftains, following the white man's example, were breaking loose from Affonso's control. Insubordination was rife in Mbanza, the Mani-Kongo's commands were defied throughout the realm, and wars between villages, tribes, provinces, and vassal kingdoms, incited to promote slaving, raged in the Congo forests.

The excessive freedom given by your factors and officials to the men and merchants who are allowed to come to this Kingdom . . . is such . . . that many of our vassals, whom we had in obedience, do not comply [Affonso wrote to King John III]. We can not reckon how great the damage is, since the above-mentioned merchants daily seize our subjects, sons of the land and sons of our noblemen and vassals and relatives. . . . Thieves and men of evil conscience take them because they wish to possess the things and wares of this Kingdom. . . . They grab them and cause them to be sold; and so great, Sir, is their corruption and licentiousness that our country is being utterly depopulated . . . to avoid this, we need from your Kingdoms no other than priests and people to teach in schools, and no other goods but wine and flour for the holy sacrament; that is why we beg your Highness to help and assist us in this matter, commanding the factors that they should send here neither merchants nor wares, because it is *our will that in these kingdoms there should not be any trade in slaves nor market for slaves.*

When this letter too went unanswered, Affonso issued an edict banning slaving in the Kongo and expelling all Portuguese who participated in the slave trade. It was an inflammatory and ultimately vain command. Both the black and white slavers not only ignored it; they seized upon it to stir up new intrigues against the ManiKongo and, within four months of the edict's promulgation, Affonso was forced to revoke it. He settled then instead for the creation of a sort of

slaving board, which was meant to inspect all coffles before they were
shipped to São Tomé to make sure that the slaves had been taken by
accepted African practices and not by kidnapping and other illegal
means. How effective this was can be seen in one of the last letters
Affonso was to write to King John III. The missive accompanied five
of Affonso's nephews and one grandson who were going to Lisbon to
be educated.

We beg of Your Highness to give them shelter and boarding and to treat
them in accordance with their rank, as relatives of ours with the same
blood . . . and if we are reminding you of this and begging of your attention it is because . . . we sent from this Kingdom to yours . . . with
a certain Antonio Veira . . . more than twenty youngsters, our grandsons,
nephews and relations who were the most gifted to learn the service of
God. . . . The above-mentioned Antonio Veira left some of these youngsters in the land of Panzamlumbo, our enemy, and it gave us great trouble
later to recover them; and only ten of these youngsters were taken to your
Kingdom. But about them we do not know so far whether they are alive
or dead, nor what happened to them, so that we have nothing to say to
their fathers and mothers.

Subsequent records show what happened to those ten: they were
seized and enslaved on São Tomé and shipped to Brazil.

Nonetheless, Affonso never could bring himself to give up his innocent trust in the Catholic rulers of Portugal. It is said that, with
increasing age and repeated disappointments, he became something of
an eccentric, exaggerating to the point of grotesqueness the Portuguese style and manners at his court. On Easter Day, 1539, an attempt
was made on his life. It occurred, ironically enough, while he was at
mass. Eight Portuguese traders, led by a corrupt priest, burst into the
church and took shots at him with their arquebuses but missed, and
after that he became ever more reclusive, dreaming in private his
grand dream of bringing the benefits of European civilization to the
Kongo while in reality the realm fragmented and plunged ever deeper
into the chaos and violence that Europe actually had brought.

Meanwhile, the Congo River remained unexplored. In the *regimento* of 1512, Manuel had specifically instructed his ambassador to
Mbanza to investigate the possibility of sailing on the river above the
cataracts to discover where it led. And we know that three of his
ambassadors—Gregorio Quadra, Balthasar di Castro and Manuel

Pacheco—at different times attempted to carry out these instructions by building and launching brigantines on the Stanley Pool. Affonso, however, blocked all three attempts. He feared that any major expedition into the interior of his country could only lead to more chaos and trouble. However, it didn't much matter. Even had Affonso not prevented it, it is highly unlikely that any of these expeditions could have succeeded, given the reputation white men had made for themselves in the Congo forests. If the terrain and the fevers had not killed off the explorers, the tribesmen, in their fear and hatred of the Portuguese slavers, surely would have.

9

---◆─◾◽◽─◆---

SLAVERS, CANNIBALS, AND A SAINT

While Affonso was still alive, the nobility of his character and his charismatic stature as monarch—if not his policies and politics—held the kingdom of Kongo together in the semblance of an independent, functioning political unity. But, once he died, sometime in 1542 or 1543, the forces of divisiveness that had developed in the half century since the Kongo's discovery burst loose and proceeded to tear the kingdom to pieces.

A battle for succession—between Nkanga Mbemba, baptized Pedro and believed to be Affonso's oldest son, and Nkumbi Mpudi a Nzinga, baptized Diogo and said to be either a second son or a nephew—erupted on Affonso's death and became the battleground for all the contending factions that intrigued around the ManiKongo's throne. It is impossible to reconstruct the politics in Mbanza at the time, who supported whom, how and why, but it appears that Pedro received the backing of the São Tomistas and he managed to take Affonso's crown. But his was a chaotic and short-lived reign. Diogo rallied his forces and, after two years of bloody conflict, he overthrew Pedro and began a 16-year reign of increasing dissolution and disintegration.

Diogo was no primitive savage, no jungle chieftain sprung from the bush. Quite the contrary; he was almost surely one of Affonso's relatives who had been educated at the College of Santo Eloi in Lisbon and was every bit as "civilized" as the old ManiKongo himself. But there the comparison with Affonso ends. For Diogo had no grand vision for the modernization and evangelization of his kingdom. Nor, on the other hand, had he any program for the expulsion of the Portuguese and the return of the Kongo to its original state. He had, indeed, no visions or programs of any kind. He was a monarch much like any number of European kings of that time, beset by all sorts of problems, concerned with fighting off his enemies, maintaining his rule, and deriving the greatest amount of profit from it.

He was not, for example, opposed to the slave trade that was ravaging his kingdom. What he opposed was the fact that not enough of the profits of that trade were reaching his royal treasury. And one of his first actions on gaining the Kongo throne was to send a certain Diogo Gomes, who seems to have been a mulatto born in Mbanza, to Europe in an attempt to do something about it.

Gomes's mission was to get the Portuguese to agree to restrict their trading activities in the Kongo to the port of Mpinda at the Congo's mouth. The São Tomé slavers—and, to a lesser degree, the white traders operating out of Mbanza—at this time roamed freely throughout the kingdom and traded directly with local chiefs and other vassals of the ManiKongo as deep in the interior as the Stanley Pool and as far south as the forests of today's northern Angola. The ManiKongo wanted to reorganize the trade so as to confine the white slavers to a single marketplace on the coast, in this case Mpinda, and force them to do business strictly through his own Bakongo middlemen. This clearly was not a scheme to reduce the slave traffic in the kingdom, but designed to give Diogo control over it.

Gomes, not surprisingly, failed in his mission. King John III was no less eager now to get all the profit he could from slaving the Kongo than he had been during Affonso's reign, and he turned Gomes down on the spot. But, as some sort of gesture to the old alliance, he decided to send four Jesuits to Mbanza, the first Portuguese priests to go out there in a decade.

Throughout its long association with the Kongo, Portugal or, more accurately, the Catholic Church never quite gave up its attempts to Christianize the Bakongo. In the early years of Affonso's reign, the attempt had a magnificently ambitious dimension to it—nothing less than the establishment of the faith as the Kongo's church. As time went on, however, the effort became ever more modest, diminishing to the rather commonplace business of saving heathen souls from perdition. But, no matter how ambitious or modest the effort, it was always a sporadic, intermittent affair, which was constantly being started all over again from scratch. First the Franciscans came, then the Dominicans, then the Austin friars and the canons of Santo Eloi; later it would be the Augustinians, the Carmelites, and Capuchins, but, no matter by which order, the effort always followed the same dismal cycle: huge enthusiasm and a burst of zealous activity at the outset, and then the good fathers would succumb to the corruption of slavery, and the effort would come to nothing until someone new came along to try it again. Now it was the Jesuits' turn.

We are told that when the Jesuits arrived at Mpinda the Kongo was in such a state of disorder that they had to be escorted by 10,000 armed warriors from the coast up to Mbanza. Nevertheless, they seem to have survived the trip with their enthusiasm intact and embarked on their missionary work with predictable zeal. In the first four months, 2100 baptisms were recorded; a school (those of Affonso's reign had fallen into ruins) was built for 600 students; and three new churches were erected, the principal one of which, dedicated to the Saviour, was called São Salvador, by which name the Jesuits rechristened Mbanza.

But, alas, even so disciplined and intellectual a group as the Jesuits could not resist the temptations of that wide-open, wicked town, and within the year we find them following their predecessors into the degrading business of buying and selling slaves and keeping concubines. And we find them also involving themselves in the political intrigues at the ManiKongo's court. To protect their slaving interests, the fathers allied themselves with the São Tomé faction and turned against Diogo. They attacked him for practicing polygamy, advised John III that he was an obstacle to their missionary work, and recommended that he be replaced. They denounced him from the pulpit as "a dog of little knowledge," and joined a São Tomista plot aimed at ousting him and returning Pedro to the throne. Diogo countered as best he could, first by limiting the Jesuits' activities, then by cutting off their allowances of food and quarantining their mission, finally by expelling them.

The expulsion of the Jesuits gave the Portuguese another self-righteous justification for further defying the ManiKongo. They boycotted Mpinda, then in the control of Diogo's middlemen, and built their own slaving port, Mboma (later more simply called Boma), on the Congo River's estuary. And, pushing further southward down the West African coast, they established yet another slave port in the Bay of Goats on the site of what is today Angola's capital of Loanda, and from there struck an alliance with the ManiKongo's most important southern vassal—the Ngola or paramount chief of the Ndongo (from whose title the name Angola derives)—and induced him to revolt against the Kongo king. Diogo attempted to put down this revolt by main force. But, though some Portuguese from Mbanza fought on his side, the white forces against him proved far too strong and, in a battle on the Dande River, the Ngola routed the army of the ManiKongo in 1556. The defeat set an inescapable example, and by the time of Diogo's death, in 1561, vassal kings, province lords, tribal chiefs, and even village headmen were entering into separate slaving compacts with the Portuguese and rising in revolt against the Mani-Kongo.

Under the circumstances, the new succession struggle was a horrendous bloodbath. The Portuguese murdered Diogo's designated heir and put a nephew with the glorious name of Affonso II on the throne. This blatant power play seems to have led to a general insurrection, in the course of which Affonso II was assassinated by his brother Bernardo. Bernardo, however, didn't last much longer. He had the bad luck to seize the Kongo throne just at the moment the vassal state of the Bateke were in rebellion, and he was killed in battle against them at the Stanley Pool. His successor was named Henrique, and he went the way of Bernardo, killed in war against another rebelling vassal state. When *his* successor, Álvaro, took the crown in 1568 an even more terrible catastrophe befell the Kongo. Out of the dark forests to the south and east, the fearsome warrior hordes of the cannibalistic Yakas descended on the kingdom.

We don't really know who the Yakas (or Jagas) were. No such tribe or people exists today and there are no accounts of their origins. For all intents and purposes, they seem to have sprung mysteriously full blown on the West African scene in the mid-sixteenth century and, after a brief and terrible history of a hundred years or so, vanished from it just as mysteriously.

The best speculation is that they were a Bantu-speaking people who originated deep in the interior of Central Africa and who might just possibly have been related to the Masai or Galla of present-day Kenya and Tanzania. Why they moved from those highland savannas down through the forests of the Congo River basin toward the Atlantic Coast is unknown, but clearly theirs wasn't a mass migration of a people in search of land. The Yakas weren't farmers; nor were they pastoralists. Their main interest in things agricultural seems to have been limited to the palm tree, which they cut down by the forestful and tapped to make intoxicating wine. As for being herders, it appears that they slaughtered and immediately ate whatever cattle they could lay their hands on.

No, what they seem to have been, and that apparently from the outset of their mysterious movement toward the West African coast, was a warrior army on the march. Much like the Nguni who came out of the Lake Malawi region to create the great Zulu empire of southern Africa, the Yakas organized themselves onto a permanent war footing early in their migration, lived in small mobile fortified camps, focused their entire social structure around their fighting men, and, attacking by surprise and exercising fierce discipline, conquered tribes more populous than their own. They killed their own babies, burying them alive at birth, so as not to be hindered on their relentless march, and, not unlike the Mamelukes of Egypt, adopted the children of the peoples they conquered and made them warriors in their army. They practiced cannibalism as much for the terror it inspired in their enemies as for the taste of it, and by the time they burst into recorded history they were a desperately feared and formidable military force.

Our best source on the Yakas is the remarkable chronicle of an English sailor who lived among them for nearly two years, called *The Strange Adventures of Andrew Battell*.

Battell was a pirate. In 1589, he shipped out as pilot aboard the privateer *Dolphin*, commanded by a certain Abraham Cocke, who made directly for the coast of Brazil to prey on vessels trading with the Portuguese settlements there. After several adventures in the region of the mouth of the Rio de la Plata, Battell and four mates went ashore to forage for food, were surprised by a gang of Indians in the Portuguese service and taken prisoners. Cocke, seeing what had happened, hastily put to sea, abandoning the men to their fate. Battell was kept prisoner for four months at the Portuguese settlement at Rio de Janeiro, then was shipped in chains to the new slaving port of Loanda on the Angola coast. There he was to spend nearly twenty years as a captive of the Portuguese, some of the time shackled in terrible dungeons, much of it serving as pilot or soldier on Portuguese trading expeditions along the West African coast and in the forests of the interior, attempting several times to escape and enduring extraordinary adventures. It was in the course of one such adventure that Battell fell in among the Yakas, whom he calls the Gagas.

The year was 1600 or 1601. Battell, with a group of Portuguese and mulatto slavers, had been on a trading mission to a tribe some two days' march into the interior from the Angola coast. When they had assembled their caravan and were ready to return to their ship on the coast, the chief of the tribe, a certain Mofarigosat

would not let us go out of his land till we had gone to the wars with him, for he thought himself a mighty man having us with him. For in this place they never saw a white man before, nor guns. So we were forced to go with him, and destroyed all his enemies, and returned to his town again. Then we desired him that he would let us depart; but he denied us, without we would promise him to come again, and leave a white man with him in pawn.

Battell tells us that at first

the Portugals and Mulatos being desirous to get away from this place, determined to draw lots who should stay; but many of them would not agree to it. At last they consented together that it were fitter to leave me, because I was an Englishman, then any of themselves. Here I was fain to stay perforce. So they left me a musket, powder and shot, promising this Lord Mofarigosat that within two months they would come again and bring a hundred men to help him in his wars, and to trade with him. . . . Here I remained with this lord till the two months were expired, and was hardly used, because the Portugals came not according to promise. The chief men of this town would have put me to death, and stripped me naked, and were ready to cut off mine head. But the Lord of the town commanded them to stay longer, thinking the Portugals would come. And after that I was let loose again, I went from one town to another, shifting for myself within the liberties of the Lord. And being in fear of my life among them I ran away.

Battell fled through the jungle only to be captured by a band of Yaka warriors and taken to their camp. "All the town, great and small," he tells us, "came to wonder at me, for in this place there was never any white man seen." The camp was overgrown with baobab trees, cedars, and palms so that its streets

are darkened with them. In the middle . . . there is an image, which is big as a man, and standeth twelve feet high; and at the foot of the image there is a circle of elephants teeth, pitched into the ground. Upon these teeth stand great store of dead men's skulls, which were killed in the wars.

Presently Battell was presented to the Yaka chief whom he calls the Great Gaga Calandola and who hath his hair very long, embroidered with many knots of Banba shells, which are very rich among them, and about his neck a collar of *masoes*, which are also shells, that are found upon that coast, and are sold among them for the worth of twenty shillings a shell: and about his middle he weareth landes, which are beads made of the ostrich eggs. He weareth a palm cloth about his middle, as fine as silk. His body is carved and cut with sundry works, and every day anointed with the fat of men. He weareth a piece of copper across his nose, and in his ears also. His body is always painted red and white. He hath twenty or thirty wives, which follow him when he goeth abroad; and one of them carrieth his bows and arrows; and four of them carry his cups of drink after him. And when he drinketh they all kneel down, and clap their hands and sing.

Evidently the Great Gaga developed a liking for the Englishman, and especially for his musket. Battell was enlisted in the Yaka army and participated in their wars, burning towns down, drinking palm wine, dancing "and banquetting with man's flesh, which was a heavy spectacle to behold." In time, Battell tells us, "I was so highly esteemed with the Great Gaga, because I killed many negroes with my musket, that I had anything that I desired of him." Battell stayed with them for nearly two years in the hope that, in the course of their rampaging march, "they would travel so far to the westward that we should see the sea again; and so I might escape by some ship." And that did eventually occur, but until it did he was a rare eye-witness to the ways of these mysterious people.

He tells us, for example, that the Great Gaga Calandola

warreth all by enchantment, and taketh the Devil's counsel in all his exploits. . . . He believeth that he shall never die but in the wars. . . . He hath straight laws to his soldiers: for those that are faint-hearted, and turn their backs to the enemy, are presently condemned and killed for cowards, and their bodies eaten. He useth every night to make a warlike oration upon a high scaffold, which doth encourage his people. It is the order of these people, wheresoever they pitch their camp, although they stay but one night in a place, to build their fort, with such wood or trees as the place yieldeth. . . . They build their houses very close together, and have their bows, arrows, and darts standing without their doors; and when they give alarm, they are suddenly all out of the fort. . . .

When they settle themselves in any country, they cut down as many palms as will serve them wine for a month: and then as many more, so that in a little time they spoil the country. They stay no longer in a place than it will afford them maintenance. And then in harvest-time they arise

. . . and do reap their enemy's corn and take their cattle. For they will not sow, nor plant, nor bring up any cattle, more than they take by wars. When they come into any country that is strong, which they cannot in the first day conquer, then their general buildeth his fort, and remaineth sometimes a month or two quiet. For he saith, it is as great wars to the inhabitants to see him settled in their country, as though he fought with them every day. . . . And when the general mindeth to give the onset, he will, in the night, put out some one thousand men: which do ambush themselves about a mile from the fort. Then in the morning the Great Gaga goeth with all his strength out of the fort, as though he would take their town. The inhabitants coming near the fort to defend their country, the Gagas give the watchword with their drums, and then the ambushed men arise, so that very few escape. And that day their General overrunneth the country.

Before the Great Gaga undertook any great enterprise, Battell tells us he would make

a sacrifice to the Devil, in the morning, before the sun riseth. He sitteth upon a stool, having upon each side of him a man witch: then he hath forty or fifty women which stand round about him, holding in each hand a zebra tail wherewith they do flourish and sing. Behind them are great store of petes, ponges, and drums, which always play. In the midst of them is a great fire; upon the fire an earthen pot with white powders, wherewith the men-witches do paint him on the forehead, temples, 'thward the breast and belly, with long ceremonies and inchanting terms. . . . Then the witches bring his Casangula, which is a weapon like a hatchet, and put it into his hand, and bid him be strong with his enemies. And presently there is a man-child brought, which forthwith he killeth. Then are four men brought before him; two whereof, as it happeneth, he presently striketh and killeth; the other he commandeth to be killed without the fort. Here I was by the men-witches ordered to go away, as I was a Christian, for then the Devil doth appear to them, as they say.

The Kongo was helpless against these ferocious people. The Yakas erupted from the forests along the kingdom's southwest frontier, crossed the Kwango River, and began their pillaging advance northward to the royal capital. The ManiKongo Álvaro, his court, the entire Portuguese settlement, and much of the population fled São Salvador in abject terror. The Yakas took the city, set it afire, and slaughtered and ate whoever remained behind. Then they split their army into several regiments and proceeded to overrun the rest of the realm, massacring the inhabitants, scourging the countryside and looting the villages. Álvaro and his black and white retainers scrambled down to the Congo River and took refuge on one of the islands in the stream.

The chroniclers of the period refer variously to this sanctuary as the Isle of Horses, Hippopotamus Island, and Elephant Island. We cannot tell for sure which of the many islands in the Congo's estuary it might have been, but we know that few of them are large enough to support the thousands of fugitives who must have sought refuge there. One can easily visualize the horrendous situation. The countryside was in turmoil. Hundreds of thousands were homeless, fleeing aimlessly through the forests, crowding down to the banks of the Congo in hopes of finding safety on the islands, while those already there, like survivors on a lifeboat, fought them off and cast them to the crocodiles in the river. Famine soon doubled the misery as the crops were left to rot in the fields or be ravaged by the Yakas. And then the bubonic plague broke out and the refugees, huddled like trapped animals on the islands, died of it by the thousands.

The only beneficiaries of this awful chaos were the slavers. Caravels from São Tomé anchored in the Congo's mouth, and the slavers rowed to the islands, their longboats loaded with food. And, Duarte Lopes tells us, "forced by necessity, the father sold his son, and the brother his brother, everyone resorting to the most horrible crimes in order to obtain food." Even the nobles of Álvaro's court were not above this practice. Lopes tells us, "Those who were sold to satisfy the hunger of the others were bought by the Portuguese merchants . . . the sellers saying that those they sold were slaves, and in order to escape further misery, the latter confirmed the story."

This situation lasted for nearly three years. But finally Álvaro managed to get a message through to the King of Portugal—Sebastião, the grandson of John III—and he responded by ordering the governor of São Tomé, Francisco de Gouvea, to go to the relief of the Kongo. In 1571, de Gouvea arrived at the river's mouth with an army of 600 soldiers, slavers, and assorted adventurers and renegades and, rallying the remnants of the ManiKongo's forces, embarked on a bloody campaign against the Yakas. It lasted for two years and in the end the Yakas were driven out of the kingdom and Álvaro was reinstated as king in São Salvador.

But he was now, in effect, a king without a kingdom. He may have

A. Paleis des Koninga.
B. Slaven en Slavinne die uit
   de Reviere water na de
   Stadt brengen.
C. Kerken.
D. Krygs-vesting of Sterkte.
E. Spring-bron met zoet
   zoet water.

The River Lelunda

D

Stadt SALVADOR
van het Rijk
O.

R the Chief
of

A

A. The Kings palace.
B. The Slaves men & women which
carry Water from the River
to ý. City.
C. The Churches.
D. The Block house.
E. a Well Spring of very Sweet water.

D
C

B

RIEVIERE LELUNDA.

View of São Salvador

ruled in São Salvador but hardly anywhere else in the Kongo. The
Yakas had been defeated but not destroyed, and they remained a force
of chaos and turmoil in the Congo River basin for years. The countryside was stricken by plague and famine and torn apart by wars, every
chief and province lord was in open revolt, and slavers, traders, soldiers of fortune, and adventurers of every ilk infested the realm.

Moreover, the Portuguese, except for a handful of Dominican
priests who came with de Gouvea's soldiers to try once again to resurrect missionary work there, did not return to São Salvador after the
fright of the Yaka terror. The slaving ports of Mpinda and Boma on
the Congo's estuary thrived, but the main Portuguese base shifted now
to Loanda, about 100 miles further south down the coast. In 1576,
King Sebastião appointed Paolo Dias de Novais, grandson of the Bartholomeu Dias de Novais who had found the way round the southern
tip of Africa, *donatário* of Loanda and dispatched him with seven ships
and 700 soldiers to build a fort and establish a permanent Portuguese
settlement there. This was to be Portugal's—and indeed Europe's—first
colonization on the African mainland. For, unlike the settlement in
Mbanza, the white presence here was not based on an alliance with a
local monarch. Loanda was taken by force. Dias's soldiers embarked on
a relentless war, which was to last for more than 30 years, against the
tribes and states of the territory, conquering some, subjugating others,
making vassals of still others, and, as always, harvesting slaves from
among their people. In this war no boundaries were recognized, and
the Portuguese soldiers, not infrequently with the cannibalistic Yakas
as their allies, struck north into the Kongo and made war against
provinces ostensibly under the sovereignty of the ManiKongo.

Álvaro did the best he could to resurrect his kingdom. He offered
to become a vassal of the Portuguese crown. He tried to make an
alliance with Dias's colony. He sent ambassadors to Lisbon. But all
came to nothing; the kingdom continued its pitiable descent into
anarchy. When Álvaro died in 1614, the struggle for succession was a
bloody and tragic farce. In the next 27 years, eight kings occupied the
ManiKongo's throne, one of them a boy barely thirteen years old,
while the lords of the provinces made war against each other and
conspired against each successive king.

It was during this period that Portugal lost its monopoly on the
West African coast. To a large degree this was due to events in Europe. Sebastião had turned out to be a foolhardy king. Trained by the

Jesuits, he visualized himself as a Christian knight and, harking back to the dreams of glory of a bygone era, he led a crusade against the Moorish infidels of Morocco, only to have his army destroyed and himself killed at the battle of Alcazarquivir. He was succeeded on the throne by his uncle, Cardinal Henrique, who, having no heir, was the last of the Aviz kings. On his death, in 1580, Philip II of Spain took the Portuguese crown, and the long so-called Spanish captivity began, involving the Portuguese in Spain's debilitating wars against the English and the Dutch. It is not surprising then that the Portuguese found it increasingly difficult and eventually impossible to protect their African, Brazilian, Indies, and other far-flung enterprises.

But the more important reason that the Portuguese lost their West African monopoly was the slave trade. With the market for slaves booming, and the fortunes to be made from them reaching astronomical proportions, it was impossible to keep other European maritime nations out of the lucrative traffic.

As early as the 1560s, French and English pirates were regularly raiding the African coast and seizing the cargoes of Portuguese merchantmen. We have the account of one such pirate, a certain John Hawkins, who "put off and departed from the coast of England in the month of October 1562 and . . . passed to the coast of Guinea . . . where he stayed some time and got into his possession, partly by the sword and partly by other meanes, to the number of three hundred Negroes at the least" from five different Portuguese vessels. Then he "sayled over the ocean sea to the iland of Hispaniola," where he went from port to port selling his cargo, for which he received "such quantities of merchandise, that he did not onely lade his owne three shippes with hides, ginger, sugars, and some quantities of pearles, but he fraighted also two other hulkes with hides and like commodities." We know that Hawkins sailed at least two more times, in 1564 and 1567, with like success, and when England went to war with Spain (and, perforce, Portugal) she gave her blessings to such pirates (Hawkins was knighted). In the 1580s and 1590s, Queen Elizabeth granted royal charters to companies to trade on the Barbary Shore, the Senegambia coast and Sierra Leone. In 1618, James I chartered 30 London merchants, who called themselves the Company of Adventurers of London Trading into Parts of Africa, to do business on the Guinea Coast; and in 1672 Charles II created the Royal African Company to trade from Morocco to the Cape.

The French followed suit, creating companies to exploit the mouths of the Sénégal and Gambia rivers, and hot on their heels came the Danes and Swedes and Prussians. In time all these countries would become major slavers along the entire West African coast. But for the moment they concentrated their activities on the coastline north of the equator. It was the Dutch who emerged in the first half of the seventeenth century to challenge the Portuguese south of the line.

In the 1570s, the Dutch were also at war with Portugal's Spanish king. Having just recently revolted against Philip II, they were fighting desperately to retain their independence, and were quite willing to carry the conflict to Africa. A highly efficient commercial and maritime people, they quickly realized that the best way to break into the rich trade was not by the interloping tactics of the English and the French but by following the Portuguese example and building settlements, forts, and factories on the coast itself. The first Dutch vessel to trade on the Guinea coast of which we have any record was in 1595, and by 1612 the Dutch had built their first African trading post. Five years later, making a deal with a local chieftain, they got permission to build two forts on an island called Goree smack in the middle of the Portuguese-held Cape Verde group, and then built a factory at Rufisque on the mainland opposite these islands. Emboldened by their success both in Africa and in Europe (the English had come to their side in their war against Spain), the Dutch attacked the Portuguese directly in 1637 and in the course of the next five years drove them from the Gold Coast entirely.

The Dutch now moved south of the equator. In August of 1641, an armada of twenty-one Dutch ships appeared off the Angolan coast at Loanda. The Portuguese, apparently, were not caught unawares, but the commander of the garrison made a serious blunder. Watching the Dutch vessels find their way into the harbor and beach at a point beyond the reach of his cannon, he concluded, rather improbably, that the Dutch had come merely to plunder the settlement, not capture it, so he ordered the evacuation of the port. The Portuguese withdrew into the interior to an upcountry post called Massangano to await the departure of the invaders. They, however, did not depart. A Portuguese counter-attack was organized, but the Dutch easily dispersed the force, and the records tell us that 200 Portuguese, including the garrison commander, were taken prisoner. Then a few months later another Dutch fleet sailed into the mouth of the Congo River, attacked the port of Mpinda and, to confirm their conquest, tore down the stone pillar that Diogo Cão had erected there a century and a half before.

As a chronicler tells us, "the chiefs of the Kongo, Angola and Matamba, who had reason to complain of the Portuguese, rejoiced at their defeat and made common cause with the Dutch." The reigning ManiKongo of the moment, called Garcia II Affonso, entered into an alliance with the Dutch and sought their support in his efforts to stop the secession of the kingdom's vassals and restore control over the realm to the throne in São Salvador. What's more, he was cunning enough to exploit the fact that the Dutch were Protestants, alarming the Vatican about the fate of Catholicism in the kingdom. The Pope responded by sending the Kongo its first non-Portuguese priests, mainly Italian Capuchins. And for a moment it seemed as if the Kongo stood a chance of recovering some of its former glory.

But as abruptly as they had arrived the Dutch departed and the Portuguese returned. By 1648, Dutch interest had shifted to the Indies trade, Asian colonization, and the building of a port-of-call for their Indiamen at the Cape of Good Hope. Meanwhile, the Portuguese had thrown off the Spanish yoke—the House of Braganza, in the person of John IV, had ascended the Portuguese throne—and were eager to reclaim their Kongo holdings. And they reclaimed them with a vengeance in 1665, invading the kingdom outright.

We have the call-to-arms issued by the ManiKongo, Antonio, at the time of this invasion:

Listen to the mandate given by the King sitting on the throne at Supreme Council of war: and it is that any man of any rank, noble or base, poor or rich, provided he is capable of handling weapons, from all villages, towns and places belonging to my Kingdoms, Provinces and Domains, should go, during the first ten days following the issue of this Royal proclamation and public notice, to enlist with their Captains, Governors, Dukes, Counts, Marquises, etc., and with other justices and officials who preside over them . . . to defend our lands, wares, children, women and our own lives and freedoms which the Portuguese nation wants to conquer and dominate.

An army was raised and it marched into battle, carrying flags bearing the cross, and met the Portuguese at a place called Ambouila, near the headwaters of the Bengo River. The date was October 25, 1665.

View of Loanda

The Bakongo were massacred and the ManiKongo was killed and beheaded.

It would not be until the late nineteenth century that Portugal would formally annex the territory of the Kongo kingdom to its colony of Angola. And between the battle of Ambouila and then we could piece together a chronology of perhaps another score of ManiKongos. But, in fact, the battle of Ambouila marked the end of this once impressive African realm. After the death of Antonio, the kingdom shattered into a hundred pieces, and those who claimed the title of ManiKongo were little more than local chieftains who happened to rule in the vicinity of São Salvador. The once royal city itself fell rapidly into ruins. The Bishop of Loanda, who visited it in the 1670s, called it "a den of savage beasts," and by 1690 its churches had all

crumbled into dust and most of the population had fled. In 1701, a Capuchin priest, Laurent de Lucques, wrote:

The news coming from the Kongo is always worse and the enmities between the royal houses are tearing the kingdom further and further apart. At present there are four kings of the Kongo. There are also two great dukes of Mamba; three great dukes in Ovando; two great dukes in Batta, and four marquises of Enchus. The authority of each is declining and they are destroying each other by making war among themselves. Each claims to be chief. They make raids on one another in order to steal and to sell their prisoners like animals.

Then in the midst of all this despair and desolation there arose improbably a Joan of Arc of the Kongo. Her name was Kimpa Vita, baptized Beatriz, and the Capuchin Father de Lucques describes her for us in this way:

> This young woman was about twenty-two years old. She was rather slender and fine-featured. Externally she appeared very devout. She spoke with gravity, and seemed to weigh each word. She foretold the future and predicted, among other things, that the day of Judgement was near.

His confrère, a Father Bernardo de Gallo, from an interview he conducted with Beatriz, provides us with her own account of how she discovered her mission:

> The event occurred in this manner, she said. When she was sick and on the point of death, at the last gasp, a brother dressed as a Capuchin appeared to her. He told her he was Saint Anthony, sent by God through her person to preach to the people, hasten the restoration of the kingdom, and threaten all those who tried to oppose it with severe punishments. She died, because in place of her soul, Saint Anthony had entered her head; without knowing how, she felt herself revive. . . . She arose then and calling her parents, explained the divine commandment to go and preach, teach the people, and hasten the departure toward São Salvador. So as to do everything properly, she began by distributing the few things she possessed, renouncing the things of this world, as the apostolic missionaries do. Having done this she went up into the mountain and in complete liberty fulfilled her duty, as God had commanded her to do, and with great success.

Thus, in the early eighteenth century, the sect of the Antonians was born. Within two years this extraordinary young woman developed a dogma and doctrine, established a rudimentary church, and gathered an immense following. She claimed Saint Anthony was the second God, who held the keys to heaven and was eager to restore the Kongo kingdom. She herself, as Father de Gallo tells us, "Was in the habit of dying every Friday," in imitation of the passion of Christ, and going up to heaven "to dine with God and plead the cause of the Negroes, especially the restoration of the Kongo" and being "born again on Saturday." She imitated the Virgin as well, and when she had a son she told Father de Lucques, "I cannot deny that he is mine but how I had him I do not know: I know however that he came to me from heaven." She preached that there was a fundamental difference between whites and blacks, saying the former "were originally made from a certain soft stone called fama" while the latter "came from a tree called musenda," and her followers wore garments made from the bark of that tree (a species of fig) .

Moreover, she claimed the Kongo was the true Holy Land, that Christ was born in São Salvador and received baptism in Nsundi, that the Virgin "was born of a slave or servant woman of the marquis Nzimba Npanghi" and that Saint Francis belonged "to the clan of the marquis of Vunda." She exhorted her disciples "not to worship the cross because it was the instrument of the death of Christ"; she rejected baptism, confession, and prayer, and declared polygamy legal. She prophesied that the roots of fallen trees would turn into gold and silver, that the reconstructed ruins of São Salvador would reveal mines of precious stones and metals, and that the "rich objects of the Whites" would come to those who followed her faith.

In time, of course, she came to be regarded as a saint with miraculous powers. It was said of her that where she walked twisted or fallen trees straightened; her followers fought to possess anything she touched; the noblest ladies of the realm cleared the paths for her; and the "lords offered her the ends of their capes as mantillas or tablecloths."

Thus it came about [Father de Gallo tells us], that São Salvador was rapidly populated, for some went there to worship the pretended saint, others to see the rebuilt capital, some to see friends, others attracted by the desire to recover their health miraculously, others still out of political ambition and to be the first to occupy the place. In this manner the false saint became the restorer, ruler and lord of the Kongo.

The Capuchins, needless to say, were not happy with Beatriz and the Antonian sect. Nor, for that matter, was the reigning ManiKongo, a puppet in the hands of the Portuguese, named Pedro IV, and with a little prodding from the missionaries he had the young woman arrested. At first, fearing the outrage of popular sentiment, he thought to exile her to Loanda. But the Capuchins, motivated, they tell us, "solely by zeal for the glory of God," wouldn't hear of it, and so the ManiKongo pronounced "a sentence of death by fire on the false Saint Anthony and his guardian angel." The execution took place on July 2, 1706. Both priests were there to describe the scene.

Here is Father de Lucques:

Two men with bells in their hands . . . went and stood in the middle of the great multitude and gave a signal with their bells, and immediately the people fell back and in the middle of the empty space the basciamu-cano, that is, the judge, appeared. He was clad from head to foot in a black mantle and on his head he wore a hat which was also black, a black so ugly that I do not believe its like for ugliness has ever been seen. The culprit was led before him. The young woman, who carried her child in her arm, now appeared to be filled with fear and dread. The accused ones sat on the bare ground and awaited their death sentence. We understood then that they had decided to burn the child along with his mother. This seemed to us too great a cruelty. I hastened to speak to the king to see whether there was some way to save him. . . . The basciamucano made a long speech. Its principal theme was a eulogy to the king. He enumerated his titles and gave proofs of his zeal for justice. Finally he pronounced the sentence against Dona Beatriz, saying that under the false name of Saint Anthony she had deceived the people with her heresies and false-hoods. Consequently the king, her lord, and the royal council condemned her to die at the stake, together with the infant. . . . They were led to the stake. The woman did all she could to recant, but her efforts were in vain. There arose such a great tumult among the multitude that it was impossible for us to be of assistance to the two condemned persons. . . . For the rest all we can say is that there was gathered there a great pile of wood on which they were thrown. They were covered with other pieces of wood and burned alive. Not content with this, the following morning some men came again and burned the bones that remained and reduced everything to very fine ashes.

Father de Gallo tells us that Beatriz died "with the name of Jesus on her lips," and then adds: "The poor Saint Anthony, who was in the habit of dying and rising again, this time died but did not rise again." Nor did the Kongo.

Part Three

THE EXPLORATIONS

10

---◆━◦◦━◆---

THE WAY TO TIMBUKTOO

It was now more than 200 years since the voyages of Diogo Cão and, while everything else in the Kongo had been catastrophically changed by them, one thing remained resolutely the same: the Congo River was still unexplored, its source and course and the lands it passed through as much a mystery as they had ever been.

Even the 100 miles of the river's estuary between the Cauldron of Hell and the sea, on which European vessels had trafficked since 1482, remained astonishingly inadequately mapped. We can see by the few mariners' charts of the river that were available in the eighteenth century that even such an obvious feature as the width of the river's mouth was still a matter of uncertainty, some making it as much as 30 miles across, others giving it as less than 10. An even greater degree of uncertainty existed about the falls and cataracts above the estuary. That they were there had been known, of course, ever since Diogo Cão first encountered them, but their full extent and true character had nowhere nearly been determined. As late as 1818, for example, the best that the renowned English geographer Jameson could offer about them, after noting plaintively that they "are nowhere particularly described," was that "They are said, however, to be of great magnitude, and their noise so tremendous, as to be heard at the distance of eight miles." He then went on to suggest, quite inaccurately, that they probably extended into the interior for no more than 70 miles.

As for what lay above the cataracts, that was open to the wildest speculation. Even though Portuguese soldiers, slavers, and missionaries had reached the Stanley Pool in the first decades after the Congo's discovery, this information had somehow been lost in the intervening years. No map or description of the river in the eighteenth century makes mention of it. The most popular notion of the river's course and its source was that it rose out of a great lake deep in the heart of Central Africa—a lake fed by streams from the Mountains of the Moon and from which the River Nile was also believed to issue—and flowed from there almost due west in an unbroken line to the sea. It was a notion dating back to the fifteenth century (we first come across it on *L'Insularium illustratum Henriei Martelli Germani* of 1489) and, while it is true that the more learned geographers of the eighteenth century were tending to dismiss it at last as "fabulous" (they recognized the geological improbability of a lake outletting by two major rivers, one to the north and the other to the west), their own ideas on the subject were, if anything, even further off the mark. D'Anville, for example, in his celebrated map of Africa of 1731, imagined that the Congo was formed by the union of three rivers, the Kwango flowing from the south, the Vambre flowing from the east and the Bancaro flowing from the north, all joining in a great confluence at the head of the cataracts, with the one from the north probably the Congo's mainstream. But when it came to describing the origin and course of these rivers, he didn't have the smallest idea.

This sort of geographical ignorance was not limited to the Congo. The whole of the interior of Africa remained a blank for eighteenth-century Europe, a blank almost as complete as it had been for Prince Henry and for very much the same reason: no European had ever been there. The brutal terrain, alien climate, killing fevers, and hostile tribes continued to play their devastating part in blocking the white man's way inland, but by the eighteenth century so did something else: an almost total lack of interest in getting there. For a hundred years or more, Europeans had had no incentive for running the risks involved in attempting to penetrate the continent's forbidding interior. For they had organized themselves quite efficiently to get from the relative safety and comfort of their coastal posts the only thing they wanted of Africa: her slaves.

The eighteenth century has been described as the cruelest hundred years of the slave trade. With the European colonies of the New World firmly established and flourishing, the demand for forced labor for the plantations of the West Indies and the Americas had become insatiable. The most conservative estimates have it that no fewer than 7 million and quite possibly as many as 10 million African slaves were landed in the New World during this bloody century. The Portuguese were still the major slavers of the Congo River basin; they took some 2 million slaves from there between the time of Diogo Cão's discovery and the end of the seventeenth century and shipped at least that many again during the 1700s, mainly to Brazil. But theirs was only a fraction of the total African trade. The Danes, settled in the sugar-rich Virgin Islands, and the French with their colonies in Mauritius, Haiti, and Guadeloupe, accounted for hundreds of thousands more. The Dutch, supplying not only their own colonies in Ceylon, Surinam, and the East Indies but those of other nations in the New World, shipped at least as many as the Portuguese. But it was imperial Britain, newly emerged as the undisputed maritime and mercantile power of Europe, that overwhelmingly dominated the trade, and more than half the slaves taken from Africa during those hundred years were carried in her ships, both to her own and to other's colonies.

Those ships sailed by the hundreds each year on what was called the Great Circuit, carrying cheap manufactured goods from the ports of Liverpool, London, and Bristol to the trading posts strung down the West African coast, there to be traded at handsome profits for slaves. They in turn were carried across the Atlantic, the infamous Middle Passage, to the West Indies and the Americas, where they were exchanged, at still greater profit, for the products of the mines and plantations the slaves worked. And these were then brought back to England to be sold for the most enormous profits of all. "How vast is the importance of our trade with Africa," an anonymous English pamphleteer wrote in 1772; "[it] is the first principle and foundation of all the rest; the main spring of the machine, which sets every wheel in motion."

But there is, of course, something else that needs to be said about the eighteenth century. If it marked the zenith of the slave trade, it also saw the flowering of the Enlightenment. This was, after all, the century of Rousseau and Voltaire, Montesquieu and the *Encyclopédie* of Diderot, of Hume and Swift and the economics of Adam Smith, of Kant and Lessing and Tom Paine. It was the century of such ideas as the Noble Savage and the Rights of Man, such movements as humanitarianism and Protestant nonconformism, such events as the American and French revolutions. Newspapers, periodicals, books, encyclopedias circulated widely and literacy spread as never before. The developments of the previous century—the discoveries of Newton, the rationalism of Descartes, the empiricism of Bacon—became part of the mainstream of thought, and the ideas of the age fostered belief in natural law, universal order, and human reason. It was a century of immense intellectual creativity and intense scientific curiosity, a century for which both the bloody traffic in slaves and the abysmal ignorance of the African interior were at first paradoxes, then insults, and finally unacceptable.

Perhaps just because she was the preeminent slaving nation, England gave rise to the antislavery movement. For a century and more, isolated protests had been heard in the land. For example, in the mid-seventeenth century, Robert Baxter, a nonconformist preacher, attacked the slave trade in his *Christian Directory,* and George Fox, the founder of the Society of Friends, made antislavery a tenet of his Quaker sect. Aphra Behn's novel *Oroonoko,* published in 1678 and turned into a play by Thomas Southerne in 1696, which described the miseries of slaves in the West Indies, stirred up the kind of public outrage that *Uncle Tom's Cabin* would a century and a half later, and such writers and philosophers of the Enlightenment as Locke, Pope, Defoe, and Adam Smith, some by satire, others by logical argument, still others by appeals to humanitarian and religious sentiment, carried the attack well into the eighteenth century. But one can fairly say that antislavery as a political movement didn't get underway until 1772, and the man who got it moving was a young, well-born civil servant by the name of Granville Sharp.

At that time there were more than 10,000 African slaves in England. They had been taken there by planters from the West Indies and the Americas who, regularly traveling back and forth across the Atlantic, expected to enjoy the services of their blacks in England just as they did at home in the colonies. The story is told that Sharp, in 1765, came across such a slave who had been savagely beaten by his master and thrown out into the street. Sharp had the black attended to and then found him a job. But the slave's master reclaimed him and then turned around and sold him to a friend. Sharp, very much a child of the Enlightenment, was outraged. He could not believe that there was any legal basis for such an action or indeed that English law sanctioned the owning of slaves in England at all, and it was on this basis that he set about bringing a challenge to slavery in the courts.

The test case he chose involved a runaway slave named Somersett who had been recaptured by his master. It was a long and arduous battle, draining on emotions and finances, and Sharp fought it with tenacity. He was vindicated for his efforts and secured the decision he had so desperately sought. In 1772, the Lord Chief Justice Mansfield handed down the judgment that "the state of slavery is so odious that nothing can be suffered to support it but positive law." And as no such positive law existed at the time, slavery forthwith became unlawful in England and any slave who set foot there automatically became a free man.

It was truly a momentous ruling, and the antislavers were quick to realize—and seize on—the opening it provided. For, after all, if slavery under English law was regarded as too odious to be legally practiced in England, it surely followed that it must be too odious to be legally practiced anywhere or by anyone subject to English law. And around this line of argument a formal antislavery movement crystallized. The Quakers led the way, forming a committee for "the relief and liberation of the Negroe slaves in the West Indies and for the discouragement of the Slave Trade on the coast of Africa." Sharp joined the committee, and soon the men who were to become the heroes of English antislavery—notably Thomas Clarkson and William Wilberforce—were part of it too.

In 1787, with Sharp as chairman, the committee made the politically astute judgment that it was unrealistic to attack the entire institution of slavery, and set itself the more limited goal of outlawing the slave traffic. Wilberforce, a Member of Parliament known because of his brilliance in debate as the nightingale of the House, carried the battle to the heart of the British government. Clarkson, recently down from Cambridge, where he had won a prize for a Latin essay on the subject "Is it right to make men slaves against their will?," visited the slave ports of Liverpool and Bristol and gathered the statistics and horror stories about the trade which served as the documentation for Wilberforce's arguments in Parliament. Others held meetings, issued pamphlets and stirred up public debate. Within a year, Clarkson wrote later, "the nature of the Slave Trade had, in consequence of the labours of the Committee and of their several correspondents, become generally known throughout the kingdom. It had excited a general attention, and there was among people a general feeling on behalf of the wrongs in Africa." In 1791 the government chartered the Sierra Leone Company to resettle in Africa those slaves in England who had been freed by Lord Mansfield's ruling, and popular support for the abolitionists reached such a peak in the following year that 300,000 people signed petitions resolving to boycott slave-produced West Indian sugar.

It is not to minimize the heroic work of the abolitionists to say that, by the beginning of the nineteenth century, political and economic changes in England and Europe substantially helped their cause. But certainly with American independence Britain's direct vested interest in the slave trade diminished, and the bloody slave revolt in Haiti in the wake of the French Revolution made slave owning a less appealing prospect. Moreover, as industrialization boomed, Europe's economy came to depend less and less on the import of plantation products and more and more on the export of manufactured goods. Thus, within a few years the slave lobby in Europe found itself isolated and with little influence. And, in 1807, Britain ruled the slave trade illegal for her subjects. (Denmark had anticipated her by three years.) The next year the United States followed suit. The Dutch outlawed the traffic in 1814, the Swedes in 1815; in 1818 a Napoleonic decree did the same for the French; and Spain joined the trend in 1820. Portugal, it is true, dragged her feet. In 1815 she agreed to restrict the traffic to her own possessions, but in 1836 she too finally felt obliged to prohibit the trade altogether.

Legislation, of course, did not halt the brutal business or, for that matter, much reduce it. In fact, the numbers of slaves shipped annually actually increased for several years in the mid-nineteenth century. Britain sent armed naval squadrons to police the West African coast but there were plenty of pirates willing to try to run her blockades so long as slavery itself, and thus profitable markets for slaves, still existed. Nonetheless, the die was cast. It took another half-century, but it was perfectly plain that the end of the profits to be made from the sale of slaves was now inevitable. And, with that, so was the end of the sole commercial value Africa held for Europe.

Indeed, ever since Lord Mansfield's ruling there had been a growing recognition that this was so and, concomitantly, a growing interest in whether or not Africa could be made to yield any other commercial possibilities. Might it not, for instance, prove to abound in "immense treasures," as Malachi Postlethwayt, the leading English economic journalist of the period, suggested, in minerals and raw materials with which to feed Europe's industrial machine? Might it not, furthermore, be developed into a huge new market for the products of that machine? "The Continent of Africa is of great extent, the Country extremely populous," Postlethwayt wrote, and then went on to ask rhetorically, "If we could so exert our commercial policy among these people [the Africans], as to bring a few hundred thousand of them to cloath with our commodities, and to erect buildings to deck with our furniture, and to live something on the European way, would not such traffic prove far more lucrative than the slave-trade alone?" All logic seemed to argue that it would. But no one could know for sure until someone at last went beyond the limits of the coastal stations and found out what was actually there.

Unquestionably then, the hope for trade to replace the dying slave traffic provided a powerful new incentive for Europe to attempt the penetration of the African interior, but it would be misleading to leave the impression that it was the only one. The antislavery campaign had stirred an intense interest in Africa and in Africans. People were suddenly avidly curious about these blacks, about who they were and where they came from. Moreover, the initial humanitarian concern for the African's political and material rights awakened a religious concern for his spiritual salvation. Churches, especially the nonconformist and evangelical sects, which had been involved in the Abolition Movement from the outset, began forming those great missionary societies which would send preachers into the heart of Africa and play a vital role in opening the continent's interior for Europe.

But perhaps the single most powerful incentive was the desire for knowledge and the confidence that not only could everything be known but that it should be, that abiding belief in science which so characterized the Enlightenment. It was considered then not only a sufficient reason but a supremely sensible one to go somewhere merely because no one had ever been there before and discover something that no one had ever known. Britain's Royal Society, its very founding an illustration of the spirit of the Enlightenment, sent astronomers to Sumatra to observe the transit of Venus. The Society of Dilettanti, a dining club of rich young English nobles, organized archeological expeditions to Ionia. Louis XVI of France dispatched Comte de La Pérouse round Cape Horn to map the coasts of Japan and Australia. Captain James Cook, in ten years of ceaseless voyaging, sailed to Tahiti and Australia, the Easter Islands and Hawaii, and meticulously recorded all the exotica he saw. In such a time, then, it is anything but surprising that the vast blank which was the map of the interior of Africa should represent an irresistible challenge.

All these forces were very much in play when, on June 9, 1788, a group of Englishmen sat down to dine at St. Albans Tavern off Pall Mall in London. They were members of the Saturday's Club, one of those small (this one had a total membership of twelve, of whom nine were present that day), elitist eating clubs to be found in London in those years, where friends of equal social standing and common interests would gather informally to enjoy an excellent roast and fine old port and discuss the ideas of the day. The members were all extremely wealthy and from the highest ranks of the establishment, but they were also wonderfully representative of the enlightened spirit of their times.

For example, Sir Joseph Banks, who was to emerge as their leader, was then president of the Royal Society as well as secretary of the Society of Dilettanti and was an accomplished botanist who had sailed on Cook's first expedition. Henry Beaufoy, a Quaker, was an active abolitionist, as was the Earl of Galloway. The Bishop of Llandaff was both an abolitionist and a scientist, holding the chair of chemistry at Cambridge. Sir John Sinclair is credited with pioneering the science of statistics and later would become governor-general of India.

Given the informal nature of the club there are, of course, no records of their discussions before the June 9th gathering, but it isn't difficult to imagine that men of this sort must have often turned their conversations to Africa, speculating on its commercial and scientific value and deploring the lack of information about it. What we do know is that on June 9 they made a decision to do something about it. Beaufoy wrote later:

While we continue ignorant of so large a portion of the globe, that ignorance must be considered as a degree of reproach on the present age. Sensible of this stigma, and desirous of rescuing the age from a charge of ignorance, which, in other respects, belongs so little to its character, a few Individuals, strongly impressed with a conviction of the practicability and utility of thus enlarging the fund of human knowledge, have formed the Plan of an Association for promoting the Discovery of the Interior parts of Africa.

And with this they founded what was to become known as the African Association and set in motion the greatest age of African exploration since the days of Prince Henry.

Before they broke up that evening the members formed a committee of five with Beaufoy as secretary and Banks as treasurer (a chairman among peers apparently wasn't deemed necessary). They were aware that the British government was unlikely to sponsor their enterprise but, with their impeccable credentials and influential connections, they knew they could count on a measure of official cooperation and would have no problem finding financing privately. Each member agreed to pay a subscription of five guineas a year for three years and "to recommend . . . such of his Friends as he shall think proper to be admitted to the new Association." (In time, more than 200 such friends, well represented by dukes and earls and generals, would become patrons.) There was nothing, in fact, to prevent the discovery of the interior parts of Africa from getting started right away. All that had to be done was to pick which interior part was to be discovered first.

They did not pick the Congo. Although the explorations initiated by the African Association ultimately would focus on the river, at the time there was nothing about it to attract the attention of Banks and Beaufoy as they scanned the map of Africa, hunting for a likely goal for their first expedition. We have to remind ourselves that Banks and Beaufoy knew little if anything about the Kingdom of Kongo, of its rich history and tragic fate, nor that it had existed at all for that matter. Nor were they more than dimly aware of the size and power of the river. Information of that kind belonged then almost exclusively to the Portuguese. For Banks and Beaufoy, in fact, the most striking thing about the Congo was that the Portuguese had already been there and that was reason enough for them to be uninterested in it at the start. For what they were looking for was a place where no European had ever been before; what they wanted was a grand challenge, an intriguing mystery, a geographical puzzle so fascinating as to have defied repeated attempts at its solution, a discovery so worthwhile as to increase immediately the fund of human knowledge and promise practical benefits to mankind. The Congo seemed to offer none of these, but there was a place that did: Timbuktoo and the River Niger, on whose banks the fabled golden city was said to stand.

Unlike the Congo and its kingdom, Timbuktoo and the Niger were part of the classic literature familiar to the scholarly gentlemen of the Enlightenment. Herodotus had written about the Silent Trade conducted by the kings of Timbuktoo, Claudius Ptolemy had speculated on the Niger's course, and such Arab geographers as Al-Idrisi and Ibn-Batuta had described this interior part of Africa as the source of the gold the Saharan caravans brought. One need read only this passage from Leo Africanus, the sixteenth-century Granada Moor, to get an inkling of the magical excitement this part of Africa generated for these Englishmen:

Tombuto [Timbuktoo] is situate within twelve miles of a certaine branch of Niger . . . there is a most stately temple to be seene, the wals thereof are made of stone and lime, and a princely palace also built by a most excellent workman. . . . Here are many shops of artificers and merchants and especially of such as weave linen and cotton cloth. . . . The inhabitants, and especially strangers there residing are exceeding rich. . . . The rich king of Tombuto hath many plates and scepters of gold, some whereof weigh 1,300 pounds; and he keeps a magnificent. and well-furnished court. . . . He hath alwaies 3,000 horsemen, and a great number of footmen that shoot poysoned arrowes, attending upon him. They have often skirmishes with those that refuse to pay tribute, and so many as they take they sell unto the merchants of Tombuto. . . . Here are great stores of doctors, judges, priests and other learned men, that are bountifully maintained at the kings cost and charges. And hither are brought diverse manuscripts or written bookes out of Barbarie, which are sold for more money than any other merchandize.

Surely alluring enough, but the best part of it all was that no European had ever been there. Moreover, the Niger posed so dark a geographical mystery that not only were the locations of its source and mouth unknown but no one knew even in which direction the river flowed. And, as Beaufoy wrote, its exploration was "made doubly interesting by the consideration of its having engaged the attention and baffled the researches, of the most inquisitive and most powerful nations of antiquity." So it was chosen as a most suitable object for the association's first expeditions.

Amazingly little time was wasted. Within four days of the inaugural supper, an explorer, John Ledyard, was recruited, and within a month he was on his way. Ledyard, an American soldier-adventurer who had sailed on Cook's last voyage and who just that year had returned from a failed attempt to cross Europe and Asia to North America, set out to traverse the African continent east to west, from Cairo to Timbuktoo and the Niger. While he was en route, the association sent a second explorer, Simon Lucas, a one-time wine merchant, who had been enslaved by Moorish pirates for three years and, after his release, had served for sixteen years as British vice consul to the Moroccan court. He was to try to make the crossing from Tripoli to the river, north to south.

The expeditions were ill equipped and ill prepared. The men went off alone into the unknown without maps, with hardly any supplies and very little money. Lucas and Ledyard each started out with only £100 and the right to draw that much again once in Africa because, curiously, Banks and Beaufoy were "persuaded that in such an undertaking poverty is a better protection than wealth." Under the circumstances, their courage was incredible and the forces driving them—a sense of adventure, a degree of curiosity—of such power as to seem unimaginable in this day.

Ledyard got only as far as Cairo, and there died of an unknown disease. Lucas, disguised in Turkish dress, managed to join a Moorish caravan in Tripoli but was turned back by warring tribes in the Fezzan. The failure of the first two missions did nothing to discourage the association but it did force a reconsideration of the plan of attack. Recognizing the difficulty of passing through the Moslem-controlled desert, Banks and Beaufoy decided to dispatch the next expedition from the West African coast. Daniel Houghton, a retired army major who had served at the British fort at Goree off the coast of Sénégal, was sent to the mouth of the Gambia, with instructions to go up that river as far as possible, learn whatever he could about "the rise, the course, and the termination of the Niger, as well as of the various nations that inhabit its borders." Houghton followed these instructions to the best of his ability, but from the outset he was in constant danger from native traders trying to rob and kill him. They finally succeeded. But before they did Houghton had penetrated further into the African interior than had any other previous European. Years later it was discovered that he had died at a village named Simbing (in present-day Mali), about 160 miles north of the Niger and perhaps 500 miles short of Timbuktoo. In the dispatches he sent to London during his journey, we see that he had correctly surmised that the Niger rose in the mountains south of the Gambia and that its course was probably west to east.

The explorer the African Association next sent out was Mungo Park, the man who would turn British interest toward the Congo. Park was a young Scottish physician with an itch for travel, who had sailed in 1791 as ship's surgeon on an East India Company vessel bound for Sumatra. When he returned two years later, he offered his services to the African Association, and the association accepted, finding him "a young man of no mean talents . . . sufficiently instructed in the use of Hadley's quadrant to make the necessary observations; geographer enough to trace his path through the wilderness, and not unacquainted with natural history." In May 1795, Park sailed aboard the brig *Endeavour*, bound for the Gambia for a cargo of ivory, and reached Jilifree, on the river's northern bank, thirty days later. From there he struck inland, following Houghton's route.

Park was gone more than two and a half years, and his adventures and accomplishments rank among the greatest in the annals of African exploration. Like Houghton, he was constantly harassed by tribesmen demanding bribes for the right to pass through the regions they controlled. And, as he pressed further inland and reached territories under Moslem influence, his life as well as his supplies were threatened. In the Moorish kingdom of Ludamar, where, he learned, Houghton had been robbed of all his belongings and left to die, the tribesmen, he later wrote, "hissed, shouted, and abused me; they even spit in my face, with a view to irritating me, and afford them a pretext for seizing my baggage. But finding such insults had not the desired effect, they had recourse to the final and decisive argument, that I was a Christian, and that my property was lawful plunder." Not long afterward he was taken prisoner by a band of Moorish horsemen and brought to the camp of a local chieftain, who ordered his right hand cut off, his eyes plucked out, and his life ended. Park escaped only because, at just the opportune moment, an enemy tribe attacked the camp. He pressed on, ridden with fever, bereft of supplies, tormented by thirst and sandstorms. But at last he was out of Moorish territory and entered the country of the Bambara. The Bambara proved friendly and he followed a group from a place called Kaarta heading east toward the town of Ségou. "As we approached the town," Park wrote in his *Travels in the Interior of Africa,*

I was fortunate to overtake the Kaartans . . . and we rode together through some marshy ground, where, as I was looking round anxiously for the river, one of them called out, "*Geo affili*" (see the water) ; and looking forward, I saw with infinite pleasure the great object of my mission, the long-sought and majestic Niger, glittering to the morning sun, as broad as the Thames at Westminister, and flowing slowly *to the eastward.* I hastened to the brink, and, having drank of the water, lifted up my fervent thanks in prayer to the Great Ruler of all things for having thus crowned my endeavours with success.

The date was June 20, 1796, and Park had become the first European on record to have laid eyes on the Niger. His task now was to follow it to Timbuktoo and then on to its mouth, wherever that might be. He did not succeed. His circumstances deteriorated rapidly as he once again moved into Moorish country. The heat was unbearable, his horse collapsed, the tropical rains began, and on August 25 he was jumped by a gang of thieves and stripped naked. "I was now convinced," he wrote, "that the obstacles to my further progress were insurmountable." He had reached Silla on the Niger, still some 400 miles from Timbuktoo, when he decided to turn back. His struggle to the coast took him nearly a year. In June 1797, he reached the mouth of the Gambia and there boarded an American slaving vessel, which got him to Antigua, where he was able to catch a packet making for Falmouth. He arrived back in England just a few days before Christmas of 1797.

The African Association and, indeed, all of England were thrilled by Park's accomplishment. He was, after all, the first man to have penetrated the forbidding interior of Africa for the sole purpose of finding out what was there and to have come back alive. And, in a sense, by doing that he had invented a new and glorious calling, created a new and adventurous species of hero, the lone, brave African explorer, who was to capture the imagination, feed the fantasies, and fill the literature of Europe for a century to come. He was lionized by the best of English society, and the book he wrote about his adventures became an instant best-seller. And Banks, with Park's success to point to, launched an ultimately successful campaign to involve the British government in African exploration.

Speaking strictly geographically, Park had barely scratched the surface of the interior of Africa. Timbuktoo still had not been reached, and the puzzle of the Niger's course and the location of its mouth remained unsolved. No one was more acutely aware of this than Park himself, and no sooner had he returned than he began making plans for a second expedition. But, as it turned out, that would have to wait for nearly six years. For Park married and began having children. Considering the meager wages the African Association paid its explorers (Park was offered ten shillings a day for his next journey) , this meant settling down and earning a living.

While practicing medicine in Scotland, Park had plenty of time to sort out what he had learned from first-hand experience and develop his own theory about the geography of the Niger, especially the location of its mouth. There were at this time three contradictory theories about the river's ultimate destination. The oldest and perhaps the most venerated "supposed," as a geographer of the period wrote,

that the Niger has an inland termination somewhere in the eastern part of Africa . . . and that it is partly discharged into inland lakes, which have no communication with the sea, and partly spread over a wide extent of level country, and lost in sands or evaporated by the heat of the sun.

Against this theory, it was argued:

To account for such a phenomenon, a great inland sea, bearing some resemblance to the Caspian or the Aral, appears to be necessary. But besides that the existence of so vast a body of water without any outlet into the ocean, is in itself an improbable circumstance . . . such a sea, if it really existed, could hardly have remained a secret to the ancients, and entirely unknown at the present day.

Another idea was that the Niger flowed into the Nile. But the geographers of the period tended to dismiss this theory as

rather a loose popular conjecture, than an opinion deduced from probable reasoning; since nothing appears to be alleged in its support, except the mere circumstance of the course of the river being in the direction of the Nile.

The third hypothesis held

that the Niger, after reaching Wangara [present-day Mali], takes a direction towards the south, and being joined by other rivers from that part of Africa, makes a great turn from thence towards the southwest, and pursues its course till it approaches . . . the gulf of Guinea, when it divides and discharges itself by different channels into the Atlantic; after having formed a great Delta.

This was to turn out to be an amazingly accurate description of the river's course and termination, but at the time the reasoning in support of it was regarded as "hazardous and uncertain," and a host of geographical objections were raised, resulting in the widely held conclusion, as one geographer of the period put it, that "the data on which it is grounded are all of them wholly gratuitous." So it was a fourth theory entirely that Park, while not its originator, came to adopt and champion. That theory held that the Niger, taking the turn to the south after Wangara or Timbuktoo, as proposed above, but persisting in that direction rather than turning southwest, terminated through the estuary of the Congo. The two rivers, it said, were one and the same.

This idea appears to have been first put forward by a certain George Maxwell, a Scotsman who had traded on the Congo and who, more than any other person, managed to attract Britain's attention to it. For years he had proselytized among his influential friends in London about the river's importance, pointing out the then little known facts about the river's powerful current and flow, ranking it accurately as second only to the Amazon in this regard, deducing its immense size from that, and arguing that it offered a natural way for the exploration of and trade with the African interior. But it wasn't until the question of the Niger's geography became a lively subject of inquiry after Park's first expedition that he succeeded in getting the right London circles to pay him and the Congo any serious heed.

Maxwell himself had never traveled above the estuary but, as he wrote, he had long concluded, "before even the Niger came to be the topic of conversation . . . that the Congo drew its source far to the northward," and in a letter to a mutual friend of his and Park's, which he asked to be passed on to Park, he set forth his conviction that "if the Niger *has* a sensible outlet, I have no doubt of its proving the Congo, knowing all the rivers between Cape Palmas and Cape Lopes to be inadequate for the purpose." He was so convinced of this that in another letter, this one written directly to Park, he described a plan he had formulated for exploring the river which involved bringing out from England "six supernumerary boats, well adapted for rowing and sailing; each being of such a size as to be easily carried by thirty people, and transported across several cataracts, with which the course of the river is known to be impeded.

Park, as his first biographer was to write, "adopted Mr. Maxwell's sentiments relative to the termination of the Niger in their utmost extent, and persevered in that opinion to the end of his life." He was well aware of the geographical objections that could be raised against this theory, but was quick to find solutions by which to overcome each.

For example, if the Niger and Congo were one, it would have a length of well over 4000 miles (thus making it the longest river in the world). To this, Park's answer was essentially, well, why not? After all, the Amazon was then accepted to be more than 3500 miles long. As to the objection that the river would have to flow through a great mountain chain, which was then supposed to run through the middle of the continent, this was dismissed on the grounds that there was no real evidence that these mountains existed. And to get around the difficulty that the great rises and falls in the level of the Niger did not correspond to the relatively even flow of the Congo, Park supposed that the river passed through a series of 17 or 18 lakes. Moreover, as he wrote to Earl Camden, then the British colonial secretary, "the quantity of water discharged into the Atlantic by the Congo cannot be accounted for on any other known principle but that it is the termination of the Niger."

By 1804 Park was tired of his sedentary family life as a country doctor and came down to London to present a plan to Banks and Earl Camden for a second Niger expedition. This one was not to be a lone adventure. He wanted an escort of thirty English soldiers, a half-dozen carpenters to build the boats he would need to travel on the river, and authority to hire up to twenty Africans to serve as porters. Though he was convinced of Maxwell's ideas, Park chose not to follow the trader's plan of exploration up the Congo estuary. More familiar with the route he had taken on his first expedition, he planned to start again from the Gambia, strike overland to the Niger, and then sail down the river to its end. If, indeed, the river did terminate in a great lake in Wangara, he would then return across the desert to the coast at the Bight of Benin. But he was sure that he would wind up in the Congo's estuary and planned to sail from there to the West Indies and then back to Europe. If he proved correct, he told Earl Camden,

the expedition though attended with extreme danger, promises to be productive of the utmost advantages to Great Britain. Considered in a commercial point of view, it is second only to the discovery of the Cape of Good Hope, and in a geographical point of view is certainly the greatest discovery that remains to be made in the world.

A number of distinguished geographers regarded Park's ideas as wrong and tried to discourage him from embarking on such a dangerous enterprise. But Banks backed him fervently:

I am aware that Mr. Park's expedition is one of the most hazardous a man can undertake but I cannot agree with those who think it is too hazardous to be attempted; it is by similar hazards of human life alone that we can hope to penetrate the obscurity of the internal face of Africa; we are wholly ignorant of the country between the Niger and the Congo and can explore it only by incurring the most frightful hazards.

Park set off at the end of January 1805 aboard the troopship *Crescent* and arrived at Goree at the mouth of the Gambia two months later. He had brought with him five navy carpenters, who had been convicts in Portsmouth and had received pardons in exchange for volunteering for the expedition. In Goree, he recruited 32 soldiers and 2 sailors from the Royal Africa Corps garrison there, men who were also convicts—service in Africa was their punishment—and who joined the party on the promise of double pay and a discharge from the corps at the completion of the expedition. In addition, Park, who had been commissioned a brevet captain, had with him an army lieutenant, his brother-in-law, and a friend from Scotland. He, however, discovered that, as he wrote, "No inducement could prevail on a single Negro to accompany me." Nevertheless, Park and his party sailed up the Gambia aboard the *Crescent* to the town of Kayee, where an English-speaking Mandingo guide named Isaaco was hired, and from there, in April, struck out overland toward the Niger.

Park had reckoned on reaching the Niger by the end of June. In fact, he didn't get there until August 19, and by that time three-quarters of his party were dead. The rains had come and, more than the Moorish tribesmen who attacked the caravan all along the way, fever and dysentery proved the great killers. So terrible was the journey that the dead were not buried and the ailing were left behind to be stripped and killed by bandits. But on seeing the Niger again, "rolling its immense stream along the plain," although he had only ten men left and his own health was badly undermined, Park was too excited to acknowledge the seriousness of his situation and, against all common sense, decided to press forward with the journey.

Canoes were hired to take Park and the remnants of his caravan downriver as far as Ségou, where they arrived in September. There they had to wait several weeks while suspicious tribesmen argued about providing new canoes. During that time, the party suffered further losses, including the death of Park's brother-in-law. By the time the natives agreed to let Park have two canoes, his escort was down to the army lieutenant, three soldiers, and the guide Isaaco. Nevertheless, Park was determined to go on. He sent the guide Isaaco back to the coast with letters to his wife and to Banks. He wrote to Banks that it was his intention "to keep to the middle of the river and make the best use I can of winds and currents till I reach the termination of this mysterious stream." To his wife: "I think it is not unlikely that I shall be in England before you receive this . . . the sails are now hoisting for our departure to the coast." That was November 20, 1805, and it was the last anyone ever heard from Park.

We don't know exactly what happened to him, what fate he met, or how far he got before he met it, but a few years later, in 1810, the Mandingo guide Isaaco volunteered to return to Ségou in an attempt to find out, and the story he heard gives us some clues. Apparently Park, realizing that he was now moving into country controlled by Moorish tribes and remembering their hostility from his previous expedition, had been expecting trouble. He had taken fifteen muskets and plenty of ammunition aboard the two canoes, as well as enough provisions so that his party would not have to land until they were safely out of Moorish country.

From the outset, Park and his men came under attack from the shore and were required to shoot their way down the river. According to Isaaco's account, they managed to get to Timbuktoo, but there was absolutely no question of going ashore and visiting the city because of the hostility of its inhabitants. Park pushed on and, it seems, managed to sail down some 1500 miles of the Niger's total course of 2600 miles and reach a point barely 600 miles from its outlet to the sea. But it was at this point, a place called Bussa rapids, where the Kainji dam in present-day Nigeria stands, that the party was ambushed and all were killed.

Park's death, however it actually occurred (questions persisted about Isaaco's version, and it wasn't until 1819 that the London *Times* finally wrote, "The death of this intrepid traveller is now placed beyond any doubt"), did not kill off the belief that the Niger and Congo were one and the same river. To be sure, Park himself, if he did in fact get as far as Isaaco tells us, would have been forced to abandon the idea, seeing that the river, having turned to the south after Timbuktoo, turned again soon thereafter, at Gao, to the southwest and flowed in a direction that couldn't possibly have brought it to the Congo's estuary. But no one else knew this at the time; the last reports from Park were sent from Ségou, and he was then even more convinced about the rightness of the theory. For he had learned there that the until then eastward-flowing river would soon turn to the south (not yet knowing that it would later turn again to the southwest). In a letter to Banks, which Isaaco had brought back, we find Park writing, "I have hired a guide . . . he is one of the greatest travellers in this part of Africa: he says that the Niger, after it passes Kashna [presumably near Timbuktoo], runs directly to the right hand, or to the south," and in his last letters to his wife and Lord Camden he repeated his conviction that he would return to England via the West Indies from the Congo's mouth.

Ten years were to pass before Britain again would try to prove the connection between the Niger and the Congo, mainly because the Napoleonic Wars came along to divert her attention from Africa. But interest in the question had been so heightened by the drama and mystery of Park's disappearance that in 1815 an ambitious, two-pronged attack on the problem was launched. One expedition, under the sponsorship of the Colonial Office, was sent out to follow Park's course down the Niger. The second, organized by the Admiralty, was to start at the Congo's mouth and follow that river upstream. The hope, of course, was that the two would meet somewhere in the middle.

11

THE TUCKEY EXPEDITION

The Admiralty's expedition was the first real attempt to explore the Congo River ever undertaken by Europeans. And, it must be said, having waited more than three hundred years to get around to it, they undertook it in a wholly admirable manner. The expedition, like no other effort of African exploration until that time, was meticulously planned, conscientiously organized, and generously financed.

To be sure, its main purpose was to establish the identity of the Niger's mouth. Sir John Barrow, who was then the secretary of the Admiralty and the driving force behind the expedition, underscored this goal repeatedly in a memorandum he prepared for the expedition's commander. For example, at one point he noted:

The usual flooded state of the Zaire [the names Congo and Zaire were used interchangeably by this time] . . . would seem to warrant the supposition, that one great branch, perhaps the main trunk, descends from the tropical regions to the northward of the Line; and if in your progress it should be found, that the general trending of its course is from the north-east, it will strengthen the conjecture of that branch and the Niger being one and the same river. It will be adviseable, therefore, as long as the mainstream of the Zaire shall be found to flow from the northeast . . . to give the preference to that stream; and, to endeavour to follow it to its source.

Nevertheless, Barrow and the Admiralty also recognized that the Congo was in and of itself a worthy object of exploration. Barrow wrote:

It is not to be understood, that the attempt to ascertain this point [the identity of the Congo and the Niger] is by any means the exclusive object of this expedition. That a river of such magnitude as the Zaire, and offering so many peculiarities, should not be known with any degree of certainty, beyond, if so far as, 200 miles from its mouth, is incompatible with the present advanced state of geographical science, and little creditable to those Europeans, who, for three centuries nearly, have occupied various parts of the coast near to which it empties itself into the sea, and have held communication with the interior of the country through which it descends, by means of missionaries, and slave agents; so confined indeed is our knowledge of the course of this remarkable river, that the only chart of it which can have any pretension to accuracy [it was one drawn by George Maxwell], does not extend above 130 miles, and the correctness of this survey, as it is called, is more than questionable. There can be little doubt, however, that a river, which runs more rapidly and discharges more water, than either the Ganges or the Nile, and which has this peculiar quality of being, almost all seasons of the year, in a *flooded* state, must not only traverse a vast extent of country, but must also be supplied by large branches flowing from different, and probably opposite directions; so that some one or more of them must, at all times of year, pass through a tract of country where the rains prevail. To ascertain the sources of these great branches, then, will be one of the principal objects of the present expedition.

James Kingston Tuckey, a captain in the Royal Navy, was named the expedition's commander. He was then not quite forty years old, a tall, gangling man, prematurely gray and nearly entirely bald. "His countenance" as a contemporary described him, "was pleasing, but wore rather a pensive cast; but he was at all times gentle and kind in his manners, cheerful in conversation, and indulgent to every one placed under his command." His early navy service was in Britain's empire-building skirmishes against the Dutch and the French in India and Ceylon and then later against the French in the Red Sea and off the East African coast. In 1802, sent out to New South Wales to participate in the establishment of a British colony there, he gathered his first experience as an explorer, making a survey of the harbors, coasts, and adjacent unmapped country.

His career, however, appeared to come to an abrupt halt with the outbreak of the Napoleonic Wars. His ship, the *Calcutta*, escorting a British convoy from St. Helena in 1805, was captured by the French, and Tuckey spent the next nine years in imprisonment. But, in fact, he made remarkably good use of those years. "To pass away the tedious hours of a hopeless captivity," as he later wrote, he compiled a massive, four-volume *Maritime Geography and Statistics,* a work which presented

a comprehensive view of the various phenomena of the ocean, the description of coasts and islands, and of the seas that wash them; the remarkable headlands, harbours and port towns; the several rivers that reach the sea, and the nature and extent of their inland navigations that communicate with the coasts.

It was not long after his release, at the end of the war with France, that the Admiralty began planning its Congo expedition. Tuckey requested its command. He was not the only one. In a time of peace, the Admiralty's expedition provided a naval officer with the best, if not only, opportunity to distinguish himself, and several applied for the coveted position. Tuckey was selected because of his impressive *Maritime Geography and Statistics,* which gave proof that "he had stored his mind with so much various knowledge and . . . had given so much attention to the subject of nautical discovery and river navigation" as to be considered "most eligible for the undertaking." Still, in retrospect, one can't help wondering about the choice. Though still relatively young, Tuckey was not a strong man. His health had been undermined by fevers he had contracted during his service in the tropics and was seriously if not permanently damaged by his long imprisonment in France. What's more, he seems to have been a typically conservative, careful, strait-laced military man. He does not seem to have had the flair, the imagination, the innovative daring one expects of an explorer. For example, a contemporary Admiralty historian has noted:

As so very little was known of the course of the Zaire, and nothing at all beyond the first cataracts, it was at first intended to leave Captain Tuckey entirely to his own discretion, to act as circumstances might appear to require . . . but Captain Tuckey pressed with such urgency for specific instructions, that, as he observed, he might be satisfied in his own mind when he had done all that was expected of him, that his wishes in this respect were complied with.

Tuckey chose for his second-in-command John Hawkey, a navy lieutenant of about his own age who had also spent the entire Napoleonic war in captivity and whom Tuckey had befriended when they

Captain Tuckey's voyage in Africa. The market village near Embomma

shared the same prison compound in France. A party of scientists was assembled. It included a botanist by the name of Smith; a "Collector of Objects of Natural History" called Cranch; a surgeon and comparative anatomist named Tudor; the gardener from His Majesty's Gardens at Kew by the name of Lockhart; and a man named Galwey who is listed in the log simply as a "Volunteer and Observant Gentleman" and appears to have been a boyhood chum of Tuckey's. In addition, the expedition consisted of five other navy officers, eight petty officers, four carpenters, two blacksmiths, fourteen able seamen, an escort of fourteen Royal Marines, and two freed slaves who were natives of the Congo, named Benjamin Benjamin and Somme Simmons, to act as guides and interpreters.

The plan for the expedition took much of its inspiration from George Maxwell. Two ships, loaded with provisions, arms, and equipment, as well as presents for the natives such as iron tools, knives, glassware, beads, and umbrellas, would sail to the Congo's mouth. One of these, a 350-ton transport store ship christened the *Dorothy*, was meant to help carry supplies to the river, and once these were transhipped at the river's mouth to the other vessel, appropriately christened the *Congo*, she was to return to England. The *Congo* then would sail up the river until she met the impediment of the rapids and cataracts. At this point, smaller, lighter vessels, capable of being transported overland, were to be brought into play. Two double-boats, drawing very little water, were designed and built; each was 35 feet long, fitted with a canopy to keep off sun and rain and, when assembled, capable of carrying 20 to 30 men and three months' provisions. With them, the party was supposed to get around the cataracts, find where the river became navigable again, and sail on it to its source, expected to be the Niger.

The expedition departed from Deptford on February 16, 1816. The ships had some trouble getting out of the English Channel but by March they were at last on the high seas, making for Madeira, then the Canaries, and then the Cape Verde Islands. There they laid over for caulking and sail repairs and reached the mouth of the Congo on July 5, early in the dry season.

Tuckey now issued a memorandum of regulations "for our conduct in the country," which gives us another insight into his careful character. He warned:

It is highly necessary to be guarded in our intercourse with [the natives]; that, by showing we are prepared to resist aggression, we may leave no hope of success, or no inducement to commit it. . . . In the event of the absolute necessity of repelling hostility for self-preservation, it will certainly be more consonant to humanity, and perhaps more effectual in striking terror, that the first guns fired be only loaded with small shot.

Tuckey also worried about theft, which, he had learned from his studies of the experiences of other African explorers,

has been one of the most frequent causes of unhappy catastrophes that have befallen navigators; it is therefore urgently advised, not to expose anything unnecessarily to the view of the natives, or to leave any object in their way that may tempt their avidity.

He then pointed out that another

great cause of the disputes of navigators with uncivilized people is in unauthorized freedoms with their females; and hence every species of curiosity or familiarity with them, which may create jealousy in the man, is to be strictly avoided.

Tuckey was aboard the *Dorothy* and, while the more maneuverable *Congo* under Hawkey's command had little difficulty anchoring at Tall Trees (the name that British traders on the river had given the old slaving port of Mpinda) , the captain spent three days getting his "brute of a transport" around the headlands of the river's mouth and into the estuary. At last he reached Shark's Point a short way upstream from the point where Diogo Cão had erected his pillar, and there he remained. For all his efforts, Tuckey could not get the *Dorothy* any further upriver than that.

Tuckey and his party, as it turned out, weren't the only Europeans on the river. "At four o'clock," he noted in his log for July 8,

a schooner appeared off the point, hoisted Spanish Colours, and fired a gun. . . . A boat was immediately sent from her to ask what we were, and on being informed, they made some excuse for firing the shot, intended as they said, to assure the colours; their vessel, by their account, was from the Havana for slaves.

Tuckey had been forewarned by the Admiralty to expect to run into slavers on the river and specifically ordered not to get involved with them. At this time, as we've seen, most European nations had outlawed the traffic. The notable exceptions were Spain and Portugal, and the most popular ruse of pirate slavers, when they encountered vessels of the British naval squadrons policing the trade on the West African coast, was to hoist the colors of one or the other of these nations. Tuckey was convinced that this was the case with this ship. As he noted in his log, "It was perfectly evident, from their answers to my questions, that she was illicity employed in this trade, and prepared to carry it on by force, being armed with 12 guns, and full of men." However, under his orders from the Admiralty, he was obliged to assure the slavers that he had no intention of interfering in their business. Even so, the sight of a vessel flying the Union Jack commanded by a British naval officer and carrying Royal Marines made the pirates uneasy. And that they didn't entirely believe Tuckey was "put out of doubt," he noted in his log, by the slaver "getting underway and running out of the river." Seven other slavers, three schooners and four pinnaces, all flying the Portuguese flag, were anchored at the slave port of Embomma (Boma) further upriver. And, when they learned of the presence of the two British vessels, they too "precipitately . . . quitted the river, passing us no doubt in the night."

While stuck aboard the *Dorothy* at Shark's Point, Tuckey made his first contacts with the Bakongo of the lost kingdom's Soyo province, and his unflattering observations provide a striking reminder of how the centuries of the slave trade had corrupted and destroyed these once noble people.

The Mafook [trading agent of the local chief] of Shark Point came on board with a half dozen of his myrmidons [Tuckey wrote], and though the most ragged, dirty looking wretch that can be well conceived, he expected as much respect as a prince. . . . Seating himself at the tafferel, he certainly made a very grotesque appearance, having a most tattered pelisse of red velvet, edged with gold lace, on his naked carcass, a green silk umbrella spread over his head, though the sun was completely obscured, and his stick of office headed with silver in the other hand. It being our breakfast hour, he notified his desire to be asked into our cabin, to partake of our meal; but he smelt so offensively, and was moreover so covered with a cutaneous disorder, that my politeness gave way to my stomach, and he was obliged, though with great sulkiness, to content himself on deck. To bring him into good humor, I however saluted him with one swivel [the firing of a musket], and gave him a plentiful allowance of brandy. He seemed indeed to have no other object in coming on board than to get a few glasses of this liquor, which he relished so well that he staid on board all night and the five following days.

Others quickly followed. Tuckey noted with contempt:

Several of the Soyo men were Christians after the Portuguese fashion, having been converted by missionaries of that nation; and one of them was even qualified to lead his fellow negroes into the path of salvation, as appeared from a diploma with which he was furnished. This man and another of the Christians had been taught to write their own names and that of Saint Antonio, and could also read the Romish litany in Latin. . . . The Christian priest was however somewhat loose in his practical morality, having, as he assured us, one wife and five concubines; and added, that St. Peter, in confining him to *one* wife, did not prohibit his solacing himself with as many handmaidens as he could manage. . . . Our Soyo visitors were almost without exception sulky looking vagabonds, dirty, swarming with lice, and scaled over with the itch, all strong symptoms of their having been *civilized* by the Portuguese.

After more than a week at Shark's Point, Tuckey chased all the brandy-imbibing Mafooks off the *Dorothy,* gave up trying to get the transport any further upriver, and set about transhipping her stores to the *Congo.* The operation took until July 18, and now the expedition's real business of exploration could begin.

Tuckey's first object was to get the *Congo* to Embomma. But again the river current and the precarious sea breeze worked against him, and so he left the job to Hawkey and set out with the scientists in one of the double-boats. It appears to have been a pleasant trip. At one point, Tuckey noted in his journal:

This evening's sail along the banks was particularly agreeable, the lofty mangroves overhanging the boat, and a variety of palm trees vibrating in the breeze; immense flocks of parrots alone broke the silence of the woods with their chattering towards sun-set.

At another he records:

Two women, an old and a young one, came on board . . . by their dress and ornaments they appeared to be of a superior class; I therefore gave them some beads and a glass of rum, which they swallowed as greedily as the men; and, in return, the old lady offered, through our interpreter, to leave the young one on board, pour m'amuser; a civility which, under existing circumstances, I thought proper to decline; though the young lady seemed much chagrined at such an insult to her charm.

On July 25, the party reached the marketplace of Embomma, where a remarkable incident occurred concerning Somme Simmons, one of the freed slaves with the expedition, who had worked as a cook's mate on the voyage out and had served as the chief interpreter since its arrival on the river.

It was, of course, known that Simmons was from the Congo, but "the story of this man," Tuckey confessed, "I never thought of inquiring into." As it turned out, this man, who had "performed, without any signs of impatience or disgust, his menial offices" with the expedition, was from Embomma and the son of "a prince of the blood, and counsellor to the King of Embomma." His father, Tuckey learned,

intrusted him, when eight or ten years old, to a Liverpool captain . . . to be educated (or according to his expression to learn to make book) in England; but his conscientious guardian found it less troublesome to have him taught to make sugar in St. Kitts, where he accordingly sold him.

For eleven years, his father had awaited his son's return, making inquiries of every European ship that came to trade at Embomma. But it was only in the previous year that Simmons had contrived to escape his enslavement in the West Indies and get aboard an English ship and

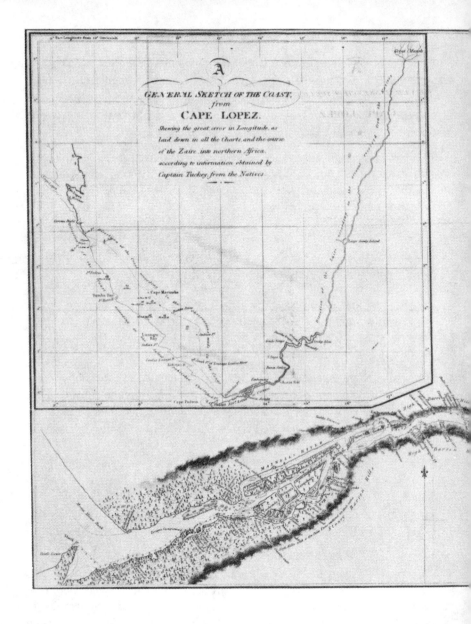

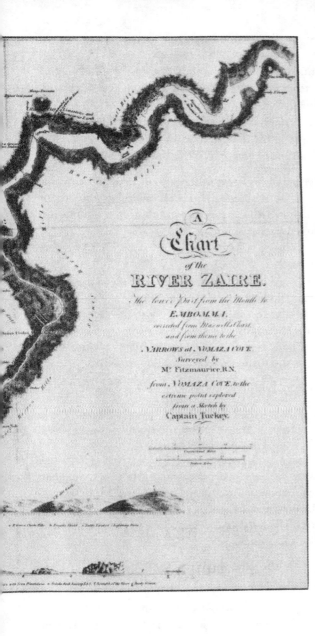

A

Chart

of the

RIVER ZAIRE.

The lower Part from the Mouth to

EMBOMMA,

corrected from Maxwell's Chart,
and from thence to the

NARROWS at NOMAZA COVE,

Surveyed by

Mr. Fitzmaurice, R.N.

from NOMAZA COVE, to the

extreme point explored

from a Sketch by

Captain Tuckey.

by that win his freedom. And the commander of that ship, hearing of the Admiralty's expedition to the Congo, had arranged to have Simmons signed over to Tuckey.

Now once again, with news of the presence of English ships on the river, Simmons's father made his hopeful inquiries about his long-lost son, and this time, we read in the journal of the botanist Smith,

unexpectedly got intelligence of his being with us, and came on board the first evening of our arrival [at Embomma]. His excessive joy, the ardour with which he hugged his son in his arms, proved that even among this people nature is awake to tender emotions.

Tuckey tells us that

The transport of joy, at the meeting was much more strongly expressed by the father than by the son, whose European ideas, though acquired in the school of slavery, did not seem to assimilate with those of Negro society, and he persisted in wearing his European jacket and trowsers; he however went ashore with his friends, and throughout the night the town resounded with the sound of the drum and the songs of rejoicing.

The next day, Tuckey informs us,

Mr. Simmons . . . paid us a visit, in so complete a metamorphosis that we could with difficulty recognize our late cook's mate; his father having dressed him out in a silk coat embroidered with silver . . . on his head a black glazed hat with an enormous grenadier feather, and a silk sash . . . suspending a ship's cutlass, finished his costume. He was brought to the boat by two slaves in a hammock, an umbrella held over his head, preceded by his father and other members of his family, and followed by a rabble escort of 20 muskets. His father's presents to me consisted of a male goat, a bunch of plantains, and a duck.

Tuckey was escorted to the compound of the Chenoo or king of Embomma and led to a seat

prepared of three or four old chests, covered with a red velvet pall, an old English carpet with another velvet pall spread on the ground. Having seated myself . . . the Chenoo made his appearance from behind a mat screen, his costume conveying the idea of Punch in a puppet-show, being composed of a crimson plush jacket with enormous gilt buttons, a lower garment in the native style of red velvet, his legs muffled in pink sarcenet in guise of stockings, and a pair of red Morocco half-boots; on his head an immense high-crowned hat embroidered with gold; and surmounted by a kind of coronet of European artificial flowers; round his neck hung a long string of ivory beads, and a very large piece of unmanufactured coral.

With Simmons as his interpreter, Tuckey explained his mission. The Chenoo and his counselors were, however, suspicious. "For two hours they rung the changes on the questions, are you come to trade and are you come to make war." Dissatisfied with Tuckey's responses, they went off to palaver among themselves. They returned and

after again tiring me with questions as to my motives, the old man, starting up, plucked a leaf from a tree, and holding it to me said, if you come to trade, swear by your God, and break the leaf; on my refusing to do so, he then said, swear by your God you don't come to make war, and break the leaf; on my doing which, the whole company performed a grand *sakilla*.

After this all seemed well. There was a grand banquet, an exchange of gifts, the offer of women, even the offer of land on which to build an English settlement. In this congenial atmosphere, Tuckey decided to set up camp and, while waiting for Hawkey, who was making slow but steady progress bringing the *Congo* upstream, spend the time surveying the river and learning whatever he could of the country.

It is striking to see how utterly lost, even among the Bakongo themselves, was the history of the ancient Kingdom of Kongo by this time.

The country named Congo, of which we find so much written in collections of Voyages and Travels, appears to be an undefined tract of territory, hemmed in between Loango on the north, and Angola on the south; but to what extent it stretches inland, it would be difficult to determine. . . . All that seems to be known at present is, that the country is partitioned out into a multitude of petty states or Chenooships, held as a kind of fiefs under some real or imaginary personage living in the interior, nobody knows exactly where.

This personage or paramount sovereign, Tuckey was told, "is named Lindy, or Blindy N'Congo, and resides at Banza Congo, six days journey from Tall Trees." There, Tuckey learned, the Portuguese once had a "fixed settlement, the natives speaking of their having soldiers and white women there."

Despite the vagueness of the information available to him, Tuckey proved a careful observer and provides a vivid picture of what the life and customs of the people along the river had come to since their contact with Europe:

The natives are, with very few exceptions, drest in European clothing, their only manufacture being a kind of cape of grass, and shawls of the same material; both are made by men, as are their houses and canoes, the latter of a high tree. . . . Their drinking vessels are pumions or gourds, and their cooking utensils, earthen pots of their own making. . . . Both men and women shave the head in ornamental figures. . . . The women seem to consider pendent breasts as ornamental, the young girls, as soon as they begin to form, pressing them close to the body and downwards with bandages. They also sometimes file the two front teeth away, and raise cicatrices on the skin as well as the men. . . . The two prominent features, in their moral character and social state, seem to be the indolence of the men and the degradation of the women! the latter being considered as perfect slaves, whose bodies are at the entire disposal of their fathers, or husbands, and may be transferred by either of them, how and when they may please.

At one point, Tuckey came upon a funeral. The corpse of a woman was lying in a hut

drest as when alive; inside the hut, four women were howling, and outside, two men standing close to the hut, with their faces leaning against it, kept them company in a kind of cadence, producing a concert not unlike the Irish funeral yell. These marks of sorrow, we understood, were repeated for an hour for four successive days after the death of the person.

Apparently though, the corpse would not be buried for several years, not until it had

arrived at a size to make a genteel funeral. The manner for preserving corpses, for so long a time, is by enveloping them in cloth . . . the smell of putrefaction being only kept in by the quantity of wrappers, which are successively multiplied as they can be procured by the relations of the deceased, or according to the rank of the person; in the case of a rich and very great man, the bulk acquired being only limited by the power of conveyance to the grace; so that the first hut in which the body is deposited, becoming too small, a second, a third, and even to a sixth, increasing in dimensions, is placed over it.

On August 1, the *Congo* at last reached Embomma and the next morning Tuckey "shook hands with the Chenoo, giving him, as a parting token of friendship, one fathom of scarlet cloth, an amber necklace, two jars of spirits, and some plates and dishes." In return, the Chenoo sent three of his sons and a half-dozen of his men to accompany the expedition as guides and pilots. Four days later the *Congo* got up to a point just below the Cauldron of Hell and "finding that we should be much retarded by persevering in the attempt to get much higher, I ordered her to be moored and directed . . . the purser to remain in charge of her; together with the surgeon, a master's mate and 15 men." In the middle of the next day, the rest of the party, in the double-boats, a long boat from the *Dorothy,* two gigs and a punt, set off to take on the rapids.

The going was tricky but not impossible. Tuckey's journal notes strong eddies and rocky outcroppings, but he also found channels, stretches of calm water, and sheltered reaches, and his party made decent headway. On August 8, they reached a village called Noki, where they "received their first coherent information respecting . . . a great cataract named Yellala" that was said to pose a formidable obstruction to further navigation. Tuckey sent his interpreter Simmons to the Chenoo of Noki

to request he would send me a person acquainted with the river higher up; but on his return in the evening, I found that nothing could be done without my own presence, and the usual *dash* of a present of brandy.

The next morning, after "a two hour's fatiguing march" into the interior from the river's left bank,

I was ushered into the presence of the Chenoo, whom we found seated . . . in much more savage magnificence, but less of European manner, than the king of Embomma, the seats and grounds being here covered with lions' and leopard skins, the treading on which, by a subject of the highest rank, is a crime punished with slavery.

Once again Simmons was called upon to explain the expedition's motives and much to Tuckey's gratification,

the Chenoo, with less deliberation or questioning than I had been plagued with at Bomma, granted two guides to go as far as the cataract, beyond which the country was to them terra incognita, not a single person of the banza having ever been beyond it. The palaver being over, the keg of brandy I had brought was opened, and a greater scramble than even at Bomma took place for a sup of the precious liquor.

Tuckey and his men returned to their boats on the river to await the Chenoo's guides, but it wasn't until the following evening that they at last arrived. The next day Tuckey set off, trying still to keep to the river.

With the aid of the oars, and a track rope at times, we got the boats up along the south shore, until we came to a large sand bank extending two-thirds across the river; here we crossed over to the other side, and ran along it as far as a little island. . . . Here we found the current so rapid, that with a strong breeze and the oars we could not pass over it. . . . In crossing the river we passed several whirlpools, which swept the boat round and round in spite of her oars and sails. . . . These vortices are formed in an instant, last but a few minutes with considerable noise, and subside as quickly. The punt got into one of them and entirely disappeared in the hollows.

Tuckey went ashore and climbed the highest hill to see what lay ahead. He reported:

From hence our upward view of the river was confined to a single short reach, the appearance of which, however, was sufficient to convince us, that there was little prospect of being able to get the double boats up much farther, and none at all of being able to transport them overland. Both sides of the river appeared to be lined by rocks above water, and the middle obstructed by whirlpools, whose noise we heard in a constant roar.

Tuckey made one more reconnaissance in the gig, which convinced him of the utter futility of trying to proceed further on the river. So on the morning of August 14 he had the boats anchored in a safe cove and, with a party of twenty and provisions to last four days, struck out overland. At noon they reached a village called Cooloo,

from whence we understood we should see Yellala. Anxious to get a sight of it, I declined the Chenoo's invitation to visit him, until my return. On the farthest end of the banza we unexpectedly saw the fall almost under our feet, and were not less surprised than disappointed at finding, instead of a second Niagara, which the description of the natives, and their horror of it had given us reason to expect, a comparative brook bubbling over a stony bed.

Tuckey climbed down to the river and on a closer inspection of the cataract realized that it was nevertheless impassable.

The party was utterly exhausted by its first march overland across the Crystal Mountains. It was not so much a matter of climate. At this time of year, in the dry season, although the sky was almost constantly overcast and the air hung with heavy, oppressive humidity, temperatures during the day didn't get much above 80 degrees Fahrenheit and at night dropped to a pleasant 65 degrees. What proved so punishing was the terrain, the "scrambling up the sides of almost perpendicular hills, and over great masses of quartz and schistus" and the slipping and stumbling down into precipices and ravines. So Tuckey had the party pitch their tents for the night in Cooloo and he went to make the obligatory call on the local Chenoo, where he

found less pomp and noise, but much more civility and hospitality, than from the richer kings I had visited. This old man seemed perfectly satisfied with our account of the motives of our visit, not asking a single question, treating us with a little palm wine, and sending me a present of six fowls without asking for anything on return.

At Cooloo, Tuckey had reached deeper into the interior along the river itself than any other white man. Smith notes in his journal that "we are constantly followed by a number of people, chiefly boys. They said they had never seen white men before," and Tuckey writes,

The higher we proceed the fewer European articles the natives possess; the country grass-cloth generally forms the sole clothing of the mass of people. . . . The women approach nearer to a state of nudity; their sole clothing being a narrow apron . . . before and behind, so that the hips on each side are uncovered . . . they flocked out to look at the white men, and without any marks of timidity came and shook hands with us. . . . We in no instance . . . found the men *allant en avant* in their offer of their women.

The next morning Tuckey engaged a guide from Cooloo and set off with the party overland to get around the cataract.

After four hours most fatiguing march we again got sight of the river; but to my great vexation, instead of being 12 or 13 miles as I expected, I found we were not above four miles from Yellala. . . . Here we found the river still obstructed with rocks and islets sometimes quite across, but at one place leaving a clear place, which seems to be used as a ferry, as we found here a canoe with four men; no inducement we could offer them had however any effect in prevailing on them to attempt going up the stream.

The party pushed a bit further, crossing through deep ravines, and at sunset camped on the side of a steep hill.

The next morning, Tudor, the comparative anatomist, and several other members of the party awoke with fever, unable to go on. Tuckey had them sent back to Cooloo and with the rest tried to proceed further.

We went across a valley and the hills on the other side, which were last night illuminated by fires [Smith tells us]. Towards the north, the country is more level and more woody. Elephants are reported to be plentiful here. A wild boar rushed forth in a valley, and though it broke through the whole line, the sailors, from their hurry and want of skill, all fired amiss. . . . We continued our route over the steep hills.

By noon though, "the people being extremely fatigued," Tuckey agreed to halt. He climbed a hill from which he had a view of a five-mile stretch of the river. It

presented the same appearance as yesterday, being filled with rocks in the middle, over which the current foamed violently; the shore on each side was also scattered with rocky barren islets. . . . Upwards my view was stopped by the sudden turn of the river from north to S.E. . . . Just where the river shuts in . . . on a high plateau of the north shore, is the banza Inga, which we understood was two days march from Cooloo (though its direct distance is not above 20 miles) and that it is out of the dominions of the Congo.

Tuckey decided to return to Cooloo, resupply his party and attempt to reach Inga along the opposite bank. The march back took eight hours; they reached the village at dark. At Cooloo, Tuckey found Tudor "in a most violent fever," unable to move on his own, and more than half the rest of the party complaining of fatigue and blistered feet. The invalids were carried down to the river where the expedition's boats had been left anchored and Tuckey had them sent back downriver to the *Congo*, anchored just below the Cauldron of Hell, and had additional supplies brought back. With a half-dozen guides and porters recruited from Cooloo and a party of about a dozen relatively fit whites, Tuckey was ready to set off for Inga on the morning of August 22.

He had awakened feeling "extremely unwell . . . directly swallowed five grains of calomel, and moved myself until I produced a strong perspiration." He hoped to be off by daybreak but it wasn't until ten o'clock that the guides and porters showed up. And then he learned that Simmons, his valued interpreter, now called Prince Schi, had deserted. The reason, as the Chenoo came to tell Tuckey, was that Simmons, "having bargained with two of the head gentlemen for their wives (one the first time I was at Cooloo, and the other the night preceding), for two fathoms a night, which having no means of paying, he had concealed himself, or ran off to Embomma." To replace him, Tuckey hired "a man whom we had picked up at Embomma and employed as one of the boat's crew," and to whom Tuckey promised to pay "the value of a slave and other etceteras on my return, if he would accompany me; to which he at last acceded, all his countrymen attempting to deter him, by the idea of being killed and eaten by the bushmen" who lived outside the Congo realm at Inga.

The party, after a march that was now becoming depressingly familiar in its punishing difficulty, reached Inga at noon the following day. The Chenoo there turned out to be blind, and the affairs of the village were in the hands of a committee of headmen. Here Tuckey ran into a degree of hostility that he had not met before and it is difficult to tell, from either his or Smith's journals, why. It may have been because these people were not Bakongo; indeed, there is some suggestion, from the repeated reference to them as cannibalistic bush men, that they may have been descendants of the Yakas, who had once overrun the ancient kingdom. But it is more likely that the trouble was with Tuckey rather than with the tribesmen. He was ill; as we've noted, his health had not been good at the outset anyway. Added to that were the punishing difficulty of the terrain and the depressingly slow progress that he was making, all of which would have been enough to make him short-tempered. But, whatever the cause, it was from this point that we see the expedition starting to go dangerously awry.

What Tuckey wanted from the headmen at Inga was a guide who knew the river still further upcountry, but to get one here, he reports,

I found it would be necessary to deviate from my former assertions of having nothing to do with trade, if I meant to go forward; and accordingly I gave these gentlemen to understand, that I was only the forerunner of other white men, who would bring them everything they required, provided I should make a favorable report of their conduct on my return to my own country. At length I was promised a guide to conduct me to a place where the river again became navigable for canoes, but on the express

condition that I should pay a jar of brandy and dress four gentlemen with
two fathoms of bast each. These terms I complied with, stipulating on my
part that the guide should be furnished immediately . . . but was now
informed that I could not have the guide till the morning. Exasperated
by this intolerable tergiversation, being unable to buy a single fowl, and
having but three days' provisions, I remonstrated in the strongest manner, and deviated a little from my hitherto patient and concilliating manners . . . ordering the ten men with me to fall in under arms; at the
sight of which the palaver broke up. . . . The women and children, who
had flocked to see the white men for the first time, disappeared, and the
banza became a desert; on inquiring for the men who had come with me
from Cooloo, I also found that they had vanished . . . in short, I was left
sole occupier of the banza. Finding that this would not at all facilitate my
progress, I sent my interpreter with a conciliating message . . . which
shortly produced the re-appearance of some men, but skulking behind the
huts with their muskets. After an hour's delay, the regency again appeared, attended by fifty men, of whom fourteen had muskets. The
Mamoom, or war minister, first got up, and made a long speech, appealing
now and then to the other people . . . and who all answered by a kind
of howl. During this speech he held in his hand the war kissey, composed
of buffaloes' hair, and dirty rags; and which (as we afterwards understood) he invoked to break the locks and wet the powder of our muskets.
As I had no intention of carrying the affair to any extremity, I went
from the place where I was seated . . . and familiarly seating myself alongside the headman, shook him by the hand, and explained, that though
he might see that I had the power to do him a great deal of harm, I had
little to fear from his rusty muskets; and that though I had great reason to
be displeased with their conduct . . . I would pass it over, provided
I was assured of having a guide.

This dispute went on for several days, with Tuckey sometimes
threatening, sometimes conciliatory. The Europeans had set up camp
on the outskirts of the village, and from time to time small parties
were sent out to see whether they could manage without a guide, but
all they succeeded in doing was exhausting themselves in the unknown, brutal terrain. Fever and illness spread, morale collapsed, and
nerves frayed, and what was worse, as Smith noted on August 26, "Last
night . . . we had the first shower of rain since our arrival in Africa."

At last, having paid an exorbitant price to the headmen, Tuckey
secured the services of a guide and set off upriver with a few of the
healthier men in his party on August 28.

We ascended the hills that line the river, and which are more fatiguing than any we had yet met with, being very steep, and totally composed of broken pieces of quartz. . . . At four o'clock we came in sight of the river . . . it is crossed by a great ledge of slate rocks . . . the stream runs at least eight miles an hour, forming whirlpools in the middle, whose vortices occupy at least half the breadth of the channel, and must be fatal to any canoe that should get into them.

With night falling, the guide suggested "a banza not much higher up, where we might get some victuals" and they proceeded toward it, "scrambling over the rocks with infinite fatigue . . . nearly choked with thirst . . . until it became quite dark" only to discover that either the guide had lost his way or the banza was no longer situated where it once had been. However, they came upon a group of bushmen camped on the hillside: "The little water brought us by the wives of these bushmen . . . was our supper, and the broken granite stones our bed." The following morning, "after a small portion of roasted manioc and a draught of water for breakfast," the party returned to Inga.

For the next few days, Tuckey continued making forays of this sort from Inga in hopes of finding the point where the cataracts ended or at least where the brutal terrain of its banks eased and overland travel became feasible. On September 2, a major attempt in this respect was organized. The seriously sick were sent back to Cooloo and all the remaining fit members of the party—now numbering only twelve—along with a handful of porters from Inga, set out. It was Tuckey's last desperate try. It lasted five days and they managed to reach perhaps another 40 miles upriver, but chances for success were doomed at the outset. All the white men, Tuckey, Hawkey, and Smith included, were sick to a greater or lesser extent. Morale was abysmally low. The countryside remained unrelenting in its cruelty and the river unyielding in its impassability.

By the second day out, Tuckey tells us,

the Inga men desired to go back, on pretence of being afraid to proceed. . . . They had not walked above a mile before they laid down their loads, and refused to go on; and in this manner they plagued me . . . putting down their loads every ten minutes, walking back fifty or sixty yards as if to return, taking them up again, and so on, with a palaver of half an hour between each stoppage.

The next day, the Inga men quit entirely and Tuckey had to hire porters from a village along the way. They did not prove more cooperative. In Tuckey's entry for September 6 we read:

After a constant battle with the natives from daylight, and after using every possible means, by threats, persuasions, and promises, I at last, about two o'clock, got them underway.

The next day the party got down to the river at a stretch where it was navigable and Tuckey managed to hire some canoes from local fishermen.

About three miles from the place of departure we passed two small rapids, but the other side of the river was clear. We came to a bay in which were ten hippopotami; as the canoes could not venture to come on until these huge creatures were dispersed, we were obliged to fire volleys at them from the shore. . . . At four, reached one of the rocky promontories, round which the current set so strong, that the canoe men refused to attempt passing it. . . . I was therefore under the necessity of attempting to haul the canoes up the stream by the rocks with our own people . . . but by the neglect of one of the men, the stern of the second canoe stuck fast in the rocks, and the current taking her on the broadside, broke her right in two, and several of the articles that were in her sunk, and others were swept away. . . . All was now confusion among the canoe men, who first ran off, and then, after a long delay, came back again, but nothing could induce them to go forward.

September 9:

In the morning some rain. . . . At two P.M. we reached the head of a deep reach . . . here we stopped to dine. After dinner I wished to proceed, but our bearers refused. . . . Finding all persuasions useless, I was obliged to pitch tent at this place, and with Dr. Smith and Lieutenant Hawkey walked to the summit of a hill, where we perceived the river winding again to the S.E. but our view did not extend above three miles of the reach: the water clear of rocks, and, according to the information of all the people, there is no impediment whatever, as far as they know, above this place.

And here we were under the necessity of turning our back on the river, which we did with great regret, but with the consciousness of having done all that we possibly could.

One has to read the entry a second time. Just at the moment Tuckey at last finds the river clear of rocks and all reports assure him that there are no further impediments upstream he decides to turn his back on the river. Just when he seems at last within sight of his goal, he decides to admit the river has defeated him. Why? It was a question that never was to be answered adequately. To be sure, illness had taken a very heavy toll of the party. Moreover, it was by then short of supplies, and there was all that trouble with the native bearers. But none of these seems an adequate explanation. After all, they were not very far into the interior. It would have taken only a week or two, three at the most, to get further provisions brought up from the *Congo* and the ailing back down to her for medical attention. The struggle to get this far had been great but not really greater than expected. An expedition of this sort was expected, on the past experiences of such explorers as Mungo Park, to be gone for years, and they had been under way only just over two months. Indeed, one might feel they were just getting started. Yet the next day, September 10, the heart for some mysterious reason gone out of him, Tuckey started back.

The return to Inga took four days. There Tuckey learned that the Inga men who had deserted "had reported that one half of us had been drowned in canoes, and the rest killed by black bushmen." The next day they got back to Cooloo.

Though ill myself, I intended to proceed; but Dr. Smith and two of our people are too ill to be moved; remained therefore this day. . . . I passed a miserable and sleepless night . . . being very weak myself and wishing to get on before the sun became too hot, I set off with Dr. Smith, leaving Mr. Hawkey behind to bring on the people. . . . Terrible march; worse to us than the retreat from Moscow."

Sept. 16. Unable at daylight to procure any canoe men, I set off with our own people, and at three P.M. reached the *Congo*.

Terrible report of the state on board: coffins.

Sept. 17. At daylight sent off all the sick in double boats . . . to the transport; hired fifteen black men to assist in taking the Congo down the river. . . .

Sept. 18. Reached the transport. . . .

Flocks of flamingos going to the south denote the approach of the rains.

This was Tuckey's last journal entry. He was taken aboard the *Dorothy,* which was anchored at Tall Trees, "in a state of extreme exhaustion." He never recovered and died on October 4. By that time

Smith, Cranch, Tudor, and Galwey were also dead, and Hawkey died two days later. Before the expedition reached England again twenty-one of the original fifty-four white men in the company (Simmons and Benjamin had remained in their homeland) were dead. In his report, the surviving assistant ship's surgeon stated "that though the greater number were carried off by a most violent fever . . . some of them appeared to have no other ailment than that which had been caused by extreme fatigue, and actually to have died from exhaustion."

The catastrophe of Tuckey's expedition came as an incredible shock to England. "It may not, perhaps, be too much to say," an Admiralty historian wrote two years later (in 1818), "that there never was in this or any other country, an expedition of discovery sent out with better prospects or more flattering hopes of success. . . . Yet, by a fatality that is almost inexplicable, never were the results more melancholy and disastrous." Its high rate of mortality and the almost embarrassing shortness of its duration were bad enough. But its lack of accomplishment was overwhelming. Not only had Tuckey come nowhere near solving "the grand problem respecting the identity of the Niger and the Zaire," his magnificently equipped expedition had failed to explore and map the latter river much more than 150 miles further than had lone, haphazard European traders before him.

Under the impact of this disaster England and Europe seem to have recoiled from the Congo. They continued their exploration of the Niger. The other prong of the expedition sent out by the Colonial Office at the same time as Tuckey's, under the command of Major John Peddie, which was to follow Park's route down the Niger and which was as expensively mounted and manned, in fact failed as miserably as Tuckey's. Yet, curiously, the reaction to that failure was not the same. In the course of the next fifteen years, expedition after expedition was sent out, until the Lander brothers finally reached the Niger's mouth in 1830 and proved once and for all that it had nothing to do with the Congo. And then, when adventurous men began looking around for another geographical puzzle to solve, they did not turn to the still mysterious Congo. Tuckey's failure was too overwhelming.

12

---·◆·●●·◆·---

DR. LIVINGSTONE AND THE NILE

No sooner had the riddle of the Niger been solved than nineteenth-century men, as if they could be happiest only when faced with the challenge of *the* superlative geographical mystery, transferred all their age's impassioned curiosity to the Nile. Barely fifty years after Mungo Park had pronounced the discovery of the Niger's mouth "certainly the greatest discovery that remains to be made in the world," Englishmen were declaring, without the least sense that they were contradicting themselves, that the location of the sources of the Nile was in Sir Harry Johnston's phrase, "the greatest geographical secret after the discovery of America."

That Europe's next great adventure in African exploration should have been the Nile, rather than the Congo, is as easily explicable as that the Niger should have been its first. For like the Niger, and so very unlike the Congo, which after Tuckey's disaster had been condemned to the darkest regions of vile savagery, the Nile had long fascinated Europe. Its delta and lower valley were, after all, the cradle of Western civilization, its flow and flood the life blood of that civilization, and the location of the source of those life-giving waters a mystery that had tantalized and defeated mankind for more than 2000 years.

As long ago as 460 B.C., Herodotus had attempted to ascend the Nile to find where it began, only to be turned back by the cataracts at Aswan. The Roman Emperor Nero, in the first century of the Christian era, sent two centurions beyond the confluence of the Blue and White Niles on the same errand, but they too were stopped, this time by the impenetrable papyrus swamps of the Sudd. A few years later,

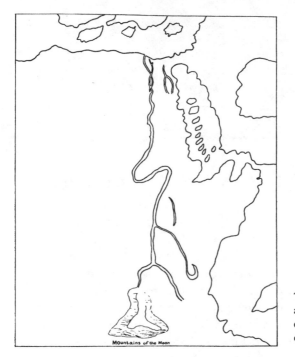

Mountains of the Moon

The course of the Nile according to the oldest extant version of Ptolemy's map

the Syrian geographer Marinus of Tyre tells us, a Greek merchant by the name of Diogenes, returning from a trading voyage to India, landed on the East African coast and then journeyed inland for 25 days in search of "two great lakes, and the snowy range of mountains whence the Nile draws its twin sources," an idea that was enshrined in Claudius Ptolemy's celebrated *mappimundi* which showed the Nile flowing from two such lakes, hidden away in the heart of Africa and fed by streams from the legendary snow-capped Mountains of the Moon.

But it wasn't until the second decade of the seventeenth century that any real headway was made in cracking the secret of the Nile sources, when two Portuguese Jesuits, on that quest for the realm of Prester John, reached Lake Tana in the Ethiopian highlands, the source of the Blue Nile. Some 150 years later, just about the time the Saturday's Club in London was forming the African Association, James Bruce, a rich and eccentric Scotsman, traveling alone from Cairo, duplicated the Jesuits' feat. In subsequent decades, Europe's abiding interest in the Nile sharpened and took on an increasingly political and economic cast with Napoleon's campaign in Egypt, Mehemet Ali's conquest of the Sudan, the Anglo-French competition for control of the Red Sea, and the first glimmerings of a grand plan to build a canal through the Suez isthmus. Then, with the Niger's mouth at last found and Europe yearning for a new geographical conundrum to solve, along came the sensational reports of three German missionaries in East Africa to rivet attention on the still undiscovered source of the river's parent stream, the White Nile.

Johann Ludwig Krapf, born in Württemberg but sent out to Africa by the London Church Mission, initially had set up a mission station in Ethiopia, but, because of the hostility of the native Coptic priests, he had been obliged to withdraw and establish himself near Mombasa, on the coast of present-day Kenya. There he was joined by two of his countrymen, Johannes Rebmann and Jakob Erhardt, and they proved a remarkable trio. Not only were they the first Protestant missionaries in this part of Africa, but they brought to their work an intelligent curiosity about the continent, inquiring ceaselessly about the geography of the interior, listening carefully to every report, rumor, myth, and tale. One story they heard repeatedly was of a mountain whose peak was said to be covered in silver but a silver so strange that when men brought it down from the mountain top it turned into water. Rebmann, a farmer's son and the strongest of the trio, was chosen to go inland, like the legendary Diogenes, and try to find that obviously snow-capped mountain. On May 11, 1848, he did. It was Mount Kilimanjaro, the tallest in Africa. The following year, Krapf, pushing beyond Kilimanjaro, discovered still another snow-covered peak, the Kenya massif, and Erhardt, following up on Krapf's work, learned that further westward was the land of Uniamwezi—the Country of the Moon—in which, it was said, lay a vast inland sea from which a river flowed northward toward the "land of the Turks."

The missionaries' findings, published in the periodicals of the London Church Mission between 1848 and 1855, created a sensation in England. After all, the map they drew of their discoveries bore a stunning resemblance to Ptolemy's, and their commentaries on it, replete with references to snow-capped mountains, great lakes, and the Country of the Moon, seemed a confirmation of the ancients' view of the White Nile's source. What's more, after centuries of futile attempts to reach that source by ascending the river from its delta, they suggested a promising new way of getting there. In 1856, Britain's Royal Geographical Society, which had absorbed the African Association, took up that suggestion and launched a campaign to find the White Nile's source by striking not southward through the desert but westward from the East African coast, a campaign which, like the African Association's missions to the Niger a half century before, though for rather different reasons, would once again awaken Europe's interest in the Congo.

The first expedition sent out by the Royal Geographical Society was that of Richard Francis Burton, although only 36 already a famous explorer for his journeys to the forbidden cities of Mecca and Harar, and John Hanning Speke, a 30-year-old officer in the Indian Army, who had accompanied Burton on the Harar expedition. Sailing on the monsoon from Bombay aboard a British sloop, the pair arrived in Zanzibar in December 1856, spent several months making a geographical reconnaissance—they took a side trip to visit Rebmann at the mission near Mombasa—outfitted and assembled a caravan, and in June 1857 crossed over from Zanzibar to the East African mainland at the village of Bagamoyo in present-day Tanzania, just up the coast from Dar es Salaam.

These were the last great years of Arab domination in East Africa, and the island of Zanzibár was the major entrepôt of their thriving ivory and slave trade with the African interior. The Zanzibari sultans, in a vague and general way, laid claim to what today is Tanzania, Kenya, Uganda, the South Sudan, Malawi, Zambia, Mozambique and even Zaire, and each year, with the onset of the dry season, Arab caravans would set out from Bagamoyo into those (at least from Europe's standpoint) unmapped parts, following well-traveled trading routes, visiting their upcountry trading stations and returning perhaps a year or two later with their harvest of slaves and ivory. It was along one of these trading routes that Burton and Speke now set off with their own caravan of locally hired porters and guides and a herd of pack animals, and by August they had ascended the escarpment from the coastal plain and struck westward across the savanna plateau toward the vast lake or lakes of Uniamwezi, from which the White Nile arrived in June.

The going wasn't particularly rough. For the most part, the track they followed led from one village to another, from one watering place to another. Still, their progress was slow. At every village the local chief would delay them with a demand for the payment of a tax for the privilege of passing through his territory. What's more, as they got further from the coast, porters deserted, and much time was wasted in hiring replacements. And then there were the fevers and disease of the African interior. One by one the pack animals died, and both Burton and Speke were soon constantly sick. So it wasn't until November that they reached Tabora, in the middle of present-day Tanzania, and, as we know now, just about equidistant from Lake Victoria toward the north and Lake Tanganyika toward the west.

Tabora was then the most important Arab town in the African interior, the crossroads of caravan routes radiating throughout Central Africa, and Burton and Speke decided to take advantage of its comparative luxury to rest up and recover their health, and to gather information from its Arab residents about the geography of the country. It was during the month they spent in Tabora that they heard the encouraging news that great lakes did indeed lie ahead, both to the west and to the north of them.

As the leader of the expedition, it was for Burton to choose in which of these directions to head. And, as it turned out, he chose wrongly. When they left Tabora in December, Burton and Speke headed west toward Lake Tanganyika, reaching the Arab trading village of Ujiji on its eastern shore in February 1858. To be sure, this was a major discovery. Burton and Speke were the first Europeans to have penetrated this far into the interior of Africa, the first to lay eyes on the great lake, the first to prove that, just as the ancients and later the German missionaries had believed, great lakes did exist in these parts, one of which might very well be the source of the White Nile. But Lake Tanganyika wasn't it.

By the time they reached Ujiji, both men were seriously sick again. Besides malaria, Speke was suffering from ophthalmia so that he could barely see and Burton from an ulcerated jaw so that he could barely eat. When they recovered enough, they hired some native canoes and sailed to the north end of the lake in hopes of finding a river issuing from it which could be the Nile. They didn't. They heard of a river further on, the Ruzizi, but the local tribesmen told them that it flowed not out of but into the lake, so they didn't bother to investigate it. The two explorers returned to Ujiji "sick at heart" as Burton wrote later, and from there made their way back to Tabora, where they arrived in June.

Here Burton made yet another wrong choice. He decided to spend some time in Tabora resupplying the expedition's caravan and compiling his notes on the discovery of Lake Tanganyika. Speke, on the other hand, was anxious to investigate the lake that they had heard lay to the north of Tabora, a lake which the Arabs claimed to be far larger than Lake Tanganyika, and Burton let him go off on his own. Speke's journey took three weeks. He arrived on the shore of Lake Victoria, near present-day Mwanza, in early August, and at the first sight of it was seized by an amazing conviction. "I no longer felt any doubt," he wrote, "that the lake at my feet gave birth to that interesting river, the source of which has been the subject of so much speculation, and the object of so many explorers." He was correct, of course, but in fact he had no right to be. He spent only three days on the lake and viewed only a tiny portion of it. He did not find any river outletting from it to the north, nor could he even be sure that the vast sheet of water he saw was a single lake and not several. Even so, he returned to Tabora in an ecstasy of enthusiasm, declaring to Burton that he felt "quite certain in my mind I had discovered the source of the Nile."

Now the green serpent of jealousy reared its ugly head. Burton wasn't about to concede to his younger, less experienced companion this most cherished prize of African discovery. He immediately pointed out Speke's failure to explore the lake properly and rejected his reasons for claiming the discovery as "weak and flimsy." Moreover, Burton had been having second thoughts about Lake Tanganyika, of which he could claim himself the discoverer, and he was now no longer willing to rule it out altogether as a possible source of the White Nile. Speke's lake, christened by him in honor of the reigning British monarch, might provide a feeder stream to the Upper Nile, Burton was willing to allow, but if so only after the Upper Nile had emerged from *his* lake, Tanganyika, perhaps as that unexplored river, the Ruzizi.

The traveling companions fell out bitterly over the issue, and with neither speaking to the other and both again stricken with fever, their return to the coast was a nightmare. They arrived back in Zanzibar in March 1859, proceeded to Aden and there parted forever. Burton chose to continue his convalescence in Aden. Speke returned to England and, going directly to Sir Roderick Murchison, president of the Royal Geographical Society, was able to make his argument for Victoria as the White Nile's source without Burton's interference. Murchison and the society were excited by the report and agreed to sponsor an expedition to follow up Speke's discovery. Speke was to head it, and James Augustus Grant, another Indian Army officer, the same age as Speke and a former hunting companion of his, was to be his traveling companion this time.

The Royal Geographical Society's second attempt to find the White Nile's source from the East African coast left the following year and Speke, now with Grant, arrived again in Zanzibar in October 1860. His plan was to follow the same caravan route to Tabora, turn north from there to Victoria, then work his way along the lake's western shore until he reached the north end, where he fully expected to find a river outletting into the Nile, which he would then follow north into the Sudan. It was a sensible plan and, except for some unexpected delays, he and Grant carried it through to a remarkable extent.

Because of tribal wars in the interior, it took the pair over a year after leaving Zanzibar to get as far as Speke and Burton had gotten in five months, and it wasn't until November 1861 that they were at last on their way northward from Tabora. Then came further and, in many ways, wonderful delays in the kingdoms of Uganda, especially at the fabulous court of Mtesa, the Kabaka (king) of Buganda, on the western shores of Lake Victoria. It wasn't until July 1862 that they were actually on the march to the northern end of the great inland sea. And here Speke again contrived to separate from his expedition partner. Unlike Burton, however, Grant never raised any complaint. He was at that time suffering from an agonizingly painful infection in one of his legs and, recognizing that he was slowing Speke down, agreed to let his companion go on ahead without him. Speke then led a column on a forced march, traveling at the rate of 20 miles a day, and on July 21, 1862, at a place called Urondogani about 40 miles from Victoria, he found a river flowing from the lake toward the north and "at last," he concluded, "I stood on the brink of the Nile."

A month later, Speke rejoined forces with Grant and then, since they had been in Africa for nearly two years, his main concern was to get back to England and report his momentous discovery to the world. For the next six months he and Grant marched to the north, sometimes in sight of the river found outletting from Victoria but, because of the rugged terrain, usually not. At one point they heard reports of still another great lake to the west of them, called Luta Nzige, which they realized might prove to be another source of the Nile, but with their supplies running low and their health failing they couldn't

afford the detour to find out. In February 1863, they reached Gondokoro, in the southern Sudan, where a relief column sent by the Royal
Geographical Society was waiting for them. From there they sailed
down the Nile to Khartoum, on to Cairo, and finally back to England,
where they arrived in June 1863.

Speke had in fact discovered the source of the White Nile, but that
was not to be conclusively proved or finally conceded for nearly fifteen
years. He had left too many unanswered questions and there were still
too many rival explorers coveting the honor for themselves. Burton,
for example, once again charged Speke with "an extreme looseness of
geography." He argued that what Speke had done was catch a glimpse
of a large sheet of water at Mwanza in 1858, then catch a glimpse of
another large sheet of water at the court of the Kabaka of Buganda in
1862 and conclude that the area between the two points, covering
nearly 30,000 square miles, comprised a single lake. But he had no
right to jump to such a fantastic conclusion because he still had not
circumnavigated the lake, still had not demonstrated that what he had
discovered was not two different lakes or more. In addition, Burton
went on, while it was true that Speke had found a northward-flowing
outlet from the lake (or lakes), he had no basis for declaring it to be
the Nile because he had not followed it downstream into the Sudan;
he had marched overland to Gondokoro and though, from time to
time, he caught sight of a river along the march, he had no way of
knowing that what he saw was always the same river. But finally,
Burton contended, even granting it was the same river, even granting
that Victoria was a single vast lake and not several, there was still no
proof that it was the source of the Nile. For, after all, Speke could not
say what river might flow *into* the lake, a river rising to the south of
the lake, rising perhaps in another lake like his Tanganyika, a river
whose source, by virtue of lying further south, would more properly
be the Nile's source than Victoria's outlet.

Arguments like these split England into two passionately contending camps. And then Samuel Baker came along to confuse matters
even further.

Baker, a rich man's son who had spent his youth in idle travel and
big-game hunting, decided in his late thirties to get in on the excitement of African exploration. In June 1861, outfitted with delicacies
from Fortnum & Mason's and equipment from the best London shops
and traveling with his beautiful Hungarian wife, he arrived in Cairo

to spend a year journeying up the Nile, shooting big game and observing the exotic ways of the natives, reaching Khartoum in June 1862. And there his aimless wandering came to an end. The Royal Geographical Society had charged the British vice consul in Khartoum, a certain John Petherick, with the job of organizing a relief column to meet Speke and Grant in Gondokoro. A few months before Baker and his wife arrived at Khartoum, Petherick and *his* wife had set off for Gondokoro. Nothing had been heard from them since, and rumors had filtered back that they were dead. What's more, nothing had been heard from Speke and Grant for more than a year, and there was a growing belief that they too had perished. So the Royal Geographical Society asked Baker to take over the job of leading the relief column to Gondokoro and, if he learned there that Speke and Grant were dead, to take up their task of finding the Nile's source.

Baker delightedly accepted the dual assignment. It took him six months to assemble and outfit the relief column, and he and his wife led it out of Khartoum in December. After a journey of over 1000 miles southward on the Nile—first through the waterless waste of the desert, then through primeval swamp of the Sudd—a journey that took forty days, they reached Gondokoro in February 1863.

As it turned out, no one had died. Two weeks after the Bakers' arrival in Gondokoro, Speke and Grant turned up, and a few days later so did the Pethericks. As a result, Baker considered "my expedition as terminated," he later wrote, "but . . . Speke and Grant with characteristic candour and generosity gave me a map of their route, showing that they had been unable to complete the actual exploration of the Nile, and that a most important portion still remained to be determined." That portion was the large lake, Luta Nzige, of which Speke and Grant had heard, lying to the west of them, during their march to Gondokoro. So, as soon as Speke and Grant left for Khartoum, Baker and his wife set out to find it. Just over a year later, in May 1864, they did. "The waves were rolling upon a white pebbly beach," Baker wrote. "I rushed into the lake, and thirsty with heat and fatigue, with a heart full of gratitude, I drank deeply from the Sources of the Nile." And so Lake Albert, as Baker named Luta Nzige in honor of Queen Victoria's recently deceased consort, was added to the dispute over the origins of the river.

In September 1864, at a meeting of the British Association for the Advancement of Science at Bath, an attempt was to be made to settle the dispute by debate. The principal contestants in what the popular press called the Nile Duel were to be the two greatest rivals on the issue, Burton and Speke. Before an audience of several hundred of the nation's most eminent geographers and scientists, they were to face each other for the first time since they had parted in Aden more than five years before. They never did. On the day before the Nile Duel, Speke killed himself. It was, as it turned out, a tragic accident. Speke had gone out that afternoon with some friends to shoot partridges on his uncle's estate and, while climbing over a wall, had fallen and his rifle discharged into his chest. But so hot were the emotions on the question of the Nile that the immediate reaction was that Speke, fearing to face Burton's arguments, had committed suicide, a view that persisted for years.

Obviously, the Nile Duel was off. (In its place, Burton read a paper on the *Ethnology of Dahomey*.) But, equally obviously, even had it taken place it would have accomplished little more than inflame the controversy even further. For the question of the Nile's source could not be resolved in a lecture hall in England by debaters. The only place it would be settled finally was in the field in Central Africa by an explorer. No one understood this better than Murchison, the president of the Royal Geographical Society, and for that job he now turned to another participant at the Bath meeting: the missionary doctor David Livingstone.

At the time of the Bath meeting, where he delivered a paper on the evils of the slave trade, Livingstone was almost 52 years old and had spent nearly half those years in Africa. He had been born in Blantyre, Scotland, the son of a respectable but desperately poor traveling tea salesman, and had worked in the textile mills of that city, from six in the morning to eight at night, six days a week, from the age of 10 until he was 23. He escaped from that Dickensian life by gaining admission to Anderson's College in Glasgow, and there he trained for a career as a medical missionary.

That was the time, at the height of the abolitionist movement, of the first real surge of Protestant mission activity in Africa. For the Scottish and English nonconformists the main field of that activity was in and around the Cape Colony, which the British government had seized from the Dutch at the outbreak of the Napoleonic Wars in order to protect its shipping lanes to India. As early as 1805, the London Missionary Society had established a mission station north of the Orange River, and by 1841, when Livingstone completed his medical studies in Glasgow and was ordained a Congregationalist minister at Albion Chapel, Finsbury, the society had a station at Kuruman, nearly 600 miles further into the African interior. And that was where Livingstone asked to be sent.

From the outset, Livingstone was an unusual sort of missionary. The London Society's prevailing practice then was to have its missionaries settle down at their first station and proceed to spend if not exactly their entire lives then at least twenty or thirty years there, devoted to the task of converting the tribesmen in the immediate region. But Livingstone had been in Kuruman barely a month when he was already restlessly looking further afield. He quarreled with his superior, found that he couldn't get along with his fellow missionaries, developed an insatiable curiosity to discover what lay beyond the confines of the station's territory, and was immediately ambitious to run a mission of his own. Indeed, it was this early in his African career that he first used the phrase that was to be the guiding light of the rest of his life. In a letter home to Scotland, he wrote, "I would never build on another man's foundation. I shall preach the gospel *beyond every other man's line of things.*"

And Livingstone got his chance far sooner than he had any right to expect. Convincing the society's directors that the tribes to the north of Kuruman offered a promising field for missionary work, he received permission to undertake a series of expeditions in search of a suitable site for a new station. And from the end of 1841 to the middle of 1843 he traveled north and northeast, often as much as 500 miles further into the interior from Kuruman, entering country where no white man had been before. Though the mission station that he finally did establish, at Mabotsa, ultimately turned out to be a failure, these travels proved decisive to his career: during them Livingstone began the steady, inevitable transformation from a missionary with an interest in geography to an explorer with an interest in religion.

Livingstone spent a little less than two years running the mission station at Mabotsa, during which time he married a missionary's daughter from Kuruman, but, having no success in converting the local tribesmen there, he abandoned it and moved further northeast and established another one at Chonunane. As this turned out just as dismally as the last, he moved on once again and set himself up in Kolobeng where he remained for two more years.

David Livingstone (From a photograph taken by Thomas Annan, of Hamilton and Glasgow)

It was at Kolobeng that he first heard of a large lake lying north-westward from the station, a lake which, he wrote to a friend, "every-one would like to be the first to see." And in 1849, determined to be that first one, he set off on the first of three expeditions which were to establish his reputation as an African explorer. Between June and October of 1849, he journeyed more than 300 miles from Kolobeng, crossing the Kalahari Desert, and reached Lake Ngami in the north-western corner of what is today Botswana. His account of this journey, which was published in the March 1850 issue of *Missionary Magazine*, brought Livingstone to the attention of the Royal Geographical So-ciety, and Murchison, just then elected its president, arranged to have a small sum raised for a second expedition. So, between April and August of 1850, Livingstone repeated the journey, this time taking his family along (there were three children by now and his wife was five months pregnant with the fourth) and this time heard of a great river lying several hundred miles further to the northeast. Because his wife and children had fallen ill, Livingstone had to turn back without attempting to find that river. But the next year, again with his wife and children in tow, he set off on the third and what was to prove the crucial journey, for in August 1851, at the town of Sesheke where the Caprivi Strip of South-West Africa divides modern Bots-wana from Zambia, he came upon the Zambezi River.

The discovery of the Zambezi is one of the great achievements of African exploration, and Livingstone devoted the next twelve years of his life to the river's exploration. After taking his family back to Cape Town, he returned to the Zambezi in May 1853, and, in the course of the next year, followed the river upstream into Angola and then pro-ceeded all the way to Loanda on the West African coast, where he arrived in May 1854 half-dead with fever. Then, after five months in the Portuguese settlement recovering his health, he turned around, retraced his steps across Angola and returned to his starting point in September 1855. But he was not done yet. In November of that year he set out to follow the river downstream, to its mouth, discovering Victoria Falls along the way, and arrived in Quelimane in present-day Mozambique in May 1856. By this stupendous journey he became the first European ever to have crossed the African continent from coast to coast and the most famous African explorer of his day. When he re-turned to England, he was treated as a national hero. The Royal Geographical Society awarded him its gold medal; Oxford University gave him an honorary doctorate; Queen Victoria granted him a private audience; and wherever he appeared in public, he was mobbed by crowds fighting to shake his hand.

But Livingstone was not yet through with the Zambezi. He believed that in the river he had found a great highway into the interior of Africa, along which "Christianity and Commerce" could be brought to the continent. And he used his popularity, fame, and prestige to promote a government-sponsored expedition to the river which was meant to open the way for missionaries and mission stations, traders and trading posts, and for the eventual British colonization of the regions adjacent to its shores. That expedition left England in March 1858, it lasted until July 1864, and it was a terrible failure. In the first place, Livingstone discovered that the Zambezi, far from being a highway into the interior, was navigable for only 400 miles from its mouth. During his journey *down* the river in 1856, he had heard about the Kebrabassa Rapids but, seeking then to avoid some rough terrain, he had left the river and bypassed them without actually seeing them. When he returned and laid eyes on the rapids for the first time, he realized that what he had heard—that they were merely "a number of rocks which jut out across the stream"—was utterly false. In fact, they turned out to be 30 miles of thundering cataracts, through which no vessel of any sort could pass. Moreover, even the short navigable stretch of the river posed problems for his expedition's boats. The Zambezi's mouth is a delta, clogged with sandbars and mudflats through which Livingstone's vessels had a devilish time entering, and not far upstream the river becomes shallow, with its channels shifting from month to month, so that the boats were constantly going aground.

After a year of struggling hopelessly with this troublesome river, Livingstone admitted defeat and turned his attention to the Shire, a major tributary which flows into the Zambezi about 100 miles above its mouth. At first this seemed a promising prospect, and, indeed, it was in the process of exploring the Shire that Livingstone scored his next noteworthy discovery, that of Lake Nyasa (now called Lake Malawi), out of which the Shire flows. But it was to be the expedition's only positive achievement. All too soon a host of problems beset the explorer. The Shire turned out to be only slightly more navigable than the Zambezi, being clogged with vegetation and blocked by rapids of its own. Moreover, the shores of the river and lake were a major hunting ground of the Arab slavers, and as a consequence the tribes in the region were extremely hostile to strangers and defeated all attempts to establish missions or trading posts among them. Then too, because of the flooding of the river and the lake, the shorelines were swampy and proved to be breeding grounds for disease, and members of the party rapidly came down with fever and dysentery. Men became delirious; Livingstone's wife died; morale plummeted. The ugliest sort of petty quarrels broke out. Defeat and failure were inevitable.

When Livingstone returned to England this time, in July 1864, he met with an entirely different reception. It would be too much to say that he was in disgrace. Among geographers at least there was a fair appreciation for his accomplishments. He had discovered an important new lake; he had mapped the Zambezi to the Kebrabassa Rapids and all of the Shire; he had provided useful new information about the tribes, the Arab slave trade, and the geographical problems of south-central and southeast Africa. Nevertheless, there were no banquets, no visits with the Queen, no medals, no mobs hailing him in the streets. For the public, at least, his expedition seemed worthy of little attention, especially since something far more exciting in the way of African exploration had come along in the meantime.

During the six years Livingstone had been struggling on the Zambezi and Shire, the search for the Nile's source had developed into the passionate issue of the day. Burton and Speke had gone out to Africa and returned during those years, and so had Speke and Grant and Baker. In fact, it was barely six weeks after Livingstone's return that the great Nile Duel was scheduled to take place at Bath.

Nevertheless, Livingstone was still accorded enough respect as an explorer for Murchison to select him to go out to Africa and settle the dispute about the Nile's source, and it was a choice that was universally applauded. For there was Livingstone's vast experience in Africa to commend him for the job. But, more important, on the touchy issue of the Nile, he was a neutral. To have sent out Burton or Grant (in lieu of the dead Speke) or Baker would have made nonsense of the project. Each too passionately had his own axe to grind, his own theory to prove. Livingstone, presumably, had none. In all his years in Africa, he had never come near the region of the supposed source of the White Nile, had never laid eyes on any of the contending lakes, and so could bring a fresh, objective view to the problem.

What Murchison wanted Livingstone to do was to proceed to Burton's Lake Tanganyika and determine whether the Ruzizi flowed from it, and, if it did, find out whether it flowed north into Baker's Lake Albert and issued from there as the Upper Nile. Furthermore, he wanted him to explore Speke's Lake Victoria and establish once and for all its relationship to the Nile watershed.

But Livingstone was the man who had written more than twenty years before that he "would never build on another man's foundation," that he would always work "beyond every other man's line of things." For him to have proceeded as Murchison suggested would have meant that he would be building on Burton's and Speke's and Baker's foundations, would be remaining within their line of things. And this simply wasn't in Livingstone's character. If he was going to settle the issue of the Nile, he would not do it by confirming one or another man's work; if he was going to find the river's origin, he would find it where other men had never looked for it before. Livingstone, as a matter of fact, wasn't quite the neutral on the question that everyone believed. Almost as soon as Murchison involved him in the great debate, he began to develop his own ideas about where the Nile's source was to be found: south of Lakes Victoria and Albert, south even of Tanganyika, further south than Burton or Speke or Baker or any other man had dreamed. Livingstone would look for the Nile's source in those savanna highlands where not the Nile but the Congo rises.

13

---◆━◆◆◆◆━◆---

THE SACRED ORACLES

Livingstone did not immediately accept Murchison's proposal to undertake an expedition to settle the Nile dispute. It was not from any lack of desire on his part to return to Africa. Of that there was never any question. He had spent more than twenty years, virtually his entire adult life, on the continent, and Africa was far more a home to him than England or Scotland. At 52 he was still youthful enough and intellectually vigorous, and his health, though it had been undermined on his last expedition, seemed fully recovered after his rest in Britain. And besides, with his wife dead and his children grown, he had no family duties to hold him back. No, it was something else that caused Livingstone to hesitate: the purely geographical purpose of the enterprise.

Livingstone had long before this severed his ties with the London Missionary Society and had so thoroughly evolved away from his original calling as a medical missionary that it was hard to think of him as anything but an explorer by this time. Yet, oddly enough, this was not how Livingstone thought of himself. If he was no longer a missionary in the classic sense, he also was not, at least in his own mind, someone for whom geographical discovery for its own sake was sufficient reason to lead an expedition into the heart of Africa. He had to have a larger, more noble reason, and on all his previous journeys he had managed to come up with one. In his earliest years, for example, he had justified his restless wanderings as the search for new and more promising fields for missionary work. And later on, when he was no longer even nominally in the pay of the London Society, he insisted that his expeditions were less matters of discovering and mapping the Zambezi or the Shire than grand pioneering ventures to open up those rivers as highways which missionaries and traders could follow to bring the civilizing influence of Christianity and commerce to the African tribes of those parts.

But no such reasons, Livingstone realized, could be used to justify an expedition searching for the Nile's source. Such an expedition would be constantly on the move, and where it went would be dictated by such strictly geographical considerations as the locations of lakes, the flow of rivers, the pattern of watersheds. As this might lead it into the remotest, most unlikely regions, it would be ridiculous to claim that its purpose was the reconnaissance of promising fields for missionary stations or commercial settlements. So other justifications entirely had to be found and, though it took him a year, Livingstone eventually found them.

The first was the Arab slave trade. On his previous expedition, while traveling up the Shire to Lake Nyasa, he had come into contact with it and witnessed the terrible havoc it wrought, and he was aware that, wherever a search for the Nile's source might otherwise lead, it surely would pass through the bloody hunting grounds of the Arab slavers. At this time, Europe cared very little about the Arab slave trade, primarily because little was known about it, so Livingstone could allow himself to believe that he was undertaking Murchison's assignment, at least in part, to make Europeans aware of this bloody traffic and arouse them to take the same sort of measures to abolish it that they had taken to end the slave trade from the West African coast.

But Livingstone found yet another reason for agreeing to take up the search for the Nile's source, a reason that infused the enterprise with a far grander significance than even the abolition of the Arab slave trade did. For he had come to believe that the agelessly elusive source of what he called, quoting Homer, "Egypt's heaven-descended spring" was somehow holy and its discovery an almost divine undertaking.

It is impossible to know when the seeds of this fantastic belief first took root in Livingstone's mind because he revealed it only after it was in its fullest flower, when he had been on his divine quest for several years. What we do know is that he was familiar with and fascinated by the ancient geographers' accounts of the mystery of the Nile's sources. For example, at one point in his journals he tran-

scribed an account of the Nile's origin, given to Herodotus by an
Egyptian scribe, in which it is described as rising from "fountains
fathomless in depth" between two mountains, half of whose water
"flowed to Egypt, towards the North Wind, the other half to Ethiopia
and the South Wind." And we know too that, with his missionary
training, Livingstone was an avid Bible student and was particularly
intrigued by a story in Exodus which tells of Moses, accompanied by
Merr, the Pharaoh's daughter, going up the Nile to Inner Ethiopia
to found the mysterious city of Meroe, going up so far that he might
possibly have reached the great river's source. And this allowed Livingstone to dream, as he wrote, of discovering "evidence of the great
Moses in those parts." Apparently these Biblical and classical allu-
sions melded in Livingstone's mind into a mystical sense of mission
"to confirm the Sacred Oracles," a mission so compelling that it was
to blind him to his expedition's true accomplishment: the discovery
of the source and headwaters of the Congo.

Livingstone departed from England on August 13, 1865, and, traveling by way of India, arrived in Zanzibar on January 28, 1866. This

A View of Zanzibar

was still the capital of the Arab slave trade, where anywhere from 80,000 to 100,000 captives were brought from the African interior each year and, given Livingstone's stated intention of campaigning against this trade, it is rather a paradox that not only did his expedition start out from this teeming slave port but from the very outset its success depended on the help of Arab slavers.

On Livingstone's side, the paradox is not difficult to explain. There can be no question of his hatred for the island and everything he saw there. In one of his first journal entries he called the place "Stinkibar" and described the humiliations that the Africans were subjected to in its slave market: "The teeth are examined, the cloth lifted up to examine the lower limbs, and a stick is thrown for the slave to bring, and thus exhibit his paces. Some are dragged through the crowd by the hand, and the price is called out incessantly." But Livingstone really had no choice. This was the only place he could properly outfit his expedition, and since all the island's firms, directly or indirectly, dealt in slaves he had no way of avoiding doing business with slavers. Moreover, all the caravan routes he would be following into the interior were controlled by the Arab slavers, as were all the trading posts upcountry where he would be calling for resupply, so he was obliged to stay on reasonably good terms with them.

What is far more difficult to understand is why the Arabs cooperated with Livingstone. They were aware of his view of the slave trade and knew well enough that one of his main objects in coming to Africa was to incite a campaign to destroy it. And yet they helped him. They outfitted his expedition with first-class goods at decent prices. The Sultan of Zanzibar loaned him a handsome house for his stay on the island and provided him with a *firman* to the sheikhs in the interior, instructing them to render Livingstone any assistance he might require. And time and again, once he was in the interior, slavers went out of their way to render him just such assistance and, in fact, on more than one occasion saved his life. Partly, one can suppose, this amiable attitude toward a man who ostensibly was their enemy was rooted in the Arabs' desire to stay on good terms with the British. But, to a greater extent, it had something to do with the kind of man Livingstone was, his courage, his indomitable will, his patience and gentleness, that quality in him which the Arabs called *baraka* and which attracted them to him and made them genuinely want to help him.

Livingstone spent seven weeks on Zanzibar organizing his caravan. He had brought out 22 members of the party from India, 13 sepoys from the Bombay Marine Battalion and 9 young freed African slaves from the British government school at Nassick. Now he recruited 13 more, including ten Johanna men sent over from the Comoro Islands and he would later bring the complement up to 60 by hiring local tribesmen once he landed on the African mainland. Among his initial party were a number of men who had served with him before. Chuma, for example, one of the Nassick schoolboys, was a slave Livingstone had freed during his explorations of Lake Nyasa, and Susi, a young Zanzibari, had worked on the boat used in the expedition up the Shire River. In addition, Livingstone assembled a train of baggage animals. He was the only white man in the party.

It was an astonishingly small party. To appreciate just how small it is only necessary to point out that Burton and Speke, who traveled nowhere nearly the great distances Livingstone now intended, never had fewer than 130 men in their caravan. The small size of the party reflected Livingstone's ideas on the best way to travel in Africa. He believed that to march in "grand array" was only to stir up the greed and hostility of the tribesmen, provoke demands for larger *hongo* or bribes, and offer greater temptations for thieving. Even so, the reality of African travel in Livingstone's time was that the larger the caravan the farther it could go, for it had to carry not only all the equipment the expedition itself needed but enough trading goods—bales of cloth, bags of beads, and items of manufacture—to buy fresh food and the right of passage along the way. Thus, to make up for the fact that he didn't have a sufficiently large party to carry as much goods as he needed, Livingstone arranged to have an advance post set up in the interior, where additional supplies were to be sent for him. And the post he chose was Ujiji, the Arab trading town on the eastern shore of Lake Tanganyika, which he hoped to reach within a year.

In March 1866 his little party landed on the East African coast at the port town of Mikindani, just north of the mouth of the Rovuma River in what is today Tanzania, and set off for the interior. "Now that I am on the point of starting another trip into Africa I feel quite exhilarated," he recorded in his journal on March 26.

The mere animal pleasure of travelling in a wild unexplored country is very great. When on lands of a couple of thousand feet, brisk exercise imparts elasticity to the muscles, fresh and healthy blood circulates through the brain, the mind works well, the eye is clear, the step is firm, and a day's exertion always makes the evening's repose thoroughly enjoyable. We have usually the stimulus of remote chances of danger either from beasts or men. Our sympathies are drawn out towards our humble hardy companions by a community of interests and, it may be, of perils, which makes us all friends.

Livingstone, as we've seen, was convinced that the Nile's source lay much further south than any of his predecessors had thought to look. And so his plan was to march almost due westward from Mikindani, following the Rovuma River much of the way, until he reached Lake Nyasa, cross it, and then begin working his way northward toward the southern tip of Lake Tanganyika, in the full expectation that before he got there he would come across a system of rivers and lakes which would be the watershed of the Nile and from which he would find a river flowing northward, very possibly into Lake Tanganyika, and from there on into Lake Albert or, alternatively, along the western shores of those lakes. Having established that, he would then thoroughly explore the watershed until he isolated the particular stream which fed it and then find that particular stream's source, and thus discover the precise fountain of the Nile.

But things turned sour almost immediately, and the exhilarating tone of the early entry vanished tragically quickly from Livingstone's diary. The area he was passing through proved to be far more brutally ransacked by the Arab slavers than even Livingstone had expected. He records at one point:

We passed a woman tied by the neck to a tree and dead, the people of the country explained that she had been unable to keep up with other slaves in the gang, and her master had determined that she should not become the property of anyone else if she recovered after resting for a time. I may mention here that we saw others tied up in a similar manner, and one lying in the path shot or stabbed, for she was in a pool of blood. The explanation we got invariably was that the Arab who owned these victims was enraged at losing his money by the slaves becoming unable to walk, and vented his spleen by murdering them.

But Livingstone's real troubles developed within his own caravan. Barely ten days after leaving the coast, he became aware that the sepoys were mistreating the baggage animals, flogging, goading, and

Slavers revenging their losses

stabbing at them with such ferociousness that he suspected that they were deliberately bent on killing the beasts and sabotaging the expedition. What was worse, they dawdled incorrigibly, constantly making excuses for stopping or falling back.

At one point, his patience tried to the breaking point, Livingstone gave two of the sepoys "some smart cuts with a cane." But this was very much not in the gentle Livingstone's style, and he wrote after the incident, "I felt I was degrading myself, and resolved not to do the punishment myself again." Discipline meted out so half-heartedly served more to encourage than discourage defiance and the rot spread, slowing the march, destroying the baggage animals, which died off one by one, and finally infecting the Nassick boys and Johanna men. "It is difficult to feel charitable to fellows," Livingstone wrote of the sepoys, "whose scheme seems to have been to detach the Nassick boys from me first, then, when the animals were all killed, the Johanna men, afterwards they could rule me as they liked, or go back and leave me to perish; but I shall try to feel as charitably as I can in spite of it all."

In June, some 200 miles inland from the coast, the caravan entered a region suffering from famine and ravaged by tribal wars as well as by Arab slavers. Under these conditions, the porters whom Livingstone had hired at Mikindani refused to go further, saying they feared capture by the slavers or death in the tribal wars, and Livingstone was obliged to pay them off and let them return to the coast. It was a serious loss. The party had been small enough to begin with and now it was more than halved in size. Then a few weeks later there was another devastating blow. Believing they had gained the upper hand because of the loss of the porters from the coast, the sepoys became increasingly mutinous, until Livingstone had no choice but to get rid of them as well. Thus, with the Johanna men, Nassick boys, some locally hired porters, and his young servants from previous expeditions, such as Chuma and Susi, Livingstone's party was down to twenty-three and growing alarmingly short of food as it marched through the famine-stricken country toward the shores of Lake Nyasa.

We came to the Lake . . . and felt grateful to That Hand which had protected us thus far on our journey [reads the entry for August 8 in Livingstone's journal]. It was as if I had come back to an old home I never expected to see again; and pleasant to bathe in the delicious waters again, hear the roar of the sea, and dash in the rollers. Temp. 71 degrees at 8 A.M., while the air was 65 degrees. I feel quite exhilarated.

But, alas, this exhilaration also was to pass quickly. Livingstone had planned to get passage for his party across the lake in one of the Arab dhows that regularly crossed it as part of the slaving route from the interior down to the coast. But here was a case—the only serious one—where the Arab slavers refused to aid Livingstone. Showing them the *firman* of the Sultan of Zanzibar was no help. "Very few of the coast Arabs can read," Livingstone discovered. "All Arabs flee from me, the English name being in their minds inseparably connected with recapturing of slaves." So, after two weeks of useless negotiations for a dhow, Livingstone was obliged to make a long detour around the southern end of the lake. He crossed the Shire, where it outlets from Nyasa, on September 13 and started up the lake's western shore toward Lake Tanganyika.

And now there were still more setbacks. On September 25, the Johanna men quit. They claimed that they had heard from a passing Arab, we read in Livingstone's journal, "that all the country in front was full of Mazitu [a tribe of nomadic warriors] . . . and all the Johanna men now declared that they would go no further. Musa [their leader] said, 'No good country that; I want to go back to Johanna to see my father and mother and son.' " Livingstone tried to convince them that the Arab's story was false and took them to a local chieftain, who told them, " 'There are no Mazitu near where you are going'; but Musa's eyes *stood out* with terror, and he said, 'I no can believe that man.' . . . When we started, all the Johanna men walked off, leaving the goods on the ground." The party was now down to a dangerously small complement of eleven as the caravan moved from the open savanna into ever more thickly forested regions.

And then the rains began. Within a matter of a few weeks Livingstone was writing, "It rains every day . . . the cracks in the soil then fill up and everything rushes up with astonishing rapidity . . . we spent a miserable night . . . wetted by a heavy thunder-shower . . . Morning muggy, clouded all over, and rolling thunder in the distance." And with the onset of the rains came diseases and fevers, taking their toll of the members of the dwindling party, including Livingstone himself. His entry for December 6: "Too ill to march." In the subsequent weeks: "We could get no food at any price . . . the men grumbled at their feet being pierced by thorns . . . we have no grain, and live on meat alone . . . we had so little to eat that I dreamed the night long of dinners I had eaten, and might have been eating." On New Year's Eve he wrote: "We now end 1866. It has not been so fruitful or useful as I intended. Will try to do better in 1867, and be better—more gentle and loving; and may the Almighty, to whom I commit my way, bring my desires to pass, and prosper me! Let all the sins of '66 be blotted out for Jesus' sake."

Barely a week into the new year there was yet another serious mishap. A porter, clambering down into a ravine along a steep path slippery from the incessant rain, fell and damaged Livingstone's chronometers, making it impossible for him to know for sure that his longitude readings were accurate, and thus where he was. Two weeks after that, a still more dangerous blow fell. Two porters deserted with their loads—and the load one carried was the expedition's medicine chest. With little exaggeration Livingstone wrote, "I felt as if I had now received the sentence of death."

He had now been more than nine months under way and had traveled more than 800 miles. He was suffering from dysentery and malaria, both of which were sure to get worse with the rains and the lack of decent food and, unchecked by drugs, they could prove fatal. To go on without the medicine chest was almost suicidal. And yet Livingstone decided to go on. He believed that he was very near his goal, that within a reasonable amount of time he would come upon that watershed of lakes and rivers where he would find the source of the Nile. He was wrong only in the name of the river. On January 24, he reached the Chambezi, the source of the Congo.

It is difficult to understand how Livingstone could have made the gross geographical error he now made. The Chambezi flows southwest into Lake Bangweolo, from which, as the Luapula, it turns to the north to flow into Lake Mweru, the outlet of which is the Luvua, which flows into the Lualaba, which is the Upper Congo. Yet Livingstone believed—perhaps wanted to believe—that the Chambezi flowed north, that it was the river he was seeking that flowed into Lake Tanganyika and thus was the beginning of the Nile. He would not realize his mistake for months, and by that time he had marched northward all the way to the southern shore of Lake Tanganyika.

It was a beastly trek. He was hungry all the time, his health deteriorated alarmingly, and added to his woes was an attack of rheumatic fever. "Every step I take jars the chest," he wrote, "and I am very weak; I can scarcely keep up the march, though formerly I was always first, and had to hold in my pace not to leave the people altogether." The only moment of consolation came when the party encountered a caravan of Arab slavers headed for the coast and its leader offered to take a packet of letters with him to Zanzibar. This was Livingstone's first opportunity to make contact with the outside world in nearly a year and he used it to describe the dismissal of the sepoys and the defection of the Johanna men, then went on to describe his own situation:

We have lately had a great deal of hunger, not want of fine dishes, but want of all dishes except mushrooms. . . . The severest loss I ever sustained was that of my medicines; every grain of them, except a little extract of hyoscyamus. We had plenty of provisions after we left Lake Nyassa, but latterly got into severe hunger. Don't think please, that I make a moan over nothing but a little sharpness of appetite. I am a mere ruckle of bones.

On April 1, Livingstone reached the southern shore of Lake Tanganyika. There was no exhilaration this time. He writes, "I feel deeply thankful at having got so far. I am excessively weak—cannot walk without tottering, and have a constant singing in the head." The next day he fell dangerously ill. "I had a fit of insensibility, which shows the power of fever without medicine. I found myself floundering outside my hut and unable to get in; I tried to lift myself from my back by laying hold of two posts at the entrance, but when I got nearly upright I let them go, and fell back heavily on my head." Chuma and Susi, who were daily becoming Livingstone's most devoted followers, got their leader into the hut "and hung a blanket at the entrance . . . that no stranger might see my helplessness; some hours elapsed before I could recognize where I was." A month elapsed before he could get up and move around again.

He had by this time realized, of course, that the Chambezi did not flow into Lake Tanganyika. What's more, he had also learned of Lake Bangweolo, into which it did flow, and of Lake Mweru, into which Bangweolo drained via the Luapula. The existence of this system of lakes and rivers suggested the very watershed Livingstone had expected to come across in his march north from Lake Nyasa, and he recognized that what he ought to do was return there and explore it. But he could not bring himself to turn away from Tanganyika—and his advance post at Ujiji 300 miles to the north, where he could hope to get medicines and other supplies. But, when he was well enough to undertake the trek to Ujiji, he discovered that the way was blocked by wars that had broken out between local tribes and Arab slavers.

For a month, Livingstone tried to decide what to do, and we find him confessing in his diary, quite uncharacteristically, "I am perplexed how to proceed." Then in May he fell in with a party of Arabs who proved extremely hospitable. Their leader, Livingstone wrote, "has been particularly kind to me in presenting food, beads, cloth . . . [and] is certainly very anxious to secure my safety." So, in his perplexed state and undermined physical condition, Livingstone decided to attach his party to the Arab caravan and let it dictate the direction of his march for the time being.

The leader of the caravan was Hamidi bin Muhammad, a Zanzibari Arab better known by his nickname Tippoo Tib, who was to become the greatest slaver and trader in Central Africa within the next few years and play, as we shall see, a crucial role in the exploration of the Congo. Now, though, he was merely an agent of his father's firm in Zanzibar, and he was headed westward to Lake Mweru. So it was to Mweru, rather than back to the Chambezi and Bangweolo, that Livingstone went. It was a journey of little more than 100 miles, but with constant stops to conduct business along the way the caravan didn't reach the lake's northern shore until November. Livingstone's interest in Mweru centered on its relationship to Bangweolo and the pattern of the rivers and streams in the watershed around it. And, piecing together information he gathered from the local tribesmen, he learned that "round the western end flows the water that makes the river Lualaba, which, before it enters Mweru, is the Luapula, and that again (if the most intelligent reports speak true) is the Chambezi before it enters Lake Bemba, or Bangweolo."

Moreover, Livingstone heard that the Lualaba was a major river, and a northward-flowing one at that, and he concluded that it could be the river he had been searching for. Now two obvious tasks faced him. One was to go south and confirm with his own eyes the geography he had learned second-hand of the Lualaba's origin in the Chambezi. The other was to go north and follow the Lualaba from Mweru as far as necessary to see if in fact it was the mainstream of the Nile. But which of the two he would undertake depended on which direction the Arab caravan chose to go. His party was now down to nine members, he was drastically short of supplies, food, and trading goods, and his health, in the absence of any proper medicines, continued to decline dangerously. Under such conditions, it was utterly impracticable for him to set off on either exploration on his own. So, when Tippoo Tib chose to move southward down the eastern shore of Lake Mweru, Livingstone went along, and on November 20 he reached the lake's southern end, not far from the banks of the Luapula, and the royal kraal of the King of Casembe.

The plain extending . . . to the town of Casembe is level [Livingstone recorded], and studded pretty thickly with red anthills, from 15 to 20 feet high. Casembe has made a broad path from his town . . . about a mile-and-a-half long, and as broad as a carriage path. The chief's residence is enclosed in a wall of reeds, 8 or 9 feet high, and 300 square yards, the gateway is ornamented with about sixty human skulls; a shed stands in the middle of the road before we come to the gate, with a cannon dressed in gaudy cloths. A number of noisy fellows stopped our party and demanded tribute. . . . Many of Casembe's people appear with the ears cropped and hands lopped off: the present chief has been often guilty of this barbarity. One man has just come to us without ears or hands: he tries to excite our pity making a chirruping noise, by striking his cheeks with the stumps of his hands."

November 24:

We were called to be presented to Casembe in a grand reception. The present Casembe has a heavy uninteresting countenance, without beard or whiskers, and somewhat of the Chinese type, and his eyes have an outward squint. He smiled but once during the day, and that was pleasant enough, though the cropped ears and lopped hands, with human skulls at the gate, made me indisposed to look on anything with favour. His principal wife came with her attendants . . . to look at the Englishman. She was a fine, tall, good-featured lady, with two spears in her hands; the principal men who had come around made way for her, and called on me to salute: I did so; but she, being forty yards off, I involuntarily beckoned her to come nearer: this upset the gravity of all her attendants; all burst into a laugh, and ran off. Casembe's smile was elicited by a dwarf making some uncouth antics before him. His executioner also came forward to look: he had a broad Lunda sword on his arm, and a curious scizzor-like instrument at his neck for cropping ears. On saying to him that his was nasty work, he smiled, and so did many who were not sure of their ears at the moment; many men of respectability show that at some former time they have been thus punished.

The town of Casembe was a major trading post for Arab caravans and, as Tippoo Tib had a great deal of business to conduct there, Livingstone was obliged to idle away his time for more than a month. To occupy himself, he wrote letters which he hoped to get to the outside world by a chance Arab caravan headed for the coast. In one of these, he provided an accurate description of the Mweru-Bangweolo watershed, and, though he was not yet quite ready to make the claim publicly that this was the Nile's source—he wouldn't do that formally for another year—the implication was there and the task that he saw before him clear. "Since coming to Casembe's," he wrote, "the testimony of natives and Arabs has been so united and consistent that I am but ten days from Lake Bemba, or Bangweolo, that I cannot doubt its accuracy." But we also find him writing, "I am so tired of exploration without a word from home or anywhere else for two years, that I must go to Ujiji on Tanganyika for letters before doing anything else. The banks and country adjacent to Lake Bangweolo are reported to be now very muddy and very unhealthy. I have no medicine." So when, at the end of December, he heard of an Arab caravan heading north again for Ujiji—Tippoo Tib planned to go westward into Katanga— Livingstone turned his back on Bangweolo and joined it.

He didn't get very far. For nearly three months the caravan trudged north along the eastern shore of Lake Mweru but managed to cover barely 50 miles. Once again the rains had set in, and they turned the land into a terrible swamp. On the last day of 1867, he wrote: "I was taken ill. Heavy rains kept the convoy back. . . . It is well that I did not go to Bangweolo Lake, for it is now very unhealthy to the natives, and I fear that without medicine continual wettings . . . might have knocked me up altogether." The next morning, New Year's Day 1868, he wrote: "Almighty Father, forgive the sins of the past year for Thy Son's sake. Help me to be more profitable during this year. If I am to die this year prepare me for it." A month later: "I am ill with fever. . . . We must remain; it is a dry spot. . . . *Hooping-cough* here." At the end of February: "Some believe that Kilimanjaro Mountain has mummies, as in Egypt, and that Moses visited it of old." On March 17, the caravan at last reached the northern end of Lake Mweru, and that was as far as it would go. The land to the north toward Tanganyika and Ujiji was by now an impassable swamp and the Arabs decided to wait for the end of the rains before proceeding any further.

For a few weeks Livingstone seemed to have accepted the Arabs' decision and resigned himself to another long period of inactivity and delay. But then on April 2 we find this entry in his journal:

If I am not deceived by the information I have received from various reliable sources, the springs of the Nile rise between 9 degrees or 10 degrees south latitude [the region of Bangweolo], or at least 400 or 500 miles south of the south end of Speke's Lake, which he considered to be the sources of the Nile.

With that he seems suddenly to have realized that for nearly a year now he had been wandering pointlessly in the tow of Arab caravans. By some inexplicable bolt of energy, he resolved to put an end to that state and turn back to find Bangweolo after all. The leader of the caravan was appalled by the decision and attempted to dissuade Livingstone by promising that the departure for Ujiji would not be much longer delayed. But Livingstone responded that even if that were the case "I would on no account go to Ujiji, till I had done all in my power to reach the Lake I sought." On April 13, he announced his plans to his nine followers. Five of them pointblank refused to go. So the next day he set off with only Chuma, Susi, and two others.

It was a heroic undertaking, a journey of 200 miles under the worst possible conditions, and miraculously it succeeded. Retracing his steps, wading waist deep through rivers and swamps for hours at a time, slogging through "black tenacious mud," floundering through

Chuma and Susi

water-filled ruts, he reached Casembe at the end of May. There, by a splendid stroke of luck, he came upon an Arab caravan making for Bangweolo, and on June 11 he headed southeast with it. It took another month, a month of suffering, constant peril, and thoughts of death. At one point, the party was surrounded by tribesmen "poising their spears at us, taking aim with their bows and arrows, and making as if about to strike with their axes." At another point,

We came to a grave in the forest; it was a little rounded mound as if the occupant sat in it in the usual native way; it was strewed over with flour, and a number of large blue beads put on it; a little path showed that it had visitors. This is the sort of grave I should prefer, to lie in the still, still forest, and no hand ever to disturb my bones.

Livingstone reached Bangweolo on July 18 and, although an attempt to circumnavigate it failed, he confirmed all the information he had heard about its geography and felt free to announce publicly that he had reached his goal. In a dispatch to the foreign office, which he hoped to send out by Arab caravan, he wrote:

I may safely assert that the chief sources of the Nile, arise between 10 and 12 degrees south latitude, or nearly in the position assigned to them by Ptolemy . . . the springs of the Nile have hitherto been searched for very much too far to the north. They rise some 400 miles south of the most southerly portion of Victoria Nyanza, and, indeed, south of all the lakes except Bangweolo.

In another letter to a friend around the same time he acknowledged:

I still have to follow down the Lualaba, and see whether, as the natives assert, it passes Tanganyika to the west, or enters it and finds exit into Baker's lake.

Livingstone was now ready to go to Ujiji to get his much-needed medicines and supplies and from there take up the exploration of the Lualaba. The rainy season had ended, and by October Livingstone was back at the northern end of Lake Mweru. The Arab caravan he had left in April was still there and so were his five deserters, and they all once again joined forces and in November set off for Ujiji.

That miraculous burst of energy, which had gotten Livingstone to Bangweolo and back proved to be just that—a burst. He had not recovered his health, and on the long, hard journey to Ujiji it steadily deteriorated. The diary entry for New Year's Day 1869 omits the usual prayers and expressions of hope for the coming year: "I have been wet times without number, but the wetting of yesterday was once too often: I felt very ill." Two days later: "I marched one hour, but found I was too ill to go further . . . I had a pain in the chest . . . my lungs, my strongest part, were thus affected. . . . I lost count of the days of the week and month after this. Very ill all over." The next entry: "About 7th January.—Cannot walk: Pneumonia of right lung, and I cough all day and night: sputa rust of iron and bloody: distressing weakness." The Arabs rigged up a litter and had him carried. "I am so weak I can scarcely speak. . . . This is the first time in my life I have been carried in illness, but I cannot raise myself to a sitting posture. . . . The sun is vertical, blistering any part of the skin exposed, and I try to shelter my face and head as well as I can with a bunch of leaves, but it is dreadfully fatiguing in my weakness."

That was the last inscription Livingstone made until February 14, when the caravan at last reached the western shore of Lake Tanganyika and set about trying to get canoes for the passage across to Ujiji on the opposite shore. "Patience was never more needed than now," Livingstone scribbled. But at last the necessary canoes were acquired, and after nearly three weeks of paddling they brought him to Ujiji on March 14, emaciated, toothless, desperately sick, practically three years to the day since he had landed on the East African coast and after traveling more than 2000 miles totally out of contact with the outside world.

And now drama turns to melodrama. There were only three things Livingstone wanted and needed at Ujiji: medicines to cure his illness, letters to soothe his loneliness, and supplies to carry on his explorations. And none of these were there.

As we have seen, Livingstone, before leaving Zanzibar, had made arrangements for goods to be sent up to Ujiji, and these arrangements had been faithfully carried out. But the goods had arrived two years before and what happened to them in the meantime is easily enough imagined. As the weeks turned into months and the months into years and Livingstone didn't arrive and the conviction grew that he was dead somewhere in the interior and would never arrive, the goods were pilfered, plundered, and finally stolen outright by the Ujiji inhabitants. "The disappointment," Horace Waller, who edited Livingstone's *Last Journal,* annotated on the page with the entry for March 14, "must have been severe indeed." But, curiously, there's no indication of the disappointment in Livingstone's own writing. It is possible that he had all along realized that setting up a depot at Ujiji was risky business and had steeled himself against the possibility that he wouldn't find his stores once he got there. Besides, when he did get there he was in terrible physical condition, and by the time he was up and around again, in the early summer, the disappointment was well behind him and he had turned his attention to other things.

It is now that we realize what a fantastic hold the quest for the Nile's source had on him. For surely the wisest thing that he could have done would have been to join one of the Arab caravans going down to the coast and return to Zanzibar for proper medical care and supplies. But he doesn't seem to have given this possibility a serious second thought. Instead, he merely sent a message to Zanzibar asking for new supplies to be dispatched to Ujiji and set off to explore the Lualaba.

Livingstone's tiny expedition party was in as bad shape as it had been for the last two years, which meant that in order to embark on any further journey of exploration he again had to rely on the help of the Arabs. On July 12, a caravan did turn up in Ujiji headed across Lake Tanganyika for a slave and ivory hunt along the banks of the Lualaba, and Livingstone attached his small party to it. He expected to be gone four or five months, long enough to determine the course of the Lualaba and be back just about the time his new shipment of supplies from Zanzibar reached Ujiji. In fact, he was gone for more than two years and in all that time never did learn where the Lualaba flowed.

He had no idea into what kind of country he was going. No European had ever been there and it was utterly unlike any Livingstone himself had ever been in before. For where he went was the rain forest of Maniema (Manyuema, in Livingstone's spelling), the forbidding home of cannibal tribes. What's more, it was a region which the Arab slavers and ivory hunters had only just barely begun to penetrate, and their shocking impact was still new enough to be met with resistance by the forest tribesmen, turning the jungle into a doubly hostile and dangerous place.

Almost as soon as he set foot on Lake Tanganyika's western shore, we find those, by now, all-too-familiar pitiful entries in his journal about the difficulties: "Marched 3¼ hours . . . very fatiguing in my weakness. . . . Any ascent, though gentle, makes me blow since the attack of pneumonia." But this was still not yet the Maniema, and the caravan made decent progress. On September 21, it reached the town of Bambarre (Kabambare in today's Zaire), about 100 miles west of Tanganyika and 100 miles east of the Lualaba, where Livingstone rested for over a month while his Arab hosts went about their business of collecting slaves and ivory. On November 1, Livingstone, resuming the westward march, entered the outskirts of the Maniema forests: the vegetation thickened and the cannibal tribesmen, never having seen a European before, became increasingly wary; then the rains came and with them the fevers. Three weeks after leaving Bambarre, the party reached the Luama, a tributary of the Lualaba, but couldn't cross it. The region ahead had been plundered by slavers, and the tribesmen were openly hostile to strangers and wouldn't let them have canoes. They were obliged to return to Bambarre. It was December 19, 1869.

The plan now was to circumvent the troubled regions by striking northwest and reaching the Lualaba further downstream. On December 25, Livingstone wrote, "We start immediately after Christmas: I must try with all my might to finish my exploration before next Christmas." And his prayer for New Year's Day, 1870: "May the Almight help me to finish the work in hand, and retire . . . before the year is out." But six months later he was back in Bambarre, again having failed to reach the Lualaba, defeated by the Maniema forests.

Trees fallen across the path formed a breast-high wall which had to be climbed over; flooded rivers, breast and neck deep, had to be crossed, the mud was awful. . . . The country is indescribable . . . an elephant alone can pass through it . . . reeds clog the feet, and the leaves rub sorely on the face and eyes. . . . Full grown leeches come on the surface.

Then two blows fell that made pushing on impossible. Six of Livingstone's nine followers deserted him (one, he later learned, was killed and eaten by the cannibals), leaving him with only the faithful Chuma and Susi and a Nassick boy named Gardner. And his feet

for the first time in my life failed me. . . . Instead of healing quietly as heretofore, when torn by hard travel, irritable-eating ulcers fastened on both feet. . . . If the foot were put to the ground, a discharge of bloody ichor flowed, and the same discharge happened every night with considerable pain, that prevented sleep.

Livingstone stayed in Bambarre for eight months, three of which he was confined to a hut unable to move. It was a terrible time. In a letter he confessed that "I am made very old and shaky—my cheeks fallen in—space around the eyes—the mouth almost toothless." And, unquestionably, his mind was also damaged by all his suffering. For it was here, in his awful isolation and loneliness, able to do little else than read and reread his Bible, that his strange, mystical conception of the sources of the Nile, and his quest for it, came into full flower.

He wrote on August 25:

One of my waking dreams is that of the legendary tales about Moses coming up into Inner Ethiopia with Merr, his foster mother, and founding a city which he called in her honour 'Meroe,' may have a substratum of fact. . . . I dream of discovering some monumental relics of Meroe, and if anything confirmatory of sacred history does remain, I pray to be guided thereunto. If the sacred chronology would thereby be confirmed, I would not grudge the toil and hardships, hunger and pain, I have endured—the irritable ulcers would only be discipline.

Several weeks later, after what we can imagine to be wandering speculation in his fevered solitude, we find him writing:

My course has been an even one, turning neither to the right hand nor to the left, though my route has been torturous enough. All the hardship, hunger, toil were met with the full conviction that I was right in persevering to make a complete work of the exploration of the sources of the Nile. . . . I had a strong presentiment during the first three years that I should never live through the enterprise, but it weakened as I came near to the end of the journey, and an eager desire to discover any evidence of the great Moses having visited those parts bound me, spellbound me, I may say, for if I could bring to light anything to confirm the Sacred Oracles, I should not grudge one whit all the labour expended.

Around this time, two Arab traders who had come to Bambarre from a journey to Katanga, visited Livingstone and told him that they had seen the "fountains" of four great rivers in that region. One flowed northward through a chain of lakes; the second, seven days away, also flowed northward but to the west of the first; the other two, about ten miles away, flowed to the south and "a mound rises between them, the most remarkable in Africa." As a matter of fact, this was reasonably accurate geography. Four rivers do rise within a few hundred miles of each other in the Katanga region: the Lomami and the Lualaba both flowing northward, the first eventually becoming a tributary of the Congo, and the Zambezi and the Kafue flowing southward. But Livingstone's mind, in its agitated state, leaped to a fabulous conclusion: "Were this spot in Armenia it would serve exactly the description of the garden of Eden in Genesis, with its four rivers, the Ghison, Pison, Hiddekel, and Euphrates." But, as it was not, Livingstone decided rather that "It possibly gave occasion to the story told to Herodotus by the Secretary of Minerva in the City of Sais, about two hills with conical tops, Crophi and Mophi. 'Midway between them,' said he, 'are the fountains which it is impossible to fathom: half the water runs northward into Egypt; half to the south towards Ethiopia.' "

And so the idea was fixed. Though he still planned to go northward and trace the course of the Lualaba to confirm that it was the Nile, he would be drawn always more obsessively by those four fountains of Herodotus, by his search for evidence of the great Moses, by his desire to confirm the Sacred Oracles, and in the end they would kill him.

His chance to try for the Lualaba again came early in the new year. On New Year's Day, 1871, he had written, "O Father! help me to finish this work in Thy honour. Still detained at Bambarre, but a caravan of 500 muskets is reported from the coast: it may bring me other men and goods." It did. The message he had sent to Zanzibar nearly two years before had gotten through, and, at the beginning of February, having been directed there from Ujiji, ten porters with supplies arrived in Bambarre for Livingstone. He was fairly well recovered and the medicines that now arrived made him feel fit enough to again undertake his explorations.

The going was as rough as ever, but now with a party of thirteen, decent supplies, and the continuing assistance of the Arabs, Livingstone made good time, and on March 30 he reached the Lualaba at Nyangwe, an Arab trading town on its banks. The next day, "I went down to take a good look at the Lualaba here. It is . . . a mighty river, at least 3000 yards broad, and always deep: it can never be waded at any point, or at any time of the year; the people unhesitatingly declare that if any one tried to ford it, he would assuredly be lost." The next step was clear: to get canoes and follow it to the north.

But he didn't. And here we see how seriously undermined, in physical and mental powers, Livingstone was after all his years of torturous wandering. The problem was acquiring canoes; the tribesmen wouldn't give, rent, or sell him any. "They all think," Livingstone wrote, "that my buying a canoe means carrying war to the left bank." It was not an unreasonable fear. Nyangwe was the furthest into the Maniema forests that the Arab traders had penetrated, and on the basis of their performance so far, it is hardly surprising that the tribesmen didn't want to see them penetrate any further. They did not distinguish Livingstone from the Arabs. They had never seen a European, so he was for them just another stranger who would unleash all the horrors of the slave and ivory hunts.

Still, given all the obstacles he had overcome to get this far, it is hard to accept the idea that getting canoes should have been such an impossible task. And yet, curiously, it seemed so to Livingstone. He settled down in Nyangwe, built himself a house, and waited passively for the canoes somehow to materialize. And he was still waiting two and a half months later when an event occurred that finally broke his spirit and caused him to turn his back on the Lualaba forever.

During his weeks of helpless waiting, Livingstone's only real pleasure had been to visit Nyangwe's marketplace. It was a lively and colorful place, jammed with hundreds, sometimes thousands of people, mainly women, for whom

it seems to be a pleasure of life to haggle and joke, and laugh and cheat: many come eagerly . . . many are beautiful . . . all carry very heavy loads of dried cassava and earthen pots which they dispose of very cheaply for palm-oil, fish, salt, pepper, and relishes for their food. The men appear in gaudy lambas, and carry little save their iron wares, fowls, grass cloth, and pigs.

After making a few visits, he felt himself very welcome there

for all are pleased to tell me the names of the fishes and other things. Lepidosirens are caught by the neck and lifted out of the pot to show their fatness. Camwood ground and made into flat cakes for sale . . . are offered and there is quite a roar of voices in the multitude, haggling. It was pleasant to be among them . . . vendors of fish run about with potsherds full of snails or small fishes . . . each is intensely eager to barter food for relishes, and makes strong assertions as to the goodness or bad-ness of everything: the sweat stands in beads on their faces—cocks crow briskly, even when slung over the shoulder with their heads down, and pigs squeal. . . . They deal fairly, and when differences arise they are easily settled by the men interfering or pointing at me.

On July 15, Livingstone made his usual visit to the market. "It was a hot, sultry day," he tells us but there was a good attendance, perhaps as many as 1500 people, mostly women. He noticed three Arabs and

was surprised to see these three with their guns, and felt inclined to reprove them . . . for bringing weapons into the market, but I attributed it to their ignorance, and, it being very hot, I was walking away to go out of the market, when I saw one of the fellows haggling about a fowl, and seizing hold of it. Before I got thirty yards out of the market, the discharge of two guns in the middle of the crowd told me that slaughter had begun: crowds dashed off from the place, and threw down their wares in confusion, and ran. At the same time . . . volleys were discharged from a party down near the creek on the panic-stricken women, who dashed at the canoes. These . . . were jammed in the creek, and the men forgot their paddles in the terror that seized all . . . men and women, wounded by the balls . . . leaped and scrambled into the water, shrieking. . . . Shot after shot continued to be fired on the helpless and perishing.

The massacre went on for two days, spreading through the town, to surrounding villages, and across the river. A gang of slaves broke loose and went on a rampage of looting. Huts were set afire, entire villages went up in flames. At least 400 people and probably far more were killed.

The open murder perpetrated on hundreds of unsuspecting women fills me with unspeakable horror: I cannot think of going anywhere. . . . I cannot stay here in agony. . . . I see nothing for it but to go back to Ujiji.

The return trip took three months and Livingstone arrived there on October 23, "reduced to a skeleton." And once again there was nothing waiting for him. As before, whatever goods might have been sent up to Ujiji from Zanzibar had been stolen.

This was distressing [Livingstone wrote]. I had made up my mind . . . to wait till men should come up from the coast, but to wait in beggary was what I never contemplated, and I now felt miserable. . . . But when my spirits were at their lowest ebb, the good Samaritan was close at hand, for one morning Susi came running at the top of his speed and gasped out,

The massacre of the Manyuema women at Nyangwe

"An Englishman! I see him!" and off he darted to meet him. The American flag at the head of the caravan told of the nationality of the stranger. Bales of goods, baths of tin, huge kettles, cooking pots, tents, etc., made me think, "This must be a luxurious traveller, and not one at his wits' end like me."

The interpreter for the luxurious traveler at that moment called out, "I see the Doctor, sir. Oh, what an old man! He has got a white beard." And the luxurious traveler, as he later would write, thought,

And I—what would I not have given for a bit of friendly wilderness, where, unseen, I might vent my joy in some mad freak, such as idiotically biting my hand, turning somersault, or slashing at the trees, in order to allay those exciting feelings that were well-nigh uncontrollable. My heart beats fast, but I must not let my face betray my emotions, lest it shall detract from the dignity of a white man appearing under such extraordinary circumstances.

So I did that which I thought was most dignified. I pushed back the crowds, and, passing from the rear, walked down a living avenue of people, until I came in front of the semi-circle of Arabs, in front of which stood the white man with the grey beard. As I advanced slowly towards him I noticed he was pale, looked wearied, had a grey beard, wore a bluish cap with a faded gold band around it, had on a red-sleeved waistcoat, and a pair of grey tweed trousers. I would have run to him, only I was a coward in the presence of such a mob—would have embraced him, only, he being an Englishman, I did not know how he would receive me; so I did what cowardice and false pride suggested was the best thing— walked deliberately to him, took off my hat, and said: "Dr. Livingstone, I presume?"

"Yes," he said, with a kind smile, lifting his cap slightly.

I replace my hat on my head, and he puts on his cap, and we both grasp hands, and I then say aloud:

"I thank God, Doctor, I have been permitted to see you."

He answered, "I feel thankful that I am here to welcome you."

14

STANLEY AND LIVINGSTONE

Henry Morton Stanley was the first European to see Livingstone in nearly six years—and he would be the last—but he was not the only one to have tried to find Livingstone in all those years.

It will be remembered that in September of the expedition's first year, 1866, when Livingstone was making his way up the western shore of Lake Nyasa, the Johanna men in his party had downed their loads and refused to proceed further in fear of the hardships that lay ahead. Unlike the sepoys, whom Livingstone had fired and paid off, the Johanna men were deserters. So, when they got back to Zanzibar in December, they were obliged to come up with a story to explain their desertion. And they came up with a cunning one. Calculating that the sepoys had already given their version of what had happened, the Johanna men told the truth about events up to the time the sepoys were dismissed. But then the self-serving lies began. They claimed that after the party had crossed Lake Nyasa it was attacked by a band of marauding tribesmen. Livingstone was at the head of the caravan, as usual, while they were at the rear and, they admitted by way of adding a convincing touch, had just grounded their loads and stopped to rest when the attack began. What happened next they saw from the hiding places they rushed into in the long grass. The tribesmen charged, shouting war cries and rattling their spears against their shields. Livingstone managed to shoot two, but, as he was reloading his rifle, a third felled him with an axe blow to the back of his neck, and the rest of the party was massacred. That evening, at sunset, the Johanna men said they had crept to the site of the battle, found Livingstone's body and buried it. There was no trace of any survivor and all the expedition's baggage had been stolen, leaving nothing for them to bring back to Zanzibar as proof of the occurrence.

The initial reaction to the story was disbelief, but the Johanna men had apparently rehearsed it so well and in such convincing detail during their march back to the coast and stuck to it so unshakably under the closest questioning that it gradually won acceptance. In March 1867, while Livingstone was struggling to Lake Tanganyika, the *Times* of London printed a letter from Murchison saying, "If this cruel intelligence should be substantiated, the civilised world will mourn the loss of as noble and lion-hearted an explorer as ever lived." Less than two weeks later, in another letter to the *Times,* Murchison had to concede, "I can now scarcely cling to the hope my dear friend should still be alive." At a meeting of the Royal Geographical Society on March 25, which had been called to discuss the matter, Murchison suggested that a search expedition be sent to Africa to determine Livingstone's fate, one way or another, as "doubt was not to be endured."

E. D. Young, a naval lieutenant who had served with Livingstone on the second Zambezi expedition, headed the search party. It departed from England in June, reached the mouth of the Zambezi in July, pushed upstream to the confluence with the Shire, reached Lake Nyasa in mid August, and by the beginning of September was in the region where Livingstone reportedly had been killed. Once on the scene, Young was able to give the lie to the tale told by the Johanna men. He found evidence of Livingstone's passage—a spoon, a knife, a razor, a mirror, a cartridge case, and other such items which had been traded at one village or another for food—well beyond where the Johanna men claimed they had buried him. Then he met and interviewed chiefs and tribesmen who had seen Livingstone alive months after the Johanna men had deserted him. With that he concluded that his mission had been satisfactorily completed. It is true he had no proof that Livingstone was *still* alive but, in all fairness, that proof would have been virtually impossible to come by. Young hadn't the least idea where Livingstone might be at that time—he was, in fact, wandering aimlessly with the Arabs 500 miles to the north—and Young's party wasn't equipped to set off on a blind search into the interior of Africa. So they made their way down to the coast, where, in December, a ship picked them up for the voyage back to England.

No sooner had Young returned than the letter which Livingstone had dispatched a year before, while he was still making his way for the first time toward Lake Tanganyika, arrived, setting forth the details of the desertion of the Johanna men and providing information on his plans and whereabouts. And in May 1868, Murchison convened a meeting of the Royal Geographical Society for the purpose of communicating the "glorious tidings" that the lion-hearted explorer was alive, then went on to caution the members that it might be years before Livingstone emerged from the African interior.

There was no further word of Livingstone for more than a year. From time to time, in the course of 1869, while Livingstone was struggling to Ujiji from Lake Bangweolo near to death, the Royal Geographical Society and letters in the *Times* speculated on his whereabouts or reported rumors of his fate. One suggested that he was on his way down the Nile and would soon emerge at Aden. Another cautioned that it was likely that he was being held prisoner by the King of Casembe. Yet another believed he had been diverted to the west and could be expected to reappear on the continent's Atlantic coast. But by and large it seems to have been a case of "out of sight, out of mind" and public interest in the lone wanderer waned. Even Murchison took a surprisingly apathetic view. In September 1869, he wrote to the *Times,* "I hold stoutly to the opinion that he will overcome every obstacle" and advised that the only reasonable course was to wait patiently until he was heard from again. The fact is that no one knew whether Livingstone was alive or dead, lost or safe, and no one seemed to care enough to send someone to find out. Except one man.

The genius of James Gordon Bennett, Jr., heir of the proprietor of the New York *Herald* and himself the newspaper's general manager, was his uncanny instinct for what made a story. Under his editorial direction the *Herald* had gained a world-wide notoriety—and a booming circulation—with its flashy, sensationalist coverage of events and its endlessly astonishing scoops and features. It was this remarkable journalistic instinct that told Bennett that Livingstone was a story, despite the general public's apparent indifference to the explorer's fate. He was convinced that if someone actually found out what had happened to Livingstone and put an end to the vague, uninteresting speculation on the matter, the news would jolt the public out of its apathy and the newspaper that carried the news would have the scoop of the century. And so on October 16, 1869, while visiting in France, Bennett fired off a telegram to his star reporter, ordering him to Paris "on important business."

The star reporter was, of course, Henry Morton Stanley. He was in Madrid at the time, covering the Carlist uprising against the Spanish throne and had just returned "fresh from the carnage at Valencia" when Bennett's telegram arrived. "Down come my pictures from the walls of my apartments," he later wrote, "into my trunks go my books and souvenirs, my clothes are hastily collected, some half washed, some from the clothes-line half dry and after a couple of hours of hasty hard work my portmanteaus are strapped up, and labelled for Paris."

He arrived in the French capital the following afternoon and was ushered into Bennett's suite at the Grand Hotel. Bennett was in bed. "Who are you?" he asked, Stanley tells us.

"My name is Stanley," I answered.

"Ah, yes. Sit down; I have important business on hand for you."

After throwing over his shoulders his robe-de-chambre, Mr. Bennett asked, "Where do you think Livingstone is?"

"I really do not know, sir."

"Do you think he is alive?"

"He may be, and he may not be," I answered.

"Well, I think he is alive, and that he can be found, and I am going to send you to find him."

Stanley was flabbergasted. "Wondering at the cool order of sending one to Central Africa to search for a man whom I, in common with almost all other men, believed to be dead," he asked Bennett,

Have you considered seriously the great expense you are likely to incur on account of this little journey?"

"What will it cost?" he asked, abruptly.

"Burton and Speke's journey to Central Africa cost between 3,000 and 5,000 pounds, and I fear it cannot be done for under 2,500 pounds."

"Well, I will tell you what you will do. Draw a thousand pounds now; and when you have gone through that, draw another thousand, and when that is spent, draw another thousand, and when you have finished that, draw another thousand, and so on; but FIND LIVINGSTONE."

Stanley was 28 years old when Bennett handed him the assignment. Although only 5 feet 5 inches tall, he was powerfully built and in prime physical condition; he had a handsome head of chestnut hair, a flamboyant Victorian mustache, intense gray eyes and a swaggering style. He was something of a romantic and very much the rough-and-ready adventurer, a combination that nicely suited his identity as the

Henry Morton Stanley

daring newspaperman, dashing off from one war zone to another, from one perilous situation to another.

But Stanley was also an extremely ambitious young man. He had acquired his reputation as Bennett's star reporter only recently—indeed, had won a staff position on the *Herald* less than two years before —and he realized, in accepting Bennett's improbable assignment, that if he succeeded at it, if he did find Livingstone, his career would be made, fame and fortune would be his, and, most of all, what he had struggled for all of his life—respectability, social standing, prestige— might at last be achieved. For Stanley was a bastard and that condition haunted him, drove him, and more than anything explains his incredible accomplishments.

He was born in Denbigh, Wales, in 1841 to a rather feckless 19-year-old daughter of a butcher; Elizabeth Parry (she was to go on and have three more illegitimate children before she was done), christened him John Rowlands, after a young farmer who was willing to admit paternity but not responsibility, and then abandoned him. Her father and brothers looked after the child, but when the father died the brothers refused to continue with the arrangement and the boy was sent to the St. Asaph Union Workhouse.

St. Asaph's, "into which I had been so treacherously taken," Stanley wrote in his *Autobiography*, "is an institution to which the aged poor and superfluous children of that parish are taken, to relieve the respectabilities of the obnoxious sight of extreme poverty, and because civilization knows no better method of disposing of the infirm and helpless than by imprisoning them." Stanley received in this institution all the formal education he was ever to get. He was six when he entered and fifteen when he left. And he left by escaping over its walls. The headmaster of the workhouse, a certain James Francis, who years later was to die in a lunatic asylum, was a brutal and violent man, and one day, Stanley tells us, "fell into a furious rage, and uttered terrific threats with the air of one resolved on massacre," then set about birching the entire senior class. When Stanley's turn came, "I felt myself hardening in resistance. He stood before me vindictively glaring, his spectacles intensifying the gleam of his eyes." Stanley refused to submit to the birching and, as a result,

I found myself swung upward into the air by the collar of my jacket, and flung into a nerveless heap on the bench. Then the passionate brute pummeled me in the stomach until I fell backward. . . . Recovering my breath, finally . . . I aimed a vigorous kick at the cruel Master . . . and, by chance, the booted foot smashed his glasses, and almost blinded him with their splinters. Starting backward with the excruciating pain, he contrived to stumble over a bench, and the back of his head struck the stone floor.

Stanley believed that he had killed the master. And so he scampered over the garden wall and fled "as though pursued by bloodhounds."

Stanley's hope was to find some kind relatives to take him in, but the fatherless boy was no more wanted now than he had ever been. So, after two years of shuttling from one family to another, he wandered off to Liverpool and signed on as a cabin boy aboard a packet bound for America. But at the packet's first port-of-call, New Orleans, he jumped ship because the captain's cruelty to his crew was no less than the headmaster's at St. Asaph's.

A long-standing legend, based on Stanley's *Autobiography* but recently called into doubt, tells us what happened next. He was then still John Rowlands, a fatherless, friendless, penniless youth of eighteen in a strange city in a foreign country, walking the streets looking for work. One day he saw a gentleman sitting in front of a general goods store, reading the morning newspaper.

"From his sober dark alpaca suit and tall hat," Stanley tells us, "I took him to be the proprietor of the building. . . . I ventured to ask,—'Do you want a boy, sir?'

" 'Eh?' he demanded with a start; 'what did you say?'

" 'I asked if you wanted a boy.' "

As it turned out, the gentleman wasn't the proprietor of the store but, the legend has it, he was a childless man who had long regretted never having a son and, startled from his newspaper reading, he thought the youth was offering to make up for this lack. In the next few words it became clear that what the youth was doing was asking for work and not offering himself for adoption, but the gentleman was so taken by his initial misunderstanding that he expressed an immediate and deeply paternal interest in the youth. This gentleman's name was Henry Morton Stanley.

The elder Stanley was a prosperous cotton broker and, although he never formally adopted the youth, he outfitted him with a new wardrobe, set about improving his education, took him into his business, and told him: "As you are wholly unclaimed, without a parent, relation, or sponsor, I promise to take you for my son . . . and, in future, you are to bear my name." The workhouse boy was overjoyed.

Before I could quite grasp all that this declaration meant for me, he had risen, taken me by the hand, and folded me in a gentle embrace. My sense seemed to whirl about for a few half-minutes: and, finally, I broke down, sobbing from extreme emotion. It was the only tender action I had ever known, and, what no amount of cruelty could have forced from me, tears poured in a torrent under the influence of the simple embrace. The golden period of my life began from that supreme moment!

It was, however, a pathetically brief period. For two years, Stanley traveled with his "father" learning the cotton brokerage business, studying the books the elder Stanley gave him, developing into a "complete gentleman." But in the autumn of 1860 the elder Stanley visited a brother in Cuba and died in Havana the next year. Stanley was fatherless and adrift again.

The Civil War broke out. After some hesitation, Stanley enlisted in a volunteer brigade called the Dixie Greys and saw his first combat at the battle of Shiloh.

I cannot forget that half mile square of woodland, lighted brightly by the sun, and littered by the forms of about a thousand dead and wounded men, and by horses, and military equipments [Stanley wrote years later]. For it was the first Field of Glory I had seen . . . and the first time that Glory sickened me with its repulsive aspect, and made me suspect it was all a glittering lie.

Stanley was wounded and captured on the second day of battle and shipped, along with several hundred other Confederate soldiers, to Camp Douglas, a prisoner-of-war center near Chicago. He was held there nearly a year and then took his only chance for escape. He deserted the Confederate cause, took an oath of allegiance to the Union, and was sworn into a regiment of the Illinois Light Artillery. He, however, never got to fight with the unit. Within days of donning his Federal army blues, he collapsed with dysentery and was discharged. And he began a period of wandering that was to last most of his life.

He returned to Wales, where he found himself as unwelcome as ever, sailed from Liverpool again to New York, there signed on as a deckhand aboard a merchant vessel trading between Boston and the Mediterranean, worked as a scribe for a time in Brooklyn, and then, in 1864, enlisted in the Federal Navy with the petty officer rating of ship's writer. He was aboard the frigate *Minnesota* at the time of the last major battle of the Civil War, the Union's combined land-and-sea attack on Fort Fisher in North Carolina, and turning his official duty of recording the engagement for the ship's log to his own account, he sent an eye-witness report of the battle to a group of provincial newspapers and launched his career as a journalist.

Though he had still two and a half years to serve, Stanley deserted the U.S. Navy at the end of the Civil War and, heeding Horace Greeley's grand cry of the times, headed west. In St. Louis he persuaded the Missouri *Democrat* and then later a string of other newspapers, including eventually the New York *Herald,* to sign him on as a free lance. For the next three years he roamed the American wilderness, covering the Rocky Mountain mining boom, the Indian wars, the coming of the railroad, the settlement of the plains, America's expansion from coast to coast. He was adventurous, recklessly brave, with a vivid writing style, a keen nose for news, and a sharp eye for the telling detail; his reputation rapidly grew and with it so did his ambition. His first big chance came when he heard that Britain was preparing to invade Ethiopia.

Theodore, the tyrannical and half-mad emperor of Ethiopia, believing himself to have been insulted by Queen Victoria, had imprisoned the British consul along with a number of other Europeans residing in his realm, and for several years all efforts to negotiate their release had failed. So in 1867 Britain declared war on the ancient kingdom of Prester John and organized, under the command of Sir Robert Napier, the largest European army to invade Africa since the days of Imperial Rome. It had all the makings of an exciting story, and Stanley hurried to New York and persuaded James Gordon Bennett to send him to cover it for the *Herald.*

On the way to Ethiopia, in January 1868, Stanley stopped in Suez and made arrangements that would assure his success. Suez had the only telegraph office anywhere near Ethiopia, and Stanley bribed the head telegraphist to send his dispatches ahead of everyone else's. Then, at the end of the campaign, with the death of Theodore and the fall of his mountain fastness at Magdala in April, Stanley sped back to

Suez ahead of Napier's army (with which the other journalists were traveling) and, even though the city was in quarantine because of a cholera epidemic, managed to smuggle his dispatches to the bribed telegraphists for transmission to the *Herald*'s bureau in London.

It was an astonishing scoop. For a time, Stanley's was the only account of Napier's campaign, and the *Herald* was accused of fabricating the news. But at last the official messages from Napier arrived confirming everything the *Herald* had published, and the delighted Bennett signed Stanley on as a staff correspondent. "I am now a permanent employee of the Herald," Stanley rejoiced in his diary on June 28, 1868, "and must keep a sharp look-out that my second coup shall be as much of a success as the first." It was, and then some.

Stanley did not set off to find Livingstone straight away. First Bennett wanted him to cover the inaugural ceremonies of the opening of the Suez Canal. Then, as Samuel Baker was planning to take an expedition up the Nile from Cairo, Stanley was to file a dispatch on that, and, while he was at it, he should also write up a practical guide on Lower Egypt for tourists. "Then you might as well go to Jerusalem," Stanley tells us Bennett ordered.

Then visit Constantinople, and find out about that trouble between the Khedive and the Sultan. Then—let me see—you might as well visit the Crimea and those old battle-grounds. Then go across the Caucasus to the Caspian Sea, I hear there is a Russian expedition bound for Khiva. From thence you may get through Persia to India; you could write an interesting letter from Persepolis. Bagdad will be close on your way to India; suppose you go there and write up something interesting about the Euphrates Valley Railway. Then, when you have come to India, you can go after Livingstone.

The reason Bennett came up with this roundabout itinerary, which would take Stanley fourteen months to complete, was simple. Just three days before Bennett had summoned Stanley to Paris, Livingstone had been heard of again. Some Arab traders had arrived in Zanzibar with news that they had seen the explorer in Ujiji a few months before. Not long after that, a letter from Livingstone from Ujiji, dated May 13 of that year (1869), was received, and yet another report from traders placed Livingstone, correctly, in Ujiji as late as July (shortly after which, as we've seen, he set out for the Lualaba).

None of this particularly bothered Bennett. He was perfectly convinced that, if he let enough time pass, Livingstone would surely get "lost" again. And he was right. By the time Stanley completed his roving assignment from the Suez to Bombay and arrived in Zanzibar on January 6, 1871, Livingstone, then making his second vain attempt to reach the Lualaba from Bambarre, hadn't been heard from for over a year. The last report anyone had was in a letter to the *Times*, in which a gentleman in Donegal said that his son-in-law, the captain of the H.M.S. *Petrel*, then on naval patrol off the West African coast, had been told by a Portuguese trader that Livingstone had been eaten by cannibals. It was up to Stanley to prove otherwise.

Stanley had a few problems. He had been to Africa only once before in his life, and then in the company of Napier's well-provisioned army. He had no experience as an explorer. He had never led an expedition of any sort; in fact, he had never led men under any circumstances before, and he was going into country that not only he hadn't seen but only three Europeans (Burton, Speke and Grant) before him had. What's more, as a journalist in search of a scoop, he felt constrained to keep secret what he was up to. Even worse, his casual inquiries in Zanzibar led him to believe that Livingstone didn't want to be found and that, if he heard, as the acting British consul on the island told Stanley, "fellows were going after him . . . Livingstone would put a hundred miles of swamp in a very short time between himself and them." So Stanley thought it best to go about assembling his expedition on the pretext that he was planning only a modest news-gathering excursion along the East African coast.

Against these handicaps, however, Stanley had an advantage that no other traveler into the African interior had ever had: that flamboyant offer by Bennett of virtually unlimited funds. And Stanley made liberal use of it. In the six weeks he was on Zanzibar readying his expedition, he spent £4,000. He bought almost 6 tons of supplies and equipment, including nearly 350 pounds of brass wire, 20 miles of cloth, and a million beads to use as trading currency, 2 collapsible boats, 71 cases of ammunition, 40 rifles, tents, cooking utensils, silver goblets, champagne, Persian carpets, and a bathtub. He hired 192 porters to carry this massive load, getting many who had served with Burton and Speke, as well as two British seamen he had met on his recent travels and a young Christianized Arab, Selim Heshmy, whom he had picked up in Jerusalem to act as his interpreter. In the first week of February, he landed his party on the coast at Bagamoyo, saying, "We are all in for it now, sink or swim, live or die—none can desert his duty," and to the sound of rifles fired in celebration struck into the interior at the head of the caravan carrying the American flag.

Stanley, who was to become the greatest of all the African explorers of the nineteenth century, was described by a contemporary as "a man remarkable for strength of character, resolution, promptness of thought and iron will. . . . Difficulties did not deter him, disasters did not dismay him. With an extraordinary readiness of mind he improvises means, and draws himself out of difficulty." For all his lack of experience, these qualities—plus his physical strength, his rough-and-ready courage, his innate if untested leadership abilities, his ambition—emerged full-grown on his first African adventure. He set as his goal Ujiji, for that was where Livingstone had been last heard from, and though all the usual trials and tribulations of African travel beset him—malaria, tribal wars, mutiny in his own ranks, the death of his white companions, hunger, and dysentery (he lost 40 pounds during the trek) —he made excellent time. On November 10, the 236th day from Bagamoyo, he saw Lake Tanganyika.

It is a happy, glorious morning, [he wrote]. The air is fresh and cool. The sky lovingly smiles on the earth and her children. . . . A little further on—just yonder, oh! there it is—a silvery gleam. I merely catch sight of it between the trees, and—but here it is at last. . . . An immense broad sheet, a burnished bed of silver—lucid canopy of blue above—lofty mountains are its valances, palm forests form its fringes! The Tanganyika! —Hurrah!

Stanley had Selim lay out a new flannel suit, oil his boots, chalk his pith helmet, and fold a new puggaree around it and, shedding the tattered clothing he had worn throughout the march, changed into this fresh outfit "to make as presentable an appearance as possible." Then he ordered the American flag unfurled and volleys fired by his rifle men to announce the coming of the caravan. "We are now about three hundred yards from the village of Ujiji, and the crowds are dense about me. Suddenly I hear a voice on my right say, 'Good morning, sir!' " Startled to hear the English greeting, Stanley turned sharply to see "a man dressed in a long white shirt, with a turban of American sheeting around his woolly head."

"Who the mischief are you?" he asks.

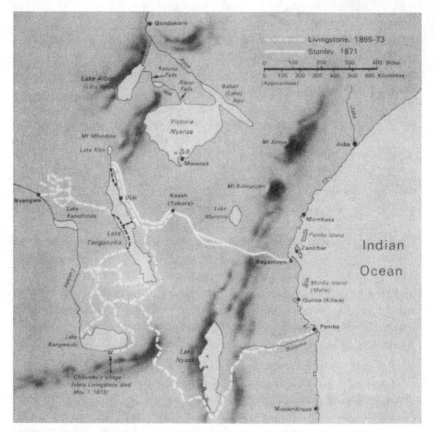

Map based on contemporary information showing the route taken by Livingstone, 1866–1873, and the route taken by Stanley, 1871

"I am Susi, the servant of Dr. Livingstone," said he, smiling and showing a gleaming row of teeth.

"What! Is Dr. Livingstone here?"

"Yes, sir."

"In this village?"

"Yes, sir."

"Are you sure?"

"Sure, sure, sir. Why, I leave him just now."

Stanley's incredulity that he should find Livingstone the very first place he looked for him was thoroughly justified. It was an amazing coincidence. One only has to remember that Stanley had been under way in an outlandishly rambling fashion for more than two years and that Livingstone had arrived in Ujiji not much more than a week and probably only a few days before Stanley got there. (The reason for doubt on the matter is that both men had lost track of time during their African travels. Livingstone's journals give October 24 as the day he got back to Ujiji and October 28 as the day Stanley arrived, but later realized his calendar could have been off by as much as three weeks. Stanley's diary gives November 10 as the day he reached Ujiji but he later discovered that he had lost a week during his travels and might have arrived there as early as November 3.)

Had Stanley arrived in Ujiji only a week or two earlier "Livingstone would not have been found there," as he himself acknowledged, "and I should have had to follow him on his devious tracks through the primeval forests of Manyuema, and up along the crooked course of the Lualaba for hundreds of miles . . . [and] I might have lost him." And had he arrived only a few weeks later, an equally likely supposition, Livingstone almost surely wouldn't have been there either. He very well might have set off on his restless wanderings again or, in his dire physical and mental condition, he might very well have been dead. As he himself told Stanley on the first day of their meeting, "You have brought me new life. You have brought me new life."

Stanley remained with Livingstone for over four months, and that

"Dr. Livingstone, I presume."

time had a profound impact on him. When he first arrived he was an ambitious journalist in search of a scoop, and his plan was to stay a week or two, provide Livingstone with supplies in return for an exclusive interview, then race back to the coast, catch a boat for Aden, from where he would telegraph his sensational story. At dinner on the first day of their meeting, even before Stanley had revealed to Livingstone who he was and why he had come, he was tempted, as he tells us, "to take my note-book out, and begin to stenograph his story." And during that night, as he records, he carried on this delighted conversation with himself:

"What was I sent for?"
"To find Livingstone?"
"Have you found him?"
"Yes, of course; am I not in his house? Whose compass is hanging on the peg there? Whose clothes, whose boots are those? . . ."
"Well, what are you going to do now?"
"I shall tell him in the morning who sent me, and what brought me here. I will then ask him to write a letter to Mr. Bennett, and to give what news he can. . . . It is a complete success so far."

And the next morning at breakfast he was happy to see that Livingstone

was not an apparition . . . and yesterday's scenes were not the result of a dream! and I gazed on him intently, for thus I was assured he had not run away, which was the great fear that constantly haunted me as I was journeying to Ujiji. "Now, Doctor," said I, "you are, probably, wondering why I came here?"

Livingstone had, indeed, been wondering but, he said, "I did not like to ask you yesterday, because it was none of my business." And so Stanley said: "Now don't be frightened when I tell you that I have come after—you!" And not long after that he did at last take out his notebook and begin scribbling down the story Livingstone had to tell.

But it wasn't long before Stanley came to believe that what he was acquiring in Livingstone's company was not merely a story, albeit the scoop of the century, but something far more precious and personal. "I knew him not as a friend before my arrival," wrote the erstwhile workhouse orphan who had been moved to tears by a paternal embrace in New Orleans less than a decade before.

He was only an object to me—a great item for a daily newspaper . . . but never had I been called to record anything that moved me so much as this man's woes and sufferings, his privations and disappointments.

And in the days and weeks that followed we find Stanley writing,

Livingstone's was a character that I venerated, that called forth all my enthusiasm, that evoked nothing but the sincerest admiration. . . . I grant he is not an angel, but he approaches to that being as near as the nature of living man will allow. . . . He is sensitive. . . . His gentleness never forsakes him; his hopefulness never deserts him . . . he has such faith in the goodness of Providence. . . . His is the Spartan heroism, the inflexibility of the Roman, the enduring resolution of the Anglo-Saxon.

Now these certainly were the qualities that the young reporter could wish for in an idealized father. And the difference in their ages—Livingstone was approaching 60, Stanley nearing 31—conspired to foster just such a relationship between them. At one point Stanley was delighted to tell Livingstone that "my men call you the 'Great Master,' and me the 'Little Master,' " and years later confessed, "I loved him as a son, and would have done for him anything worthy of the most filial."

For his part, Livingstone responded to Stanley with almost as much warmth and affection. He too acknowledged their paternal relationship and wrote of the young reporter, "He behaved as a son to a father—truly overflowing with kindness." He unhesitatingly agreed not only to the interview but to Stanley's request that he write a couple of letters himself for publication in the *Herald*. And he took it upon himself to instruct Stanley in the customs of Africans and how best to get along with them. When Stanley fell ill with malaria he nursed him with such care that Stanley would write, "But though this fever . . . was more severe than usual I did not much regret its occurrence, since I became the recipient of the very tender and fatherly kindness of the good man whose companion I now found myself." But perhaps the best measure of the closeness that Livingstone felt for Stanley is the fact that he confided to him the secret of the Nile.

Stanley recorded in his notebook:

That this river [the Lualaba] flowing from one lake into another in a northerly direction, with all its great crooked bends and sinuosities, is the Nile—the true Nile—the Doctor has not the least doubt. For a long time he entertained great scepticism, because of its deep bends and curves west, and south-west even; but having traced it from its head waters, the Chambezi . . . he has been compelled to come to the conclusion that it can be no other other river than the Nile. He had thought it was the Congo . . . but the Lualaba, the Doctor thinks, cannot be the Congo, from its great size and body, and from its steady and continued flow northward. . . . Livingstone admits the Nile sources have not been found, though he has traced the Lualaba through seven degrees of latitude flowing north; and, though he has not a particle of doubt of its being the Nile not yet can the Nile question be said to be resolved and ended. For two reasons: 1. He has heard of the existence of four fountains. . . . Several times he has been within 100 and 200 miles of them, but something always interposed to prevent his going to see them. . . . These fountains must be discovered, and their positions taken . . . he says. These four full-grown gushing fountains, rising so near each other, and giving origin to four large rivers, answer in a certain degree to the description given of the unfathomable fountains of the Nile . . . to the father of all travelers—Herodotus . . . 2. The Lualaba must be traced to its connection with some portion of the old Nile. When these two things have been accomplished, then, and not till then, can the mystery of the Nile be explained.

Stanley and Livingstone undertook a bit of joint exploration and, although it lasted only four weeks and covered only 300 miles, it had its significance. It concerned the question, dating back to Burton's day, whether the Ruzizi River at the northern end of Lake Tanganyika flowed into or out of the lake. Burton had heard that it flowed into the lake, but never having actually seen it he later theorized that it flowed out and thus could be the Nile, with Tanganyika the river's source. Livingstone, who was perfectly satisfied that the Nile rose far south of Lake Tanganyika, was interested in the Ruzizi's direction to determine whether it connected Tanganyika with Baker's Lake Albert, the outlet of which Livingstone believed joined the Lualaba, and so made Tanganyika part of the Nile watershed. Stanley and Livingstone discovered that the Ruzizi flowed into Tanganyika and not out of it into Lake Albert. Thus they removed Tanganyika from Livingstone's geography of the Nile and confirmed his belief in the four fountains of Herodotus as the river's true source.

Stanley enjoyed this, his first experience with geographical exploration, but he was still very much the journalist and he was anxious to get to civilization, file his scoop, and enjoy the fruits of his success. But he was also worried about leaving his new-found father in the wilds. During the excursion on Tanganyika, he had seen how seriously Livingstone's health was undermined and, using "some very strong arguments," as Livingstone noted, urged the doctor to return to England with him. This was very much to Stanley's credit because surely the return of Livingstone himself would take the drama out of his scoop and shift the limelight from Stanley to the long-lost explorer. But Livingstone refused to go home. He was by now completely possessed by his quest for the fountains of the Nile, and the most he would agree to was to accompany Stanley to Tabora, where he could rest and recuperate in greater comfort than in Ujiji while Stanley arranged for a well provisioned caravan to be sent up to him for his future explorations. The two men arrived in Tabora in mid-February 1872, and on March 14 Stanley departed for the coast.

It was an emotional parting. Stanley seems to have sensed that he would be the last European to see Livingstone alive. On the night before the final day, he wrote, "I feel as though I would rebel against the fate which drives me away from him . . . the farewell may be forever!" The next morning, "We had a sad breakfast together. I could not eat, my heart was too full; neither did my companion seem to have an appetite." Livingstone chose to accompany Stanley's caravan a little way down the road from Tabora. "We walked side by side. . . . I took long looks at Livingstone, to impress his features thoroughly on my memory." Then they stopped and made their last farewells. "We wrung each other's hands, and I had to tear myself away before I unmanned myself; but Susi, and Chuma . . . the doctor's faithful fellows—they must all shake and kiss my hands before I could quite turn away. I betrayed myself!" Bursting into tears, Stanley shouted to his men: "March! Why do you stop? Go on! Are you not going home? And my people were driven before me. No more weakness. I shall show them such marching as will make them remember me."

Stanley reached Bagamoyo on May 6 and the following day took a dhow across to Zanzibar. There he spent two weeks assembling the caravan he had promised Livingstone, taking every pain to make sure it was well outfitted and that it would reach Tabora quickly. Then he filed his story to the *Herald* and caught a mail steamer for England, where he arrived on August 1, 1872.

Stanley's reception was a mixed one. Bennett, of course, was delighted. Even before Stanley reached England he had received a cable from the boss saying, "You are now as famous as Livingstone, having discovered the discoverer. Accept my thanks and the whole world's." By the time he got to London, the news of his exploit had swept all others from the front pages. "He sets off and does it," wrote the *Times,* "while others are idly talking or slowly planning. Africa is a very wide target, but Mr. Stanley hit the bull's-eye at once." Other British papers echoed the sentiment: "We could, of course, have wished," wrote one, "that the honour of that discovery had fallen to countrymen of our own. But it is only in the generous sense of the word that we can be said to envy the honour which the American press has fairly won and well deserved." He was presented to Queen Victoria, he was modeled in wax for Madame Tussaud's, he was invited to address the Royal Geographical Society and awarded its gold medal. He went on a lecture tour, there were cheering crowds at railway stations, toasts and tributes at civic banquets, and his book, *How I Found Livingstone,* became an overnight best seller. It would seem that the illegitimate workhouse boy had achieved all he had hoped for when he had taken the assignment.

But the acclaim, in fact, was far from universal. Most of the British press was a great deal less sporting than the *Times.* They could barely contain their jealousy at having been scooped by the *Herald* and its American journalist. An editorial in the *Standard* stated, "We cannot resist some suspicions and misgivings in connection with his story. There is something inexplicable and mysterious about its incidents and conclusions." Other papers picked up on the line, going so far as to suggest that Stanley had never found Livingstone at all, that the whole thing was a hoax, and the letters Livingstone had written for the *Herald* were Stanley's forgeries.

The acclaim of the scientific community, though more gentlemanly than Fleet Street's, was also riddled with doubts. Henry Rawlinson, who had succeeded as president of the Royal Geographical Society on Murchison's death the year before, commented in a letter to the *Times,* "If there has been any discovery it is Dr. Livingstone who has discovered Mr. Stanley," and other members of the society held to this view, maintaining, in order to excuse their own inaction, that Livingstone couldn't have been found by Stanley because he had never been lost. But the most devastating criticism focused on Stanley's assertion that Livingstone believed the Lualaba to be the mainstream of the Nile. James Grant (of the Speke-Grant expedition) led the way in questioning this geography, theorizing, quite correctly as it would turn out, that the Lualaba was more likely the Congo than any other river.

Stanley was deeply wounded by all this and reacted rather vehemently.

Gentlemen, editors [he wrote], you have no right to feel jealous of me. . . . The whole world is as open to you as to the New York Herald. . . . The traveller whom I sought for was . . . alive. . . . I found him ailing, and destitute; by my mere presence I cheered him—with my goods I relieved him. Is the fact that I cheered and relieved him a source of annoyance to you? . . . Some of you first doubted the truth of my narrative; then suspected that the letters I produced as coming from him were forgeries; then accused me of sensationalism; then quibbled at the facts I published, and snarled at me as if I had committed a crime. With a simple tale—unvarnished, plain, clear, literal truth—you could find fault! What weakness! What puerility!

But what hurt most were the attacks on his reports on Livingstone's view of the Nile sources, for these were not only insults to him but to his new-found father. To answer them was difficult but he did his best to defend Livingstone. "What have you to say for yourselves, gentlemen geographers?" he wrote in his sharpest style.

A paper written by Colonel Grant . . . was to the effect that Livingstone had conceived a most extravagant idea when he believed that he had found the Sources of the Nile. . . . Colonel Grant was the companion of Speke . . . and he believes implicitly that Speke discovered the Nile source in the river issuing from Victoria. . . . As a friend of Speke's, and as his companion during the expedition, the gallant gentleman dislikes to hear any other person claiming to have discovered another Nile source.

The rancorous controversy raged for a few months but as with all such matters the public soon tired of it, and before the end of the year interest in Stanley and his scoop had waned, and he returned to New York to resume his career as a foreign correspondent for the *Herald*. He was confident that Livingstone would have the last word on the Nile.

15

THE LAST JOURNEY

Livingstone, alone and isolated again in Africa, had of course no inkling of the doubts his theories about the Nile's geography had raised in England. And, while waiting for the caravan that Stanley had arranged to send up to him at Tabora, he made a stunning—and thoroughly unwarranted—leap of faith in his fantastic belief.

As we have seen, when Livingstone turned back from Nyangwe and returned to Ujiji the year before, he had been on his way to prove that the Lualaba became the Nile somewhere downstream of Lake Albert, and it would be reasonable to expect that his plan, after he had been properly re-equipped and resupplied by Stanley, would be to resume that task and trace the Lualaba as far northward as necessary to find, as he told Stanley, "its connection with some portion of the old Nile." But, amazingly enough, even before Stanley left him, he had abandoned this plan. He seems to have entirely forgotten about it or simply to have taken it to be a foregone conclusion that the Lualaba flowed into the Nile. Or, what is more likely, his mind had been finally overcome by his mystical desire to reach the four fountains of Herodotus.

A month before Stanley left for the coast, we find this entry in Livingstone's journal:

It is all but certain that four full-grown gushing fountains rise on the watershed eight days south of Katanga, each of which at no great distance off becomes a large river; and two rivers thus formed flow north to Egypt, the other south to Inner Ethiopia. . . . It may be that these are not the fountains of the Nile mentioned to Herodotus . . . but they are worthy of discovery. . . . I propose to go . . . round the south end of

Tanganyika . . . then across the Chambezi, and round south of Lake Bangweolo, and due west to the ancient fountains. . . . This route will serve to certify that no other sources of the Nile can come from the south without being seen by me.

Livingstone had to wait five months for Stanley's caravan to reach him, and it was a difficult time. March 19, four days after Stanley left, was his fifty-ninth birthday, and he wrote: "My Jesus, my king, my life, my all; I again dedicate my whole self to Thee. Accept me, and grant, O Gracious Father, that ere this year is gone I may finish my task." But he was acutely aware that if he were to finish his task within the year he couldn't afford to be sitting idly in Tabora month after month. First of all, he realized that his health, though improved by the food and medicines Stanley had brought, was in fact incurably undermined, and it could not stand the rigors of African exploration too much longer. Secondly, there was the matter of weather. It soon would be the dry season in the part of Africa where he intended to travel (at the end of April) and he wanted to take advantage of that. The longer he delayed, the more of his traveling would take place after the rains started (in the beginning of December), and that would mean facing impassable terrain and killing fevers again.

But, perhaps most worrisome, the longer he delayed the more he was assailed by doubts.

Ptolemy [he wrote] seems to have gathered up the threads of ancient explorations, and made many springs (six) flow into two Lakes situated East and West. . . . If the Victoria Lake were large, then it and the Albert would probably be the Lakes Ptolemy meant, and it would be pleasant to call them Ptolemy's sources, rediscovered by the toil and enterprise of our countrymen Speke, Grant, and Baker.

A few weeks later he wrote,

I pray the good Lord of all to favour me so as to allow me to discover the ancient fountains of Herodotus, and if there is anything . . . to confirm the precious old documents, the Scriptures of truth, may He permit me to bring it to light, and give me wisdom to make proper use of it.

But then:

I wish I had some of the assurance possessed by others, but I am oppressed with the apprehension that after all it may turn out that I have been following the Congo; and who would risk being put into a cannibal pot and converted into black man for it?

And then ten days later:

In reference to the Nile source I have been kept in perpetual doubt and perplexity.

A month later:

The medical education has led me to a continual tendency to suspend judgement. What a state of blessedness it would have been had I possessed the dead certainty of the homeopathic persuasion, and as soon as I found the Lakes Bangweolo, Moero . . . pouring out their waters down the great central valley, bellowed out, "Hurrah! Eureka!" and gone home in firm and honest belief that I had settled it, and no mistake. Instead of that I am even now not at all "cock-sure" that I have not been following down what may after all be the Congo.

In a letter to London, in which he described the route he intended to take to the fountains of Herodotus, he wrote: "But what if these fountains exist only in my imagination!"

But all he could do now was wait, read books Stanley had brought him, write in his journal, organize and reorganize his notes, conduct Bible classes for native children under the mangoes, count the days.

Dr. Livingstone at work on his journal

If Stanley arrived the 1st of May at Zanzibar—allow 20 days to get men and settle with them = May 20th, men leave Zanzibar 22nd of May. . . . On the road may be 10 days, still to come 30 days . . . ought to arrive 10th or 15th July . . . then engage pagazi half a month = August, 5 months of this year will remain for journey, the whole of 1873 will be swallowed up in work, but in February or March 1874, please the Almighty Disposer of events, I shall complete my task and retire.

Then: "Stanley . . . 100 days gone: he must be in London now." In July: "Wearisome waiting, this; and yet the men can not be here before the middle or the end of the month." A few days later: "Weary! weary! . . . Waiting wearily here, and hoping that the good and loving Father of all may favour me, and help me to finish my work quickly and well."

But then at last the wearisome waiting was over. On August 9 an advance party arrived, and on August 14 the full caravan Stanley sent marched into Tabora. It was, in Stanley's best style, a splendidly outfitted party: 57 carefully chosen porters (one of whom, Jacob Wainwright, deserves to be mentioned by name because of the role he was later to play in Livingstone's service), plus muskets, ammunition, flour, sugar, tea, canned foods, riding donkeys, thousands of yards of trading cloth, and hundreds of pounds of beads and wire. Added to the 5 men, including of course Susi and Chuma, who had remained loyal to Livingstone from the beginning, he now commanded a caravan that would last at least two years, the most luxurious he had ever had in his whole life.

Because wars between Arab slavers and tribesmen blocked the route west back to Ujiji, Livingstone struck off to the southwest and, in early October, reached Lake Tanganyika a little more than halfway between Ujiji and the lake's southern end and there turned southward. All the familiar hardships and mishaps beset the caravan during this leg of the journey: a couple of porters decamped carrying off precious loads of trading cloth; the tsetse fly got to the baggage animals and killed them off one by one; food became increasingly hard to come by; the climate and the terrain along the mountainous eastern shore of Tanganyika proved brutally punishing. And it became quickly apparent just how superficial Livingstone's recovery had been, how unequal his health was to the rigors of African travel. Within a month of setting off he was suffering from malaria, and by the beginning of November from dysentery and anal bleeding. Nevertheless, it was at least still the dry season and, plodding steadily on, the caravan rounded the southern end of Lake Tanganyika in the second week of November, turned west and then south toward Lake Bangweolo.

But then the rains came. For some weeks Livingstone had been listening to the thunder in the east with growing anxiety. On October 30, he had recorded, "Thunder all the morning, and a few drops of rain fell." Then, on November 19: "There are heavy rains now and then every day." By the end of that month: "Very heavy rain and high gusts of wind, which wet us all." And, from the beginning of December onward, the rains became the lamenting refrain of his days, falling in a steady drizzle, bursting from the heavens in sudden, violent downpours, lashing across the land in blinding, impenetrable sheets. "Rain, rain, rain as if it never tired on this watershed." Rivulets and rivers flooded their banks; the terrain was transformed into vast and terrible swamps (which he called sponges) ; snakes and leeches came out; and there was never ever getting dry and warm again.

A leech crawling towards me in the village this morning elicited the Bemba idea that they fall from the sky. . . . 29th or 1st January, 1873.—I am wrong two days. . . . The sponges here are now full and overflowing, from the continuous and heavy rains. . . . Detained by heavy continuous rains. . . . Got off in the afternoon in a drizzle; crossed a rill six feet wide, but now very deep, and with large running sponges on each side . . . then one hour beyond came to a sponge, and a sluggish rivulet 100 yards broad with broad sponges on either bank waist deep, and many leeches. . . . Never was in such a spell of cold rainy weather. . . . The country is covered with brackens, and rivulets occur at least one every hour of the march. These are now deep, and have a broad selvage of sponge. . . . I don't know where we are. . . .

. . . Carrying me across one of the broad deep sedgy rivers is really a very difficult task. One we crossed was at least 2000 feet broad. . . . The first part, the main stream, came up to Susi's mouth, and wetted my seat and legs. One held up my pistol behind, then one after another took a turn, and when he sank into an elephant's foot-print, he required two to lift him, so as to gain a footing on the level, which was over waist deep. Others went on, and bent down the grass, to insure some footing on the side of the elephant's path. Every ten or twelve paces brought us to a clear stream, flowing fast in its own channel, while over all a strong current came bodily through all the rushes and aquatic plants.

"The main stream came up to Susi's mouth."

Under these conditions, Livingstone's health, not surprisingly, steadily disintegrated. From time to time, he would note in his journal:

I lose much blood. . . . I remain because of an excessive haemorrhagic discharge. If the good Lord gives me favour, and permits me to finish my work, I shall thank and bless Him, though it has cost me untold toil, pain, and travel; this trip has made my hair all grey.

And equally unsurprisingly, in his weakness and pain, his mind began to play tricks on him. He started composing imaginary dispatches:

I have the pleasure of reporting to your Lordship that on the —— I succeeded at last in reaching your remarkable fountains, each of which, at no great distance off, becomes a large river. They rise at the base of a swell of land or earthen mound, which can scarcely be called a hill, for it seems only about —— feet above ground level. . . . Possibly these four gushing fountains may be the very same that were mentioned by Herodotus. . . . The geographical position of the mound or low earthen hill, may be for the present taken as latitude —— and longitude ——. The altitude above the sea, ——.

In mid-February, Livingstone reached Lake Bangweolo, but he now had only the vaguest notion where he was. Because of the cease-

less rains, the lake had monumentally overflowed its banks, giving it a
configuration far different from what it had had when Livingstone
had seen it five years before. Because of the relentlessly overcast sky, he
couldn't fix his position by shooting the sun or stars. And the bleak,
featureless marshland all around him provided no landmarks to help
him out. All he knew was that he was somewhere on the lake's northeastern shore. His plan was to go round to the southern end, from
where he would strike out to the southwest toward Katanga and his
fabulous fountains, but he could not see the way to get around. In
fact, he could not properly see the lake's shoreline at all because the
waters of the lake merged imperceptibly with the waters of the flooded
marshland, in places seven feet deep and broken only occasionally by
islets, the crowns of anthills, clumps of reeds, and lotus plants. The
only course that seemed open was to go into the lake, that is, to cross it
from the northeastern to the southeastern shore. But for that canoes
were required.

Canoes could be gotten, apparently, only from a certain Matipa,
the leading chief of the neighborhood, and that involved endlessly
tedious negotiations. In the meantime Livingstone was forced to camp
in the dreadfully unhealthy mosquito-ridden swamps, suffering the
relentless rains and cold, the attacks of driver ants, the painful anal

Discovery of Lake Bangweolo

bleeding. At one point Matipa agreed to hire out some canoes in return for five bundles of brass wire, but reneged on the arrangement. At another, after Livingstone had given him a sharp talking-to, he again agreed but again no canoes were produced. "Matipa says 'Wait' . . . Time is of no value to him. His wife is making him pombe, and will drown all his cares, but mine increase and plague me. . . . I spoke sharply to Matipa for his duplicity. He promises everything and does nothing. . . . Ill all day with my old complaint. . . . The delay is most trying." Livingstone's sixtieth birthday came, March 19: "Thanks to the Almighty Preserver of men for sparing me thus far on the journey of life. Can I hope for ultimate success? So many obstacles have arisen. Let not Satan prevail over me, Oh! my good Lord Jesus."

That morning, nerves stretched to the breaking point, Livingstone, in an uncharacteristic act of violent desperation, marched into Matipa's village, took possession of the chief's hut, and fired a pistol through the roof. That did the trick, for in a few days Livingstone had six canoes and on March 24 had them loaded with his men and goods and set off into the lake.

We punted six hours to a little islet without a tree, and no sooner did we land than a pitiless pelting rain came on. We turned up a canoe to get shelter. . . . The wind tore the tent out of our hands, and damaged it too; the loads are all soaked, and with the cold it's bitterly uncomfortable. . . . Nothing earthly will make me give up my work in despair. I encourage myself in the Lord my God, and go forward.

For some two weeks, he went forward, southeasterly, the canoes trying to follow as closely as possible the reed marshes that vaguely marked the lake shore, each night stopping at another sodden islet in the endless expanse of water.

The flood extends . . . for twenty or thirty miles, and far too broad to be seen across . . . got into a large stream. . . . One canoe sank in it, and we lost a slave girl. . . . Fished up three boxes, and two guns, but the boxes being full of cartridges were much injured. . . . A lion roars mightily. The fishhawk utters his weird voice in the morning, as if he lifted up to a friend at a great distance . . . it is quite impossible at present to tell where land ends, and Lake begins; it is all water, water everywhere. . . . I am pale, bloodless, and weak from bleeding profusely ever since the 31st of March last: an artery gives off a copious stream, and takes away my strength.

That last was the entry under April 10. The party had reached the southeastern shore of the lake, had abandoned the canoes, and was preparing to set off southwestward through the endless marshlands. But Livingstone was now slowly bleeding to death, and it was virtually impossible for him to walk.

Tottered along nearly two hours, and then lay down quite done. Cooked coffee—our last—and went on, but in an hour I was compelled to lie down. Very unwilling to be carried, but on being pressed I allowed the men to help me along by relays.

Two days later he wrote:

After the turtle doves and cocks give out their warning calls to the watchful, the fish-eagle lifts up his remarkable voice. It is pitched in a high falsetto key, very loud, and seems as if he were calling to someone in the other world. Once heard, his weird unearthly voice can never be forgotten—it sticks to one through life.

He had to submit to being carried, and Chuma and Susi constructed a litter for him. His diary entries become shorter, punctuated with pathetic confessions of weakness, the copious loss of blood, the relentlessness of the driving rains, the murderous difficulty of making way through the flooded lands. On April 19, he wrote, "It is not all pleasure this exploration. . . . No observations now, owing to great weakness; I can scarcely hold the pencil." But he still had not given up his quest. On April 25, upon reaching a village where the party intended to spend the night, Livingstone called some of the tribesmen around him and asked them if they knew of a hill around which four rivers took their rise. The chief replied that they had no knowledge of such but went on to explain that they themselves were not travelers and all those who once went on the trading expeditions from their tribe were now dead. Livingstone thanked them and asked them to leave him. On April 27 he scrawled his final diary entry: "Knocked up quite and remain—recover—sent to buy milch goats. We are on the banks of the Molilamo."

Livingstone lived four days longer, and our knowledge of what happened in those days comes from an account provided by his most faithful followers, Chuma and Susi. On April 29, after a day of rest, Livingstone ordered the party to march on southwestward, obviously still in quest of his mystical fountains. He himself was, however, com-

The last mile of Livingstone's travels

pletely unable to walk, and since the door of the hut in which he rested was too small for his litter to be brought through, the walls of the hut had to be broken down before he could be carried from his cot. That day's traveling was brutal. A small river had to be crossed, but Livingstone was unable to sit up in the canoe, and he had to be lifted off his litter, put down gently in its bottom and then lifted again onto the litter after the crossing. Chuma and Susi tell us that his pain was so great from the movements of the march that he repeatedly begged them to set him down and allow him to rest. But, just when it seemed that he wouldn't be able to stand the anguish of being carried a step further, the outlying huts of a village came into sight, Ilala, the village of a chief called Chitambo.

Livingstone was set down under the eaves of a hut to shelter him from the rain while a lodging of reeds and grass was built for him. It took until nightfall, and inquisitive villagers gathered around to peer at the prostrate white man. At last he was moved into the hut. The cot was placed on sticks to keep it out of the muddy water; a crate beside it held the medicine chest and a young boy was put on guard outside the hut to listen in case the master called out for something during the night. But Livingstone slept.

The next morning the chief, Chitambo, came to pay a courtesy call on the white man, but Livingstone was too weak to speak to him and was obliged to ask him to return the next day, when he hoped to be better. In the afternoon he sent for Susi and had him bring his watch so that he could wind it. Then he dozed off again and, as night fell once more, a fire was lighted outside the hut, and the boy took up his vigil there. Around 11 P.M. Livingstone sent for Susi and inquired about some sounds he heard off in the distance. "Are our men making the noise?" he asked faintly. "No," Susi replied, "I can hear from the cries that the people are scaring away a buffalo from their fields." After a few moments, Livingstone asked, "Is this the Luapula?" Susi told him they were at Chitambo's village. *"Sikun' gapi kuenda Luapula?* (How many days is it to the Luapula?)" Livingstone asked, reverting to Swahili. *"Na zani zikutatu, Bwana* (I think it is three days, master)," Susi replied. After a few seconds, Livingstone said, "Oh dear, dear," and dozed off again. An hour later Susi was called again and Livingstone asked him to boil some water, and then, with great difficulty, Livingstone took a dosage of calomel from his medicine chest and had Susi mix it with the hot water in a cup so he could take it. "All right," he said, "you can go now." Those were his last words.

Around 4 A.M. the following morning, May 1, with the first pastel shades of the sun streaking the horizon, the boy who had been placed on guard outside Livingstone's hut called for Susi and Chuma. He said that before he had fallen asleep by the fire he had seen Livingstone pull himself off the cot and kneel by it in prayer. Now, when he awakened a few hours later, he saw that the master was still in the same position. Susi, Chuma, and a few others hurried to the hut. A candle stuck by its own wax to the crate by the cot shed sufficient light for them to see. Livingstone was kneeling by the side of the cot, his body stretched forward, his head buried in 'his hands on the pillow. They watched him for a moment, not sure whether to disturb him at his prayers. But they saw that he didn't move; there was no sign of breathing. At last one went into the hut and placed his hand gently against Livingstone's cheek. It was nearly cold. Livingstone had been dead for some time.

What happened now remains one of the most remarkable stories in the annals of African exploration. By all rights, Livingstone's death should have shattered his party. The sixty or so Africans of the caravan were hundreds and in some cases thousands of miles from their homes. For more than eight months they had followed Livingstone from

Tabora, going where he chose to go, wandering through the endless swamps with him, suffering the cold and the rain and the fevers with him, facing all the terrors he led them into, leaving all the decisions to him, relying completely on him to get them to their goal and back again. And now suddenly he was dead and they found themselves stranded in the middle of the wilderness, in a strange land with no real idea where they were. There would be every reason to expect them to panic, to abandon Livingstone's body and his journals, to plunder the stores of the caravan for its most precious goods, and set off in a disorderly and desperate flight in whatever direction they thought might lead them homeward. But they did none of these things. Rather they acted with a calm and courage and discipline and intelligence that must still elicit admiration a century later.

The news of Livingstone's death was quietly spread to each member of the caravan, and in the first light of morning they all gathered in front of the master's hut to discuss what they should do. Two decisions were made without any hesitation. The first was that Susi and Chuma, who had been with Livingstone for more than seven years and who, in the words of the others, were "old men in travelling and in hardships," were to take over as the leaders of the caravan. The second was that they would not abandon Livingstone: they would take him home. The second of these decisions was remarkable enough in revealing just how profound was the affection Livingstone had elicited from his followers. But it is all the more remarkable in that these followers were well aware of the problems they would create for themselves by trying to carry a corpse halfway across Africa. The tribesmen through whose regions they intended to pass believed that the spirits of the dead caused terrible trouble and destruction among the living. Thus, to carry a stranger's corpse through a tribe's territory was extremely dangerous. At the very best, the punishment for such a horrendous deed would be the payment of a stiff fine. At the worst, the bearers of the corpse could expect, if discovered, to be attacked and killed as evil witches. Nevertheless, Livingstone's followers resolved to run the risks. What they had to do, however, if they hoped to have any chance of succeeding, was keep what they were doing a secret.

The first person they had to keep it a secret from was Chitambo, the chief of the village they were in. So Chuma went to the chief later that morning and, telling him that Livingstone was still too ill to be seen, asked Chitambo for permission to move the white man out of the village to a quieter, more secluded place. Chitambo consented, and so that afternoon a new hut was built and Livingstone's corpse, covered with cloth and a blanket, was carried to it on a litter. However, not long after, Chitambo learned the truth and hurried to the new hut to confront Susi and Chuma. The two men stood their ground tensely, ready for the first of the series of troubles they could expect from their extraordinary decision. But it seems that Chitambo himself had some-how been affected by the force of Livingstone's personality. And we find him saying, "Why did you not tell me the truth? I know that your master died last night. You were afraid to let me know, but do not fear any longer. . . . I know that you have no bad motives in coming to our land, and death often happens to travellers in their journeys." Encouraged by his attitude, Chuma and Susi then told him of their plan to carry Livingstone home. Chitambo tried to dissuade them, urging them to bury the body then and there. But, when he saw the two men's determination, he agreed not to interfere with whatever they wanted to do and brought a party of mourners, including his wives, drummers, and warriors with bows and arrows, to Livingstone's hut and led them in wailing lamentations for the dead white man.

Within, Susi, Chuma, and another member of the caravan held a thick blanket as a screen in front of the emaciated body lying on the cot. Jacob Wainwright, who had joined the party in Tabora and could read and write English, stood to one side with his prayer book. And a porter by the name of Farijala, who had worked as a servant for a doctor on Zanzibar, stepped forward to begin the operation. He made a careful incision upward from the abdomen. Then he removed Livingstone's heart and viscera and poured a quantity of salt into the body. (During this process all noticed a clot of coagulated blood as large as a man's fist blocking the lower intestines, which, if it was not the reason for Livingstone's death, must have caused him horri-fying pain in his final days.) The heart and internal organs were then placed in a tin box, and, while Jacob Wainwright read the ser-vice from his prayer book, the box was buried in the earthen floor of the hut. Some brandy was then poured into the corpse's mouth as an additional preservative and, as at long last the dry season was return-ing again, the roof of the hut was removed so that the body could be exposed to the drying power of the sun. This took fourteen days, and once each day Susi or Chuma would go into the hut and change the position of the corpse. When the body was judged tolerably dry, it was wrapped in calico and then placed in a cylinder of bark. Over this, sailcloth was sewn and heavily tarred to make it waterproof, and this strange bier was then lashed to poles so it could be carried by two men. Wainwright now carved an inscription on a tree near where the body had lain—Livingstone, May 4, 1873. Two strong posts with a crosspiece were erected in the form of a doorway, and Chitambo promised to guard both the tree and this doorway from destruction. And so, sometime in the middle of May, Susi and Chuma led the caravan out of Chitambo's village on the more than 1000-mile journey back from whence it had come. It is a measure of Susi's and Chuma's magnificent leadership abilities that, despite the ruggedness of the terrain, the ravages of disease, and the hostilities of tribesmen to the strange burden they carried, the caravan reached Tabora, with the loss of only ten men, in five months' time.

Meanwhile, back in England, ever since Stanley's successful expedition, the Royal Geographical Society had been suffering from a guilty conscience for having taken a far too sanguine view of Livingstone's fate and for having left it to an American newspaperman to find and help him. Determined never to let that happen again, the Royal Geographical Society decided to send out *two* relief expeditions just to make doubly sure that Livingstone was all right. Both departed from England the same day, November 30, 1872, when Livingstone was, in fact, still all right, making his way around Lake Tanganyika toward Lake Bangweolo before the rains had fully set in.

One of these, headed by a young naval lieutenant by the name of William J. Grandy, is of interest only because it reveals that at last there was a growing recognition of the true significance of Livingstone's discoveries. More and more geographers were coming around to the opinion that the system of rivers and lakes that Livingstone had found formed the watershed not of the Nile but the Congo. Convinced that Livingstone himself would come to realize this as well, they believed that he would ultimately trace the Lualaba along its great westward arc, and therefore the most likely way to meet up with him would be in his inevitable journey down to the Atlantic. Thus it was Grandy's task to push up toward Livingstone along the Congo River and provide him with whatever assistance he might need. But, even if he failed to meet Livingstone by this route, the expedition would not be a waste because Grandy was further instructed to explore and map the Congo's course upstream into the interior as far as he possibly could. This was the first expedition to the Congo since Tuckey's and, if it wasn't as terrible a catastrophe as Tuckey's, it was even less successful.

Grandy's party arrived at Loanda, in Angola, on January 22, 1873, and from there struck overland northeastward toward the Congo. Because by then the rainy season had started in this part of Africa, because too of the difficulties of getting porters, and perhaps mainly because of Grandy's inexperience, it wasn't until October that the party reached the old royal capital of the vanished Kingdom of Kongo, São Salvador. By this time Livingstone, of course, was dead and his body was on its way home with his faithful followers. But Grandy could not know this, and he pushed his caravan down to the banks of the Congo. There he was stopped for the next six months, engaged in interminable negotiations for guides and porters and canoes for the journey upriver. By the time he was ready to move on upriver into the interior, however, the news of Livingstone's death had at last reached him, and he abandoned the project.

The second expedition was under the command of Verney Lovett Cameron. He also was a young naval lieutenant (28 years old) but he had had some experience in Africa before this assignment. He had served with Napier in the British punitive campaign against Theodore in Ethiopia, after which he had been posted to Zanzibar, where he participated in the British fleet's efforts to blockade the Arab slave traffic. Often taking his shore leaves to visit the East African mainland, he developed an appetite and ambition for African exploration. This was his first chance and, unlike Grandy, he wasn't going to let anything—even Livingstone's death—deter him from making a success of it. As a consequence, he in fact was to add more to Europe's understanding of the Congo's geography than Grandy or Tuckey ever did, even though he was never expected to come anywhere near the river. For he was sent out to meet Livingstone by the conventional route from the East African coast westward into the interior.

Cameron's party, which included three other white men—a naval surgeon by the name of Dillon, an army lieutenant by the name of Murphy, and Robert Moffat, a nephew of Livingstone's by marriage—arrived in Zanzibar just about the same time that Grandy arrived in Angola. Following what was then an increasingly routine procedure, Cameron assembled his supplies and porters, including some who had served with Stanley, then took a dhow across to Bagamoyo, where he arrived in the beginning of February, and, after all the usual delays, struck off inland along the familiar Arab caravan route at the end of March 1873. During the trek, Cameron and his white companions were struck down with severe cases of malaria. By May, Moffat was dead of it, and by August, when the caravan reached Tabora, the others were half crazed and half blind from the fever, so they halted the march until they were sufficiently recovered to go on. It was a painfully slow recovery and, indeed, never completed—within a few months Dillon was to blow his brains out and Murphy was to desert the expedition—and on October 20 they were still there, bedridden and virtually helpless.

Then, Cameron tells us,

as I lay on my bed, prostrate, listless, and enfeebled from repeated attacks of fever; my mind dazed and confused with whirling thoughts and fantasies of home and those dear ones far away . . . my servant . . . came running into my tent with a letter in his hand. I snatched it from him, asking at the same moment where it came from. His only reply was, "Some man bring him."

Tearing it open, this is what Cameron found:

Sir, We have heard in the month of August that you have started from Zanzibar for Unyenyembe, and again and again lately we have heard your arrival—your father died by disease beyond the country of Bisa, but we have carried the corpse with us. 10 of our soldiers are lost and some have died. Our hunger presses us to ask you some clothes to buy provisions for our soldiers, and we should have an answer that when we shall enter there shall be firing guns or not, and if you permit us to fire guns then send some powder. We have wrote these few words in the place of the Sultan or King Mbowra. The writer Jacob Wainwright. Dr. Livingstone Exped.

Cameron tells us that

Being half-blind, it was with some difficulty that I deciphered the writing, and then, failing to attach any definite meaning to it, I went to Dillon. His brain was in much the same state of confusion from fever as mine, and we read it again together, each having the same vague idea—Could it be our own father who was dead?

At last, Cameron thought to have the bearer of the letter brought to him. It was Chuma, and then Cameron understood. Susi, Chuma, and the others, on their long hard journey bearing Livingstone home, had come across an Arab caravan from Bagamoyo which told them that an English expedition had arrived on the east coast, headed for Tabora, commanded by one of Livingstone's sons. It is not clear how this misunderstanding arose. It is possible that the Arabs misunderstood Moffat's relationship to Livingstone and converted the nephew by marriage into a son. But in any case, on hearing the news, Chuma had run on ahead with Jacob Wainwright's letter, and a few days later the rest of the troop arrived, carrying Livingstone's body into Tabora.

The reaction to the arrival of Livingstone's body was curious. Murphy immediately seized on the occasion to quit the expedition and return to the coast, on the grounds, as Cameron tells us, "that nothing further remained for us to do." Dillon was clearly too sick to consider doing anything, and it was agreed that he should be carried back to the coast in a litter (he would kill himself before he got there). But Cameron was all for going on. He intended to make a name for himself as an explorer and he wasn't about to let Livingstone's death forestall him. He rummaged through Livingstone's effects and took a number of instruments that he felt would be useful for his explorations, and though Chuma and Susi were appalled at this there was nothing they could do to prevent him. But, when Cameron went on to suggest that they bury Livingstone's corpse in Tabora and not bother to carry it down to the coast, they firmly declined. They were taking Livingstone home and they would not stop until they had completed the sacred task they had set for themselves. On November 9 they once more took up their burden and, with Murphy and Dillon now a part of their caravan, set off on the final leg of their journey to the coast while, Cameron tells us, "my cry was 'Westward ho!' "

Cameron reached Ujiji just about the same time that Livingstone's cortege reached Bagamoyo, February 15, 1874. Chuma had gone ahead to Zanzibar, and the next day, February 16, a British cruiser, the H.M.S. *Vulture* arrived at Bagamoyo and took Livingstone's body aboard and transported it to the island. There it was taken from its coffin of sailcloth, bark, and calico, and a medical examination revealed a skull of European shape with white straight hair and, though the features were no longer recognizable, there could be no doubt that this was Livingstone's body. It was then laid in a simple coffin of zinc and wood and put aboard the next mailboat bound for England, where it arrived on April 15.

Only one of the Africans—Jacob Wainwright—accompanied Livingstone on this journey. Chuma and Susi and the others, who had shown themselves so brave and devoted and who would never understand the callous lack of response to their courage and devotion, were paid off and sent on their way. To be sure, a few months later Susi and Chuma were taken to England to help edit Livingstone's last journals and fill in the narrative of the days after his death, but by that time they were too late to attend his funeral. A year later the Royal Geographical Society thought to strike commemorative medals for the sixty men who had carried Livingstone out of the heart of the interior, but by that time those men were scattered all over East Africa, and most never received the medals. When Livingstone's journals were published, an attempt was made to acknowledge the remarkable and noble deed of these men.

Nothing but such leadership and staunchness as that which organized the march home . . . and distinguished it throughout, could have brought Livingstone's bones to our land or his last notes and maps to the outer world. To none does the feat seem so marvellous as to those who know Africa and the difficulties which must have beset both the first and the last in the enterprise. Thus in his death, not less than in his life, David Livingstone bore testimony to that goodwill and kindliness which exists in the heart of the African.

16

---◆━◆━◆---

THE EXTRAORDINARY ENTERPRISE

Stanley learned of Livingstone's death on February 25, 1874, ten days after the explorer's body had been brought to Zanzibar and the news had been telegraphed around the world. As it happened, Stanley was himself just returning from Africa. He had spent the preceding four months in the Gold Coast, covering a British punitive campaign against the Ashantee for the *Herald,* and it was on his way home, when the British warship H.M.S. *Dauntless* on which he was traveling called at St. Vincent in the Cape Verde Islands that he received the cable telling him that he had once again lost a father.

Stanley reached England a month before Livingstone's body, and, taking rooms at the Langham Hotel in London, he used that time to go through all the file stories at the *Herald*'s office on Livingstone's death to convince himself that it was really true and not just another of those many false reports that had dogged the explorer in his last years of wandering. And, once he was, he wrote, "Dear Livingstone! another sacrifice to Africa! His mission, however, must not be allowed to cease; others must go forward and fill the gap." And then: "May I be selected to succeed him in opening up Africa to the shining light of Christianity!"

On April 15, Stanley went down to Southampton to meet the funeral cortege. It was a wet and windy day, but massive crowds, the mayor and aldermen of the town, a military band, a company of the Royal Horse Artillery and a procession of black-draped carriages had been waiting on the quay since dawn. At nine o'clock the mail steamer from Zanzibar entered the harbor with Livingstone's coffin, draped in the Union Jack, on the open deck. Then, as it was brought down the gangway, the Royal Horse fired the first of a series of twenty-one-gun salutes and the band began the mournful refrain of the "Death March" from *Saul*. The waiting carriages escorted the coffin to the railway station, where a special train carried it to London. There it lay in state in the map room of the Royal Geographical Society for two days. On the morning of April 18, declared a day of national mourning, it was transported through the crowded silent streets to Westminster Abbey, where, down the nave beyond the tomb of the Unknown Soldier, it was interred. Stanley was one of the pallbearers. Another was Jacob Wainwright.

Stanley confided to his diary that day that the effect the news of Livingstone's death had on him "after the first shock had passed away, was to fire me with a resolution to complete his work, to be, if God willed it, the next martyr to geographical science, or, if my life was to be spared, to clear up not only the secrets of the Great River throughout its course, but also all that remained still problematic and incomplete."

Stanley's desire to finish Livingstone's work was for him unquestionably genuine. He loved and admired the man; he could deeply sympathize with Livingstone's tragic disappointment at having failed to settle the mystery of the Nile; and as the last European to have spoken to the explorer, he felt personally called upon to vindicate Livingstone's geographical theories.

But there was something else at work in Stanley's psyche at this time. He was still suffering bitterly from the mixed and often insulting reception he had received when he had returned from Africa after finding Livingstone. He could not forget that his accomplishment at first had been dismissed as a hoax and then belittled as a publicity stunt, and he was painfully aware that he remained in the eyes of the geographers and social establishment and the educated public merely a journalist, a daring and adventurous journalist to be sure, but merely a journalist nevertheless. He had gained a certain kind of fame and something of a fortune but he had not acquired the respect and reputation accorded to the true heroes of African exploration. And more than anything else that was what he craved. "What I have already endured in that accursed Africa," he wrote, "amounts to nothing in men's estimation. Surely if I can resolve any of the problems which such travelers as Dr. Livingstone, Captains Burton, Speke, and Grant, and Sir Samuel Baker left unsettled, people must needs believe that I discovered Livingstone." And it was this, perhaps more than his love for Livingstone, that inspired him to plan the most amazingly audacious journey of African exploration that had ever been conceived let alone undertaken, one that would make him inarguably the greatest African explorer of them all.

It consisted of three parts. First, he would resolve the problems left unsettled by Speke. As we've seen, Speke believed Victoria to be a huge single sheet of water whose outlet was the source of the White Nile. Since Speke's death, this view, although correct, had fallen into disrepute. The most definitive map of Africa published around this time—that of Georg Schweinfurth's in *The Heart of Africa*—showed Victoria as five separate lakes, and even Grant, Speke's faithful companion on his second expedition, had tired of arguing otherwise. So Stanley proposed to settle this matter one way or the other by doing what no one else had yet done: circumnavigate the lake.

Second, there were the disputes about Burton's Lake Tanganyika and Baker's Lake Albert. Each of these men also believed *his* lake was a single body of water and the Nile's source. Baker was willing to concede that Albert might share the distinction with Victoria, that its outlet might join Victoria's to form the great river. But Burton held that Tanganyika was the Nile's only source, arguing that its effluent river, which neither he nor anyone else had yet found, flowed into Albert. So Stanley decided to undertake answering these questions as well.

And, finally, there was Livingstone's Lualaba. From the explorer's last journals, which had been brought home with his body, Stanley could see that Livingstone had done a fairly complete job of mapping the watershed of this river. What he hadn't done, however, allowing his obsessive quest for the four fountains of Herodotus to divert him, was to trace the Lualaba far enough northward to prove whether it was the Nile, as he had contended, or the Congo, as a growing number of geographers now believed. So Stanley planned, after settling all the outstanding questions about Victoria, Albert, and Tanganyika, to follow the Lualaba wherever it took him, down the Nile to the Mediterranean or down the Congo to the Atlantic Ocean.

This was the scheme for a journey of more than 5000 miles, most of it through country where no European had ever gone before and further in distance than Livingstone had traveled in all the seven years of his final wanderings. Stanley realized that it would require massive financial backing. He estimated it at over £12,000 sterling or $60,000 and he knew that the New York *Herald* could not be expected to put up that much. (For all Bennett's largess when he sent Stanley off to find Livingstone he had been appalled at the amount of money the scoop had cost him.) So Stanley first turned to the London *Daily Telegraph.* The *Telegraph,* which around this time had emerged as the leading British newspaper, had a popular, racy style much like that of the *Herald,* and what's more its deputy editor, Edwin Arnold, was a fellow of the Royal Geographical Society and one of the few backers Stanley had in that group. Thus, Stanley could count on an intelligent hearing for his plans from Arnold, and he could expect Bennett's competitive spirit to be aroused by the idea that an opposition newspaper might beat him to a scoop.

As Stanley tells the story, he was out strolling the streets of London not long after Livingstone's funeral and decided to look in on Arnold at the *Telegraph*'s offices. Their conversation drifted to Livingstone and from there to the work he had left incomplete. "What is there to do?" Arnold asked. Stanley outlined his threefold scheme. "Do you think you can settle all this, if we commission you?" Arnold asked. Stanley tells us he replied: "While I live, there will be something done. If I survive the time required to perform all the work, all shall be done." A telegram was sent off to Bennett in New York asking him if he would be willing to split the cost with the *Telegraph* of "sending Stanley out to Africa to complete the discoveries of Speke, Burton, and Livingstone." There was only a twenty-four-hour wait. Stanley had judged his boss's temper correctly. Bennett's cable in reply contained only one work: "Yes."

Stanley was anxious to get started as quickly as possible so as to be under way in Africa by the beginning of the dry season. He made a brief trip back to New York in June to put his personal affairs in order and then spent the next two months in London preparing the extraordinary enterprise. He bought every available book on Africa and African exploration, more than 130 he tells us, and cluttered up his rooms at the Langham Hotel with maps and newspapers and manuscripts. "Until late hours I sat up, inventing and planning, sketching out routes, laying out lengthy lines of possible exploration." During the day, he went out shopping in the London stores for the hundreds of items on the endless lists of supplies he drew up. As he intended to spend so much of his time exploring lakes and rivers, he decided to bring along his own boats and put in orders for a yawl, a gig, and a barge, the last of which he designed himself so that it could be disassembled into sections for easier portage.

Stanley also used this time to recruit some white assistants. There was no dearth of volunteers. At the time the papers announced the joint Anglo-American enterprise, "applications by the score poured into the offices of the *Daily Telegraph* and the *New York Herald* for employment," Stanley tells us.

Over 1200 letters were received from generals, colonels, captains, lieutenants, midshipmen, engineers, commissioners of hotels, mechanics, waiters, cooks, servants, somebodies and nobodies, spiritual mediums and magnetizers, etc., etc. They all knew Africa, were perfectly acclimatized, were quite sure they would please me, would do important services, save me from any number of troubles by their ingenuity and resources, take me up in balloons or by flying carriages, make us all invisible by their magic arts, or by the science of magnetism would cause all savages to fall asleep while we might pass anywhere without trouble.

At the end, though, Stanley chose three rather conventional young British lads. The brothers Edward and Francis (Frank) Pocock were Kentish fishermen and accomplished boatsmen, "who bore the reputation of being honest and trustworthy," while Frederick Barker was a desk clerk at the Langham Hotel, "who, smitten with a desire to go to Africa, was not to be dissuaded by reports of its unhealthy climate, its dangerous fevers, or the uncompromising views of exploring life given to him." Additionally, and for some inexplicable reason, Stanley bought five dogs to take with him, and then after a few farewell dinners departed from England on August 15, 1874. Six weeks later he was once again in Zanzibar, 28 months after he had left it with the scoop of the century, but this time he was there as an explorer and not a journalist.

The island was in the midst of great changes. Since the opening of the Suez Canal, it was no longer quite the remote, exotic, clove-scented outpost. The island's European colony now numbered over 70, and America as well as practically every major European power maintained a consulate there. A mail steamer called every month, and the harbor was jammed with the vessels of a dozen nations plying the Indies trade. But the biggest change that had occurred since Stanley left it was the end of the island's booming market in slaves. Largely owing to Livingstone's propaganda, and most especially his vivid, heart-breaking account of the massacre at Nyangwe, the British government had been incited to threaten the sultan of Zanzibar with a naval blockade if he didn't shut down the island's slave market. And, though slaving continued in the African mainland, with the bloody traffic passing through other markets, Zanzibar's marketplace had been bought up by the Anglicans, and a huge red-brick church was under construction on the site when Stanley arrived.

In characteristic fashion, he immediately set about assembling his caravan, recruiting first a reliable cadre from among the men who had served with him or Livingstone before and with whose help he meant to select and hire the rest of his force. But, before this could begin, Stanley tells us, "a preliminary deliberative palaver" or *shauri* was necessary. "The chiefs arranged themselves in a semicircle . . . and I sat *a la Turque* fronting them." After a few minutes of formalities, a spokesman for the group said, "A traveller journeys not without knowing whither he wanders. We have come to ascertain what lands you are bound for." Stanley, using a

low tone of voice, as though the information about to be imparted to the intensely interested and eagerly listening group were too important to speak it loud . . . described in brief outline the prospective journey, in broken Kiswahili. As country after country was mentioned of which they had hitherto but vague ideas, and river after river, lake after lake named, all of which I hoped with their trusty aid to explore carefully, various ejaculations expressive of wonder and joy, mixed with a little alarm, broke from their lips, but when I concluded, each of the group drew a long breath, and almost simultaneously they uttered admiringly, "Ah, fellows, this is a journey worthy to be called a journey!"

"But, master," said they, after recovering themselves, "this long journey will take years to travel—six, nine or ten years." "Nonsense," I replied. "Six, nine, or ten years! What can you be thinking of? It takes the Arabs nearly three years to reach Ujiji, it is true, but, if you remember, I was but sixteen months from Zanzibar to Ujiji and back . . . If I were quick on my first journey, am I likely to be slow now? Am I much older than I was then? Am I less strong? Do I not know what travel is now? Was I not like a boy then, and am I not now a man? You remember while going to Ujiji I permitted the guide to show the way, but when we were returning who was it that led the way? Was it not I . . . ? Very well then, let us finish the shauri, and go."

By mid-November they were ready to go. Some 356 pagazis (porters) and askaris (armed soldiers for an escort) had been hired and, though he planned to travel nearly three times as far and had almost twice as many men as on his previous expedition, Stanley assembled only 8 tons of supplies versus the 6 tons the last time. He had learned from experience what was really needed and, what's more, this time he wanted to travel light for speed. The goods were broken down into 60-pound loads for each porter to carry, and they included (among the usual wire, beads, cloth, bedding, ropes, tents, medicines, ammunition, guns, scientific instruments, and so on) photographic equipment (the first ever to be taken into Africa), five cut-throat razors in a case, shaving mirrors, ivory-backed hairbrushes, eau de cologne, and a few meerschaum pipes, one with Stanley's monogram on the bowl. But clearly the centerpiece of the caravan was the portable barge that Stanley had designed. It was 40 feet long, 6 feet wide and 30 inches deep, made of Spanish cedar, equipped with oars and a sail and capable of being disassembled into five sections, each light enough to be carried by two men. It was to prove to be the single most valuable piece of equipment on the expedition, and Stanley christened it the *Lady Alice*.

Who the lady named Alice was has long been a titillating mystery of the Stanley expedition, and only recently, in Richard Hall's biography of the explorer, was it at last cleared up. It seems that Stanley, just a few weeks after Livingstone's funeral, had fallen in love. The girl who had won his heart was Alice Pike, the 17-year-old daughter of an American whiskey millionaire, who was visiting London with her family at the time. They met at a dinner party at the Langham Hotel arranged by a mutual friend, and they seem to have seen each other practically every day after that. Although Alice had other suitors, Stanley was able to write only a few days after meeting her, "I fear that if Miss Alice gives me as much encouragement long as she has been giving me lately, I shall fall in love with her." Stanley, whom Alice preferred to call by his middle name Morton because it had a more melodious ring, was then already in the midst of his preparations for his African journey, but when the Pikes returned to New York, Stanley, on the pretext of needing to see Bennett, followed shortly thereafter. In mid-July he proposed to Alice and they signed a marriage pact: "We solemnly pledge ourselves to be faithful to each other and to be married to one another on the return of Henry Morton Stanley from Africa. We call God to witness this our pledge in writing." On their last evening together, they took a walk in Central Park and "She raised her lips in tempting proximity and I kissed her on her lips, on her eyes, on her cheeks and her neck, and she kissed me in return." She gave him two photographs of herself to carry with him on his travels, and he promised that he would return in two years.

And so, on November 17, when he set off from Bagamoyo, he was intent on keeping this rendezvous with love.

The bugle mustered the people to rank themselves. . . . Four chiefs a few hundred yards in front; next the twelve guides clad in red robes of Jobo, bearing the wire coils; then a long file 270 strong, bearing cloth, wire, beads, and sections of the Lady Alice; after them thirty six women and ten boys, children of some of the chiefs and boat-bearers, following their mothers and assisting them with trifling loads of utensils, followed by the riding asses, Europeans and gun-bearers; the long line closed by sixteen chiefs who act as rearguard . . . in all, 356 souls. . . . The lengthy line occupies nearly half a mile of the path which at the present day is the commercial and exploring highway into the Lake regions.

Stanley knew that he was not the only European traveling in those regions at this time. As we have seen, Verney Lovett Cameron, who had been sent out to assist Livingstone and who, after learning of Livingstone's death, had decided to continue on his own expedition of exploration, had reached Ujiji in February, nine months before Stanley left Bagamoyo. Moreover, as Stanley knew at this time, Cameron had sailed from Ujiji down the eastern shore of Lake Tanganyika, around its southern end, and part way up the western shore, and had then returned to Ujiji in May. From there, Cameron could be expected to have set off from Ujiji again, this time in an effort to reach the Lualaba and do what Livingstone had failed to do, sail northward on it to see if it was really the Nile or rather the Congo. All reports indicated that Cameron was having a very difficult time of it, and his progress was desperately slow, but he had eighteen months' headstart on Stanley, and by the time Stanley completed his explorations of Victoria and Albert, which he intended to do before ever heading for the Lualaba, that lead would have lengthened to over three years. So, as Stanley now led his caravan into the African interior, he was a man not only hurrying to a rendezvous with love, but in a terribly handicapped race with a rival for the most cherished prize of African exploration.

And the way he proceeded showed it. Nothing could have been more different from Livingstone's march into the interior. He himself had acknowledged it would be. "My methods will not be Livingstone's. Each man has his own way," he had written before setting out, and his way was a series of forced marches, an overpowering of obstacles, harsh, relentless discipline, a heavy loss of life, but finally a speedy attainment of the objective. He reached the town of Mpwapwa, about halfway between the coast and Tabora, in less than a month, whereas it had taken Cameron four. Here Stanley turned off the well-beaten track of the Arab caravan route and blazed a new trail north for Lake Victoria.

The rains began and with that all the Europeans, including Stanley, came down with fevers, and, to make matters worse, the country they were passing through was beset by famine. The further northward they went the more difficult it became to acquire food. The local tribesmen either just didn't have any or what little they had was too precious to barter away for Stanley's beads, wire, and cloth at anything less than exorbitant prices. On Christmas, he wrote to Alice Pike:

How your kind woman's heart would pity me and mine. . . . I am in a centre-pole tent, seven by eight. As it rained all day yesterday, the tent was set over wet ground. . . . The tent walls are disfigured by large splashes of mud, and the tent corners hang down limp and languid, and there is such an air of forlornness and misery about its very set that it increases my own misery. . . . I sit on a bed raised about a foot above the sludge, mournfully reflecting on my condition. Outside, the people have evidently a fellow feeling with me, for they appear to me like beings with strong suicidal intentions or perhaps they mean to lie still, inert until death relieves them. It has been raining heavily the last two or three days, and an impetuous downpour of sheet rain has just ceased. On the march, rain is very disagreeable; it makes the clayey path slippery, and the loads heavier by being saturated, while it half ruins the cloths. It makes us dis-spirited, wet, and cold, added to which we are hungry. . . . I myself have not had a piece of meat for ten days. My food is boiled rice, tea and coffee, and soon I shall be reduced to eating native porridge, like my own people. I weighed 180 lbs. when I left Zanzibar, but under this diet I have been reduced to 134 lbs. within thirty-eight days. The young Englishmen are in the same impoverished condition of body, and unless we reach some more flourishing country . . . we must soon become mere skeletons.

But it would be some time before more flourishing country would be reached, and in the meantime matters steadily deteriorated. Porters deserted, others were killed off by disease or hunger, the riding donkeys and the dogs Stanley had brought with him dropped off one by one, and on January 17 the first of the Europeans, Edward Pocock, died of typhus. Then, when it appeared that the situation couldn't possibly get any worse, the local tribesmen turned openly hostile. Bands of warriors armed with spears and knobsticks began harassing the caravan, attacking and killing stragglers and stealing their loads, and in one pitched battle, which lasted three days, 22 of Stanley's men were killed. Yet through it all Stanley never once faltered in his harsh, disciplined, single-minded methods, and with bulldog persistence he reached his objective. The cost was high: of the 356 men who had started out with him from Bagamoyo only 166 were left. But on February 27, 1875, having covered the 720 miles in the record-breaking time of 103 days, Stanley reached Lake Victoria at the town of Kagheyi, near present-day Mwanza in Tanzania. He was only the fourth European to lay eyes on it since Speke discovered it nearly seventeen years before, and he would be the first to prove that it was a single lake and not several, map its shoreline, and establish its incredible extent. (At 26,000 square miles in area, Victoria is the largest lake in Africa and the second largest, after Lake Superior, in the world.)

Food was plentiful here and the people of Kagheyi friendly, so Stanley selected the spot to set up a base camp for the second stage of his expedition: the circumnavigation of Lake Victoria. He gave himself a week to recuperate from the grueling march from the coast, during which time he hired on additional pagazis and askaris to bring the party's strength up to about 280, resupplied the caravan, and had the *Lady Alice* assembled and launched on the lake. His plan was to leave the bulk of his caravan at Kagheyi under the command of the two remaining Englishmen, Fred Barker and Frank Pocock, while he sailed once around the lake with a small party and, on his return, collect all the men for the next stage of the expedition: the exploration of Lake Albert.

The day he was ready to depart, he called for volunteers. There were none. Victoria had a fearful reputation among the tribesmen.

There were, they said, a people dwelling on its shores who were gifted with tails; another who trained enormous and fierce dogs for war; another tribe of cannibals, who preferred human flesh to all other kinds of meat. The lake was so large it would take years to trace its shores, and who then at the end of that time would remain alive?

Again he asked for volunteers and again the response was dead silence. "Will you let me go alone?" he then asked. "No," was the reply. "What am I to do?" Stanley asked. Manwa Sera, the chief captain of the caravan, said: "Master, have done with these questions. Command your party. All your people are your children, and they will not disobey you. While you ask them as a friend, no one will offer his services. Command them, and they will go."

So Stanley selected eleven men, had the *Lady Alice* provisioned with flour and dried fish, bales of cloth and beads and other odds and ends, gave final instructions to Barker and Pocock, wrote a love letter to "my darling Alice," signing it Morton, and set sail on March 8, traveling in a counter-clockwise direction up the lake's eastern shore. The first half of the circumnavigation was essentially uneventful. On a few occasions, lakeshore peoples launched war canoes from their villages and made as if to attack the *Lady Alice,* but in every case the encounters ended amicably, without any shots being fired and with an exchange of gifts. But what it lacked in adventure this leg of the journey made up for in its contribution to geography. By the time Stanley reached the Kingdom of Buganda at the northern end of the lake in the beginning of April, he could report that it was indeed a vast single expanse as Speke had guessed, and he wrote:

Speke has now the full glory of having discovered the largest inland sea on the continent of Africa, also its principal affluent as well as outlet. I must also give him credit for having understood the geography of the countries we travelled through better than any of those who so persistently opposed his hypothesis.

Stanley spent a little less than two weeks in Buganda. The same Kabaka or king, Mtesa, was on the throne as when Speke and Grant had visited the kingdom in 1862 but he was apparently a much changed man. Mtesa then was a slim, well-built youth in his early twenties, who affected a weird stiff-legged walk, which he imagined resembled that of a lion, and who was given to having people killed in the most atrocious ways for the perverse fun of it. He ruled by pure terror and Speke regarded him as a savage, blood-thirsty monster. But the intervening thirteen years had done much to mature the king, for we find Stanley writing in his diary on the evening of his first visit with him:

Speke described a youthful prince, vain and heartless, a wholesale murderer and tyrant, one who delighted in fat women. Doubtless he described what he saw, but it is far from being the state of things now. Mtesa has impressed me as being an intelligent and distinguished prince . . . a prince well worthy the most hearty sympathies Europe can give him.

Mtesa treated Stanley grandly. He sent out a fleet of six beautiful war canoes to escort the *Lady Alice* to his royal capital, on the Victoria lakeshore (near present-day Kampala in Uganda), where 1000 warriors greeted the arrival of the white man with volley after volley from their muskets while drums sounded, banners waved, and another thousand people roared cheers of welcome. A compound of handsome grass huts was put at Stanley's disposal, and he was loaded down with gifts. A naval display was arranged in which 40 war canoes containing a total of 1200 men "went through the performance of attack and defence on water." The Kabaka took him on a crocodile hunt accom-

Mtesa, the Emperor of Uganda

Stanley is received by King Mtesa's bodyguard

panied by 200 riflemen and invited him each day to his sumptuous palace for hours of discussion on every conceivable topic. Stanley's admiration grew.

He has very intelligent and agreeable features [he wrote after a few days], reminding me of the great stone images at Thebes, and of the statues in the museum of Cairo. He has the same fulness of lips, but their grossness is relieved by the general expression of amiability blended with dignity that pervades his face, and the large, lustrous, lambent eyes that lend it a strange beauty.

Stanley was so overwhelmed that he himself felt constrained to suggest that

either Mtesa is a very admirable man, or that I am a very impressionable traveller, or that Mtesa is so perfect in the art of duplicity and acted so clever the part, that I became his dupe.

Stanley, of course, didn't believe for a moment that he was being played for a dupe. Everything he saw in Buganda—the magnificence of the court, the richness of the dress, the abundance of goods including manufactured items of all kinds, the immensity of the army (the Kabaka was said to be able to raise a force of at least 150,000), the beauty and intelligence of the people, the sense of law and order in the realm—all this convinced him that Mtesa was

the Foremost Man of Equatorial Africa . . . I think I see in him the light that shall lighten the darkness of this benighted region. . . . In this man I see the possible fruition of Livingstone's hopes, for with his aid the civilization of Equatorial Africa becomes feasible.

There was one problem. Mtesa was a Muslim, converted to the faith by the Arab traders who did business at his court, and much of the grandeur and prosperity of the court and much of the change in the Kabaka's character since Speke's day were, as Stanley himself had to admit, a result of the influence of Islam. But Stanley had no trouble rationalizing this away. In his view, since Christianity was infinitely superior to Mohammedanism, even greater improvements could be wrought if Mtesa would embrace Christ. And so Stanley set out to convert the Kabaka of Buganda.

Since 5th April [he tells us], I had enjoyed ten interviews with Mtesa, and during all I had taken occasion to introduce topics which would lead to the subject of Christianity. Nothing occurred in my presence but I contrived to turn it towards effecting that which had become an object to me, viz. his conversion. There was no attempt made to confuse him with the details of any particular doctrine. I simply drew for him the image of the Son of God humbling himself for the good of all mankind, white and black. . . . I showed the difference in character between Him whom white men love and adore, and Mohammed, whom the Arabs revere; how Jesus endeavoured to teach mankind that we should love all men, excepting none, while Mohammed taught his followers that the slaying of the pagan and the unbeliever was an act that merited Paradise. I left it to Mtesa and his chiefs to decide which was the worthier character.

Mtesa proved an interested pupil. Not unlike the ManiKongos hundreds of years before, the Kabaka was perfectly aware of the practical values of European civilization and perfectly willing to consider adopting Christianity if by that he could bring those values to his kingdom. In years to come, Mtesa would reveal that his conversion was little more than a useful bit of politics, but at the time Stanley was elated by the progress he was making in his daily Bible classes with the king. "I have, indeed, undermined Islamism so much here," he wrote, "that Mtesa has determined henceforth, until he is better informed, to observe the Christian Sabbath as well as the Muslim Sabbath, and the great captains have unanimously consented to this."

But, just a few days after having written this, Stanley abruptly abandoned his missionary role. In one of those incredible coincidences that no novelist could write into his story without blushing, another white man turned up at Mtesa's court. This was Linant de Bellefonds, a young French colonel in the service of Charles Gordon, who was then the governor of Equatoria, with his headquarters at Gondokoro (and who would later, as governor-general of the Sudan, die in the siege of Khartoum by the fanatical Mahdists). Gordon's main mission was to extend Egyptian control as far up the Nile as possible, including the annexation of Buganda, and he had sent Linant de Bellefonds to make a reconnaissance of the situation. The young French officer's arrival jolted Stanley out of his missionary fantasies. For the very first words Linant de Bellefonds addressed to him on meeting him at Mtesa's court were: "Have I the honor of speaking to Mr. Cameron?" And that served as reminder enough of the vast amount of work that still lay in front of him, work of exploration, which he feared Cameron might beat him to.

On April 15 he departed from the Kabaka's court to complete his circumnavigation of Lake Victoria. This leg of the journey, however, wasn't quite as uneventful as the first. Sailing down Victoria's western shore, the *Lady Alice* put into an island called Bumbireh (offshore of the present-day town of Bukoba) on April 28 to barter for food. But the tribesmen weren't particularly friendly. About 200 gathered around the cove which the *Lady Alice* entered, with spears and shields, bows and arrows. Stanley was certain he could master them. He was wrong. When the *Lady Alice* came within the tribesmen's reach, Stanley tells us,

with a rush they ran the boat ashore . . . seizing hawser and gunwale, dragged her about 20 yards over the rocky beach high and dry. . . . Then ensued a scene which beggars description. . . . A forest of spears was levelled; thirty or forty bows were drawn taut; as many barbed arrows seemed already on the wing; thick, knotty clubs waved above our heads; two hundred screaming black demons jostled with each other and struggled for room to vent their fury, or for an opportunity to deliver one crushing blow or thrust at us.

Stanley sprang to his feet, brandishing a cocked revolver in each hand, "to kill and be killed," but he quickly realized the hopelessness of the gesture and instead ordered his Zanzibari interpreters to try to negotiate with the tribesmen, invoking the name of Mtesa, while he scooped up beads and cloth and wire to offer to them. This had the effect of calming the warriors momentarily. A *shauri* was called. Half the tribesmen remained surrounding the boat while the other half retreated to talk things over. But, just as Stanley was beginning to relax, six men suddenly seized the boat's oars and rushed off with them. The situation was now dangerous. The *shauri* went on. A messenger arrived and demanded the payment of cloth and beads as tribute, but no sooner was this paid than drums began to beat and hundreds of other warriors gathered on a hill overlooking the beach in full war costume, their faces smeared with black and white paint.

Stanley decided to take a reckless gamble. He gave one of his men two expensive pieces of red cloth and told him to walk slowly toward the enemy as if to barter but to turn and run back to the boat as soon as he was called. To the others of his crew he said, "And you, my boys, this is for life and death, mind; range yourselves on each side of the boat, lay your hands on it carelessly, but with a firm grip, and when I give the word, push it with the force of a hundred men down the hill

The reception at Bumbireh Island

into the water." He waited for his man with the cloth to get fifty yards up the beach, then gave the signal, and, when the boat began to move, leaped into it, snatched up his double-barreled elephant gun, and shouted for his decoy to return. But "the natives were quick-eyed. They saw the boat moving, and with one accord swept down the hill uttering the most fearful cries." The boat reached the water's edge and shot out into the lake with the men swimming after it. The decoy raced back with the warriors in hot pursuit. "Spring into the water, man, head first," Stanley shouted, and then fired into the ranks of the tribesmen, killing two with a single shot. "The bowmen halted and drew their bows. I sent two charges of duck-shot into their midst with terrible effect." The crew now scrambled into the boat and were about to take up their rifles, "but I told them to leave them alone, and tear the bottom-boards out of the boat and use them as paddles; for there were two hippopotami advancing upon us open-mouthed." Stanley whirled and killed one with a shot between the eyes and wounded the other severely enough to drive it off. Then he turned back to the Bumbireh warriors, who had launched four canoes in pursuit of the *Lady Alice*. "My elephant rifle was loaded with explosive balls for this occasion. Four shots killed five men and sank two of the canoes. The two others retired to assist their friends out of the water. They attempted nothing further." Stanley, however, would not forget this incident and, vowing revenge the first chance he got, completed his voyage around the lake, and on May 6 was back at Kagheyi.

Fred Barker was dead. He had died of fever only twelve days before Stanley returned and so had a number of the Zanzibaris. Then Stanley himself came down with a severe attack of malaria, which reduced his weight to under 110 pounds and put him out of action for nearly a week. Then came still further delays. Stanley's plan now was to take his entire caravan back to Buganda, from where he would strike out for Lake Albert. But, rather than make the return trek overland, he intended to take them by water back up the western shore of Lake Victoria. For all the people of his party, though, he needed more boats than he had with him and he had arranged with Mtesa to have Buganda canoes sent down to him at Kagheyi. But weeks turned into months before they arrived, and it wasn't until the end of July that Stanley at last was on his way back to Buganda with his entire caravan.

Stanley had not forgotten Bumbireh, and when he passed it on his way up the lake's western shore he stopped there to settle the score. In his writings he gives an elaborate justification for what he subsequently did, claiming in effect that it was necessary to assure the safe passage of his expedition up the lake. But what it really seemed to come down to was that Stanley, still in a pique over his treatment at the hands of the island's warriors, sent an ultimatum to their chief to make amends, and when this was ignored he attacked. On August 4, he took a force of 250 of his men in six canoes, led by the *Lady Alice*, around to the western side of the island so that his foes would have the setting sun in their eyes, and arrayed his fleet in a line of battle across the entry of a large cove about 100 yards from the land. Anywhere from 2000 to 3000 warriors were massed on the beach and on the surrounding hills. Stanley tells us he made one last effort to parley, but the Bumbireh responded, "We will do nothing but fight." So he gave his men the order to fire. The result was a massacre.

The savages, perceiving the disastrous effect of our fire on a compact body, scattered, and came bounding down to the water's edge, some of the boldest advancing until they were hip-deep in water; others, more cautious, sought the shelter of the cane-grass, whence they discharged many sheaves of arrows, all of which fell short of us. We then moved to within 50 yards of the shore, to fire at close quarters, and each man was permitted to exercise himself as best he could. The savages gallantly held the water-line for an hour, and slung their stones with better effect than they shot their arrows . . . the spear, with which they generally fight, was quite useless.

Some 30 or 40 tribesmen were killed and at least 100 wounded before the Bumbireh gave up the fight and Stanley could feel that "Our work of chastisement was complete." Not one of Stanley's men had suffered so much as a scratch.

It would take over a year for the news of this battle to reach the outside world—via Stanley's own dispatches to the New York *Herald* and the London *Daily Telegraph*—but when it did it raised a furor. The Royal Geographical Society called protest meetings; liberal groups like the Anti-Slavery Society and intellectual journals like the *Saturday Review* vehemently expressed their disapproval of "this outrage on a peaceful and comparatively unarmed people." "Even Stanley's best friends," James Grant wrote to the Royal Geographical Society, "cannot but regret his pugnacity and want of discretion."

Stanley, of course, remained ignorant of the outcry and at the time had no expectation that it would provoke such a hostile reaction. If anything, he seems to have thought that he would be admired for the incident, and he described it in his newspaper accounts with much buccaneering gusto, justifying it on the grounds that "the savage only respects force, power, boldness, and decision." And, as he proceeded on his way up the western shore of the lake, he felt quite vindicated in this view. For the news of the Bumbireh massacre spread rapidly before him, and the lakeshore peoples, fearful of being the next victims of Stanley's riflemen, did all they could to keep from offending him, pressing gifts of food on him, lining the shores unarmed to cheer the passage of his canoes. And so, on August 14, Stanley reached the Kingdom of Buganda, ready to strike off from there northwestward to Lake Albert.

But Mtesa was at war with a vassal chief. "When I heard this news," Stanley writes, "I felt more than half inclined to turn back, for I knew by experience that African wars are tedious things, and I was not in the humour to be delayed." But on reflection Stanley realized that he couldn't do this, for he was counting on Mtesa's assistance in his exploration of Lake Albert. The region he intended to traverse, between the northwestern shore of Victoria and the southeastern shore of Albert, was populated by warrior tribes, and Stanley knew he couldn't get his caravan through without a substantial military escort of the Kabaka's soldiers. So Stanley decided to join in Mtesa's war, rationalizing that with his assistance the war, and the delay it would cause him, would be significantly shortened.

Nevertheless, for all his tactical advice and the devastating effect of his guns, the war dragged on for two months, and it wasn't until mid-October that the enemy chief sent two of his daughters to Mtesa's harem by way of tribute and the peace was concluded. Stanley was anxious to get off, but it took yet another month of negotiations with Mtesa before he succeeded in arranging for his military escort—more than 2000 Buganda warriors under the command of a young general of the Kabaka's army by the name of Sambuzi—and so he didn't set out until late in November.

This was to be the only part of his grand plan of exploration at which Stanley failed: he never reached Lake Albert, let alone explored it. One obstacle certainly was the swampy, malarial, heavily forested terrain he had to cross toward the foothills of the towering Ruwenzoris, the Mountains of the Moon. His men, after spending nearly nine months in relative immobility camped on the shores of Lake Victoria, weren't in shape for the hard march. But the main problem was the fierce hostility of the Wanyoro tribesmen along the way and the utter inadequacy of Sambuzi and his army to deal with them.

On Christmas Day, the first spear came hurtling out of a forest ambush, wounding a Buganda warrior, and by the first days of the New Year, 1876, the caravan was under constant attack. Stanley's account of this leg of his journey is anything but explicit, and it is quite impossible to trace exactly the route he took. One senses on reading his diaries that he didn't really know himself; he was probably quite lost. And Sambuzi was of no help. The Wanyoro of these forests were mortal enemies of the Bugandans, and the further from Lake Victoria they got the more fearful Sambuzi became. On January 11, however, Stanley believed that he was in sight of his goal. Gazing down from the edge of a plateau, he saw the blue waters of a lake lying 1500 feet below, which he wanted to believe was the southeastern corner of Albert. It wasn't. From the latitude and longitude he scribbled in his diary, what he was looking at was probably what years later would be named Lake George, a then unknown small body of water nearly a hundred miles to the south of Lake Albert. But it didn't really matter. Whatever lake it was, Stanley never got to it.

By this time, Sambuzi was in a complete panic. He was convinced that to descend to the lake would be to walk into an ambush of hostile tribesmen. Stanley tells us:

Large numbers of natives, posted on every hill around us, added to the fear which took possession of the minds of the Waganda [Bugandans], and rumours were spread about by malicious men of an enormous force advancing from the south. . . . The members of the Expedition even caught the panic, and prepared in silence to follow the Waganda, as common-sense informed them that, if a force of over 2000 fighting men did not consider itself strong enough to maintain its position, our Expedition of 180 men could by no means do so.

Stanley did everything he could to stem the rising panic. He called a council-of-war and tried to shame Sambuzi into pressing forward, but to no avail. Sambuzi and his lieutenants "were of the opinion that it would be best to fly at once, without waiting for night or for morning." Sambuzi said,

Stamlee, you are my friend, the Emperor's friend, and a son of Uganda, and I want to do my duty towards you as well as I am able to; but you must hear the truth. We cannot do what you want us to do. We cannot wait here two days, nor one day. We shall fight tomorrow, that is certain; and if you think I speak from fear, you shall see me handle the spear. . . . We shall fight tomorrow at sunrise, and we must cut our way through the Wanyoro to Uganda . . . once the war is begun, it is war which will last as long as we are alive—for these people take no slaves as the Waganda do. Then the only chance for our lives that I see is to pack up tonight, and tomorrow morning at sunrise to march and fight our way through them.

Stanley toyed with the idea of going down to the lake with his own men, but he discovered that, except for his last white assistant, Frank Pocock, and a handful of his most loyal Zanzibaris, they wouldn't follow him either. And so he was forced to turn away from the lake.

At dawn we mustered our force. . . . A thousand spearmen with shields formed the advanced-guard, and a thousand spearmen . . . composed the rear-guard. The goods and Expedition occupied the centre. The drums and fife and musical bands announced the signal to march. The natives, whom we expected would have attacked us, contented themselves with following us at a respectful distance . . . they permitted us to depart in peace.

By the beginning of February, they were back within the frontiers of the Kabaka's kingdom and Stanley sent off a letter to Mtesa, sharply condemning Sambuzi's cowardice, which got the young general into an awful lot of trouble with his king. But apart from this Stanley showed remarkably little disappointment over his failure to reach and explore Lake Albert. Increasingly, that part of his grand plan had become unimportant to him. His months on and around Lake Victoria had steadily moved him toward the conclusion that Victoria was, if not certainly the source of the White Nile, the river's most important watershed, and whatever Lake Albert's role might be it was surely secondary and not worth the expenditure of any more time and effort. For there were far more important questions he was determined to answer, and he was in a race with Cameron to be the first to answer them. So, without visiting Mtesa, he undertook a four months' march south to Lake Tanganyika.

At noon of the 27th May the bright waters of the Tanganyika broke upon the view, and compelled me to linger admiringly for a while, as I did on the day I first beheld them. By 3 P.M. we were in Ujiji. . . . Nothing was changed much, except the ever-changing mud tembes [houses] of the Arabs. The square or plaza where I met David Livingstone in November 1871 is now occupied by large tembes. The house where he and I lived has long ago been burnt down, and in its place there remains only a few embers and a hideous void. The lake expands with the same grand beauty before the eyes as we stand in the marketplace. . . . The surf is still as restless, and the sun as bright; the sky retains its glorious azure, and the palms all their beauty; but the grand old hero, whose presence once filled Ujiji with such absorbing interest for me was gone!

Stanley had been traveling in Africa for 17 months, covering almost 3500 miles on land and water, and he was very much looking forward to finding letters from home awaiting him at Ujiji. There were none and he was deeply disappointed.

As I thought of Ujiji I flattered myself daily that I should receive letters and newspapers. I daily fed and lived on that hope [he wrote to Alice Pike]. You may imagine how I felt . . . what would you have done, oh my Alice? Tear your hair, clothes, and shriek distractedly, run about and curse the Fates? I did not do anything so undignified, but I soberly grieved and felt discouraged. . . . My cheeks are sunk, my eyes large and sickly, my bones feel sore even lying on two blankets. . . . Yet the same heart still throbs with deepest love, as it did long ago.

Stanley still held out some hope of hearing from her before he vanished again into the unreachable depths of Africa. His plan now was to circumnavigate Lake Tanganyika, which he calculated would take him about two months, so there was a chance that there would be mail waiting for him when he returned again to Ujiji. He hurriedly had the *Lady Alice* reassembled and launched on Tanganyika and, leaving Frank Pocock in charge of the bulk of the expedition at Ujiji, set sail in mid-June, with a crew of thirteen, southward down the lake's eastern shore. In 51 relatively pacific and uneventful days he mapped 810 miles of the lake's 930 miles of coastline and was back in Ujiji with virtually positive proof that Tanganyika had no outlet river which possibly could connect it with Lake Albert and make it part of the headwaters system of the Nile. And with that he destroyed Burton's theory and was obliged to take yet another step toward accepting Speke's contention that Victoria was the White Nile's true source. The only other possibility left was Livingstone's Lualaba, but it is clear that by this time Stanley was entertaining serious doubts about his grand old hero's theory. Nevertheless, he did not waver for a moment in his determination to explore it, to complete Livingstone's work no matter what the cost or where it took him.

And he was now desperately eager to get on with it. No letters had arrived while he'd been away and there was no chance of any arriving. A smallpox epidemic had broken out in Ujiji, making the town extremely unsafe to stay in. And besides there was a growing problem with desertions; a score of his men had quit the caravan while he was away circumnavigating Tanganyika, and the longer he stayed in Ujiji the more men he lost (his party would be reduced to under 140 before he finally got away).

But most important was his sense that time was running out on him. There was his race with Cameron. Stanley learned in Ujiji that Cameron had reached Nyangwe, Livingstone's furthest point down the Lualaba, a full two years before, making his chances of catching up desperately slim. And there was his rendezvous with Alice Pike. As he wrote her in mid-August, "It is now within a few days of twenty-five months since I parted from you, and nearly twenty months since leaving Zanzibar," and then he went on to confess that he now had to figure that it would take him a total of three years to complete his expedition.

just a year longer than I estimated. But the estimates are invariably wrong, and it is not fair to tie a man down to mere estimates. We have all done our best. . . . Then, my own Darling, if by that name I may call you, let us hope cheerfully that a happy termination to this long period of trial of your constancy and my health and courage await us both. . . . Grant then that my love towards you is unchanged, that you are my dream, my stay and my hope, and my beacon, and believe that I shall cherish you in this light until I meet you, or death meets me. This is the last you will get, I fear, for a long time. Then, my darling, accept this letter with one last and loving farewell.

He signed it "Morton."

A few days later, he led his party across Lake Tanganyika and struck westward on the grueling march into the Maniema forests.

Suddenly from the crest of a low ridge we saw the confluence of the Luama with the majestic Lualaba. The former appeared to have a breadth of 400 yards at the mouth; the latter was about 1400 yards wide, a broad river of a pale grey colour, winding slowly from south and by east. We hailed its appearance with shouts of joy, and rested on the spot to enjoy the view. . . . A secret rapture filled my soul as I gazed upon the majestic stream. The great mystery that for all these centuries Nature had kept hidden away from the world of science was waiting to be solved. . . . My task was to follow it to the Ocean.

The date was October 17, 1876.

17

DOWN THE LUALABA TO THE SEA

Verney Lovett Cameron had reached the Lualaba in August 1874, more than two years before Stanley, and had every intention of following the river to its end. What's more, and very much to his credit, he had a far clearer notion where that end might be than Stanley. While still in Ujiji, Cameron tells us, "I had many long yarns with the Arabs who knew these parts . . . and learned that in their opinion the Lualaba is the Kongo." Indeed, one of these Arabs boasted to Cameron that he had once traveled "fifty-five marches" along the river "and came to where the water was salt and ships came from the sea, and white men lived there who traded much in palm-oil and had large houses." Cameron calculated 55 marches at about 500 miles, added another 300 miles for the distance from Ujiji to Nyangwe and, supposing the river turned west after Nyangwe, came up with a journey of some 800 miles, which, he believed, "gives about the distance to the Yellala Cataracts. This looks something like the Kongo and West-coast merchants." Then, once he had himself reached Nyangwe, he measured the volume of river water flowing past the town and found it to be "123,000 cubic feet per second in the dry season, or more than five times greater than that of the Nile at Gondokoro, which is 21,500 feet per second." From this fact he made the wonderfully accurate assessment:

This great stream must be one of the head-waters of the Kongo, for where else could that giant among rivers, second only to the Amazon in its volume, obtain the two million cubic feet of water which it unceasingly pours each second into the Atlantic? The large affluents from the north would explain the comparatively small rise of the Kongo at the coast; for since its enormous basin extends to both sides of the equator, some portion of it is always under the zone of rains, and therefore the supply to the main stream is nearly the same at all times, instead of varying, as is the case with tropical rivers whose basins lie completely on one side of the equator.

Cameron's only real error was his supposition that the Lualaba turned west a short distance downstream of Nyangwe, whereas it continues northward for hundreds of miles before making its westward and southwestward arc to the sea. But his assumptions were based purely on hearsay, and as such, Cameron knew, would never meet the exacting standards of the Royal Geographical Society or the acceptance of rival explorers. They would demand a map of the river's course drawn from first-hand observation, and to do that he would have to penetrate along the Lualaba into the regions north of Nyangwe. And that, like Livingstone before him, he could not do.

In the first place, he too could not get canoes. From time to time, chiefs and tribesmen, Cameron tells us, "made some show of affording aid, but they always said, 'Slowly, slowly; don't be in a hurry; tomorrow will do as well as today'; and so the matter dragged along." The paramount chief of the town, named Dugambi, promised Cameron each market day that he would go to the Nyangwe marketplace and use his influence to induce local tribesmen to sell him canoes. "And he would leave me apparently on this errand. But I afterward found that he used to slip into one of the houses of his harem by a back way, and remain there until the market-people had gone." On a few occasions, boatmen agreed to make a sale but only if payment was made in slaves, knowing full well that the white man had none, and, because of his beliefs, would not acquire any. Once a man-agreed to take payment in cowries, but "when I counted out before him the correct number of cowries," Cameron tells us, "he quietly looked them over and then returned them, remarking that if he took home such a quantity of cowries they would only be appropriated by his wives as ornaments. and he would be poorer by a canoe." "One hoary-headed old fellow" told Cameron quite bluntly why he'd never acquire any canoes.

No good had ever resulted from the advent of strangers, and he should advise each and all his countrymen to refuse to sell or hire a single canoe to the white man; for if he acted like the strangers who had gone before him, he would only prove a fresh oppressor . . . or open a new road for robbers and slave-dealers.

But, even had he been able to get the canoes, it is doubtful that Cameron would have gone down the Lualaba. For, with each passing day in Nyangwe, he and, more to the point, the members of his caravan heard fresh horror stories of what lay ahead on the river. "They described the natives as being very fierce and warlike, and using poisoned arrows, a mere scratch from which proved fatal in four or five minutes, unless an antidote, known only to the natives, was immediately applied." And they were cannibals, "more cruel and treacherous than any with whom we had yet met. Consequently stragglers would most certainly be cut off, killed and probably eaten." As for the terrain, it was, they said, "a country of large mountains wooded to the summits, and valleys filled with such dense forests that they travelled four and five days in succession without seeing the sun." So forbidding was the prospect that even the Arab caravans, despite their greed for slaves and ivory and despite their armies of riflemen, did not dare venture into those regions.

Cameron's party consisted of about 100 men, including 45 askaris armed with Snider rifles, the best weapon of the day, but Cameron considered it as "being far too small . . . to make the journey by itself." And, he discovered quickly enough, he would never be able to hire an escort.

The settlers at Nyangwe declared themselves to be too short of powder and guns to spare a sufficient force to accompany me and return safely by themselves, so no volunteers were forthcoming. In addition to this, they were very much afraid to travel by roads north of the Lualaba; for several strong and well-armed parties had been severely handled by the natives in that direction, and had returned to Nyangwe with the loss of more than half their numbers. One party . . . had especially suffered, having lost over two hundred of their total strength of three hundred.

So, within a few weeks, Cameron's resolve to go down the Lualaba eroded, and when the first opportunity came along to turn away from the terrible challenge of the river, he seized it.

That opportunity came along in the person of Tippoo Tib, the very same Tippoo Tib who had met Livingstone at the southern end of Lake Tanganyika seven years before and had assisted him during his journey to the headwaters of the Lualaba. The Arab trader had prospered mightily during the years since, having amassed a huge fortune in ivory and slaves, a fearsome following of armed riflemen, and a terrible reputation for efficient cruelty. Cameron describes him as "a good-looking man, and the greatest dandy I had seen among the traders," and in his own memoirs, Tippoo Tib confessed that he always enjoyed playing the role of grand seigneur and had always felt an intense attraction toward Europeans. When he marched into Nyangwe at the head of his impressive caravan, he immediately called on Cameron and, with a show of great chivalry and courteousness, declared himself at the white man's service.

Cameron made one last, although not too convincing request for help in securing canoes for a water journey or for an armed escort for an overland trek down the Lualaba, but Tippoo Tib, for all his eagerness to ingratiate himself with this lone European, turned him down. Despite his rapacious reputation and military might he too considered it suicidal to venture into those fearsome regions to the north but, by way of compensation, he offered to escort Cameron's party *westward* from the Lualaba at least as far as the trading camp he maintained on the banks of the Lomami River, some "ten marches" from Nyangwe. From there, Tippoo Tib claimed, Cameron would have no difficulty continuing to the west all the way to the Atlantic, since native caravans constantly made that journey to trade with the Portuguese on the Angola coast.

Cameron accepted the offer. It was either that, he realized, or return via Ujiji to Zanzibar, having accomplished nothing more than Livingstone before him. So, at the end of August, 1874, Cameron set out with Tippoo Tib's caravan, and fifteen months later, in November 1875, arrived at the Portuguese settlement of Benguela on the Atlantic Ocean. It was, unquestionably, a brilliant feat of African travel. Cameron became the second European, after Livingstone, to traverse the continent from coast to coast. In the course of this monumental journey, he crossed through a substantial portion of the Congo River basin and filled in a large portion of the map of Africa. But he had left the mystery of the Lualaba unsolved, and so the way was open for Stanley.

Stanley, of course, knew nothing of this. As he made his way along the banks of the Lualaba from its confluence with the Luama toward Nyangwe in October 1876, although Cameron had in fact been back in England for nearly six months, he still very much felt himself in a race with the British naval lieutenant. And it wasn't until Stanley himself met with Tippoo Tib on the outskirts of Nyangwe, nearly two

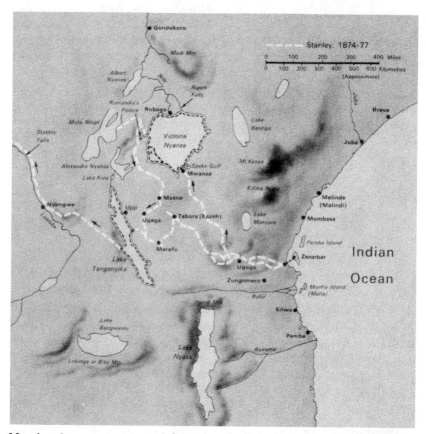

Map based on contemporary information showing the route taken by Stanley, 1874–1877

years after Cameron had parted from the Arab trader, that he at last learned it and could heave a huge sigh of relief.

He was a tall, black-bearded man, of negroid complexion, in the prime of life, straight, and quick in his movements, a picture of energy and strength [Stanley wrote of Tippoo Tib at their first meeting]. He had a fine intelligent face, with a nervous twitching of the eyes, and gleaming white and perfectly formed teeth. . . . With the air of a well-bred Arab, and almost courtier-like in his manner, he welcomed me . . . and his slaves being ready at hand with mat and bolster, he reclined vis-a-vis, while a buzz of admiration of his style was perceptible from the on-lookers. After regarding him for a few minutes, I came to the conclusion that this Arab was a remarkable man—the most remarkable man I had met among Arabs, Wa-Swahili, and half-castes in Africa. He was neat in his person, his clothes were of a spotless white, his fez-cap brand-new, his waist was encircled by a rich dowle, his dagger was splendid with silver filigree, and his *tout ensemble* was that of an Arab gentleman in very comfortable circumstances.

Stanley wasted no time in putting the question that was uppermost in his mind, inquiring of Tippoo Tib

as to the direction that my predecessor at Nyangwe had taken. The information he gave me was sufficiently clear . . . the greatest problem of African geography was left untouched at the exact spot where Dr. Livingstone had felt himself unable to prosecute his travels. . . . This was momentous and all-important news to the Expedition. We had arrived at the critical point in our travels: our destinies now awaited my final decision.

But, before he made that decision he wanted to know why Cameron had turned away from the Lualaba. And he was told in no uncertain terms: want of canoes, reluctance of the Arabs to help, cowardice of Cameron's followers, but most importantly the difficulty of the terrain and the hostility of the tribesmen ahead. To illustrate these last points, Tippoo Tib had a young Arab brought before Stanley to tell of his adventures with one of the few caravans that had ever attempted to penetrate those regions. It was, the youth related, "a forest land, where there is nothing but woods, and woods, and woods, for days, and weeks, and months. There was no end to the woods." He went on to tell of cannibal warriors, of monstrous boa constrictors, gorillas that "run up to you and seize your hands, and bite the fingers off one by one." "It is nothing but constant fighting," the youth warned.

Only two years ago a party armed with three hundred guns started north . . . they only brought sixty guns back, and no ivory. If one tries to go by river, there are falls after falls, which carry the people over and drown them. A party of thirty men, in three canoes, went down the river half a day's journey from Nyangwe. . . . They were all drowned. . . . Ah, no. Master, the country is bad, and the Arabs have given it up. . . . They will not try the journey into that country again, after trying it three times and losing nearly five hundred men altogether."

Stanley listened attentively. "These were difficulties," he realized, "for me also to surmount in some manner not yet intelligible. How was I to instil courage in my followers, or sustain it, to obtain the assistance of the Arabs to enable me to make a fair beginning, and afterwards to purchase or make canoes?" But that he would find the means to surmount the difficulties, that he would in fact go on, he was never in doubt. And he tells an anecdote that makes the point dramatically.

That night he called Frank Pocock into his hut and said to him, "Now Frank, my son, sit down. I am about to have a long and serious chat with you. Life and death—yours as well as mine, and those of all the Expedition—hang on the decision I make tonight." He then went on to review the dangers in attempting to go down the Lualaba, pointing out that "Livingstone, after fifteen thousand miles of travel, and a lifetime of experience among Africans, would not have yielded the brave struggle without strong reasons; Cameron, with his forty-five Snider rifles, would never have turned away from such a brilliant field if he had not sincerely thought that they were insufficient to resist the persistent attacks of countless thousands of wild men." Then he asked, "Now, what I wish you to tell me, Frank, is your opinion as to what we ought to do. . . . Think well, my dear fellow; don't be hasty, life and death hang on our decision." And before Frank could properly answer, Stanley sketched out an alternative route the expedition could take, south to Katanga and down the Zambezi, which in itself would represent a major feat of exploration. The young Kentish fisherman, struggling to follow Stanley's conversation, agreed that to go to Katanga and the Zambezi "would be a fine job, Sir, if we could do it." "Yet, if you think of it, Frank," Stanley said, "this great river which Livingstone first saw, and which broke his heart almost to turn away and leave a mystery, is a noble field too. Fancy, by-and-by, after buying or building canoes our floating down the river day by day, either to the Nile . . . or to the Congo and the Atlantic Ocean!" Finally, Frank came up with an idea: "I say, sir, let us toss up: best two out of three to decide it. . . . Heads for the north and the Lualaba; tails for the south and Katanga."

Stanley gave Frank a rupee coin. The youth flipped it; he flipped it in fact six times and six times it came up tails for the south and Katanga. Fate may have been trying to tell Stanley something, but he refused to listen. He decided that instead of flipping the coin they should draw straws to decide, long for the north and the Lualaba, short for the south and Katanga. Stanley held the straws and Frank drew them from his hand, and each time he drew a short straw, for the south and Katanga. But then, abruptly, Stanley flung the straws and coin away. "It is of no use, Frank," he said. "We'll face our destiny, despite the rupee and the straws. With your help, my dear fellow, I will follow the river."

Stanley had a plan. He would not bother to try to obtain canoes in Nyangwe. "Livingstone could not. Cameron failed. No doubt I shall fail," he decided realistically. Instead, he would push northward along the Lualaba overland until he came to a place where he could get canoes. But, for this to work, he would have to persuade his expedition to strike into those terrible regions from Nyangwe in the first place. He was perfectly aware that, after only a day of listening to the horror stories told about those regions, his men were fast losing courage, and he was in danger of mass desertions when he informed them of his plan. To prevent this, he would have to provide them with a large and comforting military escort. And that, he decided, he would have to get from Tippoo Tib. It would be sufficient, he felt, to have the Arab's riflemen accompany his party only a relatively short distance down the river, just far enough into the wild country so that, once they were alone again, his men would find it as dangerous to desert and try to make their way back again as they would to go on.

Tippoo Tib must have seen something special in Stanley, something he hadn't seen in Livingstone or Cameron or any other white man. It is true that when Stanley first made the proposition to him he raised all the predictable objections and concluded, "If you Wasungu [white men] are desirous of throwing away your lives it is no reason we Arabs should. We travel little by little to get ivory—it is now nine years since I left Zanzibar—but you white men only look for rivers and lakes and mountains, and you spend your lives for no reason, and to no purpose."

Stanley answered: "I know I have no right to expect you to risk your life for me. I only wish you to accompany me sixty days' journey, then leave me to myself . . . all I am anxious for is my people. You know the Wangwana [Zanzibaris] are easily swayed by fear, but if they hear Tippoo Tib has joined me, and is about to accompany me, every man will have a lion's courage."

Tippoo Tib agreed to think about it, and that night he held a *shauri* with his relatives and principal chiefs. In his memoirs, the Arab tells us that all his associates and family strongly advised him against assisting Stanley. But, at the end of the *shauri,* Tippoo Tib tells us, he declared, "Perhaps I am mad and it is you who are sane. Mind your own concerns." And the next day he told Stanley that, for a payment of $5000, he would accompany him with 200 armed soldiers plus that many more porters for a distance of 60 camps or marches, each camp to be four hours' march from the preceding camp, with the understanding that the total journey would not take longer than three months.

Stanley readily agreed, a contract was signed, and the next few weeks were spent in preparation for the extraordinary journey. Stanley's party consisted of about 150; 60 of these were askaris armed with Snider or Winchester rifles, percussion-lock muskets, double-barreled elephant guns or revolvers; the rest were pagazis (or porters) plus a handful of wives and children of the chiefs and headmen. Tippoo Tib's force numbered at first 700; 300 of these, however, were to strike off to the east after a few days on a separate ivory and slave-hunting expedition. Of the remaining 400, more than half were soldiers, armed with flintlocks, bows and arrows, spears and shields; the rest were porters, gunbearers, scouts, house servants, cooks, carpenters, and slaves. In addition, Tippoo Tib, "bland and courteous, enthusiastic, and sanguine," brought along twenty women from his harem. On November 5, 1876, the immense caravan set off from Nyangwe. Stanley writes:

We saw before us a black curving wall of forest, which, beginning from the river bank, extended south-east, until hills and distance made it indistinct. . . . What a forbidding aspect had the Dark Unknown which confronted us!

The terrain was killing.

The trees kept shedding their dew upon us like rain in great round drops. Every leaf seemed weeping. Down the boles and branches, creepers and vegetable cords, the moisture trickled and fell on us. Overhead the wide-spreading branches, in many interlaced strata, absolutely shut out the daylight. We knew not whether it was a sunshiny day or a dull, foggy, gloomy day; for we marched in a feeble solemn twilight. . . . To our right and left, to the height of about twenty feet, towered the undergrowth, the lower world of vegetation. . . . The tempest might roar without the leafy world, but in its deep bosom there is absolute stillness. . . . Every few minutes we found ourselves descending into ditches, with streams. . . . The dew dropped and pattered on us incessantly. . . . Our clothes were heavily saturated with it. My white sun-helmet and puggaree appeared to be weighted with lead. . . . Added to this vexation was the perspiration which exuded from every pore, for the atmosphere was stifling. The steam from the hot earth could be seen ascending upward and settling in a grey cloud above our heads.

Day after day the caravan fought its way through the primeval forest.

We had a fearful time of it today. . . . Such crawling, scrambling, tearing through the damp, dank jungles, and such height and depth of woods. . . . Our Expedition is no longer the compact column which was my pride. It is utterly demoralized. . . . It was so dark sometimes in the woods that I could not see the words which I pencilled in my notebook.

The men were soon grumbling and

all their courage was oozing out, as day by day we plodded through the doleful, dreary forest. . . . The constant slush and reek which the heavy dew caused in the forest . . . had worn my shoes out, and half the march I travelled with naked feet. I had then to draw out of my stores my last pair of shoes. Frank was already using his last pair of shoes. Yet we were still in the centre of the continent. What should we do when all were gone?

On November 16, barely 10 marches and 50 miles from Nyangwe, Tippoo Tib came to Stanley and said,

It is of no use. . . . Look at it how you may, those sixty camps will occupy us at the rate we are travelling over a year, and it will take as much time to return. I never was in this forest before, and I had no idea there was such a place in the world; but the air is killing my people, it is insufferable. You will kill your own people if you go on. . . . This country was not made for travel; it was made for vile pagans, monkeys, and wild beasts. I cannot go farther.

Stanley argued with him for two hours and at last persuaded him to continue for just 20 marches further. Three days later they camped on the bank of the Lualaba, which Stanley had decided to rechristen the Livingstone, at a point where the river was 1200 yards wide.

Downward it flows into the unknown [he wrote in his diary], to the night-black clouds of mystery and fable. . . . Something strange must surely lie in the vast space occupied by total blankness on our maps . . . we have laboured through the terrible forest, and manfully struggled through the gloom. My people's hearts have become faint. I seek a road.

Why, here lies a broad watery avenue cleaving the Unknown to some sea, like a path of light!

It still proved impossible to acquire or even build canoes but Stanley decided that he could at least launch the *Lady Alice* on the river. Some thirty of the party joined him in the boat while the rest under Tippoo Tib's command, continued overland along the river's left bank.

Although the traveling was slightly eased by this, the expedition now began to encounter the other great terror of the forest—its inhabitants. At first the villages they passed were deserted, the tribesmen fleeing into the dark forests at the news of the advance of the strange caravan, but there wasn't any question about what kind of people lived in them. Row upon row of human skulls lined the palisades around the villages, and bones from every part of the human anatomy could be seen scattered around the cooking sites. From time to time, a solitary, grotesquely painted savage would be caught sight of peering out from the thick undergrowth, and throughout the day and night they heard the drums beating, telling of their progress, the shrill, eerie cry—Ooh-hu-hu! Ooh-hu-hu!—calling warriors to assemble in the gloom of the woods and the blare of ivory war horns sounding from another world.

On November 23, the *Lady Alice* reached the confluence of the Ruiki with the Lualaba, and Stanley, realizing that the land party would have to be ferried across it, decided to camp there until Tippoo Tib's people caught up. Throughout the evening, warriors gathered in the forests around the camp but the night passed without incident. The next morning, as Tippoo Tib's party still had not arrived, Stanley went off to explore the Ruiki, but he had barely left when he heard the forest silence shattered by the crack of rifle fire. Rushing back to the camp, he found his men under attack by 100 screaming tribesmen. The Snider and Winchester rifles drove them off, but from then on hardly a day or night went by without trouble of this sort.

Morale disintegrated and problems multiplied. "The march through the jungles and forests, the scant fare, fatigue, and consequent suffering," Stanley tells us, "resulted in sickness." A small pox epidemic broke out; dysentery killed others. "Thorns had also penetrated the feet and wounded the legs of many of the people, until dreadful ulcers had been formed, disabling them from travel." Then there were typhoid fever, pneumonia, pleurisy. "Over fifty were infected with the itch. . . . Every day we tossed two or three bodies into the deep waters of the Livingstone." Six leaky canoes were found abandoned along the river bank and Stanley had these lashed together to form a floating hospital. Other abandoned canoes were picked up along the way or captured from the local tribesmen in the sporadic battles, but then the river turned nasty. Periodically, stretches of fast-moving rapids or whirlpools would suddenly break up "the broad watery avenue" and canoes would be overturned and precious cargo lost. And in December the rains began.

Tippoo Tib and the Arab advanced to me for a shauri [Stanley writes]. They wished to know whether I would not now abandon the project of continuing down the river—now that things appeared so gloomy, with rapids before us, natives hostile, cannibalism rampant, small-pox raging, people dispirited. . . . "What prospects," they asked, "lie before us but terrors, and fatal collapse and ruin? Better turn back in time."

But Stanley, of course, had no intention of turning back.

The river widened; sizable islands stood in its stream; the jungle all around was "a prey to gloom and shade, where the hawk and the eagle, the ibis, the grey parrot, and the monkey, may fly and scream and howl, undisturbed"; and the attacks of the natives intensified, became unrelenting.

We heard the warhorns sounding . . . we saw eight large canoes coming up river along the islands in mid-stream, and six along the left bank. . . . When they came within thirty yards, half of the men in each canoe began to shoot their poisoned arrows, while the other half continued to paddle in-shore. . . . On the 14th, gliding down the river . . . the natives made a brilliant and well-planned attack on us, by suddenly dashing upon us from a creek; and had not the ferocious nature of the people whom we daily encountered taught us to be prepared at all times against assault, we might have suffered considerable injury. . . .

On the 18th, after floating down a few miles . . . the aborigines at once gathered opposite, blew war-horns, and mustered a large party, preparing to attack us with canoes. . . . While rowing down, close to the left bank, we were suddenly surprised by hearing a cry from one of the guards of the hospital canoes, and, turning round, saw an arrow fixed in his chest. The next instant, looking towards the bank, we saw the forms of many men in the jungle, and several arrows flew past my head in extremely unpleasant proximity. We sheered off instantly, and, pulling hard down stream, came near the landing place of an untenanted market-green. Here we drew in-shore, and, sending out ten scouts to lie in wait in the jungle, I mustered all the healthy men, about thirty in number, and proceeded to construct a fence of brushwood, inspired to unwonted activity by a knowledge of our lonely, defenceless state. . . . The scouts retreated on the run, shouting as they approached, "Prepare! prepare! they are coming!" About fifty yards of ground outside our camp had been cleared, which . . . was soon filled by hundreds of savages, who pressed upon us from all sides . . . we were at bay, and desperate in our resolve not to die without fighting. Accordingly, at such close quarters the contest soon became terrific. Again and again the savages hurled themselves upon our stockade, launching spear after spear with deadly force. . . . Sometimes the muzzles of our guns almost touched their breasts. The shrieks, cries, shouts of encouragement, the rattling volleys of the musketry, the booming war-horns, the yells and defiance of the combatants, the groans and screams of the women and children in the hospital camp, made together such a medley of hideous noises as can never be effaced from my memory. For two hours this desperate conflict lasted. . . . At dusk the enemy retreated . . . but the hideous alarums produced from their ivory horns, and increased by the echoes of the close forest, still continued; and now and again a vengeful poison-laden arrow flew by with an ominous whizz to quiver in the earth at our feet. . . . Sleep, under the circumstances, was out of the question. . . . Morning dawned. . . . We were not long left unmolested. . . . The combat lasted until noon, when, mustering twenty-five men, we made a sally, and succeeded in clearing the skirts of the village for the day. . . . The next morning an assault was attempted. . . . About noon a large flotilla of canoes was observed ascending the river close to the left bank, manned by such a dense mass of men that any number between five hundred and eight hundred would be within the mark . . . blowing their war-horns and drumming vigorously. At the same moment, as though this were a signal in concert with those on land, war-horns responded from the forest, and I had scarcely time to order every man to look out when the battle-tempest of arrows broke upon us from the woods. This was a period when every man felt that he must either fight or resign himself to the only other alternative, that of being heaved a headless corpse into the river.

Just a few days before Christmas, some 200 miles downriver from Nyangwe and still eight marches short of the twenty they had agreed to, Tippoo Tib and the Arabs declared their intention of returning to Nyangwe by another route, and with such firmness of tone [Stanley tells us], that I renounced the idea of attempting to persuade them to change their decision. Indeed, the awful condition of the sick, the high daily mortality, the constant attacks on us during each journey . . . had produced such dismal impressions on the minds of the escort that no amount of money would have bribed the undisciplined people of Tippoo Tib to have entertained for a moment the idea of continuing the journey.

Not so Stanley; all the awful conditions hadn't for a moment dissuaded him. What's more, he had led his men so deep into the wild country that the prospect of returning seemed to them every bit as dreadful as proceeding further. But what most gave Stanley and his men the heart to go on without the Arab escort was the fact that they had by now found or captured more than twenty canoes. Repaired and christened with such names as *Livingstone, Stanley, Telegraph, Herald, London Town,* and *America,* they formed a fleet large enoug to transport the entire party on the river.

Before parting, Stanley and Tippoo Tib took a few days off to celebrate Christmas. Canoe races were organized; there were foot races, including one between Frank Pocock and Tippoo Tib which the Arab won by fifteen yards; there was a banquet of rice and roasted sheep, with dances by the tribesmen around a bonfire. On the night of December 27, 1876, Stanley had one of his earnest chats with his youthful lieutenant, and in it he revealed his steadily changing view of Lualaba's geography.

Here we are at an altitude of sixteen hundred and fifty feet above the sea [he told Frank]. What conclusions can we arrive at? Either that this river penetrates a great distance north of the Equator, and, taking a mighty sweep round, descends into the Congo . . . or that we shall shortly see it in the neighborhood of the Equator take a direct cut towards the Congo . . . or that it is the . . . Nile. I believe that it will prove to be the Congo; if the Congo then, there must be many cataracts. Let us only hope that the cataracts are all in a lump, close together.

At dawn, a heavy gray mist hung over the river and Stanley waited for it to lift before embarking the expedition. It numbered 149 men, women and children, 2 donkeys, 2 goats and a sheep, loaded into 22 canoes; the canoes were lashed together in pairs and the *Lady Alice* took her position at the head of the flotilla. Stanley concedes that the morale of his men was anything but high. "Sons of Zanzibar," Stanley shouted to them. "the Arabs . . . are looking at you. They are now telling one another what brave fellows you are. Lift up your heads and be men." But "with what wan smiles they responded to my words! How feebly they paddled." An attempt was made to raise a song but the voices died out into "piteous hoarseness" and the eerie silence of the jungle again descended. And again all the troubles started.

The drums beat along the river banks; the war-horns sounded their dreadful cry in the jungles; the cannibals gathered along the banks, rattling their spears against their shields, brandishing their bows and arrows, shrieking, "Bo-bo-bo-bo-o-o! Meat! Meat! We shall have plenty of meat!" Every day the flotilla had to run a gauntlet of arrows and spears, every night the party had to build fortifications around its camp and fight off attacks, and the further north Stanley went, the bolder the cannibals became. Painted half red and half white, with broad black stripes streaked across them, they came out into the river in their giant war canoes—one, which Stanley captured, was 85 feet long with a bas relief of a crocodile adorning its side. Stanley soon arranged to have all the shields taken from the enemy affixed to the sides of the boats of his flotilla so that his boats came to resemble miniature Viking ships. New Year's Day, 1877, passed as all the rest: fighting off cannibals, drenched in the rains, suffering fevers and disease. And then in the midst of all these horrors yet another horror loomed. On January 4, Stanley heard the distant roar of rapids on the river, and the next day he reached the first of the seven cataracts of the Stanley Falls.

It took him just over three weeks to descend the falls, and it was an amazing feat. Wherever there was a stretch of relatively calm water, Stanley would make use of it and relaunch the *Lady Alice* and his fleet of canoes, but no sooner were they floating downstream than they would again hear the roar of the next cataract in the series, and all hands would begin paddling for dear life to make the bank and avoid being swept to destruction. Then the horrendous labor of portage would begin again. A path fifteen feet wide had to be hacked through the jungle, sometimes two and three and four miles long, to circumvent a cataract. Half the expedition worked at this exhausting task, all day and, by the light of torches, all night as well, while the other half of the expedition dragged the boats after them. And throughout it all they had to fight off the continual, relentless, terrifying attacks of hordes of cannibals.

"Lady Alice" over the falls

On January 23, the party circumvented the sixth cataract and once again relaunched the boats on the river. They had, Stanley discovered from his solar observations, crossed to north of the equator, and a stretch of calm water lay in front of them. They halted the next day on an island to make some repairs on the *Lady Alice* and resumed their journey on the 25th. Around midday, the roar of the seventh cataract

burst upon our ears with a tremendous crash. . . . As the calm river, which is 1300 yards wide one mile above the falls, becomes narrowed, the current quickens, and rushes with resistless speed for a few hundred yards, and then falls about 10 feet into a boiling and tumultuous gulf, wherein are lines of brown waves 6 feet high leaping with terrific bounds, and hurling themselves against each other in dreadful fury. . . . I have seen many waterfalls during my travels in various parts of the world, but here was a stupendous river flung in full volume over a waterfall only 500 yards across. The river . . . does not merely *fall:* it is precipitated downwards.

So again the boats raced for the banks. Again the killing work of cutting a path for the overland portage was undertaken. Again a desperate battle with the cannibals was joined. And then on January 28, we hastened away down river in a hurry to escape the noise of the cataracts which, for many days and nights, had almost stunned us with their deafening sound. . . . We are once again afloat upon a magnificent stream, whose broad and grey-brown waters woo us with its mystery.

Stanley realized that he had cleared the last of the cataracts.

And he realized something else as well: the Lualaba could not possibly be the Nile. He was now 40 miles north of the equator and, by measuring the temperature at which water boiled, he determined that the river's elevation had dropped to 1511 feet above sea level, some 20 feet *below* that of the Nile at Gondokoro. Thus, for the Lualaba to be the Nile, as Livingstone had so fervently believed, it would have to flow uphill from here on. But, even if by some miracle it could perform such a feat, Stanley saw that "The Livingstone now deflected to the west-northwest."

For the next 1000 miles, the river, making its great sweeping arc from northwest to west and then to southwest back across the equator again, widening out from about a mile across to six and even nine miles in places, would be wholly navigable and provide Stanley's flotilla with that ideal "broad watery avenue cleaving the Unknown" of which he had dreamed months before. But even so it would take him nearly seven weeks to make the journey, for if the river itself no longer impeded his travels, the peoples of the river still did. Stanley calculated that, between the first cannibal attack at the confluence with the Ruiki River back in November and the bottom of the Stanley Falls at the end of January, he had fought twenty-four pitched battles with river tribes. He would now have to fight eight more.

We were getting weary of fighting every day [he wrote]. The strain to which we were exposed had been too long, the incessant, long-lasting enmity shown us was beginning to make us feel baited, harassed, and bitter . . . [these] combats which we had with the insensate furies of savage-land began to inspire us with a suspicion of everything bearing the least resemblance of man, and to infuse into our hearts something of that feeling which possibly the hard-pressed stag feels, after distancing the hounds many times, and having resorted to many stratagems to avoid them, wearied and bathed with perspiration, he hears with terror and trembling the hideous and startling yells of the ever-pursuing pack. We also had laboured strenuously through ranks upon ranks of savages, scattered over a score of flotillas, had endured persistent attacks night and day while struggling through them, had resorted to all modes of defence, and yet at every curve of this fearful river the yells of savages broke loud on our ears, the snake-like canoes darted forward impetuously to the attack, while the drums and horns and shouts raised a fierce and deafening uproar. We were becoming exhausted. Yet we were still only on the middle line of the continent! We were also being weeded out by units and twos and threes. There were not thirty men in the entire Expedition that had not received a wound. To continue this fearful life was not possible. Some day we should lie down, and offer our throats like lambs to the cannibal butchers. . . . Livingstone called floating down the Lualaba a foolhardy feat. So it has proved, indeed, and I pen these lines with half a feeling that they will be never read by any man.

At the confluence with the Aruwimi River, after two days of cease-less fighting, Stanley's party was attacked by a fleet of 54 monster canoes carrying a total of at least 2000 cannibals. The lead canoe had

two rows of upstanding paddles, forty men on a side, their bodies bending and swaying in unison as with the swelling barbarous chorus they drive her down towards us. In the bow, standing on what appears to be a platform, are ten prime young warriors, their heads gay with feathers of the parrot, crimson and grey: at the stern, eight men with long paddles, whose tops are decorated with ivory balls, guide the monster vessel; and dancing up and down from stem to stern are ten men, who appear to be chiefs. . . . The crashing sound of large drums, a hundred blasts from ivory horns, and a chilling chant from two thousand throats, do not tend to soothe our nerves or to increase our confidence.

When the first spears began to fly, Stanley gave the order to fire. Despite their more than ten-to-one superiority, the tribesmen were no match for the rifles, and after five minutes of awful slaughter they broke off the attack and retreated. But, Stanley tells us,

Our blood is up now. It is a murderous world, and we feel for the first time we hate the filthy, vulturous ghouls who inhabit it. We therefore lift our anchors, and pursue them up-stream along the right bank, until rounding a point we see their villages. We make straight for the banks, and continue the fight in the village streets with those who have landed, hunt them out into the woods.

And then, in a maddened frenzy brought on by nerves shredded to the breaking point, Stanley gave permission to his men to loot and plun-der the villages.

The fight below the confluence of the Aruwimi and the Livingstone Rivers

The attack of the tribesmen in their sixty-three canoes

A week later, Stanley found momentary respite at the village of Rubunga, whose chief proved friendly and willing to barter food for beads and cloth. And here the expedition found its first evidence of European civilization since Nyangwe: four ancient Portuguese muskets. At the sight of these, the men "raised a glad shout. These appeared to them to be certain signs that we had not lost the road, that the great river did really reach the sea, and that their master was not deluding them when he told them that some day they would see the sea." But this, Stanley realized, was a double-edged omen. To be sure, the presence of the muskets, which had been traded up the river along the old slave trails over the centuries, meant that the European settlements that had existed for centuries at the Congo's mouth could not be too far away. But it also meant that the one overwhelming advantage he had had in the ceaseless battles with the river tribes—his firearms—was about to come to an end. From now on, his attackers would come at him with muskets as well as spears. And only a few days later that was what happened.

"Suddenly I heard a shot, and a whistling of slugs in the neighborhood of the boat. I turned my head, and observed the smoke of gunpowder drifting away from a native canoe." Sniping of this sort steadily intensified and at one point escalated into a pitched battle, in which 63 canoes, armed by Stanley's estimate with at least 315 muskets, swarmed around his boats. All that saved the expedition from total annihilation was the fact that the tribesmen didn't have proper ammunition for their weapons, loading them with scraps of copper and iron, which couldn't do much damage except at close range.

The unrelenting hostility of the river tribes also threatened the expedition with starvation. By now, of course, Stanley's own provisions were virtually exhausted, and he had to count on trading with local people to get food. But each time he went ashore to barter there was new trouble and we find him writing:

We have been unable to purchase food, or indeed approach a settlement for any amicable purpose. The aborigines have been so hostile that even fishing canoes have fired at us as though we were harmless game. God alone knows how we shall prosper . . . we regarded each other as fated victims of protracted famine, or the rage of savages.

But fearing famine more, on March 9 Stanley took an armed party ashore to forage for food. Almost immediately, several loud musket-shots startled us all, and six of our men fell wounded. Though we were taken considerably at a disadvantage, long habit had taught us how to defend ourselves in a bush, and a desperate fight began, and lasted an hour, ending in the retreat of the savages, but leaving us with fourteen of our men wounded.

It was, by Stanley's reckoning, the 32nd fight he had had, and it was the last. Three days later,

the river gradually expanded . . . which admitted us in view of a mighty breadth of river. . . . Sandy islands rose in front of us like a sea-beach, and on the right towered a long row of cliffs, white and glistening. . . . The grassy table-land above the cliffs appeared as green as a lawn. . . .

While taking an observation at noon of the position, Frank, with my glass in his hand, ascended the highest part of the large sandy dune that had been deposited by the mighty river, and took a survey of its strange and sudden expansion, and after he came back and said, "Why, I declare, sir, this place is just like a pool; as broad as it is long. There are mountains all round it, and it appears to me almost circular."

"Well, if it is a pool, we must distinguish it by some name. Give me a suitable name for it, Frank."

"Why not call it Stanley Pool?"

Stanley had reached the end of the longest single navigable stretch of the Congo River and had entered a region of peaceable tribes at last. Around him was the Bateke Plateau, on the frontier of the ancient Kingdom of Kongo with its centuries-old familiarity with Europeans. The sea was less than 400 miles away; the long-established European settlement at Boma less than 200. In effect, Stanley had accomplished all he had set out to accomplish. He had mapped the great lakes of Central Africa, settled the mystery of the Nile's sources, and proved that the Lualaba was the Congo. All he had to do now was get home. And that, he realized, would prove the most difficult task of all. For he now stood at the barrier which, albeit from its other side, had blocked all explorers from Diogo Cão to Tuckey from exploring the Congo until now.

Taking his boiling-point measurements, Stanley determined that the river's elevation at Stanley Pool was nearly 1150 feet above the sea. How it would make the descent Stanley had no real idea. He knew that the distance to the Atlantic was now too short for the river to make the descent in easy, gradual stages. There would have to be falls, and, indeed, after half a day of floating down the length of the Pool "we heard for the first time the low and sullen thunder of the first cataract." In the best of all possible worlds, the plunge would occur in a single, albeit dreadfully precipitous fall, for then, with the expenditure of an enormous final burst of energy, the boats could be portaged around it and refloated on the river's estuary for the happy last leg of the journey by waterway to Boma. But Stanley was perfectly aware that he lived in anything but the best of all possible worlds. He had studied the maps drawn by the Tuckey expedition and realized that "Tuckey's Farthest," the Yellala Falls where the ill-fated British naval captain had abandoned his attempt to ascend the river in 1816, had to be a considerable distance from the cataract he now found plunging over the southern edge of the Stanley Pool. Thus he could be sure that there were at least two falls between him and the sea, and all he could hope and pray was that there weren't too many more than that. In this he was encouraged by a local chieftain, Itsi of Ntamo; he said there were only three, the Child, the Mother, and the Father. As we now know, there are thirty-two.

On March 16, Stanley began the descent on "a furious river rushing down a steep bed obstructed by reefs of lava, projected barriers of rock, lines of immense boulders, winding a crooked course through deep chasms, and dropping down over terraces in a long series of falls, cataracts, and rapids." It was a descent into what Stanley called "a watery hell" and he would later confess that

there is no fear that any other explorer will attempt what we have done in the cataract region. It will be insanity in a successor. Nor would we have ventured on this terrible task, had we the slightest idea that such fearful impediments were before us.

The three cataracts which Itsi of Ntamo had forecast turned out to be only the first bunch.

The Child was a two hundred yards' stretch of broken water; and the Mother consisted of a half a mile of dangerous rapids. . . . But the Father is the wildest stretch of river I have ever seen. Take a strip of sea blown over by a hurricane, four miles in length and a half a mile in breadth, and a pretty accurate conception of its leaping waves may be obtained. Some of the troughs were a hundred yards in length, and from one to the other the mad river plunged. There was first a rush down into the bottom of an immense trough, and then, by its sheer force, the enormous volume would lift itself upward steeply until, gathering itself into a ridge, it suddenly hurled itself 20 or 30 feet straight upward, before rolling down into another trough. If I looked up or down along this angry scene, every interval of 50 or 100 yards of it was marked by wave-towers— their collapse into foam and spray, the mad clash of watery hills, bounding mounds and heaving billows, while the base of either bank, consisting of a long line of piled boulders of massive size, was buried in the tempestuous surf. The roar was tremendous and deafening. I can only compare it to the thunder of an express train through a rock tunnel. . . . The most powerful ocean streamer, going at full speed on this portion of the river, would be as helpless as a cockle-boat. I attempted three times, by watching some tree floated down from above, to ascertain the rate of the wild current by observing the time it occupied in passing between two given points, from which I estimated it to be about thirty miles an hour!

Stanley devised a scheme of leashing the boats with rattan hawsers to hold them back from the rapids while teams of men on land dragged them along the bank. Where that didn't work, he had the boats manhandled over the jagged and slippery rocks and boulders along the shore. By these methods, he managed to get downstream of these cataracts by March 24, only to discover an even more terrible cataract awaiting him, which he named the Cauldron. Hawsers parted, canoes were torn loose from the hands of fifty men and were swept away to destruction. "Accidents were numerous. . . . One man dislocated his shoulder, another was bruised on the hips, and another had a severe contusion of the head." Stanley himself fell feet first "into a chasm 30 feet deep between two enormous boulders, but fortunately escaped with only a few ribs bruised." On March 28 came the first fatalities in the roaring river. The Cauldron had been bypassed and the next rapid was about to be attempted and

I was beginning to congratulate myself . . . when to my horror I saw the Crocodile [the huge canoe captured above the Stanley Falls, now with six men in it] in mid-river . . . gliding with the speed of an arrow towards the falls. Human strength availed nothing now, and we watched it in agony. . . . We saw it whirled round three or four times, then plunged down into the depths, out of which the stern presently emerged pointed upwards, and we knew then that the canoe-mates were no more.

That afternoon three more men were lost in the raging torrents. "On the 3rd April . . . I myself tumbled headlong into a small basin, and saved myself with difficulty from being swept away by the receding tide."

Often the boats had to be portaged.

If the rapids or falls were deemed impassable by water, I planned the shortest and safest route across the projecting points, and then, mustering the people, strewed a broad track with bushes, over which . . . we set to work to haul our vessels. . . . The rocks rose singly in precipitous masses 50 feet above the river, and this extreme height increased the difficulty and rendered footing precarious.

On April 12, the *Lady Alice,* with Stanley in her, was almost lost.

Strong cane cables were lashed to the bow and stern, and three men were detailed to each, while five men assisted me in the boat. . . . We had scarcely ventured near the top of the rapids when . . . the current swept the boat from the hands [of the men holding the canecables on the bank]. Away into the centre of the angry, foaming, billowy stream the boat darted, dragging one man into the maddened flood . . . we rode downwards furiously on the crests of the proud waves, the human voice was weak against the over-whelming thunder of the angry river. . . . Never did rocks assume such hardness, such solemn grimness and bigness, never were they invested with such terrors and such grandeur, as while we were the cruel sport and prey of the brown-black waves, which whirled us round like a spinning top, swung us aside, almost engulfed us in the rapidly subsiding troughs, and then hurled us upon the white rageful crests of others. . . . The flood was resolved that we should taste the bitterness of death . . . we saw the river heaved bodily upward, as though a volcano was about to belch around us. . . . I shouted out, "Pull, men, for your lives."

And as by a miracle the *Lady Alice* was tossed up on the sandy bank of a small inlet.

On April 21, 37 days after the party had begun the descent, it had advanced a mere 34 miles from the Stanley Pool. And the cataract that now faced it, the Inkisi Falls, was utterly impassable. The boats would have to be portaged around it. But the banks were utterly impassable as well, "heaps of ruin, thick slabs, and blocks of trap rock." The only way to bypass Inkisi was to back away from the river and go up and over a 1200-foot mountain. To appreciate the magnitude of the task, one need only realize that, of the some dozen or so canoes that remained, several were well over 70 feet long and, made of teak, weighed upward of three tons. Stanley hoped to recruit 600 local tribesmen to assist in the work, but they considered the project complete madness. So Stanley set out with just his own men, half of them cutting a path up the mountain while the other half dragged the canoes after them; 500 to 800 yards of advance in a day was considered good going. Ultimately, "the native chiefs were in a state of agreeable wonder and complimentary admiration of our industry" and they delegated tribesmen from their villages to help the undefeatable white man. Nevertheless, it took the caravan nearly a month to get over the mountain and back down to the river on the other side.

The further downriver the expedition moved, the greater was the evidence of the long European presence at the river's mouth. So far the tribesmen had never actually seen Europeans themselves, but the marketplaces of their villages contained Delft ware and British crockery, Birmingham cutlery, gunpowder and guns, cloth and glassware and other such items of European manufacture. To a degree, of course, this was a heartening sight, since it proved that the party was advancing, no matter how painfully slowly, ever closer to its destination. But, as was the case with the appearance of those four Portuguese muskets at Rubunga, it created new problems. For, with European merchandise fairly abundant, Stanley found that his own trading goods were not in much demand. In effect, his currency was devalued; the prices for everything, and most especially food, skyrocketed.

In the absence of positive knowledge as to how long we might be toiling in the cataracts, we were all compelled to be extremely economical. Goat and pig meat were such luxuries that we declined to think of them as being possible with our means . . . chickens had reached such prices that they were rare in our camp. . . . Therefore—by the will of the gods—contentment had to be found in boiled duff, or cold cassava bread, ground-nuts, or pea-nuts, yams, and green bananas.

On this sort of diet, the caravan became increasingly prey to ravages of dysentery and disease.

Another devastating affliction was foot ulcers, and Frank Pocock was among the first to fall victim to them. He had finally worn out his last pair of shoes and after them a series of improvised sandals. Though Stanley—who himself was down to his last pair of boots, held together by bits of brass wire and worn through at the soles—continually urged him to make new sandals, Frank had taken to going barefoot most of the time. As a result, ants, mosquitos, vermin, and insects of all kinds swarmed into every cut or bruise his feet sustained scrambling over the rocks and crags of the river bank. Infections developed; they soon turned into festering ulcers, steadily eating down to the bone, and by the end of May he was too crippled to walk, and whenever the party could not travel by boat he had to be carried in a litter.

On June 3, the party reached a long stretch of rapids and cataracts called Zinga Falls and Stanley went ahead to make a reconnaissance. The plan was for the canoes to shoot the rapids one by one in those portions where it was feasible, to portage them around where it wasn't. But Frank, because of his crippled condition, was to come the entire way overland carried in his litter. The youth, however, seems to have taken this as an affront to his manhood, and no sooner was Stanley gone than he countermanded the order and had the men lift him into one of the canoes. The first stretch of rapids was run successfully, but then they came to a booming cataract and the boatmen pulled for the bank. Ordinarily what they would have done now was portage the canoe overland, but with the crippled youth they couldn't do that. What they decided, therefore, was to leave Frank where he was while they portaged the canoe downriver, then return with the litter to carry him the rest of the way. But the youth wouldn't hear of it. "What, carry me about the country like a worthless Goee-Goee for all the natives to stare at me? No, indeed!" Then he went on to argue, "I don't believe this fall is as bad as you say it is." For some minutes he and the boatmen debated the advisability of shooting the cataract in the canoe. The boatmen insisted the river was impassable; Frank, fearful of being made a laughingstock by allowing himself to be carried, insisted that it wasn't and finally called them cowards for not daring to attempt it. Goaded beyond endurance, one of the boatmen at last turned to the others and said, "Boys, our little master is saying we are afraid of death. I know there is death in the cataract, but come, let us show him that black men fear death as little as white men."

So the canoe was relaunched.

There was a greasy slipperiness about the water that was delusive, and it was irresistibly bearing them broadside over the falls. . . . Roused from his seat by the increasing thunder of the fearful waters, Frank rose to his feet, and looked over the heads of those in front, and now the full danger of the situation burst on him. But too late! They had reached the fall, and plunged headlong amid the waves and spray. The angry waters rose and leaped into their vessel, spun them round as though on a pivot, and so down over the curling, dancing, leaping crests, they were borne, to the whirlpools which yawned below. Ah! then came the moment of anguish, regret, and terror.

Eight days later Frank's body was found washed up on the bank, "the upper part nude, he having torn his shirt away to swim."

The death of the youth was an appalling blow to the morale of the caravan. Every man sensed in it his own approaching death on this hopeless enterprise. Stanley grieved as blackly as the rest. In the almost three years that he had been traveling with Frank, he had developed a deep affection for him, had come to count heavily on his assistance, and now felt himself terribly alone. "We are all so unnerved with the terrible accident . . . that we are utterly unable to decide what is best to do. We have a horror of the river now." It took him nearly three weeks to rouse himself and the rest of his party out of a paralyzed state of despair and get them struggling onward again. Hunger and fever plagued them; more men drowned in the raging torrents or dropped from disease; mutinies were repeatedly threatened, and thirty men deserted. By July, the situation had become so desperate that the men took to thieving. The only items the local tribesmen were interested in trading for were rum and guns, and as Stanley had no rum and would not sell his guns, his party was edged ever closer to the brink of outright starvation, and the men took to stealing from the villages they passed. When they were caught, Stanley had to pay heavy ransoms of cloth, beads, and wire to free them and when, as finally happened, he had exhausted his supplies, he was forced to abandon them to slavery.

At last, at the end of July, Stanley decided he had to abandon the river. He had been making latitude measurements for the last several days, and when he reached a cataract called Isangila on July 30 he concluded this was Tuckey's Farthest. "As the object of the journey had now been attained, and the great river of Livingstone had been connected with the Congo of Tuckey, I saw no reason to follow it farther, or to expend the little remaining vitality we possessed in toiling through the last four cataracts." More important, he had learned from the local people that by striking away from the river he could reach Boma in five days, and given the condition of his party every day was a matter of life and death. So, on July 31, the canoes were beached for the last time and, as a final tribute to "the brave boat, after her adventurous journey across Africa," the *Lady Alice* was carried to the summit of some rocks and "consigned to her resting place above the Isangila Cataract, to bleach and to rot to dust!" The next morning "a wayworn, feeble, and suffering column" set off for Boma.

They couldn't make it. For three days they struggled forward through the cruel, punishing Crystal Mountains, which had defeated Tuckey.

Up and down the desolate and sad land wound the poor, hungry caravan. Bleached whiteness of ripest grass, grey rock-piles here and there, looming up solemn and sad in their greyness, a thin grove of trees now and then visible on the heights and in the hollows—such were the scenes which every uplift of a ridge or rising crest of a hill met our hungry eyes.

On the fourth day, they reached a village named Nsanda, and here Stanley called a halt. The party was finished; the people were dying.

"To any Gentleman who speaks English at Embomma," he wrote:

Dear Sir, I have arrived at this place from Zanzibar with 115 souls, men, women, and children. We are now in a state of imminent starva tion. We can buy nothing from the natives, for they laugh at our kinds of cloth, beads, and wire. . . . I do not know you; but I am told there is an Englishman at Embomma, and as you are a Christian and a gentleman, I beg you not to disregard my request. . . . We are in a state of the greatest distress; but if your supplies arrive in time, I may be able to reach Embomma within four days. . . . The supplies must arrive within two days, or I may have a fearful time of it among the dying. . . . What is wanted is immediate relief; and I pray you to use your utmost energies to forward it at once. . . . Until that time, I beg you to believe me.

He signed the letter "Yours sincerely, H. M. Stanley" and then added rather pathetically, "P.S. You may not know me by name; I therefore add, I am the person that discovered Livingstone in 1871."

He prepared two other versions of the letter, in French and in Spanish (as a substitute for Portuguese), and then called for volunteers from among his men to carry them to Boma. Four stepped forward. "If there are white men in Embomma," they said, "we will find them out. We will walk, and walk, and when we cannot walk we will crawl." Two guides were recruited from the village to accompany them.

The reply was not long in coming. Boma turned out to be just a day's journey away, and on August 6 the men returned at the head of a luxuriously provisioned caravan.

Pale ale! Sherry! Port wine! Champagne! Several loaves of bread, wheaten bread, sufficient for a week. Two pots of butter. A packet of tea! Coffee! White loaf-sugar! Sardines and salmon! Plum-pudding! Currant, gooseberry, and raspberry jam! The gracious God be praised for ever! The long war we had maintained against famine and the siege of woe were over, and my people and I rejoiced in plenty!

After feasting for a day, Stanley and his expedition set off once again and "On the 9th August, 1877, the 999th day from the date of our departure from Zanzibar, we prepared to greet the van of civilization." Four white men, three Portuguese and a Hollander, came out to meet the caravan.

They brought a hammock with them, and eight sturdy, well-fed bearers. They insisted on my permitting them to lift me into the hammock. I declined. They said it was a Portuguese custom. To custom, therefore, I yielded.

He had come 7000 miles through the dark continent to be carried the final steps into Boma.

He spent two days there, and then he and his party were transferred to the larger Portuguese trading settlement at Cabinda.

Turning to take a farewell glance at the mighty river on whose brown bosom we had endured so greatly, I saw it approach, awed and humbled, the threshold of the watery immensity, to whose immeasurable volume and illimitable expanse, awful as had been its power, and terrible as had been its fury, its flood was but a drop.

Stanley and the Congo had reached the sea.

Toward the end of August, a Portuguese gunboat took the expedition to the still greater comforts of Loanda in Angola, where it spent a month for much-deserved rest and recuperation, and from there, this time aboard a British naval vessel, they went on to Cape Colony. It was everyone's expectation that Stanley at last would part from his men here. For surely his most sensible course now would be to take a British ship from Cape Colony to England. But he had made a promise to his men when they first set out and, as he told them now, nothing shall cause me to break my promise to you that I would take you home. You have been true to me, and I shall be true to you. If we can get no ship to take us, I will walk the entire distance with you until I can show you to your friends at Zanzibar.

On November 6, 1877, the H.M.S. *Industry* sailed from Cape Colony, and two weeks later

the boat-keel kissed the beach, and the impatient fellows leaped out and upwards, and danced in ecstasy on the sands of their island; then they kneeled down, bowed their faces to the dear soil, and cried out, with emotion, their thanks to Allah! To the full they now taste the sweetness of the return home. The glad tidings ring out along the beach, "It is Bwana Stanley's expedition that has returned."

Stanley had another reason for returning to Zanzibar. He knew there must be a packet of letters waiting for him there and he was eager to read those that had accumulated during his three years in the wilderness from his beloved Alice Pike. And this is what he read: "I have done what millions of women have done before me, not been true to my promise."

Part Four

---·=◆=◆·---

THE EXPLOITATION

18

EUROPE AND THE CONGO

When Stanley returned to England from his conquest of the Congo, there was—so unlike the mixed reception he had met after he had found Livingstone five years before—absolutely no quibbling with the magnificence of his accomplishment. The dispatches he had sent from Boma and Cabinda, Loanda, Cape Town, and Zanzibar had preceded him by several months, and by the time he set foot in Europe in January 1878 the world was in a state of almost hysterical excitement and hero worship. Geographical societies heaped their highest honors upon him; kings and queens, presidents and prime ministers vied to grant him audiences; the U.S. Congress convened especially to accord him a unanimous vote of thanks; newspapers queued up to get interviews; and publishers competed to sign up his memoirs. Even his arch-rivals in the field—Burton, Grant, Baker, Cameron—were unstinting in their praise. He had done more than all of them put together; he had filled in the great blank spaces of the map of Africa and had solved the outstanding geographical mysteries of the dark continent. He was, inarguably, the greatest African explorer of them all.

It was everything that Stanley had ever hoped for, but he was unable to enjoy it. He was, as he wrote, "so sick and weary . . . I cannot think of anything more than a long rest and sleep." The grueling three-year, 7000-mile journey had exhausted him and wrecked his health. His hair had turned totally white, he was emaciated in the extreme, and although he was only 37 he looked 15 years older. Worst of all, his heart had been broken by the betrayal of his betrothed. She had been "my stay and my hope, my beacon" throughout the years of his terrible travels, but now he knew himself to have been a fool;

Alice Pike had been married in January 1876, when Stanley had been under way barely a year. He excised every reference to the faithless woman from his journals, and a friend found him "very lonely and depressed" when they met at a banquet in his honor: "He was evidently suffering acutely from a bitter disappointment . . . 'What is the good of all this pomp and show,' were his words. 'It only makes me the more miserable and unhappy.' " In his own journal Stanley described his mood in this way:

When a man returns home and finds for the moment nothing to struggle against, the vast resolve, which has sustained him through a long and difficult enterprise, dies away, burning as it sinks in the heart; and thus the greatest successes are often accompanied by a peculiar melancholy.

In his melancholy mood, Stanley secluded himself for a few months to write a massive, 1000-page account of his epic journey, and then set out to try to amuse himself with the pleasures of civilization.

I had indulged in luxurious reveries while imprisoned in the rocky cañon of the Congo, and banqueted blissfully on thoughts of how I should enjoy myself. . . . I thought the art lay in dressing *à la mode,* sipping coffee with indolent attitudes on the flagstones of Parisian boulevards, or testing the merits of Pilsen and Strasburg beer; but my declining health and increasing moody spirits informed me that these were vanities, productive of nothing but loss of time, health, and usefulness.

He went on to Trouville, Deauville, and Dieppe "but my wretchedness increased. I explored those famed seaside resorts, and discovered that I was getting more and more unfit for what my neighbors called civilised society." Then he spent three weeks in Switzerland, where he did finally recover his health but where he also concluded that his "liberty" was "joyless and insipid," that the luxury of lounging about had become "unbearable." He had to get back to work, and he had a piece of work that he wanted to get back to.

Unlike explorers in Africa before him, Stanley was determined to see his explorations profitably exploited. In the spirit of Livingstone, he believed his mission now was to "pour the civilization of Europe into the barbarism of Africa." In the tradition of the Victorian age, he was convinced that the way to do that was through commerce. In the light of his discovery, he regarded the Congo River as the perfect artery by which that commerce could be carried into the long-inaccessible heart of the continent. And, in character with his tough-minded, wholly practical nature, he counted on the "legitimate desire for gain" to serve as the motivating force for Europeans to underwrite the enterprise.

Even while he was still in Africa he had written, in a dispatch to the London *Daily Telegraph:*

I feel convinced that the question of this almighty water-way will become a political one in time. As yet, however, no European Power seems to have put forth the right of control. Portugal claims it because she discovered the mouth; but the great Powers—England, America, and France —refuse to recognize her right. If it were not that I fear to damp any interest you may have in Africa, or in this magnificent stream, by the length of my letters, I could show you very strong reasons why it would be a politic deed to settle this momentous question immediately. I could prove to you that the Power possessing the Congo, despite the cataracts, would absorb to itself the trade of the whole of the enormous basin behind. This river is and will be the grand highway of commerce to West Central Africa.

Of all the great powers, it was Britain that Stanley most wanted to take possession of the Congo. Since his expedition, financed by a pair of newspapers, had had no official standing, he had not attempted to lay claim to the lands he discovered for the British, but he now set out to convince them that they should lay claim to it themselves. He was well aware of the problems posed to the commercial exploitation of the Congo by those 200 miles of murderous cataracts between the Stanley Pool and the river's estuary but he had a straightforward plan for doing something about them. Quite simply, a road, and in time a railroad, had to be built around them to connect the 1000 miles of navigable inland waterway above the Pool with the estuary and the sea. Then, a fleet of boats would be transported up that road and set sailing between the Stanley Pool and the Stanley Falls, and a string of trading stations would be established along the riverbanks, from which commerce and civilization would radiate out into the vast hinterland of the river basin and through which huge profits would be harvested home.

Stanley took every opportunity to proselytize for this plan—in newspaper articles, on the lecture circuit, in private conversations with powerful political and financial figures. He met a number of times with the Prince of Wales and Baron Rothschild; he addressed the Chambers of Commerce of Manchester and Liverpool and other industrial cities.

There are 40,000,000 of naked people beyond that gateway [he argued], and the cotton-spinners of Manchester are waiting to clothe them. . . . Birmingham's foundries are glowing with the red metal that shall presently be made into ironwork in every fashion and shape for them . . . and the ministers of Christ are zealous to bring them, the poor benighted heathen, into the Christian fold.

The reaction to all this at first dumbfounded Stanley and then ultimately infuriated and embittered him. To be sure, the French statesmen Léon Gambetta told him, "Not only, sir, have you opened up a new Continent to our view, but you have given an impulse to scientific and philanthropic enterprise which will have a material effect on the progress of the world." And a number of missionary societies, especially the English and American Baptists, were inspired to send brethren to the lands of the old Kongo kingdom. But as for "the redemption of the splendid central basin of the continent by sound and legitimate commerce," no one responded. Again and again, the merchants and politicians with whom he discussed his plans dismissed them as impractical and dismissed him as a dreamer.

A wise Englishman [Stanley wrote] has said that pure impulses and noble purposes have been oftener thwarted by the devil under the name Quixotism than by any other insinuating phrase of obstruction . . . that word was flung in my teeth. . . . The charge of Quixotism, being directed against my mission, deterred many noble men . . . from studying the question of new markets, and deepened unjustly their prejudices against Africa and African projects.

In part, this was due to Stanley's personality and personal history. For all the honor and acclaim the British establishment was willing to shower on him, it still couldn't take this one-time bastard poorhouse boy and erstwhile scoop-seeking journalist quite seriously. In the back of all those well-bred minds, Stanley's reputation as something of a "mere penny-a-liner," something of a buccaneer, still lingered, and enough had happened on his last African journey to keep that reputation alive. The relish with which he had described his massacre of the natives of Bumbireh island in Lake Victoria hadn't helped nor did the vivid and flamboyant accounts which he later wrote of his 32 running battles with the cannibals down the Lualaba. In fact, there were those who suggested that because of Stanley's pugnacious methods the tribesmen in the Congo interior were now wildly up in arms against all white men, making any enterprise like the one Stanley proposed doubly dangerous. What's more, gossip had it, utterly falsely, that the Africans whom Stanley had captured in those ceaseless wars he had often sold into slavery and just as often he had taken their women for his personal concubines. Now and again some bejeweled lady in an establishment drawing room, raising an eyebrow innocently, could be heard to inquire how it was that of all the white men Stanley had taken with him on his African journeys (two in his search for Livingstone and three on his exploration of the Congo) not one had got out alive.

But none of this really accounts for the lack of interest in Stanley's plan. Even had his reputation been as pure as the driven snow and his social credentials as impeccable as a lord's, his ideas would have been dismissed. The best proof is the fact that Cameron, a highly respectable officer of the Royal Navy with a highly respectable family background, had met with much the same indifference when he had returned to England two years before. Like Stanley, Cameron had been enthusiastic about the commercial possibilities of the Congo River basin and had described in ecstatic and exaggerated detail the beautiful scenery, the healthy climate, and the "incalculable wealth in tropical Africa." What's more, unlike Stanley's, his expedition had had an official status, and in his enthusiasm he had formally annexed the lands he had passed through in the name of the queen. But when he got back, he was told, in effect, thanks a lot but no thanks; Britain wasn't interested in the Congo. Nor, for that matter, was any other great power. It wasn't a question of his or Stanley's reputation. It was rather that the times were all wrong for their schemes. For Europe's view of Africa just then was in transition, passing from the old but not yet having reached the new, at one of those turning points in history where for a brief moment nothing can be done.

In a very real sense, Stanley's epic journey marked the end of the old. It had solved the most intriguing geographical secrets of the continent, and with that, perforce, the great age of African exploration, impelled by adventurous intellectual curiosity, was over. What's more, the suppression of the slave trade and the abolition of slavery were by now virtually completed, and so the humanitarian enthusiasm for Africa, which had played such a vital role in awakening Europe's interest in the continent, had also much waned. But the next era—the European colonization of Africa—had not yet quite begun.

At the time, in the late 1870s, with the notable exception of South Africa (which would remain the notable exception in everything about Africa to this day), Europe still had almost no colonies worthy of the name south of the Sahara, and those few that it did have were either unimportant or unsuccessful. For example, British abolitionists had established Sierra Leone as a settlement for freed slaves and when it failed the British government felt obliged to take it over, but its only real use was as a base for its antislavery naval patrols. British colonial administrations had also been set up on the Gold Coast, at the Niger delta, and at the mouth of the Gambia River, but their prime function was to provide military protection for private traders rather than to govern natives. Similarly, France's only colonial activity on the continent at the time was in Senegal, for the protection of French traders on that river, and at Libreville in Gabon, where it too had been obliged to take over when an abolitionist attempt to set up a freed-slave settlement failed. Portugal continued to hold on to its centuries-old settlements, but these too were less colonies in the modern sense than sprawling trading stations under a governmental umbrella, with little real jurisdiction or control over the natives of the region.

And that was just about how most Europeans were content to allow it to remain. Certainly the white traders in Africa were. A rough-and-ready, individualistic band, including such legendary characters as Trader Horn, Mary Kingsley, John Holt, Du Chaillu and Douville, they were ardent advocates of laissez faire and, while they acknowledged the need for their governments' protection from time to time, they were nevertheless anxious to limit their governments' involvement in their freebooting affairs.

For their part, European governments were not anxious to get any more deeply involved in black Africa than they already were. The lucrative legitimate trade with the continent, which was expected to have boomed after the end of the slave traffic, hadn't materialized. Britain's exports to black Africa at the time, for example, amounted to less than one-hundredth of its exports to the rest of the world; apart from palm oil, groundnuts and the old standby ivory, no especially valuable imports had been developed; and because of the brutal climate, nothing in the way of meaningful white settlement had even been tried. Moreover, there wasn't any political or military advantage

King Leopold II

to be gained. Black Africa had not yet become a stage on which Europe's traditional rivalries were played out (the situation, of course, was much different in North Africa, Egypt, and along the Red Sea, since the opening of the Suez Canal). No major power exercised any greater political influence or derived any greater economic benefits than any other, nor did anyone's territorial claims, which in any case were modest, come into geographical conflict with anyone else's.

For the moment at least, what today would be called a balance of power existed in sub-Sahara Africa, and it would not be until that balance was upset, until it began to appear that one power was gaining an upper hand, that European governments would abandon their indifference toward Africa and the wild, almost hysterical scramble for colonies would suddenly get under way. But that wasn't to happen for another ten years, and when it did the force that caused it was so unexpected, so unlikely, indeed so bizarre that no one can be too seriously criticized for not anticipating it. For that force was Leopold II, king of the Belgians.

At the time of Stanley's return from the Congo, Leopold was 42 and had been 12 years on his throne, a tall, imposing man with a huge spade beard and an enormous nose, enjoying a reputation for hedonistic sensuality, cunning intelligence (his father once described him as subtle and sly as a fox), overweaning ambition, and personal ruthlessness. He was, nevertheless, an extremely minor monarch in the *realpolitik* of the times, ruling a totally insignificant nation, a nation in fact that had come into existence barely four decades before and lived under the constant threat of losing its precarious independence to the great European powers around it. He was a figure who, one might have had every reason to expect, would devote himself to maintaining his country's strict neutrality, avoiding giving offense to any of his powerful neighbors, and indulging his keenly developed tastes for the pleasures of the flesh, rather than one who would have a profound impact on history. Yet, in the most astonishing and improbable way imaginable, he managed virtually single-handedly to upset the balance of power in Africa and usher in the terrible age of European colonialism on the black continent.

He began fashioning this infamous destiny in his earliest youth. While crown prince, he traveled widely, from Egypt and North Africa to India and the lands of the Far East, including China itself, and what appeared at first a harmless fascination with geography proved to be the germ of a policy for acquiring power which was to be the central obsession of his life and reign. He believed that the only road to greatness open to little Belgium and, more especially, to her insignificant king was the acquisition of colonies. Long before he became king, he wrote:

Surrounded by the sea, Holland, Prussia and France, our frontiers can never be extended in Europe. The sea bathes our coast, the universe lies in front of us, steam and electricity have made distances disappear, all the unappropriated lands on the surface of the globe may become the field of our operations and of our successes. . . . Since history teaches that colonies are useful, that they play a great part in that which makes up the power and prosperity of states, let us strive to get one in our turn.

Leopold was related to Queen Victoria through the House of Coburg (she was a cousin) and he was influenced by this connection to believe that Belgium could achieve a measure of Britain's wealth and power by emulating her imperial policies. After all, he argued, both Britain and Belgium were small countries, both were highly industrialized, and the only real difference between them was that Britain, in her overseas possessions, had ready markets for her products and inexpensive raw materials for her industries. Belgium had lost hers when she split from the Netherlands in the 1830s, and since the Dutch had contrived to retain the entire overseas empire of the United Provinces, including the rich East Indies, Belgium had to make up for this lack. What she needed, in Leopold's words, was "some new Java." In the late 1850s and early 1860s, he set himself the task of finding one.

At one point, he expressed interest in "the Argentine Province of Entre Rios and the little island of Martin-Garcia at the confluence of the Uruguay and the Parana. Who owns this island?" he asked. "Could one buy it, and set up there a free port under the moral protection of the King of the Belgians?" Later his attentions focused on the Far East. He came up with a plan to buy Borneo from the Dutch; he offered to rent the Philippines from Spain; he suggested schemes for Belgian colonies in China, Indo-China, Japan, Fiji, the New Hebrides, and a host of other places. "I believe that the time has come to spread ourselves outwards," he wrote with growing eagerness and impatience while still prince; "we cannot afford to lose any more time, under penalty of seeing the best positions, which are already becoming rare, successively occupied by nations more enterprising than our own."

Leopold ascended the throne, in December 1865, just at the moment when the excitement generated by the exploration in search of the Nile sources was at its height. Burton, Speke, Grant, and Baker were not long back from their travels, the Nile debate raged throughout Europe, and Livingstone was about to set off on his last journey. And quite naturally, the new Belgian king's attention shifted from the far East to the dark continent. Here were "unappropriated lands" which could become the field for his operations. And here too, he saw, the best positions were not becoming rare; indeed, the great powers were making no move to occupy the territories newly opened up by their explorers and seemed to have no intention of doing so. Leopold became an Africa enthusiast. He read all the explorers' books, he joined geographical societies, he donated money for future expeditions, and he began hatching colonial schemes for Belgium in Africa. He studied the possibilities along the West Coast, between Senegal and Cape Masuradi; he proposed the foundation of an East Africa Company to operate in Mozambique and later in other Portuguese territories; he took an interest in the Lualaba question and met with Cameron; he came up with plan after plan. Yet, ten years later, in 1875, Belgium was still without a colony.

Leopold's problem was that, as much as he wanted a colony for Belgium, Belgium didn't want one for herself. Like all European governments at the time and, given her small size, with better reason, the government in Brussels was strongly opposed to incurring the costs and risks involved in establishing colonies in Africa. Since the king of the Belgians was a constitutional monarch, he was powerless to force his will on the nation. And that, by all rights, should have been the end of that. But it wasn't, and the fact that it wasn't was where the situation took its bizarre turn. For this minor and essentially powerless monarch was so determined that he decided if he couldn't acquire a colony for his country then he was going to acquire one for himself.

This was then as incredible an idea as it would be today. No individual, be he even a king, could have, would be allowed to have, his own personal colony. Leopold was perfectly aware of this. But it didn't deter him. Calling on all his cunning, all his ambition, all his ruthlessness, he devised the means by which he could have it anyway.

In September 1876, Leopold, as a well-known African enthusiast and member of a number of geographical societies, sponsored an international geographical conference in Brussels. Delegations from the scientific societies of Britain, France, Germany, Austria, Italy, and Russia attended. The purpose, Leopold stated in his speech opening the conference,

is one of those which must be a supreme preoccupation to all friends of humanity. To open to civilization the only area of our globe to which it has not yet penetrated, to pierce the gloom which hangs over entire races, constitutes, if I may dare put it in this way, a Crusade worthy of this century of progress. . . . Gentlemen, many of those who have made the closest study of Africa have come to the conclusion that their common purpose would be well served by a meeting and a conference designed to get their work in step, to concert efforts, to share all resources, and to avoid covering the same ground twice. It seemed to me that Belgium, a neutral and centrally placed country, would be a suitable place for such a meeting. . . . Need I say that in bringing you to Brussels I was guided by no motives of egoism? No, gentlemen, Belgium may be a small country, but she is happy and contented with her lot; I have no other ambition than to serve her well.

The agenda for the conference was every bit as deceptively high-minded. Only the most disinterested scientific and philanthropic topics were to be discussed: for example, the prospects for setting up supply bases and medical posts in the African interior to assist future expeditions, the methods necessary for the correlation and dissemination of maps and data gathered by past explorations, measures to be taken to accomplish the final eradication of the Arab slave trade, and so on. As the last item, Leopold called for the establishment of a permanent international committee to coordinate and oversee all these useful projects. The delegates couldn't but be favorably impressed. They threw themselves with enthusiasm into the work of the conference and, at the end, voted the formation of the Association Internationale Africaine, with headquarters in Brussels, a banner of blue with a gold star on it, and none other than Leopold II as its chairman.

The association, as it was to turn out, was a complete fiction. It, in fact, met only one more time, in 1877, and then was never heard from again. Which was precisely the way Leopold wanted it. What he had set out to create was a front organization through which he could pursue his improbable personal ambitions in Africa. And, with the subtle and sly skill of a fox, that was exactly what he had done. As the head of an ostensibly international, scientific, and philanthropic institution dedicated to good works on the continent, and not as the king of the Belgians, he was free to undertake all manner of activities in Africa without the interference of the Belgian government and without arousing the suspicions of the European powers.

Leopold's ambition had fixed on the Congo River basin. His interview with Cameron had convinced him of the potential wealth of the region, and the dispatches from Stanley, which filtered out of Africa during 1876 and 1877 and which the Belgian king read avidly, served to sharpen his appetite. So when Stanley, en route back to England in January 1878, stopped at Marseilles, Leopold sent two emissaries to meet him and, as Stanley later reported, "before I was two hours older I was made aware that King Leopold intended to undertake to do something substantial for Africa, and that I was expected to assist him." What precisely that might be Leopold was still keeping secret, but in a remarkably candid letter written at this time to a close intimate he put it this way:

I think that if I entrusted Stanley publicly with the job of taking over part of Africa in my own name, the English would stop me. If I consult them, they will again try to stop me. So I think that at first I shall give Stanley an exploring job which will not offend anybody, and will provide us with some posts down in that region and with a high command for them which we can develop when Europe and Africa have got used to our "pretensions" on the Congo.

Stanley wasn't interested. He was exhausted, sick and heartbroken, as we've seen, and, what's more, still believed that he was going to be able to interest England in backing his scheme for the exploitation of the Congo. So he politely brushed off the two Belgian emissaries, refused to pay even a courtesy call on Leopold, and went on his way to London. Leopold wasn't discouraged. He correctly judged what the British government's and, for that matter, the other great powers' reaction to Stanley's ideas would be. There was the precedent of Cameron's failure, and Leopold guessed that Stanley's somewhat soiled reputation would make him an even less convincing advocate. So, after biding his time for a bit, Leopold in June 1878 again invited Stanley to Brussels. Stanley, although by no means yet ready to give up altogether on the British but getting increasingly discouraged by their attitude, accepted. The two men discussed Stanley's ideas and especially his view that nothing substantial could be done until a road and, better yet, a railroad were built around the Livingstone Falls. Leopold agreed and revealed that he was prepared to arrange the financing of such an enterprise under the auspices of his International Association. But even so nothing definite came of the meeting, and Stanley returned to London to pursue his cause for another few, frustrating months.

In the meantime, Leopold made another cunning move. Using the umbrella of the International Association, but without consulting any of its members, he formed something called the Comité d'Études du Haut-Congo with himself as chairman. Ostensibly, this study committee was meant to sponsor a new expedition "with an essentially philanthropic and scientific point of view and with the intention of extending civilization and finding new outlets for commerce and industry by the study and explorations of certain parts of the Congo." In fact, it was simply a highfalutin name for a commercial syndicate which Leopold had formed to finance that road or railway around the Livingstone Falls and go on from there to build trading stations on the Congo. The principal stockholder in this syndicate was Leopold. Within a year, after he had changed the syndicate's name to the Association Internationale du Congo so as to deliberately confuse it with the Association Internationale Africaine, Leopold in fact became its sole stockholder. But when Stanley, early in November, once again responded to an invitation to meet with the king at the royal palace in Brussels, he tells us,

I there discovered various persons of more or less note in the commercial and monetary world, from England, Germany, France, Belgium, and Holland. . . . This body of gentlemen desired to know how much of the Congo River was actually navigable by light-draught vessels? What protection could friendly native chiefs give to commercial enterprises? Were the tribes along the Congo sufficiently intelligent to understand that it would be better for their interest to maintain friendly intercourse with the whites than to restrict it? What tributes, taxes, or imports, if any, would be levied by the native chiefs for right of way through their country? What was the character of the produce which the natives would be able to exchange for European fabrics?

But central to all their questions were those about building a way around the cataracts. Stanley suggested that, before they attempted to lay 200 miles of railway track through the rugged Crystal Mountains, a survey should be made, a wagon road built, and a string of supply stations erected for the use of the crews that would come afterward. Moreover, he pointed out, arrangements would have to be made with local chiefs, by treaty, purchase, or lease, for the acquisition of lands for the supply stations and right-of-way in order to avoid unnecessary hostilities. Once this was done, he went on, a fleet of vessels could then be transported up the wagon road and launched on the Stanley Pool, and trading, supply, and scientific stations could be erected along the Congo all the way to the Stanley Falls.

The commercial and monetary gentlemen agreed that this seemed an eminently practical approach to begin with. They were prepared to finance an expedition to implement it and Stanley was invited to head it under a five-year contract at a salary of £1000 a year. By now his hopes of interesting the British in this plan had been completely dashed and he accepted. Throughout the winter of 1878 he again engaged in the complicated business of mounting an expedition to the Congo.

There was someone else in Europe that winter who was also busily engaged in mounting an expedition to the Congo. He was Count Pierre Savorgnan de Brazza, a tall, slim, almost embarrassingly handsome 26-year-old French naval officer, who, like Cameron, was to engage Stanley in a race for the Congo but who, unlike Cameron, would win it.

Brazza by birth was an Italian from one of the most distinguished families of Rome (his correct name was Pietro Paulo Francesco Camillo Savorgnan di Brazza), and claimed descent from the Emperor Severus and from the Doges. But as a youth he had developed a passion for and joined the French Navy, and after seeing service in the Franco-Prussian War had applied for and received French citizenship. He first set foot in Africa in 1871, when the ship he was aboard carried reinforcements to French troops fighting rebel tribesmen in Algeria, and then for the next three years he served on a vessel that made frequent calls at Libreville and Port Gentil in France's Gabon colony. Though his duties as an auxiliary ensign usually confined him to his ship during these visits, he did manage on three occasions to make short excursions up the Ogowe and Gabon rivers, and in June 1874, when he was only 22 and Stanley was planning the epic journey that would discover the Congo, Brazza came forward with his own plan of exploration. "I have acquired the conviction that the Ogowe, even above

Count Pierre Savorgnan de Brazza

the first rapids, is still a very considerable river that stretches into the interior," he wrote to the French Minister of Marine, and then went on to propose an expedition, led by himself and accompanied by a couple of other navy officers and a party of Senegalese sailors, to explore the river and discover its commercial possibilities for the Gabon colony.

Three things conspired in Brazza's favor. One was that the Minister of Marine was a close personal friend of his family and had, in fact, been instrumental in getting the Italian-born youth into the French Navy in the first place. Another was that the strikingly good-looking, exquisitely mannered youth, with his impeccable noble lineage, was charmingly persuasive and made an irresistible impression wherever he went. But third and most important was the fact that there was a growing uneasiness in some influential quarters in Paris that France was allowing herself to be outdistanced, in the matter of African exploration, by her archrival Great Britain. For nearly two decades now, British expeditions, sponsored by the Admiralty, Foreign Office, or Royal Geographical Society, had been winning honors and glory for Queen Victoria with their magnificent and highly publicized quests for the Nile sources, while France had been standing aside doing absolutely nothing. Surely the time had come for the French to get into the field and take some of the prizes for their own monarch. To be sure, not everyone agreed, and it took well over a year for the Minister of Marine to win approval for Brazza's plan. But in the end the combination of these three factors won out, and by August 1875 the young count was on his way.

Stanley, who by this time had circumnavigated Lake Victoria and was headed toward Lake Albert, was completely unaware of Brazza's expedition; the only rival he knew he had in the field then was Cameron. Brazza, for his part, was aware of both Stanley and Cameron, but he did not regard himself as their rival. In his heart of hearts, he hoped that the Ogowe would stretch eastward from the coast so far into the African interior that it would bring him to the region of the great lakes and allow him to make some grand discovery in connection with the Nile sources. But he was realistic enough not to count on it. His was a modest and modestly financed expedition, and he seems to have been content just to be under way, enjoying the heady excitement of traveling in the wilds, seeking to solve the minor mystery of the Ogowe's source.

The going was rough; the terrain was thickly jungled; the tribes became increasingly hostile the deeper he penetrated from the coast; disease claimed its usual ghastly toll; and the cruelty of the slave traffic in the interior was shockingly depressing for the young, refined nobleman. It took him nearly two years to reach the point where the river, having turned from the east to the south, became unnavigable and dwindled to a stream near its source. "The Ogowe had no more secrets from us," he wrote. "It was now clear that its course was only of secondary importance, with no direct access to the center of the African continent." Although this was not unexpected, Brazza did not now turn back, for during the last several weeks of his travels he had been hearing reports of a "big water" lying further eastward in the interior, and he had begun to hope that it might turn out to be one of the great lakes. So, leaving the Ogowe, he pressed on eastward.

Early in 1878, by which time Stanley had returned to England, Brazza reached the land of the Bateke tribesmen, who showed him a river, called the Alima, which they said flowed into the big water. In fact, they claimed, the big water was only five days' journey away, but they also warned Brazza that the tribes he would now encounter were the most ferocious of all, and cannibals into the bargain. Though he was running short of supplies and, most especially, ammunition, Brazza was willing to chance it and, hiring canoes from the Bateke, set off with his party down the Alima. The first day on the river they heard the eerie and unnerving sound of the cannibal war drums beating along the jungled banks, but the first village let them pass without trouble. In the evening, however, they were fired on from shore. Fearful of traveling in the dark on the unknown river, they camped that night, and at dawn they awoke to find thirty war canoes bearing down on them in a fearsome attack. Brazza's rifles managed to drive the tribesmen off, but he decided his expedition was in no condition to survive even five days of such conditions. Leaving most of the baggage and all of the canoes, Brazza fled with his men overland through the swampy forests back from whence he had come.

Had Brazza been able to keep going, had he been, one is tempted to say, Stanley with all the latter's bulldog persistence and unflinching courage, he would have made a magnificent discovery. For the Alima is a tributary of the Congo. Five days' journey down it would have brought Brazza to the "big water" he had heard about, some 200 miles upstream of the Stanley Pool.

Brazza arrived back in France in the last days of 1878, nearly a year after Stanley's return. His reception was warm and congratulatory, and the French made something of a national hero of him as their first African explorer. But obviously his achievement was minor and the honors and acclaim bestowed on him pale in comparison to Stanley's. It wounded the young nobleman's pride. When he read Stanley's account of his journey and realized just how close he had come to reaching the Congo himself, he turned somewhat nasty. He claimed then— and, later in life, he would elaborate and embroider on his claim—that his failure was Stanley's fault. Seizing on Stanley's own accounts of the 32 battles he had fought in his progress down the river, Brazza tried to make the case that the hostility he had encountered from the tribesmen during his journey, which finally forced him to turn back from the Congo, was a result of the hostility Stanley had aroused among the tribesmen against all whites. Out of his bitter envy, Brazza became, unbeknown to Stanley, Stanley's most ferocious rival.

Brazza had a plan. He had found, although quite inadvertently, he realized, a completely new and, until now, unthought-of route to the Congo. By following the Ogowe from the Gabon coast, and then the Alima or any of a number of other tributaries that flow into the Congo from the north, he could reach Stanley's "grand highway of commerce to West Central Africa" without having to surmount the terrible cataracts of the Livingstone Falls. What Brazza wanted to do was mount a well-equipped and well-financed expedition to open that newly discovered route. He was as convinced as Cameron and Stanley had been of the commercial potential of the Congo, and he wanted to exploit that potential for France.

Unfortunately, for all his charming persuasiveness, Brazza found it as difficult to get a serious hearing for his ideas as Cameron and Stanley had for theirs. The French government was as reluctant to get involved in a colonial enterprise in Africa as the British and, for that matter, the Belgian governments had been. For months after his return Brazza raced around Paris trying to arouse support for his scheme, calling on influential friends of his family, writing articles, addressing chambers of commerce, lobbying statesmen, using every argument he could think of. He held out the prospect of a great French African empire stretching from Algeria to the Congo, promised mammoth profits from trade in the river basin, argued France's responsibility to undertake a civilizing mission among the savages there, called for the assertion of French power and glory. And all in vain.

But then Brazza got a break. The news leaked out that Stanley, having been rejected by the British, had hired on with Leopold and was to lead an expedition for the Belgian king's Association Internationale Africaine. To be sure, according to Leopold's cover story, this was meant to be a purely scientific and philanthropic undertaking, but Brazza was able to arouse suspicion in the right circles. His good friends at the Ministry of Marine were willing to sponsor a second expedition on a modest scale much like the first, lightly equipped and minimally financed, in order to give Brazza a chance to demonstrate the feasibility of reaching the Congo from the Gabon coast. And so a second race to the Congo began.

19

BULA MATARI

Stanley's expedition was cloaked in immense secrecy. So great were the stealth and deception with which Leopold surrounded it that, by the time Brazza got any inkling of it and hurriedly began preparing his own expedition in August 1879, Stanley had been under way for more than half a year.

Toward the end of January, Leopold had dispatched a chartered steamer, the *Albion*, to Suez. But Stanley wasn't on it. He left a few days later alone, traveling incognito as Monsieur Henri, on what appeared to be a private citizen's holiday ramble through France and Italy. It was only when he was sure that he had shaken off any interest in his movements and his whereabouts in Europe was generally unknown that he made a dash for Suez to rendezvous with the *Albion*. From there he sailed aboard her through the canal and down the Red Sea to Zanzibar. Meanwhile, the bulk of his expedition—a massive assemblage of over 80 tons of stores and equipment, including prefabricated houses, a fleet of 8 boats, and a party of a dozen European assistants—was dispersed in various European ports. It wouldn't set off for the Congo until May—and then by an entirely different route.

Stanley's unexpected arrival in Zanzibar in April startled the European community on the island and set it buzzing with speculations. It was obvious, of course, that he must be considering another one of his stupendous African journeys, but where or why no one could fathom. And Stanley himself deliberately deepened the mystery. Without saying a word to anyone, he hired 68 Zanzibaris—three-quarters of whom had served with him before—and then made a series of utterly pointless and completely misleading excursions with them to the East African mainland. The puzzled American consul on the island cabled Washington: "Mr. H. M. Stanley has been hovering between this place and the coast for over a month, and will leave soon for Mombassa. We don't know for what reason he is here, but presume it has some concern with some grand commercial scheme."

Then, to further compound the confusion, yet another unannounced expedition turned up on the island. It was headed by a Belgian army captain and was said to be under the auspices of King Leopold's scientific, philanthropic, and thoroughly defunct Association Internationale Africaine, sent out to establish a chain of supply stations in the African interior for the use of future explorers. Stanley busied himself helping outfit this party, as if this might have been the reason for his visit to Zanzibar, but when it departed for the mainland at the end of May (where it attached itself to a White Fathers' mission and conveniently dropped out of public view) he, of course, did not go along. Instead, he boarded his Zanzibaris on the *Albion* and steamed, not round the Cape of Good Hope toward the Congo's mouth, but once again misleadingly back up the East African coast and into the Red Sea.

For all this hugger-mugger, the biggest secret about Leopold's audacious scheme was one that Stanley himself didn't know anything about. And it was only when he was so deeply committed and so far under way that he was unlikely to pull out of the venture that Leopold felt free to let him in on it.

During his passage back through the Red Sea, Stanley received two telegrams from Brussels. The first, at Aden, informed him that Leopold had taken over all the shares of the Comité d'Études du Haut-Congo and was now the sole proprietor of the international syndicate. The second, at Suez, requested him to proceed to Gibraltar. There he was met by a certain Colonel Maximilian Strauch, a stiff-necked, pince-nezed staff officer from the Belgian War Ministry and a devoutly loyal servant of Leopold's, whom the Belgian king had designated as the secretary-general of his Comité d'Études du Haut-Congo and through whom he would henceforth communicate with Stanley about his devious Congo schemes. Strauch took Stanley to his rooms at a Gibraltar hotel and there passed on to him Leopold's latest and most startling set of instructions. Stanley was to go ahead and build that wagon road around Livingstone Falls and erect a string of trading stations up the river, as he had been instructed to do by the Comité. But now that Leopold was the sole owner of the Comité he was to do something else: create a Confederation of Free Negro Republics in the Congo River basin.

This was to be an independent black African state, taking for its precedent and bearing a superficial resemblance to the then recent American experiment in Liberia. It was to be formed through the signing of treaties with local chiefs; under the treaties they were to agree to combine in this confederation and surrender their individual sovereignties to it. And it was to have as its ruler Leopold II. "It is not a question of Belgian colonies," Stanley was told.

It is a question of creating a new State, as big as possible, and of running it. It is clearly understood that in this project there is no question of granting the slightest political power to the negroes. That would be absurd. The white men, heads of the stations, retain all power. They are the absolute commanders. . . . Every station would regard itself as a little republic. Its leader, the white man in charge, would himself be responsible to the Director-General of Stations, who in turn would be responsible to the President of the Confederation. . . . The President will hold his powers from the King.

Here then, bluntly put, was the outline of Leopold's plan to acquire his own African colony. If Stanley was in any doubt, a subsequent letter to him from Leopold reemphasized the central point:

The King, as a private person, wishes only to possess properties in Africa. Belgium wants neither a colony nor territories. Mr. Stanley must therefore buy lands or get them conceded to him, attract natives on to them, and proclaim the independence of his communities, subject to the agreement of the *Comité.*

There is no indication that Stanley found anything incredible about this idea. It is true that, knowing what he knew about African tribes, he did not think it would be an easy matter to get them to agree to any sort of political union among themselves, and in a letter to Brussels from Gibraltar he told Leopold as much. But, as his subsequent actions were to prove, he was certainly willing to give it his best try. In the context of the ideas of the times, which is to say Europe's ignorant concept that the African was too primitive to govern himself, Stanley could allow himself to believe that a confederation of this sort, ruled by a presumably enlightened European monarch, might serve to "pour the civilization of Europe into the barbarism of Africa." And so, sailing from Gilbraltar down the West African coast to the Congo's mouth, he could view his expedition as having the novel mission of sowing along [the Congo's] banks civilized settlements, to peacefully conquer and subdue it, to remould it in harmony with modern ideas of National States, within whose limits the European merchant shall go hand in hand with the dark African trader, and justice and law shall prevail, and murder and lawlessness and the cruel barter of slaves shall for ever cease.

Stanley, with his company of 68 Zanzibaris, reached the Congo on August 14, 1879. The rest of his expedition which included a polyglot crew of Belgians, Danes, Englishmen, Americans, and Frenchmen, were already there, and some 100 additional local tribesmen were hired. The flotilla of boats—three steamers, *La Belgique, Espérance,* and *Royal;* a paddle boat, *En Avant;* two steel lighters; a screw launch; and a wooden whale boat—were launched on the estuary. The massive amount of supplies and equipment, contained in over 2000 packing cases, were loaded on the boats. And on August 21 the expedition started upriver, "an event," as Stanley would later write, "that may well be called the inauguration of a new era for the Congo basin."

Stanley's first job in opening this era was the establishment of a main base camp, the first in the string of stations he was to build up the Congo. For it, he selected a village called Vivi, located on a hill on the estuary's right bank, just across the river from the present-day seaport of Matadi and just below the Cauldron of Hell. And here he took the first step to implement Leopold's ambition to bring the Congo basin under his personal sovereignty. Gathering the chiefs of Vivi together for a palaver, Stanley announced,

I want ground to build my houses, for I am about to build many. . . . I want to go inland, and must have the right to make roads wherever it is necessary, and all men that pass by those roads must be allowed to pass without interruption. No chief must lay his hand on them. . . . You have no roads in your country. It is a wilderness of grass, rocks, bush. . . . If you and I can agree, I shall change all that.

This was the first of literally hundreds of such palavers Stanley was to have in the next five years, and out of that experience he was moved to write:

In the management of a bargain I should back the Congoese native against Jew or Christian, Parsee or Banyan, in all the round world. Unthinking men may perhaps say cleverness at barter, and shrewdness in trade, consort not with their unsophisticated condition and degraded customs.

Unsophisticated is the very last term I should ever apply to an African child or man in connection with the knowledge of how to trade. . . . I have seen a child of eight do more tricks of trade in an hour than the cleverest European trader on the Congo could do in a month. . . . Therefore when I write of the Congo native, whether he is of the Bakongo, Byyanzi, or Bateke tribes, remember to associate him with an almost inconceivable amount of natural shrewdness, and power of indomitable and untiring chaffer.

The palaver went on for two days before a bargain was finally struck. Under it, Stanley agreed to make a payment of £32 sterling worth of cloth down and £2 sterling worth of cloth per month. In return, the Vivi chiefs agreed to sell him a 20-square-mile tract for his base station, granted him the right-of-way through their domains for whatever roads he wanted to build, and ceded their sovereignty over those lands to Leopold's Comité. This bargain set the pattern for the hundreds of others to come and, considering the ghastly price that they would cost the peoples of the Congo, one has to wonder about the cleverness in barter and the shrewdness in trade with which Stanley credited them. It would seem that even the American Indians made a better deal with their sale of Manhattan Island. Nevertheless, Stanley tells us, "We had the usual scenes of loud applause" at the conclusion of the negotiations.

The real work began on October 1. The local chiefs and populace gathered along the river banks "in gay robes and bright colours." Stanley had tools unloaded from his boats and then he himself picked up a sledgehammer and, in a way of instructing his men, struck the first blow. A great cry of admiration arose from the crowds and, we are told, it was for this act that the Vivi chiefs "bestowed on me the title Bula Matari—Breaker of Rocks—with which, from the sea to Stanley Falls, all natives of the Congo are now so familiar." It was a title which in time would fall into disrepute because it was to become synonymous with the governors and governments of the terrible colony which Stanley was now setting out to found for Leopold. But when it was originally bestowed on Stanley it was meant to be one of great honor, and it was then one that was richly deserved. For in the course of the next fourteen months—from October 1879 to February 1881— Bula Matari and his rock-breaking crews built a road up from the river to the Vivi hill, erected a major settlement at the Vivi station, then cut a 52-mile road around the first set of rapids and cataracts to

Isangila (where the *Lady Alice* had been abandoned), and transported by man-hauled wagons a number of the boats and more than 50 tons of equipment and supplies up it.

It was a grueling period. Stanley reckoned, what with all the marching and countermarching, that he walked 2352 miles to cover the distance from Vivi to Isangila. Ravines had to be bridged, mangrove swamps crossed, mountains surmounted, forests felled. Fevers and accidents killed 6 of the Europeans and 22 Africans, and scores of the party had to be invalided out and scores more hired to replace them. The work went on ten hours a day, six days a week, on a diet consisting of beans and goat meat and bananas. Quarrels broke out among the Europeans. Unused to commanding so many white men, Stanley found himself repeatedly embroiled in petty disputes with them over the terms of their contracts, the prerogatives of their ranks, and the perquisites of their service.

Almost all of them [Stanley later wrote in disgust], clamoured for expenses of all kinds, which included, so I was made to understand, wine, tobacco, cigars, clothes, shoes, board and lodging, and certain nameless extravagances. One said that he would not stay on the Congo unless these were granted to him freely; another asserted that if he was expected to drive a steam-launch unassisted, he must have higher pay. . . . Another—an engineer—asserted that he was engaged as sub-commander of the expedition; that he . . . would never have ventured into Africa upon such a miserable stipend; he had come for honour, reputation, fame; he would write to the newspapers, etc. Another engineer complained that he was not accorded his proper rank . . . he certainly was equal to the general accountant of the expedition. The gentleman in charge of the smallest steam-launch thought himself superior to the sailor in charge of a rowing boat, and considered himself disparaged by being requested to mess at the same table as the latter.

But most irritating of all for Stanley was the constant stream of harassing communications from Brussels.

Leopold was growing increasingly uneasy about Stanley's slow progress up the river, for at the end of December 1879, when Stanley had not yet completed the construction of Vivi station, Brazza had reached Gabon and, traveling light, was advancing swiftly up the Ogowe toward the Congo. Leopold was desperately afraid that Brazza would reach the Stanley Pool and claim it for France before Stanley got there. "Serious rivalry is threatening on the Upper Congo," he wrote, "Brazza will try to follow the Alima down to its junction with the Congo and hopes to get there before you. There is not a moment to lose." And Strauch followed up with a barrage of goading, complaining letters. Stanley responded with undisguised annoyance; he explained in detail the nature of his problems, the reasons for delays, the obstinacy of some local chiefs, the ruggedness of the terrain, the bad weather.

These and similar facts have been repeated to you since February of this year. The truths they describe should by this time be clearly obvious, so that I am ashamed to iterate and repeat them. . . . My dear Colonel, when will you believe that this is the hardest-worked expedition that ever came to Africa?

And then addressing Leopold's anxieties, he wrote haughtily,

Relative to your information about the French Expedition going over from the Ogowe River to the Stanley Pool . . . I beg leave to say that I am not a party in a race for the Stanley Pool, as I have already been in that locality just two and a half years ago, and I do not intend to visit it again until I can arrive with my fifty tons of goods, boats, and other property. . . . If my mission simply consisted on marching for Stanley Pool, I might reach it in fifteen days, but what would be the benefit of it for the expedition or the mission that I have undertaken?

On November 7, 1880, a Sunday, while the road to Isangila was still under construction, Stanley returned to his tent camp to take the day off. Around ten o'clock in the morning, he tells us, after having bathed, shaved, "dressed as becomes the Sabbath," breakfasted, and sat down to do some Bible reading, one of the local tribesmen rushed into the camp

and coming to me hastily, he hands a paper to me, on which I find traced with a lead pencil the words "Le Comte Savorgnan de Brazza, *Enseigne de Vaisseau*. . . . An hour later the French gentleman appears, dressed in helmet, naval blue coat, and feet encased in a brown leather bandage, and a following of fifteen men, principally Gabonese sailors, all armed with Winchester repeating rifles. The gentleman is tall in appearance, of very dark complexion, and looks thoroughly fatigued. He is welcome, and I invite him into the tent, and a dejeuner is prepared for him, to which he is invited. I speak French abominably, and his English is not of the best, but between us we contrive to understand one another.

And what Stanley contrived to understand was that Brazza had beaten him to the Stanley Pool. The French party had not followed the Alima to the Congo, which, as we've seen, would have brought it to the river some 200 miles above the Pool. This time, with geographical information he hadn't possessed on his previous journey, Brazza was able to strike directly for the Pool from the Ogowe and reached its right bank at a village called Mbe—site of the present-day city of Brazzaville, capital of the Congo Republic—in September 1880, less than a year after setting off from the Gabon coast.

Preceded by a bugler and by the French flag [Brazza wrote in his diary], I went into the village. . . . In front of the door of the chief's compound, we stopped, to wait for the chief to receive me. . . . At last, preceded by his wives, Makoko appeared. . . . The chief wore a big cloth robe, big bracelets on his feet and arms, a woollen hat with tapestry which is fixed to his head with an iron pin in which two long feathers are stuck. . . . Chief Makoko sat on a big carpet four metres wide, in blue and red squares, in serge, on which there was a rug with a lion. He was leaning on a big cushion of red serge. Then the men who brought me in went to kneel before him, placing their hands on the ground by his carpet, very respectfully. . . . That finished, I told Makoko that . . . hearing he was chief of all the land between Ngampe and N'coma [the right bank of the Pool], I had come to see him to talk of the views of the French about the country, where they wished to establish themselves.

Brazza was improvising. At this point the French government had no intention of establishing itself on the Pool or, for that matter, anywhere else on the river, and regarded Brazza's expedition as purely exploratory. But he spent about a month with Makoko and persuaded the chief to give him permission to build a French "fort" at his village and to put his mark on a document, which Brazza had drawn up, placing Makoko's lands and peoples under the protection of the French flag. Although nowhere nearly as impressively substantial as Stanley's stations, roads, and treaties, this piece of paper and the mud-and-grass "fort" Brazza built were to be the basis for France's claim—when a few years later she felt compelled to make it—to the north shore of the Stanley Pool and laid the foundation for her future sub-Saharan African colony, French Equatorial Africa, including what is today Congo-Brazzaville, Gabon, the Central African Republic, Cameroon, and Chad.

Having established France's presence on the Congo, Brazza was anxious to get back to Paris and pressure the French government into ratifying his improvised treaty with Makoko. He had, by then, a fairly good idea what Stanley was up to and was worried that Stanley, with his far superior force, would undo his work for France on the river. But as he had traveled with a lightly equipped expedition, which after the year's journey was much thinned out and short of supplies, the best he could do to protect his claim was to leave behind the French flag, two Gabonese sailors under the command of a Senegalese sergeant by the name of Malamine, and a copy of the document signed by Makoko, which Malamine was instructed to show to any white man who came along. "I can't give you any money or supplies," Brazza told the Senegalese. "You have your men, your hands, and your firearms . . . don't abandon your post." Then Brazza departed. He didn't return to the coast via the Ogowe, however, but chose instead to follow the Congo down to the sea. It was then, on that Sunday morning in November, that he met Stanley.

Brazza spent two days at Stanley's road camp. Stanley behaved, if not exactly warmly, then altogether correctly toward his rival. He replenished Brazza's supplies, loaned him some porters and a guide to Vivi, and provided him passage aboard one of the Belgian steamers from Vivi to Banana Point, where Brazza could catch a mailboat back to Gabon. In return, Brazza was rather less correct in his behavior toward Stanley: he never once mentioned the treaty he had struck with Makoko or the "fort" he had built at Makoko's village or the claim to the Congo he was planning to press in the name of France. Stanley was to learn all this only when he reached the Stanley Pool, and that wouldn't be for another nine months.

First the road to Isangila had to be completed and then a second station built there. Then came an 88-mile stretch of fairly navigable waterway along which the boats and goods were sailed upriver to a village called Manyanga, where a third station was to be built. But just as Stanley was about to enter his first palaver with the Manyanga chiefs he came down with a severe attack of malaria. It put him out of action for over a month and at times was so bad that he was certain he would die. But huge doses of quinine in hydrobromic acid, mixed in Madeira wine, ultimately had their effect, and in mid-June 1881 he was up and about again. He concluded his negotiations for the Manyanga station, set his crews to building it, went off on a reconnaissance trip upriver with a party of Zanzibaris, and on July 26, "we came to a square-browed hill, from whose high open summit we saw Stanley Pool far away in the hazy distance, like a blurred mirror obscured by gauze set in a gauze-covered frame of dark wood."

No sooner had he arrived, he tells us, than "we saw borne high up, a French tri-coloured flag approaching, preceded by a dashing Europeanised negro (as I supposed him to be, though he had a superior type of face), in sailor costume, with stripes of a non-commissioned officer on his arm." This was Malamine, the Senegalese sergeant whom Brazza had left behind. And with him were the two Gabonese sailors. Stanley tells us:

Malameen [sic], spoke French well, and his greeting was frank and manly. After a few words had been said on either side, he showed to me a paper, which duly translated, turned out to be a treaty, whereby a certain chief called Makoko ceded to France a territory extending . . . on the north bank of Stanley Pool, and which M. de Brazza notified, to all whom it might concern, that he took possession of the said territory in the name of France. Malameen knew a great deal about the transaction. Makoko had been generous, and for very trifling gifts had parted with a territory which, as far as I could learn, extended along the river about nine miles; the extent of it inland, was not indicated.

Later, when he heard of how Stanley had handled this situation, Leopold was furious. One of his key associates in his schemes, Baron Solvyns, the Belgian ambassador in London, declared:

Stanley is held to have been stupid to the highest degree. He ought to have begun by securing the most important part of the Congo, namely Stanley Pool, and one wonders why, as a Californian [this is in reference to Stanley's adventures as a young reporter in the wild and woolly American West], he did not think fit to lay his rival low with a rifle shot. He proved as gentle and tractable as those wretched savages that have to be civilized.

But naïve Stanley behaved gently in this instance and didn't think to shoot down Malamine and the two Gabonese sailors because he quite sincerely believed that his was a peaceful philanthropic and civilizing mission and it would be dreadfully out of character to take possession of lands by force. Besides, he didn't think that the treaty with Makoko was any good. Perfectly aware of the importance of securing the right as well as the left bank of the Pool, he crossed over two days after meeting Malamine and visited with some local chiefs there to see whether they recognized Makoko's action. One of these, a certain Gamankono, told him of Brazza's visit: "He had a few men from Makoko with him; he sent word to all of us . . . to come and see him. We went and talked with him, but I heard nothing of selling or giving away a country." Stanley asked: "But is not Makoko the great king of all this country?" Gamankono responded: "There is no great king anywhere. We are all kings—each a king over his own village and land. Makoko is chief of Mbe; I am chief of Malima . . . no one has authority over another chief. Each of us owns his own lands. Makoko is an old chief; he is richer than any of us; he has more men and guns, but his country is Mbe." On the strength of this, Stanley entered into negotiations with Gamankono for the establishment of a station at Malima. At first it seemed to be going well, but when Brazza's man Malamine got wind of what Stanley was up to he started a propaganda campaign to undermine the effort.

What fables Malameen uttered about our fondness for the meat of tender children will never be published perhaps [Stanley tells us]; but the effect of what he told them was known when the crier beat his tom-tom in the night, and shouted out along the river bank and amid the huts of the scattered village that Gamankono . . . resolved that none of the people should speak with us, or sell us anything more. By morning this notice was magnified into a mediated rupture. A woman was caught selling fish to one of my people, and beaten by some of the villagers, while some bold fellows crowded around the tent with broad knives like butchers' cleavers in their hands. The good feelings of yesterday had become replaced by suspicion, if not hatred.

Stanley made three attempts to reopen negotiations with Gamankono, then finally abandoned the effort. He realized that serious trouble could be brewing and, though his force was certainly large enough to handle it, he was not prepared to press matters to a bloody conflict. His reputation for "scrapping instincts" was, as he well knew from his previous expeditions, bad enough without adding to it now, and so, for the moment at least, he decided to withdraw and concentrate his efforts on the Pool's left bank.

The chief he had to deal with there was called Ngalyema now but he was, in fact, the Itsi of Ntamo whom Stanley had met during his first passage down the Pool in 1877.

During the four years that had elapsed, he had become a great man . . . grown richer by ivory trade . . . and become powerful by investing his large profits in slaves, guns, and gunpowder. . . . Success in life had considerably developed other ambitions. Itsi aspired to become known as the greatest chief of the country. . . . He was now about thirty-four years old, of well-built form, proud in his bearing, covetous and grasping in disposition, and, like all other lawless barbarians, prone to be cruel and sanguinary whenever he might safely vent his evil humour.

The initial meeting between Stanley and Ngalyema had all the flavor of a grand reunion. Blood brotherhood was proclaimed, toasts in palm wine were drunk, rich gifts were exchanged. Stanley gave the chief two donkeys, a large mirror, a gold-embroidered coat, brass chains, pieces of fine cloth, and a japanned tin box. Ngalyema in return presented Stanley with goats, pigs, loaves of bread, gourds of palm wine, and his own scepter, "a long staff, branded profusely with brass, and decorated with coils of brass wire, which was to be carried by me, and shown to all men as a sign that I was the brother of Ngalyema of Ntamo!" But the fraternal relationship began to fray badly as the palaver over a treaty for a station on the Stanley Pool dragged on for days and then weeks. Ngalyema very much resisted the idea of a permanent settlement of whites in his lands. At the same time, though, he coveted the white man's goods and throughout the palavering constantly demanded more. He wanted another japanned tin box, more and finer pieces of cloth, a Newfoundland dog Stanley had with him, iron boxes, cases of gin, guns, gunpowder, then Stanley's own best black suit, which the white man wore for ceremonial meetings with great chiefs. Stanley, realizing he was getting nowhere acceding to these ever-escalating demands, put an end to it by refusing to give Ngalyema the suit. The chief was infuriated; he broke off the palaver and stomped angrily out of Stanley's camp.

A few days later, word reached Stanley that Ngalyema had assembled a band of some 200 warriors armed with muskets and was returning to the camp in a foul mood. Anxious as ever to retain the peaceful, diplomatic character of his expedition, Stanley decided to deal with this threat by a clever ruse. He figured that Ngalyema would come into the camp, pretending to want to resume negotiations, then, with Stanley off his guard, attempt a surprise attack. Stanley's stratagem was to appear to be taken in by the chief, then spring an even greater surprise. He had all but twenty of his Zanzibaris hide in the trees and bushes outside the camp; the remaining twenty were told to lounge around in the camp, appearing very much off their guard and indeed half asleep. Then he had a Chinese gong, which was used to awaken the party in the mornings and call them to breakfast, placed in front of his tent and instructed all his men, those hiding and those in the camp, not to make a move until they heard the gong sounded. Finally, he seated himself next to the gong and, pretending to read a book, awaited Ngalyema's arrival.

"Ngalyema was moody-browed, stiff, most unbrotherly in his responses to my welcome," Stanley tells us, "while I looked like one almost ready to leap into his arms with an irrepressible affection." Ngalyema, as Stanley had anticipated, pretended to resume the palaver. But after only a few moments he declared abruptly, "We have no objections to trade with white men if they come for trade, but you do not come for trade; therefore you cannot come to Ntamo. My brother must go back the way he came." Stanley persisted: "I only want to get near the river and build a village of my own, whither many white men will come to trade. White men will do you no harm." But Ngalyema cut him off. "Enough, enough," he shouted. "I say for the last time you shall not come to Ntamo; we do not want any white men among us." Ngalyema turned to leave. This was the crucial moment. The chief had been carefully appraising the seeming lack of preparedness in Stanley's camp, and Stanley braced himself for a sudden attack by Ngalyema's 200 warriors. But just then, exactly as Stanley had hoped, Ngalyema's attention was drawn to the Chinese gong.

"What is this?" he asked. "It is fetish," Stanley answered. "Bula Matari, strike this; let me hear it." "Oh, Ngalyema, I dare not," Stanley said; "it is the war fetish." "Beat it, Bula Matari, that I may hear the sound," the chief insisted. "I dare not, Ngalyema. It is the signal for war; it is the fetish that calls up armed men; it would be too bad." But Ngalyema continued insisting: "Strike—strike it, I tell you." So, with feigned reluctance, Stanley relented.

With all my force I struck the gong, the loud bell-like tone sounding in the silence caused by the hushed concentrated attention of all upon the scene, was startling in the extreme. . . . They had not recovered from the first shock of astonishment when the forms of men were seen bounding . . . and war-whooping in their ears . . . a stream of frantic infuriates emerged as though from the earth . . . a yelling crowd of demoniac madmen sprang out one after another, everyone apparently madder than his neighbor. The listless, sleep-eyed stragglers burst out into a perfect frenzy of action . . . there streamed into view such a frantic mob of armed men, that to the panic-struck natives the sky and earth seemed to be contributing to the continually increasing number of death-dealing warriors.

Ngalyema's men dropped their weapons and fled the terrifying scene. Ngalyema himself dodged behind Stanley and, clutching him around the waist, cried, "Save me, Bula Matari; do not let them hurt me!" "Hold hard, Ngalyema," Stanley called out, "keep fast hold of me; I will defend you, never fear." Stanley shouted an order and his shrieking, jumping Zanzibaris suddenly formed into orderly ranks. With calm restored, Stanley let Ngalyema in on the joke. The chief, for all the humiliation he had suffered, took it in good spirits. His warriors returned to the camp somewhat sheepishly but

half-an-hour later they were all . . . retailing to one another, amid boisterous merriment, their individual experiences, while Ngalyema's loud laugh was heard above all others. . . . Over palm-wine we mutually swore faithful brotherhood and everlasting peace; and the doughty warriors of Ngalyema embraced in a fraternal manner the jolly good fellows of Bula Matari.

Stanley loved to tell this story and doubtless it played some role in softening up Ngalyema. But it took several more palavers and a number of touchy incidents with the chief before a treaty was signed that permitted Stanley to build a station on the Stanley Pool.

By the end of 1881, the road around the Livingstone Falls from the Manyanga station was completed and the paddle boat *En Avant* and a few of the smaller vessels, along with some 50 tons of supplies and equipment, were hauled up and launched on the Stanley Pool. Then, in the next four months, the fourth station was built between Ngalyema's village of Ntamo and another one called Kinshasa, on the left bank of the Pool. It was the largest and most elaborate so far, a neat settlement centered around a one-story wooden blockhouse, with broad streets, a promenade along the river front, gardens of banana trees and vegetables, prefabricated storehouses. And it was the most important. From here, with the river providing a navigable highway for more than 1000 miles, the entire Congo basin was accessible. Stanley named the station Leopoldville.

Until now, he had been totally occupied with the enormous task of building the wagon road around Livingstone Falls and erecting the four stations along it, but with the completion of Leopoldville he had his first opportunity to do some exploration. So, taking a small party aboard the *En Avant,* he sailed up the river to the confluence with the Kwa, about 100 miles above the Pool, and exploring this tributary he discovered a lake which he also named for his employer. But his heart doesn't seem to have been in the work. He had, by this time, been in Africa close to three years. He was exhausted and edgy, his quarrels with his European assistants continued unrelentingly, and then he came down with a second severe bout with malaria, complicated by gastritis, which laid him low for more than a month. "I could not disguise from myself," he wrote in his journal, "that I was not now the hardy, energetic pioneer I once was." And so, when he had sufficiently recovered from his illness, he decided to go home.

Leopold was enraged. Under his contract, Stanley had two more years to serve in the Congo, and that was where the Belgian king wanted him. By this time Brazza had been back in France for four months and had been hard at work persuading the Paris government to ratify the treaty with Makoko and stake a colonial claim to the Congo. Leopold had done his best to forestall this. At one point he even tried to hire Brazza away from France, but Brazza, fiercely patriotic, turned him down, and all he accomplished by making the approach was to give Brazza more of an insight into Leopold's Congo scheme and more fuel for his own arguments in Paris. In a sharply sarcastic document to the French government, reporting on his meeting with Leopold, Brazza wrote:

Doubtless the King of the Belgians . . . gave his millions with the sole aim of civilizing the savage tribes. I thought, however, that there was a political idea at the back of the humanitarian sentiments of the King of the Belgians. I was far from blaming him for this, but that did not prevent me from having a political idea of my own, and mine was very simple. Here it is: if it was a good thing to get hold of the Congo, I would prefer that it was the French flag, rather than the Belgian "international" flag. that floated over this splendid African territory.

Although the French government continued to be extremely suspicious of any colonial venture in Africa, imperialist notions were certainly stirred up by Brazza's campaign. And in November 1882, shortly after Stanley's return to Europe, Paris finally agreed to ratify Brazza's treaty with Makoko and back him on a third expedition to the Congo.

Leopold saw all his plans for the Congo dangerously threatened by this, and when he met with Stanley on the latter's return he is reported as saying, "Surely, Mr. Stanley, you cannot think of leaving me now, just when I most need you?" Stanley tried every argument.

I pointed out that by strenuous effort we had achieved more than we intended . . . five stations had been constructed, a steamer and sailing boat launched on the Upper Congo, while another small steamer and lighter maintained communications between the second and third station. A wagon-road had also been made at great expense and time between Vivi and Isangila, and Manyanga and Stanley Pool.

He also complained of the quality of his European assistants and the impossibility of continuing the work without better men. And he brought up the matter of his health, saying that a physician he had consulted had told him that he would be running a great risk returning to the Congo. But to no avail. Leopold promised to get Stanley an outstanding deputy to assist him in the work—Leopold, in fact, was then in communication with Charles "Chinese" Gordon, who had resigned his post in the Sudan and had expressed interest in going to work for the Belgian king—but he insisted that Stanley return to the Congo immediately.

It is indispensable that you should purchase for the *Comité d'Etudes* as much land as you can obtain, and that you should successfully place under the sovereignty of the *Comité,* as soon as possible and without losing a minute, all the chiefs from the mouth of the Congo to Stanley Falls.

So, in December 1882, Stanley was back on the Congo. To his despair, he saw that, in the short time he had been away, much of his work had fallen into disrepair because of the incompetence of his European assistants. Leopoldville was in the worst shape of all, with the streets and gardens overgrown and buildings falling into ruin. So he was forced to spend the next few months restoring order, traveling back and forth between the stations, getting crews working again, putting out fires. As he points out,

the day's notes of the 24th of March . . . will serve to show the desperate nature of my duties about this time. . . . Dispatched Lieutenant Orban with thirty-one men to Vivi, to hurry up by forced marches a caravan with brass rods. . . . Lieutenant Grang departs with sixty-four men . . . to haul the boilers of the *Royal* to Leopoldville. Received news today that a Mons. Callewart had been killed and decapitated at Kimpoko. . . . Second chief at Vivi declaims against asking him to manage the duties of chief, second chief, and storekeeper, and declares he will not—suffer who may. His letter is remarkable for impoliteness, and is replete with gross accusations against a number of people. The officer in charge of the transport of a whaleboat from Vivi to Isangila, having fifty-eight men with him, writes that he cannot and will not carry the boat with such a limited number. The Chief of Manyanga writes that the chief in charge of Vivi is acting an "infamous comedy." . . . He also writes that Mons. Luksic, an Austrian marine officer, has committed suicide by shooting himself through the head.

Finally, in May 1883 Stanley was able to get on with the work of building new stations and signing more treaties, and with a party of 80 men and 6 tons of material aboard the *En Avant* and *Royal* (which, along with 6 other vessels had by now also been launched on the Pool), sailed upriver from Leopoldville. A station was built on the Equator, and in November, six years since he had last been there, he neared the site of the farthest outpost he proposed to build on the river, the Stanley Falls.

The area was strangely silent and deserted.

On my old map [Stanley noted], it is marked Mawembe, and was strongly palisaded; but now, though I looked closely through my glass, I could detect no sign of palisade or hut. . . . As we advanced we could see the poor remnants of banana groves; we could also trace the whitened paths from the river's edge leading up the steep bank, but not a house or living thing could be seen anywhere . . . all had vanished. When we came abreast of the locality, we perceived that there had been a late fire. The heat had scorched the foliage of the tallest trees, and their silver stems had been browned by it. The banana plants looked meagre; their ragged fronds waved mournfully their tatters, as if imploring pity. . . . Six years before we had rushed by this very place without stopping, endeavoring by our haste to thwart the intentions of our foes. . . . Surely there had been a great change! As we moved up the stream slowly, another singular sight attracted our gaze. This was two or three long canoes standing on their ends, like split hollow columns, upright on the verge of the bank. What freak was this, and what did the sight signify? A few miles higher up on the same bank we came abreast of another scene of desolation, where a whole town had been burnt, the palms cut down, bananas scorched, many acres laid level with the ground, and the freak of standing canoes on end repeated. In front of the black ruin there were a couple of hundred people crouched down on the verge of the bank, looking woefully forlorn and cheerless, some with their hands supporting their chins, regarding us with stupid indifference, as though they were beyond further harm.

And then Stanley learned what had happened. The Arab slavers had come. Six years before, Tippoo Tib had watched Stanley vanish into the jungles down the Lualaba convinced that he would never be heard from again. But, when Tippoo Tib learned that he was, the thrall of horror that had kept Arab and European out of the region was broken and Tippoo Tib had sent his slaving gangs to follow in Stanley's footsteps and wreak their bloody havoc along the river he had opened up to them.

As Stanley continued the journey up to the falls, "every three or four miles we came in sight of the black traces of the destroyers. The charred stakes, upright canoes, poles of once populous settlements, scorched banana groves, and prostrate palms, all betokened ruthless ruin." At one point, "we detected some object, of a slaty colour, floating down stream." When a sailor on the *En Avant* turned it over with a boat-hook, "we were shocked to discover the bodies of two women bound together with a cord!" A few days later, they reached the camp of the Arab slavers.

There are rows upon rows of dark nakedness, relieved here and there by the white dresses of the captors. . . . On paying more attention to detail, I observe that mostly all are fettered, youths with iron rings around their necks, through which a chain . . . is rove, securing the captives by twenties. The children over ten are secured by three copper rings, each ringed leg broke together by the central ring. . . . The mothers are secured by shorter chains. . . . Every second during which I regard them the clink of fetters and chains strike my ears. My eyes catch sight of the continual lifting of the hand to ease the neck in the collar, or as it displays a manacle exposed through a muscle being irritated by its weight, or want of fitness. My nerves are offended with the rancid effluvium of the unwashed herds within this human kennel. The smell of other abominations annoy me in the vitiated atmosphere. For how could poor people, bound and riveted together by twenties, do otherwise than wallow in filth!

Stanley discovered that there were 2300 captives in this camp taken in raids on 118 villages, during which at least another 4000 Africans had been killed. "How many are wounded and die in the forest, or drop to death through an overwhelming sense of their calamities, we do not know," but Stanley reckoned that perhaps 33,000 die for every 5000 captured and enslaved.

And such slaves! they are females, or young children who cannot run away.
. . . Yet each of the very smallest infants has cost the life of a father and
perhaps his three stout brothers and three grownup daughters. An entire
family of six souls have been done to death to obtain that small, feeble,
useless child.

Stanley at first was seized by the impulse to revenge "these wholesale outrages" but then decided against it. "Who am I that I should
take the law into my hands and mete out retribution," he rationalized.
"I represented no constituted government, nor had I the shadow of
authority to assume the role of censor, judge and executioner." Moreover, he felt it was necessary to stay on good terms with the slavers,
who were clearly the true chiefs in the area. So he entered into
friendly negotiations with the Arabs and, without raising a word of
protest about their ghastly activities, went ahead and built his station
just below the last cataract of the Stanley Falls—which was to be
known as Stanleyville—and then returned downriver, making treaties
and building further stations along the way.

When he got back to Leopoldville, in January 1884, his five-year
contract with Leopold was just about up. He had hoped that by this
time Gordon would have come out to the Congo, but the British
general had decided to accept the post of governor-general of the
Sudan (where a year later he would die in the fall of Khartoum to the
Mahdists) and Leopold sent out a Belgian army officer, Lieutenant
Colonel Francis de Winton of the Royal Artillery, to relieve Stanley.
By the time he departed for Europe in June, Stanley had connected
the Congo with the sea and opened it to European exploitation. He
had signed some 400 treaties with local chiefs and brought them under
the *Comité's* sovereignty. And, while he had been unable to dislodge
the French from the north shore of Stanley Pool, he had secured the
whole of the river's left bank and most of its right bank from its
mouth well over 1000 miles into the interior to the Stanley Falls, and
had firmly built the foundation for Leopold's private Kingdom of the
Congo, a kingdom that was to be formally recognized as such by all the
great powers hardly more than half a year after Stanley returned to
Europe.

20

THE PERSONAL KINGDOM OF LEOPOLD II

Pretty much against their will, Leopold had forced the European powers to pay attention to Africa again. Stanley's stupendous pioneering work in the Congo on the Belgian king's behalf had not only awakened commercial interest in the potential of the great river basin but it also had stirred up political rivalries that had long lain dormant. The precarious balance of power in the continent was in danger of being upset, and what was to be known as the Scramble—that feverish seizure of colonies which was to bring all of Africa under European rule within the next three decades—was about to be set off.

France, albeit still reluctantly, was already moving in that direction. Even before Stanley returned to Europe, Brazza was back in Africa at the head of a third expedition to follow up on the treaty he had made with Makoko. Britain didn't like this a bit. The traditional Anglo-French rivalry had been sharpened perceptibly by Britain's recent occupation of Egypt (1882), and Britain viewed France's moves on the Congo as her way of striking back. To forestall the French, the British considered reactivating the formal claim that Cameron had made to the Congo basin. But the cabinet, under Lord Salisbury, was as opposed as ever to further colonial commitments in sub-Saharan Africa, and when another ploy came to hand for frustrating the French the cabinet grabbed for it.

Portugal provided the ploy. Awakened by Stanley's successes, the Portuguese now suddenly remembered their own centuries-old right to the Congo, based on the fact that they had discovered the river in the first place and that, in Angola and Cabinda, they currently had settlements near its estuary. At first it seemed that Portugal would do a deal with France, recognizing her claims to the Stanley Pool in exchange for recognition of Portugal's claims to the estuary. But the British moved in and offered to conclude an Anglo-Portuguese treaty, under which Britain would recognize Portugal's sovereignty over the whole river, cutting out the French, in return for Portuguese guarantees of free trade for the British.

Before this treaty could be signed, the Germans entered the picture. United under Bismarck for a little more than a decade and recently triumphant in the Franco-Prussian War, Germany was developing imperial ambitions of its own and, in an eighteen-month period between the end of 1883 and 1885, established missions and trading posts in the Tanganyika region of East Africa, in South-West Africa, and in Togoland and the Cameroons on the West African coast. Bismarck didn't want to see either France or Britain, through its deal with Portugal, control the Congo. Until now, the river's mouth had been open to the trade of every nation without the customs or duties of any, and, if Germany wasn't to control it, then that was how Bismarck wanted to keep it.

All of this represented a threat to Leopold's personal ambitions in the Congo but, as the Belgian king was cunning enough to realize, it also presented an opportunity—an opportunity to play off the contending powers against each other to his own ultimate advantage. And that is what he did, setting out in every direction at once.

He went to the French and, harping on their fears of the British, offered them a secret deal under which, in exchange for their recognition of his association's sovereignty over the Congo, he promised not only to concede their claims on the river's right bank but also to turn over to them the rest of the Congo in the event (which most thought likely) that his own personal resources proved insufficient for him to hold on to it. At the same time, he launched a provocative campaign against Portugal, reminding the world, and especially the still-influential humanitarian interests in Britain, of the Portuguese's notorious record as slavers. And to further undermine Britain's support of Portugal, Leopold let it be known in British commercial circles that if his association controlled the Congo he was prepared to grant them the same most-favored-nation trading rights on the river that Portugal had promised. Then he went to Bismarck and, conveniently forgetting about his promises to Britain, blandly assured him that under his association's control the Congo would remain a free port open to trade of every nation, including especially Germany.

But perhaps Leopold's most ingenious tack was the one he used on the United States. Though America was relatively disinterested in the brewing African Scramble, the canny Belgian king knew that her backing would influence the European powers. Sending Chester Arthur, the U.S. president, laundered versions of the treaties Stanley had signed with the Congo chiefs (and making much of the fact that Stanley was an American), Leopold emphasized the apparent similarity between his Confederation of Free Negro Republics and the American-supported state of Liberia. He argued that his association, a nongovernmental, privately financed philanthropic organization, was intended to provide the administrative, political, and technical know-how for the fledgling independent black African state, just as a private American society was doing for Liberia. Once that state was able to handle these matters for itself Leopold and his association would fade out of the picture. So convincingly did Leopold argue this case that on February 25, 1884, the beguiled U.S. Congress passed a resolution recommending that the blue flag with gold star of Leopold's association be recognized as that of a friendly government, the Congo Free State.

By now it was clear that a serious crisis over the Congo was shaping up. But it was a crisis that, for the time being at least, the major powers were anxious to avoid. For, while each was intensely suspicious of the other's expansionist plans, none was really ready yet to run the political and military risks or make the huge capital investments in expanding itself. The situation had to be defused, and on November 15, 1884, with Bismarck taking the lead, an international conference was convened in Berlin to find a way of doing that. Fourteen nations attended—Austro-Hungary, Belgium, Denmark, Britain, Holland, Italy, Norway, Portugal, Russia, Spain, Sweden, Turkey, the United States, and the host, Germany—with Bismarck himself in the chair. Leopold's association had no official representation, but Stanley, with his special knowledge, attended in the role of a technical consultant.

The meeting dragged on for over three months, but its outcome was never really in much doubt. Leopold had done his work well. He had convinced each of the major contending powers that it could expect to gain if the issue was settled in his favor. As for the others, with the United States in the lead and again thanks to Leopold's clever propaganda, they had come to believe that the safest way to cool the crisis would be by taking the Congo out of the arena of big-power

confrontation and putting it under the trusteeship of a neutral, in-
offensive, and philanthropic agency such as Leopold's association professed itself to be. And so, on February 26, 1885, the Berlin Act on the
Congo was signed. Under it, France was given 257,000 square miles of
the river basin, including a substantial stretch along the right bank,
Portugal was granted sovereignty over 351,000 square miles, including
a stretch along the estuary's left bank; all the rest, comprising nearly
1 million square miles and encompassing perhaps 15 million people,
was officially recognized as the Congo Free State and handed over to
Leopold personally. To be sure, under the agreement, Leopold was
obliged to keep this vast area open to the trade of all nations, to
welcome there missionaries of all churches, and to confine the activities of his association to the administration of the new independent
black African state. But there was no doubt whatsoever that he personally, as a private individual, was to be its sovereign.

One feels obliged to reemphasize just what an incredible arrangement this was. The Congo had not been taken as a colony by Belgium,
nor was Leopold to rule it as the king of the Belgians. A brand-new
state had been created essentially by fiat out of a vast African territory,
unbeknown to the overwhelming majority of the people who lived
there. And a private individual, whom an even greater number of
those people had never heard of, had been given that state to own
personally and had been made its king. "The sovereignty of the Congo
is invested in the person of the Sovereign," a Belgian lawyer of the
time wrote. "His will can be resisted by no juridical obstacle whatsoever. Leopold II could say with more justification than Louis XIV
did: *L'état, c'est moi.*" Leopold himself, somewhat later, put it even
more bluntly: "My rights over the Congo are to be shared with none;
they are the fruit of my own struggle and expenditure . . . the King
was the founder of the state; he was its organizer, its owner, its absolute sovereign." Perhaps an American newspaperman at that time
summed up this peculiar situation most succinctly: "He [Leopold]
possesses the Congo just as Rockefeller possesses Standard Oil."

With the establishment of the Congo Free State, Leopold dis-
carded the façade of the Association Internationale du Congo or the
Comité d'Études du Haut-Congo or whatever else people had been
misled into calling it. In its place, he erected his own personal government. The president of the new state and its "cabinet"—consisting of a
secretary of state, three secretaries-general and a treasurer-general—

were, like the king who appointed them, resident in Brussels (in all his life, Leopold was never to set foot in the Congo). Boma was selected as the capital (it would be later transferred to Leopoldville when the railroad was built to Stanley Pool), and there Leopold sent a governor-general, a vice governor-general, and a commander-in-chief of a Congo gendarmerie, known as the Force Publique. The state itself was divided into fourteen districts, each with a Leopold-appointed district commissioner in command. In turn, each district was divided into zones, each zone into sectors, and each sector into posts, with each again in the charge of a Leopold appointee, and each, it goes without saying, a white man.

Leopold's first task was to establish the authority of the new Free State as widely and as unmistakably as possible throughout the Congo River basin. The delegates at the Berlin conference might have blithely drawn a red circle around a vast territory in the heart of Africa and handed it over to Leopold, but at the time of its creation the Congo Free State in reality consisted of only the eight stations Stanley had built along the river itself from Vivi to Stanley Falls. All the rest of the basin remained pretty much terra incognita, unsurveyed rain forests for the most part, where few if any Europeans had ever gone (Cameron and some Portuguese traders being the only exceptions) and where few if any black men had ever heard of Leopold as the Belgian king, let alone as the new Congo king. Thus, expeditions had to be sent out, the numerous tributaries of the Congo explored and mapped, the commercial potential of the forests surveyed, administrative stations and military garrisons built, hundreds more treaties with local chiefs signed, the state's borders defined and secured, its gold-starred blue flag planted everywhere.

One place that Leopold would have dearly loved to plant that flag was on the Nile. His ambition was to extend his state's northeastern frontier across the Lualaba into the great lakes region and take possession of the southern Sudan itself. And barely a year after the Berlin conference he thought he saw a chance to realize that ambition.

The opportunity arose as a result of the fall of Khartoum, the death of General Gordon, and the occupation of the Sudan by the fanatical Mahdists in 1885. The catastrophe had caused a furious outcry in England, the public and the newspapers blaming the British government for failing to get a rescue expedition to Khartoum in time to save the heroic Gordon from his grisly martyrdom (he was decapi-

tated and his head paraded around on a pole in the Mahdi's camp).
Queen Victoria herself had joined in the protest: "That the promises
of support [to Gordon] were not fulfilled—which I so frequently and
constantly pressed on those who asked him to go—is to me *grief inex-
pressible!* indeed, it has made me ill." But then, just as it seemed that
the government must fall over the issue, it got a chance to redeem
itself. In the summer of 1886, a startling letter arrived in London by
way of Zanzibar. It was from a certain Eduard Schnitzer, a remarkable
German physician, who had disguised himself as a Turk, converted to
Islam, taken the name Emin Pasha, and been appointed by Gordon to
the post of governor of Equatoria, the most southerly province of the
Sudan. And what his letter revealed was that, although all the other
provinces had fallen in the wake of Gordon's death, he and his garrison were still holding out against the Mahdi's hordes at Lado, near
present-day Juba, on the Upper Nile.

Instantly, Emin Pasha became the hero of the hour; he became the
surrogate for the martyred Gordon, and the cry went up that he must
be saved. An Emin Pasha Relief Committee was formed. Tens of
thousands of pounds sterling were subscribed for an expedition. An
army of hundreds of riflemen was to be recruited, a dozen British
army officers and gentlemen volunteered for the mission, and, what
seemed a most obvious and natural choice, Stanley was invited to
head it.

Stanley, however, was still in the employ of the Belgian king. Although he had been relieved of his duties in the Congo and had spent
the last couple of years lecturing, Stanley continued to receive an
annual salary of £1000 sterling from Leopold as a retainer on his
services. So, before he could accept the command of the Emin Pasha
Relief Expedition, he was obliged to get Leopold's permission. Leopold was only too happy to grant it. He had been looking for an
excuse to get to the Nile, and, in fact, if the British hadn't beaten him
to it he would have put Stanley in charge of a rescue mission to Emin
Pasha on his own. The British-sponsored expedition, with his own
employee at its head, would serve his purposes just as well, and at a
secret meeting in Brussels he instructed Stanley what he was to do. In
the first place, he was to lead the expedition to Equatoria not from the
East African coast, which would have been the obvious and easier
route, but from the West African coast up the Congo River to the
Stanley Falls, then across the Lualaba northeast through the Ituri rain

forests to Lake Albert and from there along the Nile to Lado. Leopold was prepared to provide the expedition with all the resources of the Congo Free State—transport by its boats on the river and use of its stations along the banks—because he wanted to demonstrate the geographical integrity and easy accessibility between the Congo and the southern Sudan and by that make a case for his claim to it. What's more, once he reached Emin Pasha, Stanley was instructed to offer him, in Leopold's name, the governorship of an equatorial province of the Congo Free State.

In January 1887, Stanley set off on what was to be his last (he would be nearly 50 when he returned) and most difficult African adventure. It took very nearly three years; and it covered well over 5000 miles. It cost the lives of some 400 members of the party, who suffered all the horrors of disease and starvation and calamitous accident and all the terrors of attacks by hostile tribesmen. The expedition experienced mass desertions and violent mutinies and indulged in the worst sort of brutalities, including fatal floggings and summary executions, to contain them; it became lost time and again in the lethal jungles; it saw men go mad, murder one another, and turn into cannibals. And, in the end, it accomplished nothing.

Emin Pasha refused all offers Stanley made him on Leopold's behalf. What made the enterprise even more ludicrously pointless, Emin Pasha didn't want to be rescued. His letters to London had been meant to get him supplies and reinforcements so that he could remain in Equatoria, not be carried out of it. But by the time Stanley's ravaged column reached him it was in such desperate straits that it had only a slim chance of surviving itself, let alone providing support against the Mahdists. So Stanley was forced to rescue Emin Pasha against his will, taking him virtually as a captive down to the coast. But it was to the East African coast that he took him. On top of everything else, the expedition wound up demonstrating exactly the opposite of what Leopold had intended. The Sudan was in fact so utterly inaccessible by way of the Congo that Stanley didn't dare return from Lado the way he had come. Then, as the final irony of the entire debacle, on arriving at Bagamoyo, Emin Pasha fell and fractured his skull and had to be hospitalized on the spot. So Stanley, after all his frightful experiences, didn't even have the satisfaction of returning to Europe with the hero he had saved.

Leopold was greatly disappointed, but he did not have the luxury to dwell on his disappointment. For, although he would never entirely give up his ambition of extending the Congo Free State's northeastern border to the Nile, by the time Stanley returned from the abortive Emin Pasha expedition Leopold was engaged in a desperate struggle to hang on to the state's southwestern border in Katanga.

The year was 1890, the Scramble by now was on in earnest, and the British, in the person of one of the most ruthlessly successful empire builders of all, Cecil Rhodes, had shed their reluctance about getting involved in Africa and had taken the lead in the acquisition of colonies. Rhodes, who was at this time prime minister of Cape Colony and head of the crown-chartered British South Africa Company, sent his agents always deeper into the interior, building trading posts and mission stations, signing treaties with local chiefs, and laying claim to territories that would become Southern Rhodesia and Northern Rhodesia (today's Zambia), and then, ignoring the Berlin Act in the piratical spirit of the Scramble, on into the headwaters region of the Lualaba and Katanga. Leopold's protests to London were of no avail, and he realized that the only way to forestall Rhodes was to occupy Katanga and establish an unchallengeable Congo Free State military and political presence there, on the reasonable assumption that the British wouldn't allow Rhodes, whatever else they permitted him, to drag them into a war in the depths of Africa.

This, however, proved to be a far more difficult thing to do there than anywhere else in the Congo River basin. For at the time Katanga was under the rule of a wily, sophisticated, and powerful paramount chief by the name of Msiri. Msiri had amassed a huge fortune trading in ivory, copper, and slaves with the Portuguese on both the east and west coasts, had bought guns, assembled a great army, and had united the petty chiefdoms of the savanna plateau under his control in a series of tribal wars. His capital was at the village of Bunkeya (near today's city of Likasi), virtually at the center of the Lualaba watershed, and though his rule was despotic and unpopular it was unchallenged. He was universally acknowledged as the king of Katanga, and it was clear that any white man who hoped to possess the region would have to treat with him.

British missionaries had been the first to reach Bunkeya, and while they found Misri "a thorough gentleman" they failed to convert him to Christianity. Rhodes's agents had little better luck. At first it seemed that he might be willing to place his territories under British protection, but when he read the fine print of the treaty he balked. He couldn't see any reason why he should sign away his sovereignty for a few bits of colored cloth and some cases of gin. Leopold, however, had no intention of engaging in this sort of sham diplomacy. He was determined to secure Katanga either by cajolery or force, and he sent three well-equipped military expeditions to Bunkeya to impress this fact on Misiri. The first built a garrison near the king's capital, the second, arriving a few months later, reinforced it, and the third, coming in from the east coast, marched straight into Bunkeya itself and, without consultation, hoisted the gold-starred blue flag of the Congo Free State over Msiri's palace.

The Katanga king could see he was in trouble and retreated with his court to a neighboring village. Leopold's soldiers pursued him, brought him back to Bunkeye, and presented him with the treaty he was to sign ceding the sovereignty of his kingdom to the Congo Free State. A brief period of negotiations ensued. Misiri made one last desperate attempt to hold out, trying to amend the treaty's terms in his favor. But Leopold was impatient. The order from Brussels came down. Under mysterious circumstances, a Free State officer provoked a quarrel with the king of Katanga, and, using it as a pretext, shot Misiri dead in his palace and installed in his place a pliant puppet chief, who hastily put his mark on every document presented to him. With these, which he showed in the capitals of Europe, Leopold secured his hold on Katanga.

He was now free to turn his attentions once again to his northern and eastern frontiers. He was still dreaming of gaining a foothold on the Nile, and in the course of the next decade he would send expedition after expedition there to stake his claim. Lobbying relentlessly in Europe, he would make one arrangement after another with the British, French, and Germans in an effort to cut himself in on the regions of the Nile watershed in the Sudan, Uganda, and Tanganyika which they were partitioning out among themselves in the ferociously escalating Scramble. But his most pressing problem in the early 1890s was the challenge to the sovereignty of the Congo Free State then posed by the Arabs. For Tippoo Tib's ivory and slave hunters, following Stanley down the Lualaba from Nyangwe, had established themselves in the forests of the northern and eastern frontiers and formed a separate state within Leopold's state, interposed between the Upper Congo and the Upper Nile.

In the first years of the Congo Free State, Leopold tried a policy of coexistence and alliance with the Arabs. At one point he went so far as to appoint Tippoo Tib governor of the Stanley Falls district and enlist his aid in extending the state's borders to the Nile, encouraging the Arab to establish trading stations northeastward from Stanley Falls to the southern Sudan. But this coexistence couldn't last. The Arabs were in direct commercial competition with Leopold for the riches of the Congo River basin. And, with their highly sophisticated methods of organizing, administering, and operating their trading enterprises, they were also in direct conflict with Leopold's attempts to establish the state's political authority over its population. Tippoo Tib's satraps would not take orders from Leopold's officers nor were they willing to accept the Free State's control over their operations. What's more, the alliance was a constant source of embarrassment for Leopold in Europe. In teaming up with the last of the world's active slavers, Leopold made a public farce of the ostensible high-minded character of the state. So, professing moral indignation over their slaving but aiming at ending their political and commercial rivalry, Leopold decided to drive the Arabs out of his realm.

The Arab war was just another grisly episode in the unredeemingly grisly history of Leopold's Free State. The armies on both sides were made up largely of African tribesmen, and for the most part these Africans came from the cannibal tribes of the Lualaba forests. Stories are told of the orgies of man-eating that occurred after each battle, of how the fallen were scavenged and consumed on the battlefields, of how the captives while still living were prepared for the pot (arms and legs were broken and the prisoners were submerged in streams chin-deep, since suffering was believed to tenderize the meat for the cooking), of how some European officers developed a taste for human flesh. Both sides were undoubtedly equal in the performance of these atrocities, but in everything else Tippoo Tib's army was no match for Leopold's. The Free State's Force Publique was armed with the latest machine guns and artillery, and in battle after battle against the Arab muskets, it drove Tippoo Tib's forces back up the Lualaba. In March 1893 Nyangwe was taken, a few months later the great Arab center at Ujiji fell, and by early 1894 the war was over.

All this cost a great deal of money and, although Leopold was one of the richest men in Europe—he had made a fortune speculating in Suez Canal shares, among other things—even he didn't have enough, personally, to finance expeditions of exploration, build stations and pay their staffs, raise armies and fight wars. And he certainly didn't have the huge sums of investment capital needed for the development program—the construction of that railway around the Livingstone Falls, for example—to exploit the commercial potential of the Congo River basin. Such sums could only be had on the traditional European money markets and, at the outset, obtaining them proved to be a difficult task. It would take a few years before any of the several Congo bond issues Leopold floated would be subscribed, before any of the railway and mining syndicates he tried to form actually came into existence, before the commercial trading companies and merchant bankers that he approached were willing to take the risk and invest in his Congo enterprise. In the meantime, his personal fortune was suffering a heavy drain. Indeed, it got so bad that he is said to have melodramatized his problems by ostentatiously selling off the livery of his servants, cutting out courses at his banquets, and dunning fellow royalty for money at state funerals. His wife is said to have wailed, *"Mais, Léopold, tu vas nous ruiner avec ton Congo."* Clearly something had to be done, some other source of revenue had to be found to tide him over the first hard years, and, to his everlasting infamy, Leopold decided to find it in the Congo itself.

He had toyed with this approach before. While Stanley was still rock-breaking his way up to Stanley Pool, Leopold had suggested that European traders and missionaries be required to pay tolls for the use of the roads and stations he was building. But Stanley dissuaded him. "The mere rumour of such a course in Europe," he warned, "would bring general condemnation on our heads." Obviously, the association's philanthropic image would be damaged and just when Leopold was presenting that image as his best argument why the European powers should let him have the Congo. But now that he had it—and in view of what it was costing him to hold on to it—he was less concerned about preserving that image. So, in a clear violation of the Berlin Act, which had mandated him only to administer and police the new state, he put his Congo governmental apparatus into the business of doing business. All Free State officials—from the governor-general down to the lowliest post commander—became his personal trading agents.

He started modestly enough—and, characteristically, in secret—with the concept of *terres vacantes*. What constituted vacant or unclaimed land was left deliberately vague; presumably it represented areas where Africans didn't actually live, but it could include regions where they might hunt or farm. In any case that land was designated Free State property and Free State officials were authorized, and indeed encouraged, to engage in trade there in competition with private operators. This worked out quite nicely. One official, for example, discovered that ivory could be bought from Africans for 82 centimes a pound and sold in Liverpool for 12 francs 50 centimes, a profit, before deducting transport costs, of over 1500 percent. These transactions were meant to be secret, but the private traders of course were aware of them and they protested to their governments, arguing that besides being in violation of the Berlin Act, Leopold's officers enjoyed a grossly unfair advantage in being able to bring the full force of the state apparatus and the Force Publique into the trade. But the European powers took no notice. So, undeterred in this first experiment, Leopold got greedier. In 1891 and 1892, he issued a series of decrees—also in secret—which laid the foundation for a hugely lucrative scheme by which he could realize the maximum profits from his Congo enterprise.

The Free State was divided into two separate economic zones. The first of these was a free trading zone, which was open to the exploitation of private entrepreneurs of all nations. To attract them and their much-needed development capital, Leopold instituted a system of monopoly concessions in this zone. Under varying term leases (ten to fifteen years seems to have been average), investors were guaranteed exclusive commercial rights over a specific service or industry, product or region. And the investors responded. With the Scramble heating up, Europe's financiers and merchants, eager to get in on the profits that Africa promised, now began flocking to the Congo. An international syndicate was formed to build the railway around Livingstone Falls (it was completed and the first locomotive reached Leopoldville in 1898). The Anglo-Belgian India-Rubber Company was granted monopoly rights over vast tracts of rubber-rich forest regions; other concessionaires took over the trade in ivory, in hides, in palm oil, in forestry products. Union Minière du Haut-Katanga was created to develop the mineral wealth of Katanga, a consortium was organized to exploit the diamond fields of the Kasai, and in all of these trusts and corporations Leopold contrived to retain control of 50 percent of the voting stock.

But this Free Trading Zone, unbeknown to most, comprised less than half, probably not more than a third, of the land area of the Free State. All the rest, as a natural extension of the *terres vacantes* concept, was designated Domaine Privé, the private property of the state. And, in this zone, the state and only the state had the right to do business.

Government officials ran the state's trading monopolies, and in one of his secret decrees Leopold made it clear that their paramount duty—that is, above their administrative, military, or judicial duties— was the collection of revenue and the production of profits. As an incentive, the officials' wages consisted of direct annual salaries (pegged very low) and commissions based on how much profit their post or sector or district made for the state. To ease the job of making money, yet another secret decree stipulated not only that the native populations could not sell their products to any trader except the state's agents but that they *had* to sell to them. A quota system was installed: every village or tribal group was required to sell so much ivory or rubber to the state and, as the state held the monopoly, sell it at the state's fixed price. Failure to meet the quota was a crime punishable under the state's laws and enforced by the Force Publique. What's more, under the euphemism of taxation, Leopold also introduced a system of forced labor. Every tribal grouping of forty people was obliged to donate four people a year on a full-time basis to serve the government—one of whom was taken into the military—and ten other people part time for public-works projects. In addition, each such community was also required to provide food for the state's local post.

The money generated by this system—and it soon became substantial—went into the treasury of the Congo Free State and was used to pay its administrative and operating expenses. As this halted the drain on his personal fortune, Leopold was satisfied with it for a while. But then he became greedier still. In 1893 he created a third economic zone. It was cut out of the Free Trade Zone, centered around Lake Leopold II and Lake Tumba in the heart of the river basin, and was five times the size of Belgium. This he designated the Domaine de la Couronne. Here all the same rules and regulations as in the Domaine Privé applied and all the same operational methods were used, but the profits generated in the Crown Domain went not into the Free State treasury but into Leopold's pocket.

It is impossible to know how much money Leopold made out of the Congo. All sorts of ways have been tried to come up with a realistic number. For example, one source has pointed out that the state's exports of rubber soared from 241 tons, worth 1 million francs, in 1893, to 6000 tons, worth 47 million francs, in 1906, and Leopold owned more than half of that rubber. Another source has estimated that in a ten-year period the Crown Domain alone yielded a clear profit of over 90 million francs, and all of that went into Leopold's pocket. Still another way to look at it is that the value of each share of the Anglo-Belgian India-Rubber Company, of which Leopold owned 50 percent, rocketed in the first six years from about £5 sterling to £35. Putting it in dollars, one source has calculated that Leopold cleared at least $20 million in pure profit in the twenty years he owned the Congo. What we know for sure is that during this period he bought $13 million worth of real estate in such choice resort areas as the Riviera, Belgian beaches, German spas, and the French Midi; that he built palaces, chased young girls, kept mistresses, and won the sobriquet the King of Maxim's; and that when he died, in 1909, his will was probated at $80 million. The point is of course that he made an incalculable fortune out of his personal kingdom before it was finally taken away from him. And it was finally taken away because of that fortune—and the way he had made it.

In order to get the Congo in the first place, Leopold had kept secret his true intentions, and now he tried to keep secret what he was doing there in order to hold on to it. Independent explorers and geographers were discouraged. Casual travelers were barred. He carefully selected his officials and agents from the ranks of his most abject supporters and from the most disreputable elements in Europe—mercenaries, soldiers of fortune, adventurers, and profiteers, whom nothing was likely to shock. He even tried to control the missionaries who were allowed to enter his kingdom, giving preference to Belgian Catholics on whose loyalty he believed he could count, while hanging the threat of expulsion over the others if they did anything to cross him. But the secret he was trying to keep couldn't be kept; the things that were happening in the Congo under his personal rule were far too atrocious even for his most loyal priests, his most abject supporters, his most immoral agents, to keep from the eyes of the world.

The atrocities centered primarily on rubber, which, with the newly rising demand for bicycle and then automobile tires, was then the single most valuable product of the Congo. At the time, rubber was not cultivated on plantations; it still grew in the wild, and to harvest it natives went into the forests, located the rubber trees amid the profusion of other species, tapped their trunks, waited for the slowly running sap to collect, then brought it back to the state's agents. The work was hard and unrewarding, given the low prices the state monopoly paid for the latex, and there was very little enthusiasm for it. Thus, as often as not, the state-imposed quotas—which constantly escalated as the profits to be made in rubber escalated—were not met. So the state resorted to coercive methods.

As early as 1890, reports about these methods began to reach the outside world. They came at first from English Baptist missionaries, who were initially rather tentative in fear of Leopold's wrath, but as time went on they grew bolder and were joined by other missionaries, including the Belgian priests, and then even by officials of the state apparatus. And what they told of were the most unspeakable, inhuman cruelties. The soldiers of the Force Publique—recruited for the most part from the cannibal tribes of the Lualaba—were used to enforce the rubber quotas. Like their commanders, they were paid low salaries but handsome commissions based on how well they did their jobs—that is to say, how much rubber they coerced out of the local population—and they were taught by their white officers that terrorism was the most efficient way of getting it done. "I have the honour to inform you," a district commissioner in the late 1890s wrote to his sector and post commanders, "that you must succeed in furnishing 4000 kilos of rubber every month. To this effect I give you *carte blanche*. . . . Employ gentleness first, and if they [the natives] persist in not accepting the imposition of the State employ force."

One common use of force was the taking of hostages, usually women and children, who could be bought back by their husbands and fathers only with stipulated amounts of rubber. To make sure that they would be bought back, the conditions under which these hostages were held were awful. "In stations in charge of white men," an American missionary wrote, "one sees strings of poor, emaciated women, some of them mere skeletons . . . tramping about in gangs with a rope around their necks and connected by a rope one and a half yards apart." Brutal floggings, often fatal, with a bullwhip called the *chicotte* were freely meted out to encourage the rubber collections. If a village failed or was slow in meeting its quota, a punitive raid was staged, accompanied by rape, plundering, and wanton killing, and any protest or rebellion was dealt with by mass executions. A white officer described such a raid: "We fell upon them all and killed them without mercy . . . he [a Monsieur X who was in command] ordered us to cut off the heads of the men and hang them on the village palisades, also their sexual members, and to hang the women and children on the palisade in the form of a cross." As the American missionary wrote in 1896, "War has been waged all through the district of the Equator, and thousands of people have been killed and twenty-one heads were brought back to Stanley Falls, and have been used by Captain Rom [the station commander] as a decoration around a flower-bed in front of his house."

One particularly widespread punishment was the cutting off of hands.

If the rubber does not reach the full amount required the sentries attack the natives. They kill some and bring the hands to the Commissioner [a Danish missionary wrote]. That was about the time I saw the native killed before my own eyes. The soldier said, "Don't take this to heart so much. They kill us if we don't bring the rubber. The Commissioner has promised us if we have plenty of hands he will shorten our service." These were often smoked to preserve them until they could be shown to the European officer.

For the most part, the hands (and, for that matter, the cut-off heads) served as proof that the Force Publique soldiers were doing their job, that they were actually killing people who failed to meet the rubber quotas and not just going off into the forests and shooting off their bullets in pretense. But horribly often the hands were taken from the living.

The scenes I have witnessed [another American wrote], have been almost enough to make me wish I were dead. The soldiers are themselves savages, some even cannibals, trained to use rifles. . . . Imagine them returning from fighting rebels; see on the bow of the canoe is a pole, and a bundle of something on it. These are the hands (right hands) of sixteen warriors they have slain. "Warriors?" Don't you see among them the hands of little children and girls? I have seen them. I have seen where the trophy has been cut off, while the poor heart beat strongly enough to shoot the blood from the cut arteries at a distance of fully four feet.

The baskets of severed smoked hands, set down at the feet of the European post commanders, became the symbol of Leopold's Congo Free State. In the degenerate, brutalized atmosphere of the Congo forests—the atmosphere out of which Joseph Conrad created that chilling masterpiece *Heart of Darkness* and the malevolently evil figure of Kurtz, a station agent in the vicinity of Stanley Falls—the collection of hands became an end in itself. Force Publique soldiers brought them to the stations in place of rubber; they even went out to harvest them instead of rubber. Hands took on a value in their own right. They became a sort of currency. They came to be used to make up for short falls in rubber quotas, to replace the food that hadn't been delivered to the stations or the people who were demanded for the forced-labor gangs; and the Force Publique soldiers were paid their bonuses on the basis of how many hands they collected. A native might save his life by surrendering his right hand, but more often than not the harvesting of hands meant wholesale murder, and there are estimates that in the twenty years of Leopold's personal rule at least 5 million people were killed in the Congo.

Leopold mounted a massive propaganda campaign to counter these devastating reports. He created a phony Commission for the Protection of the Natives, which ostensibly was to track down what he maintained might be a few isolated cases of atrocities and have them corrected. He set up a secret press bureau, whose job was to influence and buy off prominent newspapers and newspapermen. He imputed ulterior motives to his accusers, claiming, for example, that the English were attacking his rule in the Free State because they wanted to take it over for themselves or that the Protestant missionaries were sending out those reports in order to undermine the Catholics. And in the Congo itself he used all his powers to terrorize to prevent the reports from getting out. An Italian officer in the Force Publique, for example, who finally had become disgusted with what he had been forced to participate in, discovered that a white man wasn't free to quit Leopold's service.

If he insists [he reported], and leaves his station, he can be prosecuted for desertion, and in any case, will probably never get out of the country alive, for the routes of communication, victualling stations, etc., are in the hands of the Administration, and escape in a native canoe is out of the question—every native canoe, if its destination be not known and its movements chronicled in advance from post to post, is at once liable to be stopped, for the natives are not allowed to move freely about the controlled water-ways.

As these horror stories circulated ever more widely and the evidence supporting them mounted always more irrefutably, Europe, and especially Britain, at last became exercised. And by the turn of the century, something amounting to a concerted political and propaganda campaign against Leopold's Congo misrule was underway, spearheaded by such men as H. R. Fox Bourne, Herbert Samuel, John Holt and Edmund D. Morel.

Morel had started his career as a clerk at the Liverpool shipping line of Elder Dempster, which imported rubber from the Congo Free State, and it was while in this relatively lowly job that he first became suspicious of what was going on in the Belgian king's personal realm. Specifically, what Morel noted was that, although the Free State had ostensibly been created and given to Leopold for the humanitarian purpose of bringing the benefits of European civilization to the peoples of the river basin, in fact very little if any European goods were exported to the Congo in exchange for the increasingly huge quantities of rubber that were being taken out. This statistic alone—the Free State's disastrous export-import imbalance—forced Morel to draw the only possible conclusion: that Leopold was stealing the Congo blind. Turning into a muckraking, investigative journalist, Morel set about substantiating this contention. He scoured the ledgers of other shipping firms and those of the Congo monopoly trusts for further damaging statistics; he collected fresh eye-witness accounts of Leopold's atrocious *modus operandi* from missionaries and disaffected Free State agents. And he published what he found in inflammatory newspaper articles and in such devastating polemical books as *Red Rubber, The Congo Scandal* and *King Leopold's Rule in Africa.*

John Holt, a Liverpool merchant who headed one of the largest West African trading companies of the time, took a keen interest in Morel's work. His interest, it is only fair to point out, wasn't entirely philanthropic. Like all British merchants, Holt was extremely annoyed at being shut out of the Congo's rich trade by Leopold's monopolistic practices and was eager to find a way of breaking the Belgian king's hold on the river basin. So, not surprisingly, he encouraged and supported Morel in every way he could, publishing Morel's articles in his company's newspaper, *West Africa,* and helping Morel start his own newspaper, *West African Mail.* At the same time, he lobbied energetically among his fellow merchants and succeeded in getting the British Chambers of Commerce to pass a resolution calling on the British government to launch an inquiry into the abuses in the Congo Free State.

Herbert Samuel, a Liberal party member of Parliament, following up on this line of attack, carried the anti-Leopold campaign into the House of Commons. Again and again he introduced the subject for formal debate and, using Morel's writings in support of his arguments, stressed Leopold's violation of the Berlin Act in not allowing free trade in the Congo and pointed out the huge, often 500 percent profits being made by Leopold's monopoly concessions and the atrocious methods by which they were making them. H. R. Fox Bourne entered the fight as the leader of the Aborigines Protection Association—the direct descendant of England's venerable anti-slavery and abolitionist movement—and he brought all the righteous fervor and propaganda techniques of that movement to the Congo cause, writing such blistering tracts as "Civilization in Congoland: A history of wrongdoing" and staging, along with Morel and Holt, fiery public rallies.

All this together ultimately aroused public opinion to a furious pitch. But unquestionably the fatal blow to Leopold's personal kingdom was delivered by Roger David Casement.

"A tall, handsome man of fine bearing," Herbert Ward, the sculptor, who knew him in his Congo days, wrote of Casement; "mere muscle and bone, a sun-tanned face, blue eyes and black curly beard. A pure Irishman he is, with a captivating voice and a singular charm of manner. A man of distinction and great refinement, high-minded and courteous, impulsive and poetical."

Casement's greatest popular fame, of course, came years later as one of the authentic martyr-heroes of the Irish rebellion. Then, just before the Easter Uprising of 1916, having gone to Berlin on the quixotic errand of trying to secure armed assistance from the Germans for the Irish independence movement, he was arrested by the British, tried for treason and hanged. But before he met this tragic and romantically futile destiny, he performed a service to the peoples of the Congo far more important than any he ever performed for the Irish.

Born in 1864 in Sandycove near Dublin, Casement developed his interest in the Congo in much the same way as Morel. Orphaned as a child and raised by guardians in Ulster, he was sent as a teen-ager to live with an uncle in Liverpool who was an agent for a West

African trading firm and who got the youth a job as a clerk at the Elder Dempster shipping line where Morel was to work ten years later. During his employment there, Casement shipped out as a purser on one of the line's packets for a rubber-hauling voyage to Boma and though the journey started out as a lark it gave him a taste for African adventure which he was to pursue for the next quarter century.

He began in the Congo itself. In 1884, at the age of twenty, he left Elder Dempster and joined that band of Europeans who were then working for Stanley on the river. This was nearly a year before the Berlin Act created the Free State, while Leopold was still cunningly manipulating the European Powers into granting him sovereignty over the river basin and while Stanley's forces were still building a roadway and stations around Livingstone Falls to the Stanley Pool. Very much a believer then in the humanitarian and philanthropic purpose of Leopold's enterprise, Casement first was employed at the road-building expedition's supply base at Matadi, then was transferred to the trading station that had been built at the equator on the river's left bank (today's Mbandaka). In 1886, after the Free State had been established and Stanley had departed, Casement returned to Matadi to take charge of the survey for the railway that was to be built from there to Leopoldville.

On completion of this work, in 1887, Casement found himself without a job. Leopold by then was growing wary of having idealists like Casement around and was weeding out all but the most hardened adventurers from the Free State's employ. Casement, however, wasn't yet ready to return to Europe so he took a post as lay helper at a British mission on the Stanley Pool, looking after the station's river transport and managing its accounts and correspondence. But then, in 1890, when it seemed he would at last have to leave Africa, construction on the Matadi-to-Leopoldville railway began and, despite the Belgian king's unease with Casement's type of idealistic enthusiasm, he was signed to a one-year contract on the project because of his experience in preparing the original survey. And it was while on this job that Casement met the young Polish-born sea captain, Teodor Jozef Konrad Korzeniowski, who was to gain literary fame under the pen name of Joseph Conrad.

Since boyhood, Conrad had been drawn to the Congo—in *Heart of Darkness,* his protagonist, Marlow, reminiscing on "when I was a little chap," remembers thinking then that the river resembled "an immense snake uncoiled, with its head in the sea, its body at rest curving afar over a vast country, and its tail lost in the depths of the land. And as I looked at the map of it in a shop-window, it fascinated me as a snake would a bird"—and in the fall of 1890 he signed on as captain on one of the Free State's steamers plying the Congo from Leopoldville to Stanley Falls. All things considered, this was a very brief interlude in Conrad's relentlessly adventurous life, lasting in fact barely four months. But the impact of the experience was enormous. Out of it came his masterpiece, *Heart of Darkness*, which, when published in 1902, gave literary expression to an entire age's perception of the Congo as a place of horror and dread and which forever characterized in men's minds Leopold's agents as sadistic lunatics. And out of it also came his life-long friendship with Casement which was to stand the anti-Leopold cause in good stead in the years to come.

I can assure you [Conrad wrote of Casement], that he is a limpid personality. There is a touch of the conquistador in him too; for I've seen him start off into an unspeakable wilderness swinging a crook-handled stick for all weapons, with two bulldogs, Paddy (white) and Biddy (brindle), at his heels, and a Loanda boy carrying a bundle for all company. A few months afterwards it so happened that I saw him come out again, a little leaner, a little browner, with his stick, dogs, and Loanda boy, and quietly serene as though he had been for a stroll in a park.

Returning from his last such stroll on the Matadi-to-Leopoldville railway project, Casement, now twenty-seven, joined the British foreign service and, though he remained in Africa, it was eight years before he again returned to the Congo. His first posting, in 1892, was to Britain's Niger Coast Protectorate where he was put in charge of a survey of regions until then unexplored and, in some cases, never visited by Europeans. Then, in 1895, he was named Her Majesty's Consul in Lourenço Marques, capital of Portuguese East Africa (today's Mozambique), where he got involved in the Boer War, then raging just across the frontier in South Africa, by planning a raid on the Pretoria railroad. And three years later, in 1898, he was assigned as Consul to Loanda in the Portuguese colony of Angola.

By this time, concern about what was going on in the neighboring Congo Free State was rapidly on the rise so, while still in Loanda, Casement unofficially began checking out the situation there and

became increasingly horrified by what he found. For example, about
this time on a visit to his old base of Matadi, he made the same
discovery that Morel was to make a few years later: namely, that no
European goods beneficial to the peoples of the Congo were being
imported to the Free State. Instead, he learned, the loads of rubber
on the Matadi wharfs, destined for Antwerp, were being exchanged
for guns and ammunition with which to arm the forest sentries of
the Force Publique who in turn used them to terrorize the populace
into harvesting ever more rubber. Casement's disturbing dispatch
to this effect convinced London to transfer the consulate from Angola
to the Free State and so, in 1900, Casement once again returned to
the Congo, now as British Consul in Boma.

Once officially on the job, Casement followed up on his initial
discoveries and began looking into all the alleged abuses of Leopold's
rule and firing off sharply worded dispatches to London. "There is
no free trade in the Congo today," he wrote at one point. "There is,
it might be said, no trade, as such, at all in the Congo. There is
ruthless exploitation at the hands of a savage and barbarous soldiery
of one of the most prolific regions of Africa, in the interest of and
for the profit of the Sovereign of that country and his favoured Concessionaires." At another point he complained angrily that the entire
Congo "has become by the stroke of the pen the sole property of the
governing body of that State, or, it should be said, in truth, the
private property of one individual, the King of the Belgians." And
throughout these dispatches, he repeatedly urged the British government to intervene, to take action so that the Free State's "rotten
system of administration either be mended, or ended."

Casement's scorching dispatches from Boma came pouring into
Whitehall just as the anti-Leopold campaign of Morel, Holt, Fox
Bourne and the others—Conrad's *Heart of Darkness* appeared at this
time—was reaching a fever pitch. And the combination proved irre-
sistible. In 1903, under the management of Herbert Samuel, the
British Parliament voted a motion stating that

the Government of the Congo Free State, having at its inception guaranteed to the Powers that its native subjects should be governed with humanity, and that no trading monopoly or privilege should be permitted
within its domains, and both these guarantees having been constantly
violated, this House requests His Majesty's Government to confer with the

other Powers signatories of the Berlin General Act by virtue of which the Congo Free State exists, in order that measures may be adopted to abate the evils prevalent in the State.

The British government then sent a note to the thirteen other powers of the 1885 Berlin Convention, requesting a meeting to discuss their possible intervention. And it also instructed Casement to undertake an extensive tour of inspection of the Free State and make a detailed official report of what exactly was going on there.

Traveling light—just with his crook-handled stick, two bulldogs and Loanda boy—Casement set off in June 1903. He was gone just a little over three months but what he saw and heard in this brief period confirmed at first-hand all the atrocity stories that had been circulating for years. He saw women chained in sheds with their babies, being held hostage for the delivery of their village's rubber quota. He saw men beaten mercilessly with the *chicotte* for having brought insufficient latex to the collecting point. He heard of whole tribes migrating across the Congo River to escape the Force Publique's brutalities, of mass executions by the state's agents, of punitive raids in which obscene mutilations were committed.

He interviewed a handless boy of eleven or twelve who had been wounded in such a raid on his village and who, while playing dead, had been "perfectly sensible of the severing of his wrist, but lay still fearing that if he moved he would be killed." Another youth, taken prisoner in a raid, told Casement that he had had his hands tied so tightly with thongs that they "had swollen terribly in the morning, and the thongs had cut into the bone. . . . The soldiers beat his hands with their rifle butts against the tree. His hands subsequently fell off." And a woman told of fleeing with her son from soldiers "when he fell shot dead, and she herself fell down beside him—she supposed she fainted. She then felt her hand being cut off, but she made no sign."

All this, and more, Casement described in chilling detail in his official report, "confident that once any decent man or woman . . . learns and appreciates the ghastly truth of the wrong done to the Congo man and woman—aye, and the poor hunted child!—they will not desert them." And when the report was published, in February 1904, the effect was electrifying. A contemporary English statesman declared that "no external question for at least thirty years has moved the country so strongly and vehemently as this in regard to the Congo." Of the report itself, Moral wrote,

The scenes so vividly described seemed to fashion themselves out of the shadows before my eyes. The daily agony of an entire people unrolled itself in all the repulsive and terrifying details. I verily believe I *saw* those hunted women clutching their children and flying panic-stricken through the bush; the blood flowing from those quivering black bodes as the hippopotamus-hide whip struck again and again; the savage soldiery rushing hither and thither amid burning villages; the ghastly tally of severed hands.

And Conrad wrote,

It is an extraordinary thing that the conscience of Europe, which seventy years ago has put down the slave trade on humanitarian grounds, tolerates the Congo State today. It is as if the moral clock has been put back many hours. . . . In the old days, England had in her keeping the conscience of Europe. The initiative came from her. But I suppose we are busy with other things—too much involved in great affairs to take up the cudgels of humanity, decency and justice.

An immediate consequence of the Casement Report was the founding of the Congo Reform Association. Led by Morel (Casement, as a civil servant, could not participate but he gave it considerable behind-the-scenes support) and using the organizational set up of Fox Bourne's Aborigines Protection Association, it soon had active chapters not only in Britain but throughout Europe and the United States as well, lobbying their governments and marshalling their citizenry's outrage against Leopold. And nowhere was that outrage greater than in Belgium.

The Belgians had never been happy with their king's African adventure and now they found themselves embroiled in a nightmare of ugly worldwide publicity because of it. Something had to be done. Under pressure from his own Parliament, Leopold was forced to agree to the creation of a Commission of Enquiry—consisting of distinguished lawyers from Belgium, Italy and Switzerland—to investigate the conditions revealed in the Casement Report. The king hoped, of course, that the Commission would refute or, at least, ameliorate the charges against him. But that wasn't the case. When the international panel returned from an on-the-scene tour of inspection in 1905, it confirmed every one of Casement's findings.

Leopold made one last-ditch attempt to hang on to the Congo by promising to undertake a program of wide-ranging reforms. But it was rejected. In the first place, it was clear that the promised reforms would not go to the source of the problem: the state's participation in and monopoly control of the Congo's trade. In fact, with incredible imperial arrogance, at the very moment that the furor was at its height, Leopold had the audacity to extend his Crown Domain and reorganize his monopoly trusts so as to increase his personal profits from the river basin. But, additionally, the European powers had at last recognized the outlandishness of a situation in which an individual owned a country and ruled it as the most absolute of absolute monarchs without even the pretense of democratic controls. And they decided that the Congo must be taken away from him. The only question was to whom should it be given. In those days of the Scramble and ruthless colonialism, it never occurred to anyone that it might simply be given back to the Congo people. No, the belief then was that Africans couldn't rule themselves, that it was the God-given right and duty of European governments to do the job for them. And in this case the European government that seemed the natural choice for the task was that of Belgium.

Belgium, however, was no more eager now for an African colony than it ever had been and so for the next two years the matter was a subject of intense national debate. Elections were fought over it, governments fell because of it and the Parliament was occupied with no other question. But the outcome was inevitable. In August 1908, the Belgian Parliament, albeit reluctantly, voted an annexation treaty and on November 15, 1908, twenty-three years after its formation, the Congo Free State became the Belgian Congo.

EPILOGUE

In retrospect, we know that there never was any such thing as a good colony, and the Belgian Congo proved to be among the worst, but it was a considerable improvement over the Congo Free State. It couldn't help but be.

The Belgian government dismantled Leopold's apparatus of personal rule and put the administration of the Congo in the charge of a colonial ministry, answerable to the democratically elected Parliament, and set about correcting the most flagrant abuses. For a while many of Leopold's agents remained at their posts, especially at the more remote jungle stations, but in time the worst of them, the foreign mercenaries, soldiers of fortune, and sadistic adventurers, were weeded out and a conventional colonial service of Belgian civil servants and military personnel was created. The government was removed from the business of doing business. The rights of the Congolese to own and work their lands and to trade in their products were restored. The system of forced labor was abolished. The state's monopoly in trade was ended. The Domaine Privé and Crown Domains were thrown open to all comers. And they came.

Missionaries and entrepreneurs, settlers and traders flocked into the Congo. The European population rose from about 3000 in 1908, when Belgium took over from Leopold, to more than 100,000 on the eve of independence in 1960. Thousands of businesses were established. Huge plantations were put into cultivation for rubber, cotton, coffee, and palm oil. Banking consortiums were formed. The diamond fields of south Kasai, the tin and gold deposits of Kivu, the rich copper and uranium ores of Katanga were developed. Mines, factories, roads and railways, and astonishingly modern industrial cities were built. Passenger and cargo steamers were launched on the rivers, hydroelectric power dams were constructed at the cataracts, dock facilities and port towns burgeoned along the navigable stretches. In the great rush of development, the Congo became something very close to "the grand highway of commerce to West Central Africa" that Stanley had visualized, and its vast basin seemed at last to have received the wonders of European civilization of which the ManiKongo Affonso had so long ago dreamed.

There was a time, especially during the fifteen years after the Second World War, when the Belgian Congo was considered the very model of an African colony. Its economy boomed. Its colonial service seemed to administer its affairs with even-handed justice. The missionaries and mission stations offered primary and secondary education. The business concerns and industrial conglomerates provided an admirable array of enlightened social services—employment, housing, medical care, decent wages and working conditions—and the Congolese were said to be the happiest and most prosperous of all of Africa's colonized peoples.

But it was a tragic illusion; the "civilization" that Belgium appeared to have cast over the Congo proved the most fragile of façades, behind which seethed the savage anger of a people too long abused, of tribal nations too much invaded, and when the opportunity came this savagery and anger erupted in what was the bloodiest epoch of the Congo's relentlessly bloody history.

"The winds of change" was how Harold Macmillan termed the demand for independence from European rule that arose among the colonized of Africa in the wake of World War II. But those winds, with amazing swiftness, gathered the strength of a howling hurricane and, from the guerrilla wars in Algeria to the Mau Mau terror in Kenya, ripped across the continent with such irresistible force that it swept away all but a remnant of Europe's colonial power within little more than a decade. Nowhere in Africa, however, was the transition from colonialism to independence quite so agonizing as in the Congo.

Blame for the horrors of that era falls heavily on Belgium's shoulders. Having corrected the most outrageous abuses of Leopold's reign, it settled self-righteously into fifty years of what it regarded as enlightened colonial administration, never once giving a thought to the possibility, let alone the necessity, of eventual decolonization. And, when that eventuality was suddenly at hand, it did next to nothing to prepare the Congolese for it. As late as 1958, the Belgian government officially—and proudly—was describing its colonial policy as "paternalistic." No civil rights were thought necessary for the Congolese. They were citizens neither of Belgium nor of the Congo. They participated not one jot in the governing of the colony. The highest ranks they were allowed to attain in the colonial administration were as minor clerks in the civil service and as noncommissioned officers in the Force Publique. Elections were unheard of. Political parties and publications were banned. Racial segregation was the order of the day. Until 1955, Congolese were forbidden to go to college, and even after that they were not permitted to study at universities abroad; a special native school, Lovanium University, under close colonial supervision, was created in Leopoldville to insulate the "children" from dangerous foreign influences.

Nevertheless, the Congo was no more impervious to the winds of change than any other African colony. Political unrest stirred first among the so-called *évolués*—Congolese with secondary-school educations. Barred from organizing politically, they formed social, religious, and cultural clubs, usually along tribal or regional lines, and at clandestine meetings, discussed, planned, and plotted how to get better pay, improve working conditions, end racial discrimination, gain civil rights, and ultimately, win independence. These clubs became the Congo's political parties of the 1960s. In the 1950s they served as the training ground for the country's future political leaders. For example, out of the government workers' club in Stanleyville emerged a charismatic postal clerk by the name of Patrice Lumumba. In the Bakongo tribal club in Leopoldville, a pudgy civil servant named Joseph Kasavubu won popularity by stirring up memories of the lost greatness of the Kingdom of Kongo. In Katanga, at the Union Minière mining complex, a white-collar worker named Moise Tshombe organized a club among the Luba-Lunda tribesmen. And the leader of a soldiers' club in the Force Publique garrison at Thysville was a young NCO by the name of Joseph Mobutu.

Belgium's view of the *évolué* clubs and their leaders was remarkably sanguine, and its response to the political discontent that they signified was confined to token gestures. For example, a system of *immatriculation* was introduced by which a Congolese "who demonstrated a state of civilization implying the aptitude for enjoying laws and fulfilling duties" could gradually gain Belgian citizenship. The idea, essentially, was to defuse any political threat posed by the *évolués* by making a privileged class of them and thus separating them from the masses they might lead. "The time will come which will assure to each, white or black, his proper share in the country's government, according to his own qualities and capacity," the Belgian King Baudouin, on a trip to Leopoldville in 1955, declared. "But before we realize this high ideal, gentlemen, much remains to be done." Just how much, in the Belgian view, was revealed by a University of Antwerp professor. In a scholarly article in 1956, he outlined a scenario for the Congo's gaining independence—in thirty years.

But the winds of change were blowing too hard for such a leisurely timetable. In 1957, Britain granted Ghana its independence. In August 1958, Charles de Gaulle chose Brazzaville, just across the Stanley Pool, to announce that France was granting independence to all her colonies. In December 1958, newly-independent Ghana held an All-African People's Conference in Accra, at which the call went out to all the continent's blacks to rise up and throw off their colonial chains. Patrice Lumumba managed to attend that conference, and when he got back to the Congo the drive for independence surfaced in earnest. The *évolué* clubs revealed their true political character. They sent petitions to Brussels, organized rallies, staged demonstrations and strikes, circulated inflammatory pamphlets, clashed with the police.

Under the impact of this unexpected political activity, the Belgian government in January 1959 vaguely promised that "Belgium intends to organize in the Congo a democracy capable of exercising its prerogatives of sovereignty and deciding on its independence." To the nationalists, this sounded like a meaningless placebo, and the wave of rallies and strikes went on. In October, Belgium took another step to mollify the nationalists: it set a timetable under which independence would be granted in 1964. But the nationalists rejected this as not soon enough. So in January 1960, Belgium convened a conference in Brussels with black delegates from 62 *évolué* clubs and 19 tribal associations and, in a stunning capitulation, agreed to grant the Congo its independence virtually immediately.

Why Belgium reversed herself so abruptly is a question that will probably never be answered to everyone's satisfaction. There are those who say that Brussels feared that revolutionary violence would rapidly escalate and draw Belgium into a long, debilitating guerrilla war that she could ill afford, and so, never particularly happy about having an African colony anyway, decided to abdicate all further responsibility and be rid of the problem once and for all. On the other hand, there are those who believe that Belgium was perfectly aware that the Congo was in no way yet ready for independence, that chaos would surely follow its granting on such short notice, and that, as a result, she could expect to be called back to restore order and, in effect, to resume her rule. Whichever the true reason, Brussels set independence for June 30, 1960. This allowed barely six months for the Congolese to formally organize political parties, choose slates of candidates, conduct elections for a bicameral national assembly and a host of provincial and local governments, and take over the civil service bureaucracy and colonial administration from the Belgians. Considering that at the time there were hardly a score of Congolese college graduates in the country—and among them not a single military officer, engineer, lawyer, architect, doctor, economist, or anyone with any practical experience or training in government—it was a patently impossible job.

The troubles began during the election campaign. Candidates made wild promises of miracles to come. In one case, a candidate advised his constituents to bury stones because they would be turned into gold once the Congo was independent. Another promised that, if elected, he would resurrect all his voters' dead relatives. More dangerously, candidates used the campaign to vent long-repressed hostilities against whites, and they sought to gain political advantage by stirring up old tribal feuds. By Independence Day, the country was in a state of high nervous excitement. Crowds roamed the streets of the major cities, impatient for the miracles of freedom to begin, nursing tribal grudges, eager to become lords over the whites and take vengeance for past injustices.

King Baudouin, either out of gross ignorance or even grosser insensitivity, intensified the country's edgy mood when at the Independence ceremonies in Leopoldville he devoted much of his formal address to paying homage to King Leopold. Patrice Lumumba, the newly elected prime minister, was enraged, and when his turn came to speak on behalf of the new Congo government, he launched into a vitriolic diatribe on the cruel and inhuman rule of the Belgians. Joseph Kasavubu, the republic's new president, rebuked Lumumba and later Lumumba tried to calm the situation in a second speech, but his original words had touched a raw nerve in the Congolese people.

As Independence Day wore on, the crowds turned into mobs, there were repeated clashes with the Force Publique, attacks on whites, outbreaks of tribal feuding. The mood rapidly worsened during the first week. With the wholesale departure of Belgian civil servants—and the lack of trained blacks to replace them—the public services broke down. And, when government employees didn't get their paychecks, wildcat strikes erupted which turned into riots when the Force Publique attempted to quell them. But the most devastating blow fell when the Force Publique itself mutinied.

At the time, Lumumba, who was eager to replace Belgians with Congolese in every other sector of the new administration, was unwilling to risk running the Force Publique with inexperienced blacks. He believed that, for the obviously difficult times ahead, he had to have a well-disciplined gendarmerie and so intended to keep the 1000 Belgian officers in command of the 24,000-man force until Congolese could be trained to replace them. To the NCOs and soldiers, though, this was discrimination, and on July 1 the Force Publique garrison at Leopoldville staged a protest demonstration against the policy. When they refused to obey orders to return to barracks, the Belgian commanding general ordered out the Thysville garrison. But that garrison mutinied as well and, as if a string of dynamite had been set alight, one by one so did virtually every other garrison in the country.

The soldiers went on a rampage, attacking their officers, raping officers' wives, looting stores. On July 6, Lumumba capitulated and agreed to replace all Belgian officers with Congolese NCOs and promote everyone else at least one rank, thus creating an army without a single private. But he was too late. The mutinies had started a tidal wave of violence. Blacks attacked whites and each other as anti-European hatreds and intertribal rivalries exploded with savage fury. The sudden chaos was exacerbated by the panicked flight of whites. In the first week some 40,000 Belgians fled. All services shut down, food shortages developed, epidemics broke out. Then another disastrous blow fell.

Moise Tshombe, who had been elected premier of Katanga Province, called on Lumumba and Kasavubu to ask Brussels for troops to restore order. Fearing that this would bring back Belgian rule, they refused, and so, on July 11, Tshombe declared the secession of Katanga. He called for and got Belgian paratroopers to round up and disarm the Force Publique mutineers in his province. And he also asked for and got Belgian civil servants to take over the shattered administration in Katanga.

Lumumba was desperate. The Congo's richest province had seceded, and violence was sweeping the rest of the country. He had only one place to turn. On July 15, he appealed to the United Nations for help.

While overall the UN's performance in the Congo must be judged positively, at the outset its presence only further complicated the rapidly deteriorating situation. Lumumba wanted the UN troops to attack Katanga and end Tshombe's secession, but the UN wanted to avoid a military confrontation with a member nation, Belgium. First the Belgian paras had to be gotten out of Katanga. In the meantime, the polyglot army of soldiers from Ghana, Tunisia, Guinea, Mali, and Ethiopia concentrated on bringing the Force Publique mutineers under control and on putting down the tribal warfare. While it did, the whirlwind of chaos raged throughout the summer.

In September, the situation took another bizarre turn. Declaring him unable to handle the affairs of state, Kasavubu fired Lumumba. Hearing this, Lumumba commandeered the Leopoldville radio station and broadcast to the nation that he had fired Kasavubu. The bewildered Congolese assembly didn't know which of the leaders to support so it wound up supporting neither. All pretense of a functioning government came to an end. And, as might be expected in such a situation, a military man stepped in. Joseph Mobutu, the young former NCO of the Force Publique who had been promoted to the command of the army when Lumumba ousted the Belgians in July, seized power.

His first move was to arrest Lumumba. On hearing this, Antoine Gizenga, a close associate of Lumumba's, declared the secession of Oriental Province, of which Lumumba's hometown and power base, Stanleyville, was the capital. The soldiers of the province's garrisons opened an attack on Mobutu's forces, and by Christmas they had overrun Kivu Province and northern Katanga. A renewed wave of savagery ravaged the country; whites were murdered and the most horrendous kind of tribal warfare, marked by wholesale massacres and cannibalism, raged in the rain forests. Blaming Lumumba, Mobutu decided to get rid of him. In January 1961, he had Lumumba flown to Katanga. What he had in mind in turning Lumumba over to Tshombe has never been made clear. Perhaps he only meant to exile him to a distant corner. But in February the news came that Lumumba was dead, killed by Katangese soldiers. The world-wide outcry—which made Lumumba a martyr-hero of Africa—was so furious that Mobutu resigned and Kasavubu resumed command.

In the midst of the turmoil, the United Nations at last began to make some progress. Belgium had been persuaded to withdraw its troops from Katanga and, though Tshombe recruited white mercenary soldiers to replace them, the UN troops were finally authorized to attack Katanga and bring its secession to an end. That war lasted eighteen months. On several occasions, Tshombe was ready to concede defeat and offered a ceasefire with the United Nations (it was while flying out to meet Tshombe to negotiate one such ceasefire that the UN Secretary-General Dag Hammarskjöld was killed in a plane crash) only to reneg and keep the bloody fighting going. But finally in January 1963, with his mercenary troops in full retreat, Tshombe threw in the towel and fled into exile in Spain. The Katanga secession was over and, after two years of political controversy about their presence there, the UN forces withdrew.

But the Congo's agony was not over. The economy had collapsed; strikes and riots were endemic in the cities and towns; tribal warfare raged in the jungles. And, above all, Oriental Province was still in secession and had fallen into the grip of an increasingly savage rebel regime. In an attempt to bring the province back into the fold, Kasavubu had arrested Gizenga, but his place in Stanleyville had been taken by a wild-eyed revolutionary named Christophe Gbenye, who received military aid from Russia and China and who claimed to be in possession of "the magic Golden Book containing all the powerful secrets of the Congo, given by Lumumba to Gizenga and by Gizenga to me." He enlisted witch doctors in his cause, called his rebel soldiers Simbas (Swahili for "lions") and convinced them that a special *dawa* (magic) he dispensed made them impervious to bullets. Dressed in monkey furs, armed with poisoned arrows and spears as well as Russian rifles, largely recruited from the once-cannibal tribes of the Lualaba, and often doped up on *mira* (a local marijuana-like drug), the Simbas struck terror before them as they marched through the jungles to the beat of the ju-ju drums. The Congo army fled before their horrifying advance, and in the course of some eighteen months they overran more than half of the Congo.

Kasavubu declared a state of emergency, and, in June 1964, in yet another bizarre twist in the Congo melodrama, he called Tshombe out of exile to head a government of national unity to meet the frightening threat of Gbenye's Simbas. Tshombe's idea of how to meet that threat was brutally simple: he would put into the field an army even more terrible than that of the Simbas. As it was clear that the Congo's own soldiers weren't up to the job, he turned to those who had helped him in the Katanga secession: white mercenaries. The call went out; the pay was $300 a month, all you could loot, and the most savage kind of excitement. And the mercenaries answered the call. Former French Foreign Legionnaires, ex-Nazis, white racists from Southern Rhodesia and South Africa, soldiers of fortune, demented sadists, adventurers and fugitives of every description—the descendants, in spirit and temperament, of the brutal agents of Leopold's Free State— enlisted in Tshombe's army. Once unleashed into the rain forests, they proved more than a match for the Simbas in savagery. Looting, massacring, raping, committing atrocities, they rolled back the Simba tide.

By September, Gbenye's forces had been driven into the northeastern corner of the Congo basin. All they held of any consequence was Stanleyville itself. In this desperate situation, Gbenye played one last horrifying card. He held 1300 white hostages from 25 countries in Stanleyville and, in a message to the United Nations, he warned that unless the mercenaries' drive on the city was halted, all the hostages would be executed and "we will wear their hearts around our necks like fetishes and dress ourselves in their flayed skins."

The fate of the hostages riveted the world's attention. An attempt was made to negotiate for their lives. But Gbenye remained adamant: Tshombe's advance on Stanleyville had to be turned back first. The negotiations dragged on, frustratingly, frighteningly, for weeks. And each day the hostages' situation grew more menacing. They were herded into barracks. They were manhandled, brutalized, tortured. Groups of them were periodically taken out to face firing squads, surrounded by howling mobs. Though no whites were executed yet, the Simbas began machine-gunning blacks whom they considered "enemies of the revolution." As the mercenaries tightened the siege around Stanleyville, water and food ran low and the Simbas turned ever more savage.

On November 24, 1964, a lightning military blow was struck at Stanleyville in a desperate gamble to save the hostages' lives. Using planes supplied by the U.S. Air Force, 600 Belgian paratroopers jumped on the city center as the mercenaries smashed into its outskirts in a coordinated attack. As soon as they realized what was happening, the Simbas drove the hostages into the streets and, as loudspeakers blared hysterically, "Kill them, kill them all—men, women, and children," the Simbas opened fire with rifles and Sten guns. A wild melee broke out; the paras and mercenaries moved in fast, the hostages scrambled for cover. It was a brief battle. The Simbas were no match for the modern military force thrown against them, and they soon broke and ran for the darkness of the rain forests. Gbenye himself fled, never to be heard of again. Twenty-nine hostages were found dead. Later, 51 more bodies of whites were found, hacked to pieces and cannibalized. The secession of Oriental Province was over.

The Congo smelled of the graveyard. It has been estimated that at least 200,000 Congolese had been killed in the less than five years since independence. The roads, bridges, railways, and communications network were a shambles. The rubber and palm-oil plantations had been abandoned, the mining industries crippled. There were shortages of everything, refugees everywhere, and every sort of tribal, racial, and regional strife had been stirred up to a killing pitch. Despite the submission of Oriental Province, the conditions in the Congo in 1965 were such that the chaos and bloodshed of the past five years seemed likely to go on for five years more. And they very well might have. For, in a chilling reprise of his action with Lumumba, Kasavubu suddenly fired Tshombe; and this immediately threatened to lead to still another round of tribal and civil wars. But then, just as he had done in the first year of independence, Joseph Mobutu stepped in. This time, though, the army chief made sure his seizure of power would last.

Mobutu's second regime can be taken to mark the Congo's final passage—for better or worse—from the mysterious mythological darkness of its savage past into the rather banal light of the modern age and, as such, provides an entirely appropriate point at which to end this book. For, from 1965 onward, the story of the river belongs less to the history of its discovery, exploration, and exploitation by Europe than to the politics of modern independent Africa. This politics is characterized by the struggle going on all over the continent—with some admirable successes and many dismal failures but always with much agony and hope—to recover the virtues and values that prevailed in Africa before the white man came, to combine them with the inarguable advantages of the civilization the white man brought, and out of that combination to forge a new but genuine African identity and society. It is a struggle that has seen, on the one hand, the undertaking of such monumental industrialization projects as a multibillion-dollar hydroelectric complex to harness the enormous power of the Livingstone Falls and, on the other hand, the introduction of Mobutu's *authenticité* campaign to change not only all the European place names but all the river people's Christian names as well. (Mobutu changed his from Joseph to Sese Seko.) It is, in short, the struggle by which the Congo is, in fact as well as name, being transformed into Zaire.

SELECTED BIBLIOGRAPHY

Anstey, Roger. *Britain and the Congo in the Nineteenth Century.* Oxford, 1962.

Anstruther, Ian. *I Presume: Stanley's Triumph and Disaster.* London, 1956.

Archer, Jules. *Congo: The Birth of a New Nation.* New York, 1970.

Armattoe, R. E. G. *The Golden Age of West African Civilization.* Londonderry, 1946.

Ascherson, Neal. *The King Incorporated.* London, 1963.

Axelson, Eric. *Congo to Cape.* New York, 1973.

Axelson, Eric. *Portuguese in Southeast Africa.* Johannesburg, 1960.

Axelson, Eric. *Southeast Africa.* London, 1940.

Balandier, Georges. *Daily Life in the Kingdom of the Kongo from the Sixteenth to the Eighteenth Century.* London, 1968.

Beazley, C. Raymond. *Prince Henry the Navigator.* New York, 1894.

Bell, Christopher. *Portugal and the Quest for the Indies.* London, 1974.

Bentley, William Holman. *Pioneering on the Congo.* London, 1900.

Blake, John W. *European Beginnings in West Africa, 1454–1578.* London, 1937.

Bovill, E. W. *The Golden Trade of the Moors.* London, 1958.

Boxer, C. R. *Four Centuries of Portuguese Expansion, 1415–1825.* Johannesburg, 1961.

Brode, Heinrich. *Tippoo-Tib: The Story of His Career in Central Africa.* London, 1907.

Burton, Richard Francis. *The Lands of Cazembe: Lacerda's Journey in 1798.* London, 1873.

Burton, Richard Francis. *Two Trips to Gorilla Land and the Cataracts of the Congo.* London, 1876.

Cameron, Verney Lovett. *Across Africa.* New York, 1877.

Campbell, Reginald John. *Livingstone.* London, 1929.

Clarkson, Thomas. *History of the Rise, Progress and Accomplishment of the Abolition of the African Slave Trade* (2 vols.) . London, 1808.

Conrad, Joseph. *Heart of Darkness.* New York, 1923.

Coupland, Reginald. *The British Anti-Slavery Movement.* London, 1933.

Coupland, Reginald. *East Africa and Its Invaders.* Oxford, 1938.

Coupland, Reginald. *The Exploitation of East Africa, 1856–1890.* Evanston, Ill., 1967.

Coupland, Reginald. *Livingstone's Last Journey.* London, 1945.

Crone, G. R. *The Voyages of Cadamosto.* London, 1937.

Cuvelier, Jean. *L'Ancien Royaume de Congo.* Brussels, 1946.

Davidson, Basil. *The African Awakening.* London, 1955.

Davidson, Basil. *Black Mother: The African Slave Trade, 1450–1850.* London, 1961.

Debenham, Frank. *The Way to Ilala: David Livingstone's Pilgrimage.* London, 1955.

Donnan, Elizabeth. *Documents Illustrative of the History of the Slave Trade to America,* Vols. I and II. Washington, D.C., 1930.

Dos Passos, John. *The Portugal Story.* Garden City, N.Y., 1969.

Duffy, James. *Portuguese Africa.* Cambridge, Mass., 1968.

Eannes de Azurara, Gomes. *Conquests and Discoveries of Henry the Navigator.* London, 1936.

Farwell, Byron. *The Man Who Presumed.* London, 1958.

Fisher, H. A. L. *A History of Europe* (2 vols.) . London, 1938.

Foran, W. Robert. *African Odyssey: Life of Verney Lovett Cameron.* London, 1937.

Gramont, Sanche de. *The Strong Brown God: The Story of the Niger River.* Boston, 1976.

Hall, Richard Seymour. *Stanley: An Adventurer Explored.* Boston, 1975.

Hallett, Robin. *Africa to 1875.* Ann Arbor, Mich., 1974.

Hallett, Robin. *The Penetration of Africa.* London, 1965.

Hallett, Robin. *Records of the African Association, 1788–1833.* London, 1964.

Hird, Frank. *The Authorized Life of Henry Morton Stanley.* London, 1935.

Ihle, Alexander. *Das Alte Koenigreich Kongo.* Leipzig, 1929.

Jameson, Robert. *Narrative of Discovery and Adventure in Africa.* New York, 1831.

Jeal, Tim. *Livingstone.* London, 1973.

Johnston, Harry H. *A History of the Colonization of Africa by Alien Races.* Cambridge, 1905.

Johnston, Harry H. *Livingstone and the Exploration of Central Africa.* London, 1891.

Johnston, Harry H. *The River Congo.* London, 1884.

July, Robert W. *A History of the African People.* New York, 1970.

Laman, Karl. *The Kongo.* Uppsala, 1953.

Legum, Colin. *Congo Disaster.* Baltimore, 1961.

Leo Africanus. *History and Description of Africa.* London, 1896.

Livingstone, David (Horace Waller, ed.) . *The Last Journals of David Livingstone in Central Africa.* London, 1864.

Livingstone, David. *Missionary Travels and Researches in South Africa.* London, 1857.

Livingstone, David. *Narrative of an Expedition to the Zambesi and Its Tributaries.* New York, 1866.

Major, Richard Henry. *The Discoveries of Prince Henry the Navigator.* London, 1877.

Martekki, George. *Leopold to Lumumba: A History of the Belgian Congo.* London, 1962.

Moorehead, Alan. *The Blue Nile.* London, 1962.

Moorehead, Alan. *The White Nile.* London, 1960.

Morel, Edmund D. *King Leopold's Rule in Africa*. London, 1904.

Morel, Edmund D. *Red Rubber*. London, 1907.

Morison, Samuel Eliot. *Admiral of the Ocean Sea: A Life of Christopher Columbus*. Boston, 1942.

Murray, Hugh. *Historical Account of Discoveries and Travels in Africa*. Edinburg, 1818.

Oliveira Martins, J. P. *The Golden Age of Prince Henry the Navigator*. London, 1914.

Oliver, Roland A. *The Dawn of African History*. London, 1961.

Oliver, Roland A., and J. D. Fage. *A Short History of Africa*. New York, 1963.

Pacheco Pereira, Duarte (G. H. T. Kimble, trans.). *Esmeraldo de Situ Orbis*. London, 1937.

Park, Mungo. *A Journal of a Mission to the Interior of Africa*. London, 1815.

Park, Mungo. *The Life and Travels of Mungo Park*. New York, 1840.

Perham, Margery, and Jack Simons (eds.). *African Discovery: Anthology of Exploration*. London, 1942.

Pigafetta, Filippo, from Duarte Lopes. *A Report of the Kingdom of Congo*. London, 1597.

Prestage, Edgar. *The Portuguese Pioneers*. London, 1933.

Ravenstein, E. D. (ed.). *The Strange Adventures of Andrew Battell of Leigh, in Angola and the Adjoining Regions*. London, 1901.

Robinson, Ronald, John Gallagher and Alice Denny. *Africa and the Victorians*. London, 1961.

Sanceau, Elaine. *The Land of Prester John*. New York, 1944.

Schiffers, Heinrich. *The Quest for Africa*. New York, 1957.

Silverberg, Robert. *The Realm of Prester John*. Garden City, N.Y., 1972.

Slade, Ruth. *King Leopold's Congo*. London, 1962.

Stanley, Henry Morton (Dorothy Stanley, ed.). *The Autobiography of Henry Morton Stanley*. Boston, 1909.

Stanley, Henry Morton. *The Congo and the Founding of Its Free State* (2 vols.). New York, 1885.

Stanley, Henry Morton. *How I Found Livingstone*. New York, 1872.

Stanley, Henry Morton. *In Darkest Africa* (2 vols.). New York, 1890.

Stanley, Henry Morton. *Through the Dark Continent* (2 vols.). New York, 1878.

Stanley, Henry Morton. (Albert Maurice, ed.). *Unpublished Letters*. London, 1957.

Stanley, Richard, and Alan Neame (eds.). *The Exploration Diaries of H. M. Stanley*. London, 1961.

Sterling, Thomas L. *Stanley's Way*. New York, 1960.

Stevenson, E. L. (trans. and ed.). *The Geography of Claudius Ptolemy*. New York, 1932.

Tuckey, J. K. *Narrative of an Expedition to Explore the River Zaire*. New York, 1818.

Vansina, Jan. *Kingdoms of the Savanna*. Madison, Wisc., 1966.

West, Richard. *Brazza of the Congo*. London, 1972.

INDEX